Dr. Max Gerson

New York, 1954

Dr. Max Gerson
Healing the Hopeless

Howard Straus

with Barbara Marinacci

QUARRY
HEALTH
BOOKS

The publisher acknowledges the support of
the Government of Canada, Department
of Canadian Heritage, Book Publishing
Industry Development Program.

ISBN 1-55082-290-x

Design by Susan Hannah.

Printed and bound in Canada by
AGMV Marquis, Cap-St-Ignace, Quebec.

Published by Quarry Press Inc., PO Box 1061,
Kingston, Ontario K7L 4Y5 Canada.

Contents

Dedication

To live for a time next to great minds is the best kind of education.
– John Buchan, 1875-1940

This book is dedicated with love to my grandfather, Dr. Max Gerson, his wife Gretchen Gerson, and my mother, Charlotte Gerson (Straus). I knew my grandfather, not as a medical genius or a beleaguered innovator in the world of human health, but as "Opa," the German familial term for "Grampa." He was a gentle, quiet man who was only partly present in my world, spending most of his time and energy in expanding his knowledge and helping his patients. He left most of the details of day-to-day life to his wife, Gretchen (later, Margaret), who raised their three daughters and several grandchildren, packed up and moved their household repeatedly and often alone, and managed their home and finances.

No one person has had more influence on my life than my mother, Charlotte Gerson (Straus), whose qualities I describe as combining the best of Billy Graham's fiery evangelism, Ralph Nader's stern caution and June Cleaver's warm, solid and loving motherhood. She has kept her father's work alive for the past 30 years by doing the daily work in the trenches with the doctors and patients. She is the most powerful human being I have ever met, bar none, continuously helping others overcome diseases that stump medical science—and all the while going head-to-head with the American Medical Association and winning by her solid integrity. She has provided me with a granite foundation that has supported me for my entire life. I owe her more than I can ever hope to repay.

Foreword

D r. Max Gerson's life story deserves to be told. He was a pioneer physician of dietary therapy for chronic diseases such as tuberculosis and cancer, recognizing the value of good nutrition in enabling the healing process and maintaining good health. He was also what one might classify as a health ecologist, a practitioner of environmental medicine, concerned about the adverse effects of modern technology upon the natural world and the human body. And he was possibly the first truly holistic physician to practice in the United States, in the time just before holistic medicine became the watchword for a new medical philosophy that addressed the whole person, integrating body, mind and spirit. Gerson called his own approach to medicine "totality"—originally known as *Ganzheit* in his homeland, Germany.

Many alternative or complementary practitioners now employ facets of the Gerson's dietary and detoxifying therapies, often without recognition of their source, yet a large body of scientific literature published in the 1920s and 1930s confirms Gerson's pioneering work in diet therapy — work that might have been recognized with a Nobel Prize in Physiology or Medicine had the political situation gone very differently in his native Germany prior to World War II under Nazi rule … or had the American medical profession, after this German-Jew fled Nazi persecution to the United States in the mid 1930s, been more open to investigating the methods and results of his treatment of cancer and other intractable, degenerative diseases. Few if any references to Gerson's name and work can be found in American medical literature after 1946, unless they are defamatory.

The sheer immensity of Dr. Gerson's achievements is staggering. He was able to prevent and cure, not simply arrest or slow, a wide range of degenerative diseases, including the top four killers in the United States — heart attack, cancer, stroke and diabetes — which together account for between two and three million deaths annually. Dr. Gerson also had remarkable success in treating rheumatoid arthritis, multiple sclerosis, muscular dystrophy, multiple chemical sensitivity and other immune system-connected or toxin-associated disorders. He did this without the financial or academic support of any university, government, institute or laboratory — working alone, while treating patients and maintaining a practice—though for brief periods of time, small private foundations did provide limited support. Yet Dr. Gerson's name remains unmentionable in medical literature, even as his principles regarding the importance of diet as prevention of and therapy for a wide variety of diseases are becoming accepted as standard medical thinking. His emphasis for health maintenance on sticking to a saltless, low-fat, largely vegetarian diet with ample fresh fruits and vegetables and whole-grain products, with no (or much restricted) stimulating or alcoholic drinks, no longer seems threatening to the establishment, but for over 60 years, the medical, pharmaceutical and governmental health authorities in the United States and abroad have seemingly done their utmost to maintain a total blackout on Gerson's therapies. Clinics have been shut down and physicians expelled from practice when they began to use the Gerson's therapeutic methods, specifically as a cure for cancer.

Max Gerson and Albert Einstein were born at opposite ends of Germany only two years apart. Both ended their lives in the United States of America, having been hounded from Nazi Germany by the anti-Semitic prejudices of the times. Einstein, working alone, formulated his Theory of Relativity and revolutionized physics, but he searched in vain for his holy grail, the grand unifying field theory in physics. Within his chosen profession of medicine, Max Gerson searched for the underlying principles that connected the seemingly disparate causes and effects of good and ill health. Early in his career, almost by accident, Gerson discovered a portion of a tantalizing, unifying theory of human immunity and well-being. He then developed the concept of "totality in medicine"—the holism of today—by continuously, for the rest of his days, testing out and proving its efficacy on his patients. Both men proposed ideas that were so radical, yet simple in their bases, that other scientists could not readily accept them. Like Einstein, Gerson was attacked by many of his colleagues. But Einstein's reputation grew so great that he is considered the most famous and influential scientist of the 20th century, whereas Max Gerson's name is scarcely known.

This biography is a labor of love. Dr. Max Gerson was my grandfather; in fact, he ushered me into the world. When my mother, Charlotte Gerson, first proposed the project to me, I was rather hesitant to take it on. My reluctance did not stem from the fact that I had never written a book before; after all, there is a first time for everything. Also, I had written many types of documents in the past: some technical, stemming from my work as a computer systems analyst, and some reflecting my understanding of the Gerson Therapy gained from a lifetime of absorbing it—sometimes by osmosis, sometimes by intent.

I was not hesitant either about the subject itself. On the contrary, Dr. Max Gerson's life story is intertwined with some of the greatest and most dramatic happenings of the 20th century. My misgivings instead stemmed from the immensely tragic nature of Gerson's journey, due mostly to his persecution by colleagues in the medical profession. As a child, I had personally witnessed or heard about enough of the incidents to know how painful it would be for me to revisit them in detail. I was not mistaken. The deeper into the story I delved, the angrier and more depressed I became at the incredible behavior of the medical profession when confronted by a true healer. Whether it was by overt conspiracy or petty jealousy, the result was the same. Max Gerson was prevented from giving to the world his message of a powerful curative technique.

When I set out to resurrect the important lifework of Dr. Max Gerson for public viewing, I also wanted to reveal some of the "underside" of standard medical practice, particularly when it is directed by an entrenched orthodox medical establishment that seeks to retain power and absolute control over its physician members. Some organizations — most notably the Medical Society of the County of New York, the American Medical Association, the Congressional Office of Technology Assessment (OTA) and the National Cancer Institute — still will not release their voluminous records regarding Dr. Gerson's results, even after 50 years. Any records that remain will have to be uncovered in the future by other people with more resources and political power than I could muster.

The medical establishment should by now recognize and publicize that diet and health are intimately connected, for better or for worse. In other words, what we eat and drink — always taking into full account the conditions of our food and water sources, which may be contaminated or poisoned — is going to make us healthy or unhealthy. This being so, it should often be possible to reverse the course of a patient's illness, and even totally cure it, by using a therapeutic diet and detoxification tactics. Which is what Max Gerson did, and did with extraordinary success, again and again in his medical practice.

Though the pain of researching and recounting the attacks on Gerson was more than I anticipated, the rewards of examining the accomplishments of this truly good, decent and honorable healer have been far greater than I ever expected.

If I have done my job, I trust that you will feel inspired by Dr. Gerson's exemplary life and his experiential medical wisdom — and therefore be motivated to improve your own health by using the techniques so clearly set forth by him over 60 years ago. If this book about Dr. Gerson can save so much as one human life from affliction by an incurable disease, my own efforts to tell his life story and describe the value of his therapies will be worthwhile.

～

In writing this book, I relied on a host of resources. My late grandmother, Gretchen (Margaret) Rose Gerson, after her husband's death in 1959, wrote a memoir of his formative years in Germany and his medical career. Calling it "Max Gerson, a Life Without Fear," she mostly focused on his medical practice following their marriage in 1916. The basic sequence and many of the incidents recounted in my biography are based on this 100-page typescript. Originally written in German, the manuscript was translated into English years ago by my sister, Margaret Straus Dego. As Gretchen Gerson had no experience in the art and craft of biography, names and dates were often omitted. These have been filled in by painstaking research. And since she wrote it in her later years, some of the dates and circumstances long past may have been imperfectly preserved in her memory. She also stopped her writing effort some-what short of the end of Gerson's life, since the chronicle of the medical profession's attacks and sabotage became too painful for her to relive.

More of Max Gerson's history was passed on verbally when Mrs. Gerson told her children about their father's early years, or recalled for her grandchildren various sto-ries about life with her husband in Germany, Austria, France and England—and then, for over 20 years, in the United States. Occasionally, too, when I was young, my grand-father would recount incidents of his past, but also of his present, including news of his current patients' progress.

Many incidents related in this biography were gleaned from my mother's mem-ories and her files, backed up as often as was possible by using her own words and by researching historical documents in her possession or obtained elsewhere. A large number and variety of unpublished manuscripts, often written by Dr. Gerson in rough-draft form and incomplete, handwritten or typed, now on crumbling paper, were located in Charlotte Gerson's "archives" concerning her father's lifework. Photographs and other visual materials are also there. Most fortunately, the originals of many of Max's letters to his close friend Professor Henry Schaefer-Simmern had been returned to the Gerson family in the distant past; other letters of Gerson's were there in carbon-copy or retyped form. Originals of Albert Schweitzer's letters to Gerson are also extant — good evidence of their excellent rapport.

My mother most obligingly has translated from the German various paragraphs in her father's correspondence, lectures and published papers that she or else I, in my less perfect German, had identified as probably useful to the book. Mining old correspondence documenting the medical and political atrocities perpetrated by Dr. Gerson's detractors was an often painful yet inspiring process for us both. Charlotte would lay down one or another document she was translating, sigh, and say, "Poor Daddy." But we both persevered, because Dr. Gerson's insights into health and disease belong to all of humanity.

My mother also contributed earlier in another way to my own knowledge of the Gerson Therapy, which came to me in an experiential, "hands-on" way. She was instrumental in my starting in 1997 a Gerson clinic in Arizona — a state that is less antagonistic toward the use of alternative medicine in treating various degenerative diseases, including cancer, than is California, or for that matter most other states. Unfortunately, problems with the facility building's landlord forced the closing of the promising clinic 15 months after it opened. Also, to assist my mother, at several times in the past I participated in public relations and educational efforts at the Gerson Institute, which Charlotte Gerson founded in 1970 and with which at times she is still associated as a consultant.

Dr. Gerson's granddaughter, Suzanne Oberlander Brandt, happily contributed some of her memories of life with the Gersons in New York. Thanks, also, to Dr. Gerson's niece, Mrs. Inge Levin Schneider, who was willing to recount her family's experiences on the SS *St. Louis*, and their subsequent internment in Holland and the concentration camp at Bergen-Belsen. It cannot have been pleasant to exhume those long buried memories, but she courageously did so in order that they might be accurately presented in the book.

Several of Dr. Gerson's former patients — Bill Schickel, Eddie Braun and Gail Allen Bogue (who tell their own stories here)—spoke with me at length about their illnesses and recoveries from incurable cancer, as well as their interactions with Dr. Gerson. Their living voices, transcribed from audiotaped interviews, offer invaluable evidence of Max Gerson's skill as a true healer. I can only wish that the readers of this book could directly witness, as both my mother and I have done since our early childhoods, the great many people with cancer and other supposedly incurable or fatal diseases who were returned to good health by Dr. Max Gerson ... or have been later by others following his exacting therapeutic guidelines either as practitioners or as patients.

To add a sense of immediacy to Max Gerson's story, I occasionally dramatized some scenes in his life, especially in his early years, basing these stories and conversations on ones often recounted within the Gerson family or originally told by my grandmother in her memoir. Elsewhere I have done my utmost to stick to a literal portrayal of the significant events in Dr. Gerson's professional and personal life, relying on documentary evidence wherever possible, and often using quotations from letters, articles, lectures, unpublished manuscripts and audiotaped interviews.

In providing this documentation, I have quoted extensively from Max Gerson's own book, A *Cancer Therapy: Results of Fifty Cases*. I have used excerpts and cited references from the biography by S.J. Haught, first published in 1962: *Censured for Curing Cancer: The American Experience of Dr. Max Gerson*. There are lengthy passages cited from Dr. Patricia S. Ward's extraordinary evaluation of the Gerson Therapy, written after she researched it under contract with the U.S. Congressional Office of Technology Assessment (OTA). I also quoted from the text of documents reprinted in the biographical novel on the theme of Dr. Gerson's life, *Doctor Max*, by Giuliano Dego. Passages have been extracted from Ferdinand Sauerbruch's autobiography, *Master Surgeon*, about his clinical work with Gerson in the 1920s; from John Gunther's *Death Be Not Proud*, pertaining to Dr. Gerson's treatment of his teen-age son Johnny in 1946-1947; and from editorials and articles in the *Journal of the American Medical Association (JAMA)*.

If inaccuracies have crept into my interpretation of any of the data, the fault is mine alone. If readers wish to take issue with the strong opinions that I occasionally express which derive from my deep knowledge of the American medical establishment's mistreatment of my grandfather, Dr. Max Gerson, they are, of course, free to do so.

~

Among those people who assisted with this book were several friends from my youth who have helped me in some material way. Gitta Block-Erwig of Hanover, Germany and Anneliese Schütte Irmer of Berlin, Germany, assisted me with my research, and Eve Fielding Franconeri of Forest Hills, New York, has tended Dr. Gerson's grave out of respect and caring for his family. Rhena Schweitzer Miller generously helped with her recollections concerning her father's contacts with Dr. Gerson. Dr. Bernard Jensen kindly recalled for me his experiences with Max and Gretchen Gerson at his health ranch in Escondido, California, in the late 1950s.

Among the librarians and libraries that provided assistance of many kinds: Donna Arrowood, document-retrieval specialist, was able to locate and obtain for me copies of most of the papers that Max Gerson wrote over his long career—quite a task, considering the age of the publications. Nikki, the Herbal Education assistant at the American Botanical Council in Austin, Texas, provided the Latin name for tausend-guldenkraut, the medical herb that probably saved Max Gerson's life when he was deathly ill from typhus in childhood. Julie Herrada, Assistant Curator of the Labadie Collection, Special Collections Library at the University of Michigan, who was particularly helpful and encouraging, enabled me to acquire almost unavailable literature. Several research librarians at the University of California at Berkeley, Stanford University and the University of Chicago generously supplied me with facts and resources or pointed me in the right direction. The reference librarians at the Carmel and Carmel Valley public libraries helped me locate and borrow reference volumes from all over the United States.

I am also pleased to acknowledge that I made ample use of a relatively new and very powerful research tool, the Worldwide Web. This amazing collection of information enabled me to find information censored by other media, and also allowed me rapid communications with the people who could help me ferret out the underlying documentation to which it pointed.

My deepest thanks go to Barbara Marinacci, who began as my editor but evolved into a trusted, precise and exacting co-author. Barbara is an accomplished writer and researcher in her own right — having published a number of books, including O Wondrous Singer! An Introduction to Walt Whitman, California's Spanish Place-Names, and Linus Pauling in His Own Words. She was perfect for this work because of the extensive knowledge of nutritional medicine gained during her years of involvement with the Linus

Pauling Institute. If I, in my first attempt at biography, got vague or omitted things, Barbara insisted on facts, dates, documents, publications and precision. She also added many of the historical contexts that would have informed or affected Gerson's life and times.

I would especially like to thank my wife, Sally, for her support in my effort. It wasn't easy for her when I made the transition from computer systems analyst to hospital founder to biographer, but she has provided me with unstinting love and sustenance during the entire time, bearing the burden with good cheer and faith in the future.

Above all, I am extremely grateful to my mother, Charlotte Gerson, for her constant encouragement, not only in the writing task itself but also in the considerable investigations in a number of different areas connected with her father's work. She has spent the best part of the past 30 years ensuring that Max Gerson's unique dietary and detoxification regimen is not relegated to the dustbin of medical-cure anomalies. She has kept the Gerson Therapy alive by founding a series of treatment centers in Mexico where this admittedly stringent treatment has been practiced daily for over 25 years. The T in Therapy is capitalized because the specific term is now a registered trademark.

Charlotte Gerson has sent thousands of people, given up for dead by their allopathic physicians, back into the world to live in health, and to inform their own friends and acquaintances of the power of the Gerson Therapy. She has trained the physicians, monitored the food preparation, and worked tirelessly to maintain the high standards of quality and integrity that mark the provision of the Gerson Therapy. It is important for patients to be aware that various practitioners and clinics that claim to use the Gerson Therapy may not, in fact, be *certified* providers or centers; therefore they may fail to employ faithfully the therapeutic techniques originated by Max Gerson, which have been slightly altered in the last 40 years in accordance with new knowledge and materials.

For readers interested in the certified Gerson Therapy, please contact the Cancer Research Wellness Network, Carmel, California (831-625-3565) or the Gerson Institute, San Diego, California (888-4-GERSON).

Howard Straus
Carmel, California

Introduction

~

Thank God for physicians who are intelligent, curious, determined — and suffering from an illness or symptoms for which medicine has no remedy. Dr. Max Gerson was afflicted with migraine headaches, did not know how to prevent them, nor how to deal with them. Since he could get no help from his medical colleagues, he had to develop his own treatment program. He discovered that his headaches were food related: when he followed a special diet, his headaches no longer occurred.

Dr. Gerson became noted for his expertise in treating migraine. Gradually his interest in the therapeutic potential of this diet expanded to tuberculosis, for which there was also no treatment at that time. He observed that some of his patients with tuberculosis on the same or similar diet recovered. Gerson's work marked a new way of dealing with a very common untreatable disease, but the medical establishment found this to be threatening, as had been the discovery a century or more earlier by Sir Thomas Sydenham that one got better results in treating small pox if the fever is lowered. The ancient and honorable treatment for small pox had been to increase the fever, but this, according to Sydenham, also increased the death rate. For his therapy, Sydenham was challenged to a duel. Dr. Gerson, as far as I can tell, was not, but reaction to his dietary treatment was no less threatening to his career, if not his life.

The fact that many of Gerson's tubercular patients recovered was not accepted. His colleagues refused to see anything new in his dietary therapy, and when pressed they would fall back on the old trick of declaring that the disease being treated was not tuberculosis (the diagnosis was wrong) or that the recoveries were really not true recoveries. I have faced this same problem for 40 years since I began to claim that schizophrenic patients can become normal if their diet is supplemented by vitamin B-3 (niacin) and vitamin C. Dr. Gerson was subject to every dirty trick in the book employed by the establishment when one paradigm defends itself against change. Even today the idea that nutrition can play a role in the treatment of infectious disease is generally frowned upon by orthodox medicine. Steeled by this kind of opposition and inspired by some early successes, Dr. Gerson began to look into cancer. He found that a nutritional regimen consisting of certain foods prepared in a special way has value in the treatment of cancer, and eventually developed what is still known as the Gerson therapy. This includes a diet of fresh vegetables and fruits, coffee enemas and nutrient supplements such as niacin. Dr. Gerson should have been awarded the Nobel Prize for introducing this entirely new concept into medicine.

By this time in his career, the Holocaust was on the horizon, and Dr. Gerson and his family had to flee to Austria, from there to France and England, and finally to New York. In New York he found personal freedom, but unfortunately did not find any more freedom for his medical views about cancer. He was subjected to the same tactics he had to face in Europe, and even though he became well known for the results he was obtaining, the opposition continued. After he died his daughter Charlotte maintained the program at a clinic in Mexico.

This biography should be required reading for every medical student so that they will know that the history of medicine progresses through the conflict of ideas. One paradigm becomes established and gives way to new knowledge, not without a struggle. Dr. Gerson's dietary and detoxification ideas are now well established — although the establishment will certainly not acknowledge this. Almost all the complementary treatments for cancer of which I am aware use elements of Gerson's work. Significantly, since the nutrients have become more readily available, they can now be used in larger amounts and greater variety than was possible for Dr. Gerson.

Max Gerson was a brilliant, dedicated, innovative medical scientist willing to set aside prejudice and an old paradigm to follow where his observations and good instincts led him. Through his work he brought nutrition and diet back into medicine. Nutrition is now recognized as important both in the cause and treatment of diseases like cancer.

In the Bible, it is written that it took Moses 40 years to march the Israelites from Egypt to Israel. A good walker can do this in two weeks. But Moses needed time for two generations of men and women to die. They were born into and raised in slavery. He needed young men and women raised in freedom who could take over the promised land. By now, we have lost several generations of medical men and women enslaved by the old paradigms of the medical schools. We are ready for the new generation to come forth and carry on the course blazed by Dr. Max Gerson.

— *Dr. Abram Hoffer, MD*

Bielefeld, 1925

~1~
Boyhood in Wongrowitz
(1881-1899)

The Tale of a Worm

Young Max Gerson crouched down to inspect closely the potato crop on either side of the pathway because his grandmother had told him that she wanted to see whether the crop could be improved this year by adding some new fertilizer. "They are saying that it does much better than nature," she had explained to Max. "But I wonder about that." On the left side of the path, the seed potatoes were dug into the soil with manure, wood ashes, rotted leaves and plant stems, as they always had been. On the other side, the farm manager had recently amended the soil by adding a dry chemical fertilizer. In the late 19th century, especially in Germany, industrial chemists were claiming that by condensing and packaging vast quantities of several minerals deemed important to plant growth, they could make the soil more productive and crops more abundant, even healthier. Soon nobody would go hungry anymore, anywhere on earth. And no crop was more basic to the German diet than the potato. Few meals were ever served that did not contain the white tuber in at least one form, whether baked, fried or boiled, whole or in pieces, in pancakes, salad, soup dumplings, bread.

Max noticed the green stems and leaves emerging from the planted tuber 'eyes' that had sprouted below his view underground, but soon his gaze shifted, no longer focused on the little potato plants. He was watching a curious phenomenon. All along the dirt pathway, hordes of earthworms wriggled along, crossing one field to go to the other. They were heading toward the untreated plot of ground on the left — apparently fleeing the soil that had been artificially fertilized.

Max picked up a worm and watched it inch across his palm. The moist, segmented body looked vulnerable in its pinky nakedness, almost like his own skin. When the worm came to the edge, he lowered his hand and let it fall gently so that it could rejoin its companions on their exodus. Something in those chemicals must be bothering or even hurting the worms, Max speculated. What might people themselves feel if chemicals like these were put down all around them, in places where they were living? Well, maybe they could just move away, as the worms were doing. But what would happen if people were to eat the potatoes raised on these chemicals?

His grandmother's agricultural experiments with chemical fertilizers seemed to prompt Max to do the same. Besides growing potatoes and other vegetable cash crops, Max's grandmother kept extensive fruit and flower gardens. Max was especially entranced with her flowers. He began experimenting with different species, growing them in different mixtures of natural fertilizers, soil types, and light exposures. Day by day he gained insight into the relationships between plants and the nutrients they derived from the soil, people and the plants and animals they ate as food.

With his curiosity and respect for all living things, young Max Gerson seemed destined for a career as a biomedical researcher and physician. Many years later, when he had been practicing medicine for half a century — all the while attentive to the adverse effects on human health created by overuse of the soil in agriculture and misuse of manmade chemicals in growing food — he would invoke that image of the earthworm fleeing from the toxic soil while discussing the medical effects of the environment in his book, A *Cancer Therapy*.

> The damage that modern civilization brings into our lives begins with the soil, where artificial fertilization leads to the displacement of mineral contents and changes in the flora of microbes combined with the exodus of the earthworms. Consequently, frequent erosion of arable land takes place. These changes bring about, at the beginning, an irritation of the plants; later they cause their degeneration. Spraying with poisonous substances (insecticides) increases the poisons in the soil, and these poisons are transferred to plants and fruits.
>
> We must conclude from these and many other observations that the soil and all that grows in it is not something distant from us but must be regarded as *our external metabolism*, which produces the basic substances for our internal metabolism. Therefore, the soil must be cared for properly and must not be depleted or poisoned; otherwise, these changes will result in serious degenerative diseases, rapidly increasing in animals and human beings. (A *Cancer Therapy*, pp. 14-15)

Max Gerson's interest in what has become known as environmental medicine and dietary therapy was abiding.

Family Life

Max Gerson had been born into a large and prosperous Jewish family on October 18, 1881, in Wongrowitz, in northeastern Germany. The town lay about 100 miles south of the Baltic Sea and around 50 miles north-northeast of the city of Posen. (The region is now part of Poland. The town is called Wagrowiec; the city, Poznan.) Through the centuries, political control over the entire Posen region had often changed, as did other shifting borders within much of Eastern Europe. In 1795, after Polish patriot Tadeusz Kosciuszko's unsuccessful rebellion against Catherine the Great of Russia, this territory had been divided up among Russia, Prussia and Austria. In 1872 Chancellor Otto von Bismarck, in the effort to integrate the Prussian-held Posen area into his visionary plan for a modern Germany, ordered the 'Germanization' of all government-sponsored functions. At the time of Max's birth, Posen province had been annexed into the recently founded German Reich. Although the general population, chiefly Polish in ancestry, retained its own distinctive language and culture, officials, teachers and schoolchildren were expected to speak German. Within the Gerson family itself, German was spoken. It is probable that both sides of Max Gerson's ancestry originally came from the west, possibly from the Berlin area in Prussia, and migrated to the east where there were fewer social restrictions and greater economic opportunities. Max Gerson always considered that he had been born in Germany, not Poland. Not until 1919, following World War I and the Treaty of Versailles, did Poland renew its existence as a independent nation.

As a young boy, Max spent much of the time at his grandmother's house, which was close to his parents' home. The widowed Hannchen Abraham had told Max's mother — her daughter Ulricke — that she liked to have the boy with her as a companion. He was bright, inquisitive, helpful. Max customarily stayed on weekdays with his grandmother, but he always went home on the weekends, to spend Friday evening and Saturday with his parents and siblings so that he could take part in the formal family meal at sundown on Friday and then attend next day's Shabbat services at the synagogue.

Though she had other grandchildren, Frau Abraham felt particularly fond of Max, who reminded her of her recently deceased husband, Nathan. Max's mother also noticed his resemblance to her father, which at times seemed uncanny. Max was her third child. Over the years Ulricke Gerson would give birth to nine children altogether. But somehow none of the others ever seemed quite as special to her as this middle child. Though he normally seemed so healthy, he would urgently need her devoted and protective care.

Since Max hadn't been long out of infancy when his maternal grandfather died, any traits he showed of his maternal grandfather's character must surely have been inherited. Throughout Max's childhood, fond yet humorous stories about *Grossvater* Nathan were often told within the family, giving him a legendary sort of afterlife. Both Max and Nathan possessed some rather special qualities: a keen and original intelligence; a fixed focus on matters of particular interest, causing them to be absent-minded; a gentle, generous concern for the welfare of others; and an overall "other-worldliness" that was inattentive to the usual human propensities toward materialistic gain, status and power over others.

Before his untimely death in the mid 1880s, Nathan Abraham had been a successful grain merchant in the eastern German province of Posen. He had traveled around among large local landowners to negotiate purchases of wheat, rye and flax. As a middleman, he then resold them in bulk to wholesalers and commercial flour mills in various cities in the area, while his wife handled the smaller sales to local retail shops.

This energetic German-Jewish businessman had another side, a humanitarian one known particularly to family members and neighbors. Nathan Abraham, familiar with the ethical teachings of the Torah and the Talmud, followed the time-honored Jewish tradition of providing hospitality and charity to strangers and travelers. For instance, after the Friday evening services at the synagogue, two or three traveling artisans or poor students might be invited home for a succulent Shabbat meal. Welcomed as honored guests, these visitors would be placed at the head of the table, and there Nathan entertained them lavishly. Occasionally, guests admired his fashionable clothes, warm coat or fine hat. Promptly their host would invite them to come around next morning to pick up the item, for it was now theirs. Nathan's wife Hannchen, a practical woman, would scold him afterwards for giving away good clothing that he had scarcely worn, but she could never halt this habit, for it obviously gave him pleasure. Nathan Abraham also purchased gifts for his wife and children. On one occasion, he brought home a large box of brand-new shoes, to be distributed among the children. But as soon as Hannchen and the children began sorting through them, they noticed a small problem: Nathan had brought them only *left* shoes.

Max's father, Bernhardt Gerson, was an enterprising merchant, as both his father and father-in-law had been. He conducted a large retail business. He also owned and operated a mill, which did not grind grains as flour mills did, but instead pressed them so as to extract oils. The pulverized residue of the process, press cakes or solid mash, provided nutritious foods for livestock, so were much in demand.

Bernhardt Gerson's press chiefly produced rapeseed oil from rape or *Brassica napus*, a plant in the mustard family widely grown in Europe in the 19th century as forage for pigs and sheep. The oil extracted from the mature seeds (often combined with turnips) could be used as a lubricant, as lamp oil, or as cooking oil. Some time later this oil was considered dangerous if ingested in large quantities, as it contained a toxin, erucic acid. In the latter part of the 20th century a variety of rape plant with less erucic acid was cultivated in Canada, and a new process was devised for processing oil from its seeds. To differentiate this cultivar from the ill-reputed rape, the plant was called *canola*. Although canola oil is now often and widely declared to be the most healthful of all vegetable oils because of its monounsaturated fatty acids, some researchers and nutritionists still pronounce it unsuitable for human consumption, especially when frequently used in foods.

Gerson's mill could press other seeds as well. Among them were flaxseeds, which yielded linseed oil. For centuries flax had been grown in Europe for the thick, dry stem which was processed into a thread that was then woven into linen cloth. Flaxseed oil also had multiple uses: as a shiny, protective coating for wood products; as a components in such industrial products as paint, varnish, printing ink and linoleum; as a medicinal substance soothing to skin and mucus membranes; and even in cooking. Linseed or flax oil is increasingly regarded as healthful oil. Flaxseeds, too, are known to have dietary value from many beneficial phytochemical and fibrous properties, if rendered digestible.

In his early schoolboy years, Max enjoyed watching the seed pressing process. His mother knew that if she could not locate him at mealtime, he most likely would be found at his father's mill nearby, so would send one of his older siblings to summon him. His fascination with the whole process of extracting valuable essences from plant foods by applying strong pressure, not by grinding or whirling them, would be reawakened later on, when as a physician he developed his special dietary therapy that relied on drinking various juices and ingesting flax oil.

Since most employees at Herr Gerson's oil press were drawn from the local working-class population, they usually spoke their native Polish among themselves and with their employer. By spending much of his free time at his father's mill, Max learned to speak Polish fluently. His ability to learn languages would be important during his years as an emigrant.

Jewish Heritage

Max Gerson's identity as a German Jew would shape both his personal and professional lives, for better and for worse. He was afforded excellent opportunities in education and access to a professional career and a marriage partner. But as a European Jew, he was also subject to major social disruptions and displacements. Although Max Gerson survived the Holocaust, his medical achievements were constricted by his religion and culture

Max's parents took the practice of their Jewish faith seriously. Friday evenings were always celebrated as true holy days in the Gerson household. Ulricke Gerson, a kindly, capable and intelligent woman, took special pains to set a beautiful and festive table for a generous meal, doubtless following her own parents' custom. Every Saturday morning the whole family would attend the early Shabbat service. Then Bernhardt returned home with his three boys — Gustav, Max and Siegfried — to recite Hebrew prayers and read Bible stories. Later, on afternoons when the weather was pleasant, the family would make the transition from holy day into holiday by taking long walks in some beautiful oak forest at the edge of one of the region's many nearby rivers and lakes. In his childhood, Max learned to love being out in the natural world away from urban life. Later, wherever he went, this penchant accompanied with him.

In religious Jewish households, charity and hospitality are not simply desirable qualities; they are considered *mitzvah* — duty. Ulricke prepared food and clothing for needy families at the approach of the Jewish High Holy Days, and delivering the gift parcels became her children's responsibility. Ulricke also participated in the local Jewish community's sponsorship of promising children in families that could not afford to pay for their children's tuition and lived in outlying areas. The wealthier families in the congregation, including the Gersons, provided these children with food and shelter for one month at a time, while their school fees were paid out of community funds. Though Max's religious practice in attending Jewish services waned over the years, he always reflected his family's attitude toward taking care of those less fortunate than themselves. He was gentle and generous with others — especially with his patients — often almost without regard for his own welfare.

Schooldays

Like the other Jewish children in Wongrowitz, Max attended the Jewish primary school. The headmaster there had to be very strict, since he was expected to prepare his students thoroughly for their future education. Jewish families wanted their offspring to excel at the *Gymnasium*, the town's only secondary school, as one way to offset the community's, and in fact all of Europe's, enduring prejudice against Jews. When students neglected their elementary-school studies, parental disapproval and punishment by the teacher would be swift and certain.

At the age of 10, Max went on to the Royal Gymnasium at Wongrowitz, where he and other classmates joined the other children in town being educated at the German equivalent of a combined middle and high school. Max began a long course of instruction that lasted seven years: the traditional classical studies based on Latin, along with German literature, history, geography, mathematics and natural history (as a general introduction to science). Some attention was also given to music, with its rich German heritage.

The children who had come from the Jewish primary school always ranked high in their Gymnasium classes, but discovered they were not liked by other students and some instructors, who were Christians. The young *goyim* aimed taunts and insults at the young Jewish students, but their parents usually counseled them to ignore the ugly words and not to fight back. Instead, they were told to concentrate on doing superior work in school, so that they could graduate with honors and go on to a university. There they would gain the necessary knowledge for succeeding as adults in some highly respected profession or prosperous business, leaving far behind them the ignorant tormentors of their youth.

As a child, Max himself seldom suffered persecution for being Jewish, though. Easygoing and likable, he even looked like a typical German or "Aryan" boy — tall, blue-eyed, with fair skin and light brown hair. It is possible that a few non-Jewish ancestors were in Max's genetic background. Also, the gene determining these striking, clear blue eyes somehow appears to be dominant rather than recessive among Gerson descendants. Like many other highly educated and often secular Jews, Max Gerson would locate his primary self-identification within his chosen profession, believing himself entitled to equal status with colleagues from all backgrounds. He would be shocked when any people without academic qualifications or public respect would persecute him or anyone else who happened to be born Jewish.

At school Max had many friends, including the two sons of the Gymnasium's headmaster. On many occasions, he and other boys would meet after the school day was over to play at ball games out in the field or to go rowing or swimming in a nearby lake, instead of heading home to work on school assignments. He preferred the age-old pursuits of healthy, high-spirited and risk-taking boys. In their mischief-making adventures they might filch fruit from a neighbor's garden or shoot small air pistols at the small glass bulbs that decorated walls and houses around town. This lack of serious attention to school work didn't pose a problem for Max, since learning came easily to him. He had an acute memory that was both visual and auditory, so he could often repeat verbatim a world history or geography lesson, whether it was something the teacher had said an hour before or information given in a book he had read earlier. He did well on tests and maintained high grades without much effort. His remarkable memory would stay with him all his life. "He had a phenomenal photographic memory," his daughter and my mother Charlotte recalls. "Very frequently he wrote papers giving the references largely from memory — though not page numbers and other such details."

Max's Latin teacher seemed to resent his student's facility for learning without working hard. The first year shortly before summer vacation began, Max handed in yet another poorly prepared paper. The Latin teacher had reached the end of his patience. "I will see to it that you will not be promoted out of this second-year class," he vowed. It was a critical moment for Max, since a failure at this level would affect his ability to get into university or get a professional job, and thus affect his

When working with Professor Boruttau, Max learned a great deal about the latest techniques in laboratory testing of bodily fluids, most notably the components of blood and lymph, as well as the body's waste products: perspiration, urine and feces. This apprenticeship in physiological chemistry with Dr. Boruttau made an extremely valuable contribution to Max Gerson's future practice of medicine, when so often in determining a patient's overall health status and then delivering a diagnosis and prognosis he would rely on intricate laboratory assays of serum and plasma in blood, lymphatic fluid, various tissues and excreta (particularly urine), along with X-rays and microscopic tissue studies. These would also offer baselines for judging the effects of treatment upon the hoped-for regression or the unfortunate progression of some disease. But another valuable instructive connection almost certainly was made.

As a physiologist mainly concerned with body chemistry, Professor Boruttau would have been fascinated with new evidence of the importance to health of nutrition — the foods that the body took in, digested and possibly stored away. The major nutrients, known to be protein (in the form of amino acids), carbohydrates and fats, were carried in the blood stream throughout the body, to fuel the metabolism that supplied energy for movement, growth and reproduction. Undoubtedly, the professor communicated his nutritional information and interests to his protégé.

Furthermore, an array of restricted-diet experiments in various laboratories by now had determined that animals and humans absolutely required, for well-being and long-term survival, some as yet unidentified substances in food beyond the major nutrients and a few minerals now known to be important for their functions. In the late 1890s, Christiaan Eijkman, a Dutch researcher in the East Indies, had proven that beriberi, a potentially fatal nervous disorder, was caused by removing something in the bran covering of brown rice while converting it to the more fashionable 'polished' or white form. The terrible scourge of scurvy, which for centuries had afflicted sailors and other people whose diet (as in wintertime) did not contain fresh fruits or vegetables, was now suspected to be due to some crucial yet mysterious ingredient — and not an infectious agent that microbiologists insistently had searched for in spite of centuries of evidence indicating that eating certain plants prevented or cured scurvy. Rickets, or bone softening, was another disease that appeared to be due to some dietary deficiency.

By 1906, as Max Gerson was just finishing medical school, the eminent British nutrition scientist Sir Frederick G. Hopkins had declared that it was impossible for animals to live on artificial food mixtures that contained a good balance of protein, carbohydrate and fat. It was apparent that this was because their bodies were designed to live on the tissues of plants or other animals, which contained something other than these basic components of nutrition. He called them "accessory food factors." What substances they were, and how many, still had to be determined, but evidence of their existence was already mounting.

In 1912 the Polish biochemist Casimir Funk, transplanted to the United States, would give the name "vitamines" to these microconstituents of food, and the term stuck, in a slightly altered form. The three vitamins that prevented beriberi, scurvy and rickets were early ones among a growing list of vitamins or potential vitamins targeted for investigation; they became known eventually as thiamin or vitamin B_1, ascorbic acid or vitamin C, and calciferol or vitamin D, respectively. When vitamins were discovered and their molecular structures were defined, they could be tracked in various foods and their presence quantified; eventually all would be synthesized for convenient and low-cost use as supplements.

This growing awareness in medicine of a new health condition classification, "deficiency diseases," initially considered vitamins, minerals and essential amino acids that could not be manufactured within the body but needed to be consumed either in food or in the form of dietary supplements. Only gradually would it become evident that plant foods contained many hundreds of other ingredients, such as enzymes and other beneficent biochemicals, that might be important as well in maintaining health and even in curing disease. Some researchers — certainly Dr Max Gerson among them — would declare that their effective actions could not remain viable under conditions other than their perfectly fresh and natural state.

Food Sensitivities and Dietary Changes

Through the long years of his intensive medical education, Max had searched in vain for a solution to the terrible migraine pain he periodically experienced. As a resident physician he had more opportunity to explore the resources of some of the world's finest universities. Whenever possible, he headed for medical libraries, to access and read whatever he could find there on the subject of migraines. If an interesting paper was written in a language he did not understand, he had the paper translated into German.

After much fruitless research, Max came across an obscure reference by an internist in a 17th-century Italian medical text. The physician had recorded that patients had told him that when they were careful about what they ate, their migraines were not so severe. This was the first piece of encouraging information Max had found in all his research. Max then recalled, possibly with a start, that his own mother earlier had suggested that changing his diet in some way might help stop the headaches from coming. Some members of her own family, for at least four generations, had suffered from migraines, and she knew that they had tended to avoid certain foods, maintaining they were headache triggers.

Gerson decided to use his own body as an experimental subject. Not surprisingly, Dr Boruttau in Berlin offered his cooperation, since he himself was very interested in the subject of diet. The first progress Max made in his research project was noticing that when he used salt in his food, the migraine attacks seemed worse. It became obvious that the first food element he must avoid was salt. Taking weekly blood and urine samples, he found that just before an attack his urine became quite clear and was noticeably lacking in waste products. After one or two days of a migraine, however, the urine became cloudy, thick and dark, and would have a very high sodium content, as if some of his tissue cells had been retaining an abnormal and detrimental amount of this mineral. Oddly, too, when the attack had passed, Max felt reborn, with his physical energy and mental faculties at peak condition, indicating that his body had just flushed out some harmful, even poisonous substance. Was there something in sodium chloride (NaCl), or table salt — the sodium or the chlorine, or both of them together — that his body could not tolerate in an excessive quantity?

Max now began to experiment with radical changes to his dietary intake. For a while, he ate only meat and vegetables, without salt; then he substituted milk products for meat. Later, he tried more and more raw plant foods and other modifications. It was a long and tedious process, but the goal pursued, after all, was his own health and well-being. The total process of methodically undertaking what we now call an elimination diet took Max about two years, but at the end of that period of experimentation, he finally knew how to avoid his migraine attacks, but he occasionally was reminded of his vulnerability. He often visited some relatives who lived in Berlin. Always glad to see their young physician nephew, they entertained him handsomely. Knowing that potato salad with sausages was one of his favorite dishes, they would prepare it specially for him. On a visit to them after he had discovered how to keep himself migraine-free, he took a generous helping of the dish. The next morning, he awakened with a severe migraine. His body, no longer at all accustomed to this kind of food, couldn't handle it. His experience in testing foods on his own body now told him that if he was to remain free of migraines, he needed to eliminate potato salad with sausages from his diet. Since no culinary delight was worth the terrible suffering that followed a misstep, he did this easily.

Dr Gerson did not know whether or not his body was peculiarly hypersensitive to specific chemical compounds in foods, such as the sodium chloride that was salt, that worsened when combined with the fat, as in the sausages; or perhaps he was actually allergic to various dietary substances, so that an immune response—about which little was known at that period—was initiated when the substance entered his bloodstream. Either way, there was a strong physiological reaction to the chemical's presence in his blood and tissues, which then caused the intense, throbbing pain, inflammation and other unpleasant symptoms of a migraine attack.

Max began considering that his body might be like a chemical barometer, providing an early-warning system for detecting harmful ingredients in certain foods and condiments. If he was adversely affected by the substances that bothered him, might not other people also be, without knowing it? Or perhaps other individuals would have their own distinctive hypersensitivities and allergies to factors not only in food but also in the external environment, that affected their digestion and subsequent metabolism—and consequently their total well-being over time. If people had specific food intolerances, perhaps because they lacked certain digestive enzymes, yet they continued to eat these troublesome foods, they would surely become ill in some way. The longer they suffered such assaults on their bodies, the sicker they were likely to become. At the same time, the foods that Max found had positive value for him might possibly prove equally beneficial to other people. And so, therefore, might the special diet that he was gradually developing for his own needs.

In this same time period, other medical researchers and nutritionists, in Europe and the United States, were extending and expanding the earlier explorations of 'whole foods', such as unrefined grains and fresh produce, but now by using scientific research methodologies. Germany became a fertile ground for avid proponents of a 'back to nature' dietary regimen, and some exceedingly nefarious political figures were among its most enthusiastic advocates.

Private Practice in Breslau

With the long period of his clinical and research training completed, in 1913 young Dr. Max Gerson settled in Breslau, where he had first entered the German university system 14 years earlier. He rented a ground floor apartment, which doubled as a dwelling and convenient office space from which he could conduct his practice.

The apartment came with a garden—a bonus in Max's estimation, recalling the pleasures and curiosity his grandmothers garden had inspired. He soon began to experiment. In his new plot he planted roses and imported Dutch tulips, since he was particularly fond of these flowers. He paid two young boys to bring horse manure from the street to fertilize the roses bushes, and he cared for them lovingly. Before long, Max was experimenting with plants as a hobby, just as he had done as a boy. He attempted to influence their colors with different combinations of fertilizers and light filters. From experience, Max discovered how far he needed to keep the filters from the buds and flowers so that they would not cause the sunlight to burn their delicate petals. Using various combinations of soil, fertilizers, exposures to sunlight, light filters and watering schedules, Max was able to produce long-stemmed roses of many different and unexpected hues. The most unusual plants had green blossoms with red stems and leaves.

One day, while taking one of his vigorous, therapeutic walks in the moist and fragrant woods around Breslau, Gerson noticed a tiny movement near the base of a tree. On closer inspection, he found it was a baby squirrel with a broken leg.

Evidently it had fallen out of its high nest, or failed to complete a trial leap from high branch to high branch. Max took the young animal home and nursed it back to health. The squirrel, having been raised by the gentle doctor, became quite tame. It would happily travel everywhere with Max, surprising his colleagues by peeping out of the pocket of his overcoat at odd times, begging for a peanut. Max named the squirrel "Bushy Semmelweiss": *Bushy* was for the shape and quality of his tail, and *Semmelweiss* honored the memory of Dr. Ignaz Semmelweiss. The Hungarian medical researcher had been literally hounded out of the profession in the middle of the past century because he had dared to suggest that surgeons should wash their hands and change their bloody aprons between the dissections of cadavers and their work in the delivery room with mothers and babies. Here was an early sign that Max recognized that any new ideas or unorthodox methods, especially those that merited serious consideration, were apt to be summarily rejected by hidebound traditionalists protecting their own professional turf. Bushy's name served as a constant reminder to him not to reject innovations — whether someone else's methods or new theories of his own. In an oddly coincidental manner, Bushy Semmelweiss died in a fashion similar to his beleaguered namesake. Ignaz Semmelweiss had died of infection incurred from an accidental cut in the dissection room. Bushy died of an infection contracted from an accidental scratch on a sharp wire in his cage.

Dr Gerson took such small interest in discussing and reading about political matters which did not directly pertain to medicine and health that probably it shocked him when the Great War — World War I — erupted in early August of 1914, as Germany began declaring war on several nations, and other nations declared war on Germany and Austria. For years, Max had been so engrossed in the process of becoming a doctor, then in acquiring advanced clinical training in several fields and finally setting up a practice of his own, that he had little time or reason to focus on the increasingly tense political and socioeconomic situation within Germany and elsewhere in Europe during the first decade and a half of the 20th century. Later, this same absorption in his own medical practice and research work in the chaotic period in Germany after the First World War would prevent him from paying sufficient heed to another far greater hazard to his career and life.

For some decades Germany, and most especially its principal state, Prussia (formerly a kingdom of its own), had stressed and indeed glorified the military's role in protecting the comparatively new nation's interests at home and abroad. Young men were often raised with the goal of entering and making noble careers in the military service, either on land or sea — or, as became possible in the new century's first two decades, in the air. Militaristic leaders were apt to take an active role in governmental policy making and administration. Germany had become an empire centered in Prussia after various states were united through Chancellor Bismarck's antagonistic policies toward neighboring nations. In 1888 Kaiser Wilhelm I's reign passed to his even more aggressive grandson, Wilhelm II, who was determined to make his nation the dominant world power. In its imperialistic activities Germany especially competed with near neighbors Great Britain and France by acquiring colonies in Africa and Asia, building a large naval force that prowled the high seas, promoting advantageous foreign trade and developing key state-supported industries, particularly those involved with mining and machinery and chemical manufacturing.

Germany's closest ally was with the Austro-Hungarian Empire just to the south. When the heir-apparent to the empire's throne, Archduke Francis Ferdinand, was assassinated in Sarajevo in June of 1914 by a Serbian nationalist, Austria-Hungary demanded extreme reparations, and when these were refused, war was declared against Serbia. Within a few weeks the Great War had begun between the Central Powers, in which Austria-Hungary and Germany were joined by the Turkish Empire, and the 'Allied' nations, Britain, France, Italy, Russia, the Low Countries (Belgium and Holland), and most of the Balkan nations.

In the Franco-Prussian War of 1870-71 and other territorial struggles, German Jews had been recruited into the military service with all other healthy young men. They served loyally in Bismarck's victorious effort, but their rise to high rank as officers inevitably encountered difficulties. Although a degree of anti-Semitism lurked in all fields of European human endeavor with the concern that they might eventually 'take over' if given high-ranking positions, this abiding fear was essentially a defensive, envious recognition of the good results of Jewish culture's emphasis on cohesion, education and professional success — which in turn was a survival response to the centuries-long prejudice against Jews. As in its previous wars, Germany during the First World War was scarcely reluctant to bring male Jewish citizens into its fighting ranks. Also, when wars come, young doctors are scarcely permitted to decline serving the urgent medical needs of their embattled nation. Almost immediately after war was declared, Max Gerson was called up for military service. Physicians would be needed to treat the battlefield casualties; some were already coming from the war's Eastern Front, to the east and the south of Breslau, where the action, immediate and heavy, for some while went mostly in the Central Powers' favor. They had struck where their foes seemed most vulnerable.

Before Dr Max Gerson left Breslau to take up a proffered commission in the Army Medical Corps, he decided to keep his apartment, and arranged to hire a gardener to tend his extraordinary flower garden during the duration of his tour of duty. Doubtless, he hoped that the German and Austrian-Hungarian military leaders, their standing armies and navies and their recent recruits were well prepared for combat. He also trusted that they knew well what they were doing in starting up this convoluted conflict with other European nations. He neither expected nor wanted to be long away from his recently launched medical practice.

3
Military Doctor
(1914–1918)

Dr Förster's Military Hospital

When Dr. Max Gerson reported for military duty, he was commissioned as a *Hauptmann* (Captain) in the German Army. Stationed in Oels (now Olesnica, Poland), some 20 miles east-northeast of Breslau, he initially worked at a military hospital that treated wounded or ailing soldiers from the war's Eastern Front, where the Central Powers had routed Russian troops at Tannenberg and the Masurian Lakes. Afterwards, Max was transferred briefly to northern Italy. There the mounting combat was less conclusive, resulting in drawing Austrian military attention away from assisting the Germans in the Western Front, where the earlier assaults on the Allies were now stalling.

After Dr. Gerson had been absent from Breslau for about a year and a half, Professor Dr. Ottfried Förster, a well-known neurosurgeon, requested his return to Breslau. Förster had first become acquainted with Max while he was attending the University of Breslau. Impressed with what he knew now of the young doctor's abilities and wanting him as an assistant physician, Förster was highly placed enough in the military hierarchy to get his wish granted. Soon Gerson was on his way back to Breslau, to serve as a surgeon in the military hospital there under Dr. Förster's command. And despite three attempts later by the military to transfer Max away from Breslau, Förster always got him reassigned to his surgery post in that city.

Upon his return to his apartment in Breslau, Max was very perturbed to find his beautiful and unusual flower garden plundered by the gardener whom he had hired to tend it during his absence. As soon as his employer was gone, this putative caretaker, amazed at the unusual and colorful flowers that the young doctor had produced, had cut all the flowers and sold them. Max was so disappointed that he never went back to working in his garden, though he kept the apartment. Still, his personal experience with gardening and experimenting with different species and varieties of plants, nutrients, light conditions and other growing factors laid the basis for his future interest in the science of agriculture. (In his later life, much as he loved to have plants around him, he would always much too busy with his urban medical practice and research to devote time and energy to the hands-on gardening at which he had once excelled. In the future, his novel experiments would largely be devised and conducted on human beings, on patients — always with the intention of discovering better ways to improve their health, which he could do especially through food plants and their nutrients.

The military hospital in Breslau occupied buildings that prior to the war had served as the seminary within the Catholic Faculty of Theology at the University of Breslau, and therefore it bore the name *Konvikt* (conviction). Since tradition is ever strong in Europe, the medical facility continued to use this old name. The hospital was large, containing 500 beds, and Professor Förster required a staff of three trained senior assistant physicians. Each of the three senior doctors in turn had two junior doctors as assistants.

In his mid '40s when the war broke out, Dr. Förster was of medium height, lean, nervous and energetic, but his most prominent characteristic was a burning ambition. Among this neurosurgeon's claims to fame was his having perfected a successful technique for suturing nerve tissue. It was an extremely useful surgical skill now with so many frontline soldiers and sailors sustaining serious wounds to their arms, legs or backs. Because of Förster's special expertise, the Konvikt received only nerve injuries from the battlefront. There was much work to be done, as the constant carnage from the war's seesawing onslaughts and retreats, using modern rapid-fire weapons, heavy artillery shelling, land mines, even submarine attacks and aerial bombardments, produced more than enough casualties to fill the hospital beds.

Förster's nerve-suturing method consisted of two separate operations, each of which normally took several hours. In the first operation, the bones near the injury were exposed and serrated. The next day, the patient's nerve endings would be electrically tested. The assistant surgeons would hold the nerve endings between their fingers, then sew together the separate ends with specially prepared hairs, which had to be ultra-fine and were collected from women. The operations often lasted six to eight hours. When the operation was successful, with proper rest and care the nerves grew together in about six months, so that the limb would become responsive and mobile again.

Dr. Gerson's daily duties at the military hospital in Breslau often left time for other challenging medical work. Besides fulfilling his military duties as the chief neurosurgeon at the Konvikt, Förster had a private clinic in Breslau where he performed operations, and he invited Gerson to be his assistant there as well. The workday at Charlottenhaus began at 6 a.m. Some of the cases at this clinic were injured and disabled officers awaiting their discharge from war service. Dr. Lübke was one of these casualties. Partially buried by a bomb explosion, the young military doctor had spent two days praying to be exhumed. After he was finally rescued, his saviors found that one of his legs, damaged by the long burial, was almost unmovable. By the time he arrived at Charlottenhaus, Dr. Lübke had been shuffled from one military hospital to another. None had been able to treat him successfully, and the Konvikt had proved no better.

Since Lübke's leg was still stiff and unusable, there was no alternative to releasing the young doctor from military service. However, discharging a military officer from the German Army during wartime required considerable paperwork, since German bureaucracy was already notorious for being more tediously efficient than that of most other organizations in the world, military or otherwise. So there were signatures and certifications and copies to be obtained. Dr. Förster had to countersign the papers, as did Breslau's head physician. Requests for the discharge of an officer then would be sent to the War High Command in Berlin. An officer still could only be released from war duties after Kaiser Wilhelm II himself had affixed his signature to the document.

Dr. Förster, called away for two days to consult at a military hospital elsewhere, assigned Max the medical responsibility for the patient during his absence. Dr. Gerson examined Dr. Lübke at the earliest opportunity, though Lübke declared it unnecessary, since he would be going home the next day. But Gerson insisted on doing some electrical tests on the leg first. Soon thereafter he came back to talk with the patient. "Dr. Lübke, I must report some interesting results from the nerve tests on your leg. Your leg appears totally normal. There is no functional problem with either the nerves or muscles."

"But how can that be, Dr. Gerson? I can barely put my weight on it when standing. And you have seen how I need crutches to move about."

"Nonetheless, the problem is not with the leg. Look at the test results, Lübke. You are a physician, you can see for yourself. The leg is fine."

"Impossible! My leg is obviously crippled. You can't just suddenly tell me I'm fine and send me back to war."

"Perhaps not, Dr. Lübke, but the test results are clear. If you wish to be a physician in civilian life, you cannot simply ignore facts that don't agree with your preconceived notions. Some people might even see this disability of yours as malingering."

"Gerson, I am not faking this injury. It is real! Besides, I am to be discharged tomorrow."

"Dr. Lübke, I am afraid I must insist on my diagnosis. If you fail to use a perfectly good leg and thus avoid your service obligation, I will be forced to make a notation to that effect in your permanent military record—and of course it will be considered when you apply for your medical license. I will also write a letter to your father explaining my actions." Max knew from reading the patient's history that this latter remark would hit a sensitive nerve.

Lübke went pale. "Please, Dr. Gerson, don't write to my father. I can't afford to lose both my dream and my father's! He is a minor official in a small town, and he has scrimped and saved all his life to put me through university and medical school. It would destroy him if I couldn't work as a doctor."

"Well, you can't be a doctor under false pretenses. So what is your decision, Lübke?"

"I will do my best now to try to use the leg, Dr. Gerson. But please let me have some time. It has been unused for too long for me to just stand and walk normally. Will you give me a while to work on it? I promise I will do everything I can."

"All right, Lübke. I'll give you a couple of days to get back on your feet. And I won't write your father about this incident."

The grateful Dr. Lübke immediately started working on getting his leg to function.

When Dr. Förster returned to Breslau the following day, he inquired of Gerson, "Is Lübke ready for his release?"

"No, sir. We've discovered that his leg is basically fine. He is walking about his room without crutches, and will be totally recovered in a few days. I have disapproved his discharge."

Förster went white. "You've done *what?* My God, are you mad, Gerson?" Rushing out of the office, Förster bounded up the stairs, three at a time, and ran down the hall toward Lübke's room. When he burst into the room, he was astounded to see Dr. Lübke tentatively but competently walking about the room without the assistance of crutches. Dismayed, turning without saying a word, he stormed back to the office where he had left Gerson.

"Do you realize what you have done, Gerson?" He was shouting by now. "I have signed papers certifying that this man was crippled and unfit for military service. My chief has countersigned the papers. The papers have been sent to Berlin, where more senior officers have signed them. Now the request is on its way to be signed by the Kaiser himself. And you have just shown the whole affair to be a fraud. This could disgrace the hospital and charges could be filed. It could end my career! I'll throw you out of here myself!"

By this time, the other doctors had heard the commotion and joined Dr. Förster and Dr. Gerson in the office.

"What I have done, Dr. Förster," Max said calmly, "is cure the patient, and return a desperately needed military doctor to active duty. I am sorry if that is inconvenient, but the truth is that the patient was not physically disabled."

Förster stopped for a moment. With the damage already done, nothing further could be accomplished by bluster or shouting. It was far more important now to salvage the situation by retrieving the paperwork. That meant intercepting the discharge request parcel in Berlin before it was presented to the Kaiser for his finalizing signature. Förster sprang into action. After several urgent telephone calls, he determined what should be done to stop the papers. He also informed his chief of the problem. He immediately dispatched a military doctor to Berlin to rescue the discharge papers from Army headquarters. Because this was highly irregular, it was only accomplished with great effort and innumerable explanations. Headquarters, operating with Teutonic efficiency, had already passed the request up the line, and it was now ready to be sent to the Kaiser for his signature. Fortunately, the papers were halted just in time, and the incident caused no further harm.

This was the first time, but scarcely the last time, that Max Gerson experienced a conflict with colleagues over curing a patient. Healing someone whom the experts have already declared incurable has always been politically dangerous. Dr. Gerson, a healer by nature, could never properly grasp the reality of this concept, and his integrity would cause him tremendous difficulty over his long career.

The Case of the Leaky Spinal Fluid

A surgical operation conducted by Dr. Förster that Dr. Gerson often assisted with involved the suturing of damaged or severed nerves in the spinal column. Unfortunately, this procedure almost invariably claimed the life of the patient, no matter how skillful the surgeon.

Gerson's usual task of administering the anesthetic and monitoring respiration and pulse rates was not unduly demanding, so he could observe each operation in detail. Before the operation, the patient was stretched out level and face down on the operating table. When the spine was opened, the natural curve of the structure made the opening lower than the rest of the spinal column. Gerson was particularly struck by the slow and inexorable seeping away of spinal fluid during the operation. Usually the patient would die, either during the operation or shortly thereafter, never having regained consciousness after being administered the anesthesia.

It occurred to Gerson that perhaps the loss of spinal fluid caused these deaths, and that it drained out simply due to gravity. He wanted to suggest to Dr. Förster a way to modify the surgery so as to prevent the leakage: to elevate the patient's hips by tilting the operating table toward the head, not radically but just enough to make the opening into the spinal column higher than the rest of the structure. In this way, he reasoned, gravity would work to keep the vital spinal fluid *within* the spinal column, rather than allow it to seep out. No matter what the outcome, it could not possibly be worse than the results Förster usually got.

Max discussed his idea with his colleagues. They pointed out two drawbacks in his proposal. The first was minor, considering the potential benefit: the position for operating would be more difficult and uncomfortable for surgeons. Max's associates judged the second obstacle insurmountable. Dr. Förster had the reputation of being dictatorial, domineering and arrogant. The other doctors repeatedly warned Gerson never to speak out, because suggesting any procedural change to the chief surgeon would only result in his immediate dismissal. Finally, his discomfort overcame his fear of Förster's wrath. He made the suggestion he had long been considering.

Förster's response was nearly as negative as the other assistants had predicted — he reacted angrily. Förster summarily rejected Max's idea. Still, he did not dismiss Gerson. And Max continued to watch the young war casualties die — unnecessarily, he believed. The tragedy of this possibly avoidable loss of life impelled him to beg his chief, again and again, to simply try the technique once, but Förster would not budge, and the soldiers kept dying.

For some years Dr. Förster had been a Professor of Neurology at the University of Breslau, where his father also was a professor. He retained this teaching and research position during the war, while carrying on his clinical practice at the military hospital and his private clinic. One day a young girl whom Förster had been treating at the clinic died of a neurodegenerative disease. Since the case was a very interesting one to the surgeon, he badly wanted the girl's brain for autopsy examination and then preservation for research and instructional purposes at the university. But the girl's family would not give him permission to extract the brain.

Förster's ambition would not be impeded, however. He now asked Gerson and another assistant doctor to go to the cemetery and, prior to the burial service, fetch the girl's brain for his purposes. This was quite a major request to put to any subordinate, as it placed the two junior physicians in legal and ethical peril. If apprehended in the act of virtual grave robbing, they could be imprisoned, cashiered from the army and lose their medical licenses.

Still, Förster was insistent, and he was their commander. So, on a frigid winter night the two young doctors set out for the cemetery. The snow lay in high drifts. An icy wind, blowing off the frozen Oder River, cut through their heavy army greatcoats. The unauthorized entry took them longer than anticipated. The men could not find the cemetery's entrance in the dark, so they decided to climb over the six-foot high wall, though ill prepared for this activity. Besides wearing bulky clothing, they had brought with them a lantern, a bag of surgical equipment and a container for the extracted brain. Finally inside, they located the mortuary, where the young girl's body still lay in the coffin, awaiting burial the next day. In accordance with Professor Förster's plan, they compensated the night watchman generously to busy himself elsewhere, in a remote corner of the lot. Then the men got down to their grisly task.

It could have been a scene right out of *Frankenstein*. By the light of a flickering lantern, the two junior doctors opened the girl's skull, removed her brain and placed it carefully in the special box. They quickly closed up the skull and sewed the scalp shut so skillfully that the incision would not be noticed without close inspection.

It was well past midnight before they returned to the Konvikt, their mission accomplished. Professor Förster was exceedingly pleased with the results. The brain in the box before him would likely bear fruitful knowledge for both his research and reputation—always an important consideration for an ambitious surgeon.

Gerson now saw a good chance to ask once more for a trial of his modification to the spinal cord procedure. This time, albeit reluctantly, Förster agreed to try the tilted operating table. Next time the surgical spine repair was attempted, Förster did it with the patient's pelvis raised above the level of his head, as Gerson suggested. For the first time, there was no post-operative coma. The patient survived—an extremely rare outcome. Before the procedure could be established as a standard, more operations were performed, with similar results. Patients now had a good chance to live after undergoing this risky operation. Förster greeted the repetition of the good results with excitement and praise. Naturally, the doctors who had begged Gerson not to speak of his innovation were amazed at the chief's reaction. The eminent surgeon was so happy, in fact, that he threw a lavish party in the best hotel in Breslau, where all the staff doctors drank and feasted in Gerson's honor, despite the desperate food shortages. Förster also published this successful new spinal-cord operating procedure under his own name—standard procedure for professors, whether or not they themselves had participated in developing some new idea or method initially proposed by some subordinate.

As for Max Gerson, he was pleased that his suggested innovation was now saving lives.

An Arranged Marriage

The Gerson family over the years got increasingly concerned about Max's seeming lack of interest in getting married. Max's mother, Ulricke, was determined to convince Max to marry and have children. She and Bernhardt now lived in Berlin with their youngest children. After the war began, they had moved to Germany's capital city from Wongrowitz, possibly to seek expert medical treatment for Bernhardt, who had a serious liver ailment.

Ulricke, in her desire to find a suitable mate for Max, resorted to the time-honored method of advertising, which she did in German-Jewish newspapers. One of the responses came from a family in Westphalia, an area in northwestern Germany about 100 miles west of Berlin. Gretchen Hope was the daughter of a prosperous merchant in the small town of Verl, which at the time had only about 300 inhabitants. Max Hope, her father, owned the general store, as well as land, cattle and horses.

Gretchen's family had been able to provide her with an excellent education. She had spent time at a Swiss finishing school for young women, where she had learned the finer points of keeping a beautiful home. She had also become fluent in

French and was an accomplished pianist. Then with her studies in Switzerland completed and World War I not yet looming, she had been sent to live with relatives in London so that she could learn to speak English. Knowledge of the two languages would serve her well, and her husband also, in her later life.

On her return to her family home, Gretchen's prospects were slim for meeting any eligible young men locally, since the Hope family was the only Jewish family in town. After the Great War broke out, all able-bodied young bachelors in the Westphalia region went into military service. So the Hopes answered the personal advertisement placed by Ulricke Gerson, and the two families soon mutually arranged for the two young people to meet in Verl.

Gretchen's first impression of Max was highly favorable. Not only was he tall, about six feet, but he was slender and handsome as well, with intense blue eyes and a gentle demeanor. He wore the full uniform of a captain in the German Army, which in that military-admiring period automatically claimed a status only slightly less than nobility. The elegant and well-educated young lady was instantly impressed. Gretchen's admiration for men in dress uniform (with the notable exception of Germans leading up to and during World War II) remained strong for the rest of her life.

Max, in turn, saw a strong, attractive, intelligent and talented young woman with exquisite manners and bearing, from a prosperous Jewish family. They became engaged on November 1, 1916, and married less than three weeks later in Verl, on November 20.

The Hope family faced a real challenge in arranging for the wedding feast, due to stringent wartime food rationing. Living out in the countryside and having ample financial means made the problem of obtaining enough supplies for a banquet less arduous, however. Max Hope went around the neighborhood from farm to farm, purchasing what he could from his customers and neighbors.

Most of Gretchen's relatives lived in Gütersloh, about 15 miles distant, or in the city of Bielefeld, an additional 15 miles away. A good number of people attended the reception, including family members of Max's. Ulricke, of course, was there for the happy event, but sadly without her husband, Bernhardt, who had died only five weeks earlier, shortly before Max's engagement to Gretchen. Dr. Gerson had received a short leave from his medical duties, to enable him to get married. But their honeymoon could last only a few days, after which Max brought his young bride to the apartment in Breslau.

Early on, Gretchen became aware that her husband did not share her admiration for uniforms and other military paraphernalia. Gerson's lack of attention to displaying the various accoutrements of his rank as a captain actually became a cause of daily consternation to his wife. The sword was a mandatory part of a German officer's uniform, so Max was required to wear it wherever he went. Gretchen had to constantly remind him to buckle on his sword and sheath when he went off to work at the hospital. But since she could not follow him around all day, he would often return home without his sword, having removed it at the Charlottenhaus clinic, the Konvikt or the home of one or another of his private patients. Their maid was then sent scurrying about Breslau to retrieve the sword that Dr. Gerson, absentminded and scarcely vainglorious, had abandoned somewhere.

Wartime Diet Discovery

The young couple had also started their domestic life together under trying culinary circumstances. The food supply had dwindled during the war as many German farmers enlisted and fertile land was transformed into battle zones along the French, Belgian, Russian and Italian borders. Severe rationing had been imposed, which grew much worse as food scarcities increased, so that even rationed goods were unobtainable. To make matters worse, the onset of an unusually cold winter had frozen the potato crop, so no spuds were available — a terrible blow to the Germans, who were accustomed to serving them at nearly every meal, where their high carbohydrate content supplied needed calories and a sense of fullness.

As the Great War stretched on and on, the near-famished civilian population made do with amazing creativity. A housewife's industrious search would occasionally yield poor-quality meat, butter, eggs, lard and flour, but these prizes were the exception rather than the rule. Tobacco and alcohol were almost impossible to obtain. 'Horse beets'—giant turnips which when cooked had an unpleasant taste that children especially loathed—were substituted for potatoes, bread was stretched by adding sawdust, dried vegetables were mixed with sand to expand their bulk. Though this fare was barely palatable at best, people were near starving, especially in the winter months, and usually ate anything that might fill their bellies.

Dr. Gerson was naturally aware that many medical experts in wartime Germany feared that the health of the general population would suffer because of most people's inability to get the quantities of animal protein and fat that seemed essential to their well-being. It was simply assumed that the habit of eating a high-fat diet originated from necessity. To everyone's surprise — and certainly Max would take great note of this later— the population's overall health actually *improved*. Corpulent people, usually a fixture in beer- and Wurst-consuming Germany, were no longer the norm, and mortality rates declined sharply under the conditions of undernutrition. Not everybody became healthier, of course — the frail elderly and poor people already on the edge of starvation were apt to decline and die.

Scientific observations and experiments on both animals and humans have borne out this epidemiological phenomenon of improved health and extended longevity in a population during a period of reduced food and caloric consumption. World War II repeated the effect on a large scale. Experiments have demonstrated that severe calorie restriction may actually triple immune-system function, and the elimination or extreme reduction of animal protein has a similar effect. Studies also have shown that rats fed near-starvation diets live twice as long as well-fed mice. An additional health-conferring factor in wartime was the widespread consumption of unrefined — whole grain, not bleached and processed — cereals and breads, with much higher vitamin and mineral contents as well as fiber.

Max Gerson realized another benefit during this food-deprivation period: his migraine headaches, which occasionally afflicted him in spite of his careful attention to diet, completely disappeared. This was a special blessing to a physician involved in painstaking neurosurgery, when a disruptive migraine attack would be wholly unacceptable, since operations often required hours of intensive, highly focused attention.

During those lean years of war-related food shortages, it was a major coup for a housewife to find some rare or tasty delicacy to break the monotony of whatever tasteless *ersatz* food could be found. One winter's day in 1917, Gretchen found a bonanza: genuine sauerkraut, made from fresh cabbage. She eagerly brought some home to serve to her hardworking new husband. She knew it would be a treat for him. Gretchen prepared the midday meal with joy, anticipating the pleasure that it would give to Max. Knowing that he was always careful about salt consumption, she first rinsed the sauerkraut to remove most of the brine. The sauerkraut was delicious, she thought, with its taste doubtless enhanced by the rarity of the acquisition.

When Max came home from the Konvikt, however, he looked utterly exhausted and quite pale. He had no appetite at all. But when he saw the eager expression on his sweet bride's face, he sat down at the table, where Gretchen had set the precious dish. When he took his first bite, he could scarcely swallow it. "Do you really expect me to eat this, Gretchen?"

"Why, Max, isn't it prepared the way you like it?"

"Gretchen, surely you can taste it! It tastes like an old rusty barrel!"

Gretchen was crushed. The sauerkraut had tasted fine to her. She sampled Max's dish, and it tasted no different. Max, who hadn't felt like eating anyway, got up from the table and went to lie down for a while before returning to work. He could not understand his fatigue. Though he had been involved in a long operation earlier in the day, he was quite used to these lengthy, intricate procedures, and they normally did not affect him this way. But today he could not shake the tiredness.

Depressed, weak and still unfed, Max returned to the hospital. There he found that the other doctors who had assisted at the operation that morning were complaining of the same symptoms as his: lack of appetite, a bad taste in their mouths, unusual fatigue. The reason was soon discovered. Before each operation, as an antiseptic measure the part of the patient's body to be operated on would be swabbed with an iodine solution. That morning, the hospital pharmacist had provided an iodine solution that later was discovered to be much too concentrated. The combination of iodine fumes and ether inhaled by the assisting physicians had given all of them iodine poisoning.

It took several days for the worst of the symptoms to disappear, but some degree of loss of taste and smell remained with Max Gerson for the rest of his life.

Two Shocking Experiences

During World War I, Dr. Gerson's duties as a military doctor continued to occupy most of his time. On one occasion, when ready to give a patient an injection after an examination, Max requested that the nurse prepare a syringe containing the desired medication. When he was about to insert the needle into the patient's vein, he noticed that the fluid in the syringe was slightly pink instead of being colorless. Calling the nurse back, he told her to bring the bottle from which she had drawn the fluid. When he looked at the bottle, he was shocked to see that the bottle contained a strong disinfectant instead of the requested medication. Had Max not spotted the slight difference in color, the injection would have killed the patient, and Gerson's career as a doctor would have been over. But there were consequences: Gretchen noticed that within a week after the incident, her young husband had developed a white streak of hair over his forehead.

In addition to working at Dr. Förster's own clinic on the side, Dr. Gerson was occasionally invited to consult at another clinic in Breslau, which was operated by two of his colleagues. This well-equipped private clinic was a pleasant work environment. One day, as Gerson was assisting an associate in the X-ray room, making diagnostic roentgen plates of a patient's body, a poorly fastened high-voltage cable suddenly fell from the ceiling and landed directly on Gerson's head. If he had simply been standing on the wooden floor at the time, probably he would have only been affected by the blow itself, but, coincidentally and most unfortunately, he was standing on a metal chain. His body thus provided the path for the electricity to travel to the ground.

The sudden jolt of thousands of volts of electricity knocked Max unconscious. He collapsed heavily onto the floor. To the great relief of his colleagues, they found that though he appeared to be dead, he was only unconscious, but then they saw that the metallic fillings in his teeth had actually melted. The other doctors quickly took Gerson to a room in the clinic and put him in a bed, where he lay unconscious for nearly 24 hours. When he regained consciousness, he was dazed and disoriented. It took a while longer for him to register the full extent of the damage done by the high voltage. He realized that he was almost completely paralyzed.

Gerson's knowledge of the nervous system, refined by his years of working with Dr. Förster, told him that the electrical shock had burned out circuits in his brain that affected motor control. He knew that he would probably be permanently paralyzed.

As Gerson lay there in his hospital bed, the horrifying vision of his future overwhelmed him. Unable to move much at all, of course he could no longer be a physician, nor could he be a proper husband to his young and talented bride. Max could not stand the prospect of this, and sank deeper and deeper into depression. The hospital room was on the third floor of the clinic, and as soon as he could muster enough strength in his partly paralyzed arms, he dragged himself out of the hospital bed and headed for the unlocked window. Before he could reach his goal and hurl himself out and onto the courtyard below, a nurse passed by the doorway. With the alarm raised, the staff nurses put Max back into the bed and applied restraints. Exhausted first from his electrocution and now from his attempted suicide, Max fell into a deep and dreamless sleep.

During the night, his body's healing system did its silent and mysterious work. Awakening the next day, Max found that he could once again move all his limbs almost as well as before. He could not understand his recovery — he could only surmise that he was the one in ten thousand individuals who had 'backup' circuitry in his brain, nerve pathways that took over the task when the primary nerves were destroyed or disabled. Delighted with his great good luck, Gerson went home and then back to work in a few days.

And Max had much to live for — on August 8, 1917, Gretchen presented him with his first daughter, Johanna.

The End of the World War

In the spring of 1918, the savage international conflict seemed at last to be approaching an end. In the East, the Russians' withdrawal from combat during the Bolshevik Revolution had encouraged the Central Powers to expand their territorial acquisitions, unwisely, drawing off more manpower in that direction. Meanwhile, on the Western front, especially after the 1917 entry of the United States into the international conflict, Germany and Austria-Hungary were exhausting their troops in persistent combats and shipping blockades against the now superior military and industrial resources of the Allied nations. Citizens questioned the sagacity of their nations' ruling class and demanded more political power; and turmoil and rebellions mounted even among the military and government ranks. Finally, the collapse of the Austrian-Hungarian and Turkish empires and Bulgaria in the summer of 1918 left Germany on its own. Knowing that Germany could no longer sustain the war by itself, some of its leaders negotiated with U.S. President Woodrow Wilson, who had been asked to arrange peace terms. Faced with the Allied demand for a democratic government and the ultimatums of advisors, Kaiser Wilhelm II abdicated the throne on November 9 and fled from Berlin to Holland. On November 11 hostilities were officially ended.

While realizing that his once powerful homeland was now vanquished, Max Gerson enjoyed an endearing domestic compensation. On October 12, 1918, Gretchen had presented him with another pretty little girl, Gertrude, who was named after Gretchen's sister.

During his four years of service at the Konvikt, Dr. Gerson had been promoted to the position of senior staff physician. He was also slated to receive the Iron Cross, on white ribbon — a decoration that would acknowledge his valuable service to the nation during wartime. However, in the general chaos accompanying Germany's defeat, the arrangements needed for giving this promised award to Dr. Gerson were totally overlooked by the beleaguered bureaucracy. This omission was of far greater concern to Gretchen than to Max, who had never cared anyway for military baubles. He was a doctor, which was reward enough for him for his past work. What he really needed now was a plan for his future life as a civilian.

~4~
Medical Practice in Westphalia
(1918–1922)

The Move to Bielefeld

The Great War had exhausted Germany and deeply wounded its pride. The nation would be more vulnerable than ever before to the agitations of political groups with extreme economic and social agendas, each diametrically opposed to the others and often incapable of any compromise. The newly declared Weimar Republic, headquartered in Berlin, had replaced the warmongering, imperialistic one and was trying to establish a full-fledged democracy in a land that still held feudal titles.

After the Armistice was signed in November of 1918, the German Army began disbanding its medical staff. Dr. Förster was unhappy at the prospect of seeing Dr. Max Gerson leave the military hospital and his private clinic—and Breslau altogether. Because he had developed a deep appreciation and respect for Gerson's insight, medical knowledge and skill, he often discussed cases with him when they were en route from one clinic to another. When it came time to discharge Max from military service, Förster urged him to continue working with him at the University of Breslau, as well as at his own clinic. Although honored by the invitation, Max doubtless looked forward to breaking free from this noted neurosurgeon's inevitable domination. Dr. Gerson gracefully declined, explaining that he had already decided to move away and set up his civilian practice elsewhere. Because of his earlier training and his years of clinical work with Förster, he qualified as a specialist in both internal medicine and neurology.

Max never considered returning to his birthplace, Wongrowitz. That region was being returned to the resurrected, newly independent Poland. Max's family no longer lived there, since his now-widowed mother and most of his siblings had settled in Berlin during the war. Gerson might have liked to join them in Germany's foremost city, where he had already spent several stimulating and productive years, first as a medical student and then as a resident physician. But as an incoming physician without good connections he would encounter stiff competition in trying to set up a successful practice. With a wife and two small children depending on his support, he could take no such chance. He chose to relocate in the city of Bielefeld, less than 20 miles northeast of the town of Verl, where Gretchen's large family still lived.

Situated in the rich agricultural plain of northern Westphalia, Bielefeld seemed a good place for Max Gerson to start his full-time civilian practice anew. The city in 1919 had about 85,000 inhabitants. In the postwar period it was quickly reviving its earlier peacetime industries, such as producing sewing machines and bicycles, and weaving and manufacturing linens.

The Gersons took over half of a big three-story house at Gütersloherstrasse 9B, which Max's father-in-law had helped them purchase. Though it was a duplex, with another family renting the other half from them, the quarters were large enough to accommodate both Max's family and a separate office and waiting room on the first floor for his medical practice.

Max's choice of location followed his lifelong preference for proximity to forests. Bielefeld was separated from its western suburb of Brackwede by a low ridge covered with dense ancient growths of large oak, linden, birch and several types of beech trees. The ridge had one gap, and through this narrow defile passed all rail, motor and foot traffic between the two communities. The Gersons' new residence was situated in this gap, near a pleasant, wooded neighborhood known as Bethel—a location favored by physicians and other professionals

Directly behind the Gersons' new home, steep, winding paths led up through the woods to the ancient fortress of Sparrenburg, built to dominate traffic through the gap and repel any invaders. The thick forest (which still cloaks the ridge) is a remnant of the vast Teutoburger *Wald* (forest) that once covered large portions of Germany; from it the population derived the name Teutons. (Three Roman Legions were annihilated in A.D. 9, probably near Osnabrück, about 50 miles northwest of Bielefeld. This event—the first time indigenous colonials anywhere had defeated Roman legionnaires—is so deeply imprinted in Germans' ethnic memories that no fewer than 44 cities today claim the site of the massacre,.)

Dr Gerson did not encounter much medical competition in Bielefeld, for the city had only two other neurologists, one being rather unpopular, and the other nearing retirement. His practice grew quickly and steadily, providing solid support for the young Gerson family, which included two-year-old Hanni and nearly one-year-old Trudy—the parents' nicknames for Johanna and Gertrude.

Gretchen was proving to be a good manager of the business side of Dr. Gerson's practice—always an essential role, it turned out. After marrying Max, she had noticed, with concern, his utter lack of interest in monetary matters. In Breslau, his billing routine for private patients and as a consultant reflected his disregard for financial compensation—highly unusual among his fellow practitioners, who tended to be sharp businessmen. After his secretary initially billed patients, if they did not get around to paying him, Gerson would not send out reminders. Many consultations never even found their way into his invoices. Some patients at least gave him gifts instead of payment: it was not unusual for him to receive carpets, paintings, cigarettes, cigars or other goods in barter for his services. Other patients were quite content never to receive a bill or reminder from him at all. As long as Max was a bachelor, this didn't matter much, especially after he began receiving a regular salary from the German Army, but Gretchen realized that if Max were ever to be able to support a family, the financial side of his doctoring would need to be rectified. Although her husband was initially uncomfortable with the businesslike methods she instituted in his medical work, he soon saw his patients were not insulted by being billed. After they moved to Bielefeld, Gretchen had good reason for continuing her attention to assuring a decent income. In the fall of 1921 she quietly informed her husband that she was again pregnant. Little Charlotte ("Lotte") arrived the following March 27. Three daughters would complete the Gerson menage.

The Quadronal Story

Despite Gretchen's vigilance, unscrupulous individuals and organizations sometimes seriously abused Dr. Gerson's generosity. Most notable among them was a company that built a billion-dollar industry on his invention, then shut him out of any of the proceeds.

Once well settled in Bielefeld, Dr. Gerson set into motion one of his pet projects. During his medical military service in Breslau, he had often noted that some patients had a low tolerance for aspirin; others could not tolerate salicylic acid at all, especially in causing gastric distress. He had experimented with combinations of medications that were better tolerated by most patients and actually seemed to work better than straight aspirin in alleviating pain. He kept improving his formulation, and over the course of three years, added several minerals often low or even absent in the blood and tissue chemistry of sick bodies.

Since the town's pharmacists, whose chemical stock varied widely in purity and potency, mixed Gerson's concoction for him, the resultant medications proved more or less effective, depending on the pharmacist's stock and his precision. Occasionally, the unreliably manufactured formula would do more harm than good. The same problem had bedeviled Max during his previous work with patients in Breslau. On an effort to solve this problem, Gerson arranged for a local chemical manufacturer, Hennig and Kipper, to create tablets made from his formula, to be called Quadronal. A small factory was established in 1919 in Brackwede, outside Bielefeld, to manufacture the remedy. Produced now with quality-controlled, consistent ingredients and effectively marketed, these tablets proved so effective that they began to replace aspirin use not just in Westphalia, but in much of Germany. Several other manufacturing facilities were started elsewhere.

In 1923, as Max's invented medication was heading toward a financial bonanza, Gerson met with August Stauch, a wealthy German rancher from South Africa. He then introduced Stauch to Hennig and Kipper. After buying into the company with a major investment, this entrepreneur renamed it ASTA-Werke (from his name, August STAuch). For an initial investment of 400,000 marks, plus already having contributed his formula to the enterprise, Dr. Gerson received 16.4% of the new company's stock; additionally, his father-in-law, Max Hope, got an additional 4.5%. An agreement was struck to provide Gerson with a royalty that would escalate as the remedy's sales increased; it was scheduled to continue for at least 20 years.

Later, when Gerson began to ask about the royalties he should be receiving based on profits from the skyrocketing international sales of the popular medication, the company replied with legalistic arguments that claimed he was not keeping his part of the research-cooperation agreement; therefore, no royalties were due him. Dr. Gerson retained an attorney, who took up the fight with ASTA. He stayed with it for several years and proved how Gerson had indeed provided continuing scientific research. But the company chose to interpret this obligation to mean that Gerson was required to share with them *all* his medical records — something no ethical physician would ever agree to. Thus ASTA seized upon Gerson's refusal as a pretext to deny him any payments.

In time, Max could see that ASTA was determined never to pay him anything, so abandoned the apparently fruitless legal battle. He never got any money out of his investment or for developing the product for the commercial distribution. Understandably, Gretchen was very bitter about the company's treatment of her husband, but Max, never much interested in business dealings, just let it go. He had more interesting medical projects to pursue.

In December 1933, the government of Peru awarded a gold medal to ASTA for the development of their excellent medication, Quadronal. ASTA never bothered to inform Gerson of the prize; by then he was living in Vienna. In 1949, on the occasion of the 30th Anniversary Jubilee of the factory, ASTA-Werke published a small celebratory pamphlet. On page 15, it says, "With the exception of Quadronal, all of our other manufactured preparations were of temporary importance and limited duration." And on page 31 it continues: "Only Quadronal remained until the spring of 1929, when the second specialty, Quadronox, also by Dr. Gerson, came onto the scene. We quickly resolved to cast all the ballast of the past overboard." Although Dr. Gerson never received compensation for either preparation, for over 40 years Quadronal was the mainstay of the ASTA product line, remaining on the market in Germany, South America and Asia until the late 1980s. ASTA-Medica today has sales of $1 billion annually, and is wholly owned by Degussa-Hüls, one of Europe's largest firms. Though they readily acknowledge Gerson's original contribution to their success, they never paid a penny to him or his family, nor honored his early ownership of shares in the company.

Health Discoveries

After he had settled down in Bielefeld, Max Gerson, by now in his late 30s, began to notice an occasional but rather consistent writer's cramp in his right hand whenever he wrote up his medical notes. He was concerned about the pain, fearing that it might indicate a brain tumor. He frequently traveled to medical congresses and other gatherings, and on one occasion, at a congress in Köln (Cologne), arranged a consultation with Professor Ottfried Förster about these troubling cramps. His old medical supervisor and mentor from Breslau examined Gerson, but found nothing definitive to indicate any specific condition. He asked Gerson to keep him informed.

Once again, Gerson's attention to his sensitivities to certain foods and other facets of his immediate physical environment served him well. He began to notice that this painful condition was worse on Mondays, following the family's regular Sunday visits to relatives in the country. The only different or unusual thing that he did there on weekends was to indulge his occasional smoking habit after meals. Like many of his colleagues, Max had taken up smoking cigars as a medical student, in part to mask the unpleasant odors of the cadaver-dissection room. Then in Breslau during the war, patients would sometimes pay him with tobacco products. But considerate of his family and patients, he now refrained from smoking at his own home and office in Bielefeld. When it occurred to him that his weekend indulgence might have something to do with this hand cramping, Gerson stopped smoking entirely. The problem simply disappeared over the course of the next week. He concluded that his "writer's cramp" was, in fact, a symptom of nicotine poisoning. He then happily reported this fact to Förster.

Max Gerson never again smoked, and began making a maximum effort to persuade both his patients and colleagues to refrain from smoking. He also insisted that his patients should rid themselves of the noxious habit, and in future years he would not permit smoking in any of his clinics or sanatoriums. Gerson was scarcely alone in this early awareness of the health dangers in the pernicious habit. One of the strident public health campaigns launched later by the Nazis attempted to eradicate smoking. Adolf Hitler himself did not smoke—among various efforts of his, including near-vegetarianism to maintain bodily purity.

Not surprisingly, because of his own adverse reactions to certain foods and to smoking, Dr. Gerson had begun to wonder how many health conditions in other people might be due to defective diets, allergies or unusual sensitivities to particular substances, whether natural or manmade, that were breathed in, ingested or came in contact with the skin.

Neurologists were expected to be experts in analyzing and treating headaches. As a specialist in internal and nervous-system disorders, Dr. Gerson often received patients who complained of migraine headaches. He discovered that migraines were so common a complaint that he printed up the "migraine diet" that he himself sedulously followed, and gave the small pamphlet to each patient with the malady. Patients were advised to eat from the "required foods" list and to avoid the "forbidden foods" list. Max knew that the diet would be difficult for Germans to maintain, since much of their regular fare consisted of the fatty, highly spiced, smoked and salted meats found on the "forbidden" list; nor were they inclined to favor more vegetable fare than meat. Nonetheless, as a group, Germans — schooled in obedience at home and school, and often in the armed services as well—usually heeded 'doctor's orders'. Gerson even noticed with pleasant surprise that his Westphalian patients were more careful in following his instructions than his patients elsewhere in Germany. Years later he observed that Germans in general tended to be far more tractable than Americans in this way. Most of his patients stuck closely to his prescribed diet, with predictably good results.

Gretchen Gerson later recalled the family's daily diet that had been devised by her husband in those early years (which would not differ much in later years, either): "Since after the war Max wished to continue testing foods on himself, all the family lived without salt or sharp spices, on raw fruits and vegetables, no animal fats and little meat, occasionally chicken or veal. Every new idea was first tried out in the family."

The Pension Examiner

During the postwar period the German military pension administration was seeking a physician in northern Westphalia who could serve as an examiner to interview and examine veterans, especially ones from the Great War. All maintained that they required pensions to sustain them because they had been wounded or otherwise claimed to be suffering physical or mental disabilities that made them incapable of holding jobs. Some were new applicants; others had received pensions for some years and their cases needed reviewing.

The military administrators had frequently encountered references to Dr. Max Gerson in official documents where his judgment and honesty were repeatedly confirmed. When the government approached Dr Gerson, he agreed to perform this duty, for which he would be reasonably compensated. He would be sent the medical records of veterans who had been treated in one or more military and civilian hospitals, as well as a preprinted postcard for each patient. After he had evaluated the records, he would send the patient the postcard with a time and date for an examination filled in. Depending on Gerson's total evaluation of the patient and his medical records, pensions could be increased, decreased or totally withdrawn. Some of the veterans wanted to have tattoos removed that had been applied during the war; Dr Gerson would inject hydrogen peroxide under the skin in that area, and in time the dark design faded away.

Psychology played a large role in this new line of work. Gerson found that many of the cases that were sent to him had been faking disability so that their pensions could be increased or continued. In one case, a young man had a stiff leg and limped badly as a result of a bullet wound that had long healed. The man, a teacher at a Catholic school in a village outside Bielefeld, was receiving a 50% disability pension. The priest, for whom the schoolteacher worked, had a large fruit orchard adjoining the property of some of Gretchen's relatives. Since Max and Gretchen frequently spent weekends at their home, they were familiar with both the priest and the young teacher. A few days before the teacher's scheduled physical examination, the priest appeared in Dr. Gerson's Bielefeld office. He was very pleasant and stressed his good relations with the Hope family, then he requested that Gerson, if he would be so kind, could be a bit nearsighted with the young teacher, not examine him too closely. He explained that the small village had no high school, that the pupils he prepared in Latin, history and mathematics would otherwise have had to leave the village to attend a high school. Max's answer, of course, was polite but very firm; he could not violate his code of ethics. The examination, which would be thorough, objective and complete, would have to determine the status of the young man's pension. The priest left, disappointed in his mission.

In fact, Max and Gretchen had been visiting their relatives next door to the priest just the prior weekend, and had seen the young man high in the branches of a cherry tree, picking fruit for the Sunday meal. Gerson's physical examination later bore out the observation: the young man's muscle and ligament responses were quite normal. He had been faking his disability for years. In his case, the pension was withdrawn completely. Max was sympathetic, but the priest and the teacher would have to work out some other arrangement for the older students to complete their education.

Another pensioner happened to be the owner of a large property. He had lost his speech after a bomb explosion had buried him alive for almost two days, and in the several years since the war ended, he had not regained it. He always had a nurse with him to help communicate. Dr Gerson, suspecting that the condition was part- ly due to nervous shock, but also partly faked, told him that during the examination he would need neither the nurse nor his writing pad. Much later, Mrs. Gerson recalled the examination: "The patient was worried and upset when the nurse was sent out and the paper taken away. Max used hypnosis in this case. After the patient woke up from the hypnosis, he was completely confused. He was able to speak, although somewhat unclearly. The doctor could not demand that he speak well again so suddenly. He soothed him and gave him a few days in which to become accustomed to speech once again. Max pointed out that it was important for him to oversee his estate himself, rather than letting his employees manage it. After the initial shock, he understood and agreed that he should for a short time still receive a 25 percent pension and that it would then be terminated."

Yet another time, a middle-aged veteran was called for examination; his repeated complaints had finally jarred the administration into action. The examination was needed to determine the course of his petition to receive a pension. He had been injured by a nearby shell explosion that killed several of his comrades, giving him such a nervous shock that his voice had been reduced to a whisper. Since the man had worked on a large farm and his training and experience prior to military service consisted of working with the horses, he was unable to earn a living — he needed a loud, clear voice for giving commands. Dr. Gerson's recommendation was instrumental in the veteran being awarded a 100% disability pension.

For several years, Dr. Gerson carried out this extra responsibility of examining the government-pension applicants, though he realized that this activity was placing an additional burden on the normal activities in his practice. These had begun to include not only migraine patients but people with other conditions, who came from near and far to consult with a physician who often used special diets as his main form of treatment.

The Diet Therapy Expands: Curing Lupus and More

One of Dr Gerson's patients, the manager of a large legal practice, came to him for help with severe migraines. Tormented by these headaches, this patient often fell into deep depressions. He had consulted numerous other physicians with no noticeable relief. Since this affliction affected his practice, he feared he would lose his position and then be unable to support his large family. Admitting his despair, he confessed he would consider suicide if Dr. Gerson could not help him. Dr. Gerson gave him the "migraine diet" pamphlet, with his usual admonition: the results would be proportional to the patient's care in sticking to the strict diet. The desperate man was only too eager to comply precisely with his instructions. Dr. Gerson told him to return for follow-ups every two to three weeks for the next few months.

Within two months, Dr. Gerson had no doubt that the man would achieve a positive outcome, as he saw that his patient was adhering closely to his recommended dietary regimen. Gradually but steadily the patient began improving, and

Gerson knew that he would soon be able to discharge him. After five months of treatment, the patient came to Gerson's offices for his last visit.

"Well, Herr Müller, how are your headaches?" Max asked.

"Completely cleared up, Doktor. I feel wonderful! I can't begin to tell you how grateful I am."

"Excellent. And the depression?"

"Also gone. I am no longer worried about holding onto my position. In fact, I have more energy than I have had in a long time. But I also have a surprise for you, Dr. Gerson."

"Ah? And what is that, Herr Müller? Has Frau Müller baked me one of her famous and forbidden cakes?"

"Not at all, Herr Doktor. Look at this, if you will." He proceeded to undo the buttons on his shirt, and soon stood before Gerson, bare to the waist. "Tell me what you see."

Gerson examined him briefly. "Hmm. It looks as if you have recently suffered burns over a large area on your chest . . . here, here and here. But the skin seems to be healing nicely, with a little inflammation that will disappear as the scars heal. Why do you consider this a surprise, Herr Müller?"

"Doktor Gerson, the scars have nothing to do with burns. Until I started your 'migraine diet,' I also suffered from lupus. I thought I would be cursed with it for the rest of my life. But it has improved along with the migraines. What you are looking at are the scars from my healed tuberculosis!"

Dr. Gerson was stunned. Skin tuberculosis, *lupus vulgaris*, was said to be completely incurable by any known medical treatment. Once patients had it, they would have it forever, and they often died from its effects as the disfiguring disease progressed, destroying facial structures and other external tissues; it could even spread to vital organs or bones. The result was similar to leprosy, with ears, noses, cheeks, lips and other features missing, and gaping holes in the remaining tissue. Indeed, it got its name because it looked as if a wolf (*lupus*) had eaten a person's face. Its presence also endangered other people, especially those living in close proximity to the sufferer. Caused by the tubercle bacillus, it is highly infectious, as is all tuberculosis in confined spaces where people are living in poor nutritional and sanitary conditions. (The *vulgaris* in the disease's medical name is the Latin word for "of the common people.")

No, Max thought, it must surely be something else. "Herr Müller," he said after recovering his composure, "you are mistaken. *Lupus vulgaris* is *never* curable. You almost certainly had some other ailment that you or some inexperienced diagnostician mistook for lupus."

The patient beamed. "Ah, Herr Doktor, I thought you would say that, for I know well what other doctors have said about the disease. I have visited so many of them for treatment, just as with the migraines. But none could help me." Now he reached down for his briefcase and opened it. "Here are the medical records from years of treatment at the University Clinic at Köln." He handed him a thick package of files, reports, tests and records of medications given. As Dr. Gerson inspected the medical records from this prestigious university clinic, he became more and more excited. There was no mistaking the diagnosis consistently given: lupus vulgaris. Just as his patient had said.

This patient was not done yet. "During my long treatment for this disorder, I met a number of people who suffer from the same condition. I have told some other patients about my cure," he said. "Now they want you to treat them as well."

"But I don't have any idea what I have done. I have never seen anything like this before! I couldn't possibly assure them of a favorable outcome in treatment."

"Not necessary, Herr Doktor. They are all quite willing to release you from any responsibility for curing them. They just want you to try to do for them what you did for me. Three of my acquaintances are in your waiting room as we speak."

Max Gerson was an internal medicine specialist, with particular knowledge of nerves. He knew he didn't know enough about lupus to speak with authority. But he resolved now to learn as much as he could about the disease.

The patients who initially came to Gerson to be treated for lupus were duly placed on his "migraine diet," even though some did not suffer from migraines. Gerson would not accept a fee from these patients, since they were, in essence, voluntary experimental subjects. Nor did he feel confident that he could ameliorate, let alone eradicate, their supposedly incurable disease. But one after another healed in the next few months. The course of the healing became predictable, and Dr. Gerson gained confidence in this treatment.

After some months of obtaining good clinical results, Max Gerson began planning to write up his methodology and its surprisingly positive and permanent outcomes in an article, eventually to be submitted to a medical journal. He wanted to take his time, accruing as much material evidence as possible of rapid and permanent healing, based on other physicians' diagnoses, test results and before-and-after photographs. Otherwise his patients' full recoveries would not be believed by the medical community. The prospective article would scarcely be Gerson's first publication. His medical-school dissertation in 1907 had been on "The Influence of Artificial Hyperemia and Blood Transfusions in the Treatment of Fractures in the Hip Joint," written at a time when transfusions were becoming far more possible and much safer now that the blood groups had been identified and compatibilities were established. In subsequent years, he had published other titles that showed his wide-ranging interests: "Bromocol Poisoning" (1910), "Myasthenic Bulbar Paralysis" (1916), "Reflex Hyperesthesia" (1918), "Paralysis Found in Diphtheria Carriers" (1919), "Concerning the Etiology of Multiple Sclerosis" (1921), and the forthcoming "Constitutional Basis for Nervous Symptoms" (1924). More papers and books would come from Max Gerson in future years, of course — though the total number would undoubtedly have been far greater, and far more widely influential within the medical profession, had he been able to remain in Germany and continued to write in his native language.

Dr. Gerson continued to treat migraine patients in the normal course of his practice, though now he was also getting a number of patients with *lupus vulgaris*. Often he noticed that people with skin tuberculosis or migraines would present other symptoms as well, like his first migraine-lupus patient. If the presenting condition was lupus, it might have spread to other organs; or the lupus or chronic migraine headaches might be accompanied by arthritis or some other condition seemingly wholly unconnected with them. And he and his patients were both cheered and fascinated when the other ailments cleared up along with the lupus or headaches.

One day a 32-year-old woman came to his office, looking very weak and ill. Saying that she suffered from severe migraines, Dr. Gerson treated her no differently than his other migraine patients. He gave her the dietary rules to follow and told her to return for checkups every two to three weeks. By now, he had great confidence in the method, since it produced such regularly positive results. This new patient, however, did not respond nearly as favorably as his other patients had. In fact, after nearly three months there were no improvements in the frequency or severity of the woman's migraine attacks.

Dr. Gerson had learned patience in his practice as a physician. He knew that each person's illness had its own timetable for recovery or, failing that, eventual mortality. These differences were due to such factors as heredity, constitution, climate, prior nutrition, current stress and history of traumas, including previous diseases. Medicine is not an exact science, but even considering individual variations in the patients' responses, Gerson became concerned about this patient's lack of progress. Questioning the patient about her compliance with the dietary regime — the usual explanation for an inability to improve — he found no problem there. Like his other Westphalian patients, she followed his instructions very strictly. But after further inquiry, the patient told Dr. Gerson that some months before coming to him, she had undergone surgery to remove a tubercular kidney. The resulting scar, running diagonally across her abdomen, at first would not heal, and constantly oozed a smelly, pussy discharge. She noted, however, that under Dr. Gerson's dietary regime, the discharge had stopped completely, and then the wound had very quickly healed. He was again dumbfounded. Once more, a patient had presented with migraine headaches, for which he had treated her. And now her kidney tuberculosis had cleared up, even before the migraines could be conquered!

Max Gerson started thinking about what might be happening to his patients because of his unique approach to treating them. What he was witnessing went against all the principles he had learned in medical school and the conventional wisdom. He and the other future physicians had always been taught: one illness, one treatment. (In fact, that is the way in which orthodox, allopathic medicine is still being practiced.) Yet here, a particular dietary therapy was evidently not only curing his patients' migraines, but also *lupus vulgaris* and even another form of tuberculosis. Might it also work with tuberculosis infections elsewhere in the body? Subsequently, Dr. Gerson did indeed begin discovering that his diet could ameliorate not only tuberculosis in various other sites, such as the lungs and bones, but also conditions wholly different from these and each other — such as rheumatoid arthritis, diabetes, multiple sclerosis, cardiovascular and other degenerative diseases, whether caused by an infection or some other agent, known or unknown.

Toward a Unified Concept of Dietary and Environmental Health

Dr. Max Gerson certainly had witnessed firsthand the negative effects on his own health and well-being of his own habits, dietary and otherwise. He had discovered the need to limit or avoid certain ingredients in foods, such as salt and fats, and at the same time, he realized that he felt better when he ate far more vegetables, fruits and grains than meats. Besides finding a key to his health in the food he ate, he had discovered that when he gave up smoking, his health improved. And his observations of patients suffering from similar problems had demonstrated that nutrition and the influences of the external world had a powerful effect on human well-being. A thought now was taking shape in Dr. Gerson's mind. Could the diseases really all stem from the same root? Could improper nutrition be exacerbating, even causing, such ailments? If so, what were the mechanisms involved? The attempt to understand the nature of the disease process would almost constantly occupy Gerson's mind during the 1920s as he became increasingly confident that that human health involved the integrity of the whole organism, not just the suppression of symptoms of malaise.

The more Max Gerson considered food as a provider and restorer of health, the more questions he had. For example, he targeted for concern the effects on health of a diet largely consisting of foods that had been preserved — foods from plant and animals prevented from spoiling so that they could be conveniently and safely consumed long after being harvested or slaughtered. The techniques of drying, smoking, pickling in brine or vinegar, fermenting, being stored in cold places and being immersed in alcohol had long histories in different cultures. Then in the 19th century came the commercial and home canning or bottling of fruits, vegetables and even meats by subjecting them to sustained high heat in metal cans or glass containers, as a way to kill the microbes that caused spoilage and food poisoning. In the 1920s the robust international chemical industry, no longer distracted by having to focus mostly on producing a variety of munitions and caustic or poisonous gases for use in the Great War, was creating and marketing more and more preservatives—special substances for adding to processed foods to retard or prevent spoilage and confer long duration, even something close to immortality. But when canned foods were tested for nutritional value, they compared poorly with comparable fresh ones. Moreover, there was growing evidence that certain metals in the "tin cans" leached into the liquids within them and thence into the foods. They were harmful to ingest and became more so as the foods remained within these containers. Lead used in soldering was particularly harmful, but there was also concern about aluminum, oxidized iron and tin.

Dr. Gerson was almost certain that all such preservative processes would involve a partial or even total destruction of enzymes, vitamins and other living microconstituents of foods—being identified at the time by nutritional biochemists in laboratories around the world—from long exposures to air and heat or from chemical additives, whether naturally occurring ones (including sodium chloride or salt) or artificial ones, such as nitrates, nitrites and synthetic dyes, which could prove harmful, especially if ingested in quantities over time. Nutritionists were demonstrating that the nutritional value of plant foods could rapidly decline prior to eating, and the nutritional value of preserved foods deteriorated further while sitting on shelves, retaining little if any of the substances important to health, except for the minerals. Minerals were not destructible in the way that cells and molecules taken from recently living substances were; yet within these preserved food substances, some might recombine in adverse chemical reactions. Dr. Gerson also knew that experiments were going on in fast-freezing some foods as a means of preserving them—and suspected that this method might not retain the value of fresh foods, even though they might resemble them far more than dried or canned foods.

Besides considering whether people were better off eating primarily fresh instead of preserved foods, Max Gerson was acutely aware, as he always had been, of the important issue of what basic elements were in the soil where plants grew, either for direct human consumption or as fodder for livestock. Did it matter whether vegetables were grown in earth where beneficent bacteria that convert decaying matter and resident minerals into natural plant fertilizers had dissipated or been destroyed? What happened to the nutritional value of plant food when the soil was depleted of certain necessary minerals, whether they were chief ones like nitrogen, phosphorus and potassium (abbreviated as N-P-K), or trace minerals such as copper, chromium and boron? What was the effect of an unfavorable imbalance in the critical acid/alkaline ratio created by soil additions and subtractions, when growing particular crops with definite requirements on the pH scale? What toxins remained on foods coming from plants that had been grown in soil artificially fertilized or sprayed with pesticides? Ever since he had observed the effect of artificial fertilizer on those earthworms in his grandmother Hannchen's garden, Max had been concerned that these additives would affect the life forces of the human beings. What might happen to the health of people who regularly eat foods with toxic residues?

As Dr. Gerson wrestled with these complex questions, a unified answer began to take shape. He recognized that humans and animals have evolved over millions of years in such ways as to extract efficiently the necessary nutrients from the plants that grow around them. Food is the way in which minerals, vitamins and nutrients required for our health become available for sustenance. The more directly and purely we receive these materials from the Earth through its plant intermediaries, the more value the food will have to our bodies. But if we interfere with this natural process anywhere along the continuum, as modern civilization does, we do so at our peril.

Max Gerson was not alone in this line of inquiry. During the early decades of the 20th century, a growing number of scientists and physicians were conducting nutritional and epidemiological research, and sometimes theories and methods were tried out in clinical applications, as Gerson was doing. Always a voracious reader of medical journals, Max absorbed many ideas, right and wrong, from others. As references in his own papers and books would show later, work already being done by nutritional researchers — particularly by Max Oskar Bircher-Benner and E. Abderhalden in Germany, and by Frederick L. Hoffman in the United States — contributed to his own speculations and trial-and-error work with patients. Even the Nazis' much-admired natural-foods and healthful-living proponent, the physician Erwin Leik, must have exercised some influence on his early speculations.

As he explored this theory, Max Gerson continued his practice, which was becoming quite large. He now had a reputation not only for being able to help migraine sufferers, but also for eradicating skin tuberculosis and possibly other forms of tuberculosis as well. His special dietary regimen often appeared to ameliorate other previously intractable conditions in patients who came to him — often initially despairing of relief, let alone cure. Relying on both his own observations and research done by others, Dr. Gerson now asked his patients — virtually prescribed for them — a daily intake of freshly pressed citrus juices along with meals that contained as many fresh vegetables and fruits as possible, along with whole grain cereal products. Yet the sign outside Dr. Max Gerson's medical office still read "Internal and Nerve Diseases."

~5~
Dietary Discoveries
(1922–1924)

Family Life

By 1923, Dr. Max Gerson's reputation for successfully healing many patients suffering from a variety of ailments, often mostly by having them change the foods they ate, had grown in Westphalia. Not everyone was willing to comply with his dietary regime without question, however, as his daughter Charlotte remembers. Often, when some local farmer would receive the dietary regimen, he would be startled at what he was required to do.

"Dr. Gerson, there is no meat in these meals!"

"That is correct."

"How can that be? Everyone knows one cannot live without meat!"

"Do you really believe that? Then I need to show you something."

Max Gerson delighted in taking the two dozen steps to the side of the sturdy building that contained both the family home and his medical office. Opening a gate leading into a outdoor yard, he would beckon to his young daughter playing industriously in a sandbox with her companion, Willi. "Lottchen," he would say, "come with Papa for a moment, please."

Little Lotte stopped her labors and ran up the steps to the house. Hand in hand, Gerson returned to his office with his youngest daughter. The patient, looking puzzled, saw a sturdy, alert and glowing—if invariably smudged and sand-covered—little girl.

"This is my daughter, Charlotte," Gerson said. "She has never eaten meat, and, as you can see, is certainly not suffering because of it. Many children would be delighted to have the robust good health that she and her two older sisters enjoy. If you follow my recommendations, you will also have much better health than you now do."

Both father and daughter took pleasure in these little demonstrations, which provided them with some contact during the workday.

May years later, Charlotte Gerson could still recall that home in Bielefeld, where she spent her first eight years with her parents and two older sisters:

Each half of the building was three stories high, with a big entry hall lead-ing into the rooms. The two parts of this very large building were totally sepa-rate. There was a fence between our two gardens, and very rarely we would see our neighbors — a widow with three teen-aged boys who looked very large to me. While we were on friendly terms, we had almost no contact with them, socially or otherwise.

On the Gerson side, to the left of the hall (as one entered the house), there was a large space which my father used as his office, with a huge desk and all kinds of medical equipment. Off to its side, next to the office, and with a door leading into the hall as well as into the office, was a much smaller waiting room, with the usual chairs lining the walls, small tables and reading material.

Straight over from the entrance, in the hall next to the office and waiting room, was the entrance to a spacious dining/living room. The room opened to the left into the "music/sitting room," with armchairs and bookcases and my mother's large piano, a wedding present from her parents. It was a Bluethner — famous for excellent sound quality in the high range. My mother frequent-ly played the piano in the evenings, for the gathered family. I was usually found under the piano, occasionally, to her annoyance, playing with the foot pedals.

The large dining table often held more than the family. For instance, I was a very poor eater and even after ages four and five a nursemaid sat at the table specifically to make sure that I was eating. Also, since my father's practice was extremely busy, he had an assistant — Dr. Lepene, from one of the Baltic States — who ate at the table with us. And occasionally there was Uncle Otto, my mother's brother, who was born with a half-sided paralysis and often needed assistance. This table was very adequate to accommodate everybody comfortably.

In the dining room were a loveseat sofa and a table that held one of the ear-liest radios, which looked like the famous trademark, "His Master's Voice," with the large funnel-like speaker. It was very soft and difficult to hear. One of my earliest memories is of climbing up on a chair and softly whispering into the funnel, "A little louder, please!"

Regularly, at about 2:30 or 3:00 p.m. my father would leave his office for a little break and come in to sit on the sofa. Then the cook would serve him a lit-tle weak tea and I would climb on his lap. He would dip the teaspoon into a lit-tle sugar, add some tea, and I would share the little teaspoonfuls of tea with him during those breaks.

Further to the right of the dining/living room was an exit to a very large open porch, formed by the balcony above, which ran alongside the master bed-room. Due to the poor climate in Bielefeld — similar to London, with frequent rains and cool weather — our gym equipment was kept under that balcony in the open porch outside the living room. We had various rungs and swings attached to the balcony above, and spent a good deal of time swinging, doing gym and playing there, even in bad weather.

From there was an exit to the garden, a very large area running steeply up the rest of the hill to the path which led to the Sparrenburg. In the garden we had some flower beds and trees. Right off the porch was my favorite tree: a beautiful large lilac. It was uncanny, but every year that tree would burst into bloom exactly on May 16th, so we could always pick some fresh new lilacs for Mother's birthday, May 17th.

The last room downstairs was a very large kitchen. It had a gas stove, sinks and tables, but no refrigerator, since those appliances were not yet commonplace in homes.

The second floor held bedrooms, but also a large room devoted to an ultraviolet lamp for irradiation of us kids during the winter months. I remember the sweet smell of ozone when lying on the comfortable couch. There was the very large master bedroom, another large bedroom with three beds for us kids, and a smaller room off our room where the nursemaid slept. There were three additional rooms on the third floor, with slanted ceilings from being under the roof. They were occupied by the maid, the cook and some storage items.

In their leisure time, Max and Gretchen loved to take their three little girls for long walks. Max especially enjoyed walking in the woods with his family on Sunday afternoons — just as he had once done with his own parents. They trekked through the hilly areas in the wooded ridge line behind their home. Later, as the girls grew older, the family would hike in the forested mountains around Kassel, the location of their second home. The children always found these walks with their father most interesting. He would talk about such fascinating things as how and why the trees shed their leaves in the fall, or how the stomach produced acid necessary for digestion. His illustrative stories and explanations of nature's ways had an almost hypnotic quality, Charlotte remembers. But their father was such a serious person that it never seemed appropriate for his daughters to have a pet name for him, even though he had pet names for all of them. They all called him *Vater*, the German word for Father. Curiously, only some years after his death did Charlotte begin thinking and speaking of him as the more familiar and endearing Daddy.

Often Max would read aloud from his favorite author for the pleasure of his daughters, as Charlotte recalls:

> Father owned a set of his favorite author Goethe's works, which he read for his own enjoyment. On Sunday evenings after supper, he often read aloud to us. The book was always the same: Goethe's *Reinecke Fuchs* (Reynard the Fox), a beautifully bound volume of animal fables. Sometimes, as we grew older, he also discussed with the family his opinions of *Faust*. He stressed that in Part I Goethe tried

to bring out the good of the human soul; but in the deeply philosophical Part II, the author was unable to get the good to triumph over the evil. This failure not only impressed my father deeply, but also depressed him more than a little.

But much of the time, Max was busy reading articles and books connected with his medical practice, including the new studies on nutrition. This mental absorption had a perilous side: Gerson was often so engrossed in thought that he didn't always watch his surroundings carefully, as Charlotte recollects:

> One day he was walking toward the house, on the wide sidewalk of the Guetersloher Strasse, which had small manholes that usually were covered with heavy metal lids. Below each of them was a convenient entry for crushed coal; it would be run down a steel chute for an easy delivery directly into a basement. That particular day, the delivery was completed but the manhole cover had not yet been put back in place — and Max fell right through the hole. It wasn't large enough to let him drop all the way into the building's cellar, because his arms and shoulders held him above the sidewalk. Nevertheless, he was badly hurt and could hardly make it home. He was then bedfast for a few days with an inflamed sciatica. I was about four years old then. Having him at home in his bed like that was a very unusual occurrence. I would creep up to his bed and put my cool hand on his forehead to help him. I think it may just have done some good.

Charlotte's father normally used a bicycle to travel to his patients' homes, not without incident. The street in front of the Gersons' home in the Bielefeld suburb carried all the traffic from one side of the city to the other. Cars, trucks, bicycles and an electric streetcar all had to pass together through the gap in the ridge. One day, as Dr. Gerson was returning home from a patient's house on his bicycle along the crowded Gütersloher Strasse, he suddenly found himself caught between a flatbed truck and a streetcar whose paths were converging. He could see that there was not going to be enough space for him and his bicycle between the two vehicles, nor could he extract his bicycle from the situation. Somehow, miraculously, he swung himself off his bicycle seat onto the flatbed truck just in time to see his bicycle reduced to scrap metal under the heavy wheels of the two vehicles. He completed his journey on the bed of the truck.

By the mid 1920s automobiles were coming into general use, and the family acquired a car, a "Wanderer"—a tan-colored four-door sedan with gray and tan uphol-stery. For a time they had a chauffeur, who taught Gretchen how to drive. Although she got a driver's license, she was always uneasy behind the wheel, so whenever she drove, she insisted upon having the chauffeur at her side. For Dr. Gerson to take the time away from his work to learn how to drive, however, was completely out of the question. Besides, as Gretchen well knew, he was probably too absorbed in his own thoughts to be a safe driver. Eventually, the family automobile was dispensed with.

The three little girls — Hanni, Trudy and Lotte — loved to spend time with their grandparents in the countryside. Max Hope's general store was right in the center of the little village of Verl, just beyond Gütersloh, and the girls enjoyed the comings and goings of the local farmers with their 'flocks' of children. And what child born in the earlier years of the 20th century has not spent fascinating hours in an old-style general store, poking around the many interesting and sometimes mysterious implements and goods available there? Outside were unlimited fields and pastures in which to roam and play. But not everything was idyllic there. Before the era of universal vaccination of children for diphtheria, the children were prone to contracting this highly infectious disease. If it is not recognized in time and properly treated, diptheria can leave the victim blind in one or both eyes.

During one of their extended vacation visits to their grandparents' home in Verl, the two older girls developed red streaming eyes, runny noses and fever. Their ailment could well have been diagnosed as a cold, but their parents were at the Hope home for the weekend, and when Max saw small scabs building up in his daughters' noses, he immediately took smears and sent them off to the nearest university clinic in Göttingen. He was very concerned since one of the children's little friends had only recently had his eyes badly infected with diphtheria. By the time the local doctor recognized the nature of the disease and sent him to a specialist, it was too late — the child was blind in one eye.

Without waiting for the results to come back from the laboratory, Dr. Gerson immediately gave his three girls anti-diphtheria injections. In two hours, the swelling in their eyes and noses had gone down; by the next morning the fever was gone, too. Four days later, the results came back from the university: positive for diphtheria. By then, the serum had done its job, and the children were almost normal again.

Folk Wisdom

Over the years Dr. Gerson had learned to listen carefully to his patients. By keeping his ears and eyes open when working as a clinical doctor, he gained many invaluable insights as a medical researcher that could have never come from simply working in a laboratory. One day an elderly farm couple who came into Bielefeld every month to sell their produce used the trip as a chance to consult with Dr. Gerson. The husband sought treatment for a hard, red lupus lesion on his cheek. Accordingly, Dr. Gerson wrote out a 'prescription' book for the man: the first half of the preprinted book contained basic information, while the second half was blank, to be stamped with changes and alterations in treatment and medication at each future visit. Patients customarily were told to return for examination every three to four weeks, bringing this book with them.

The elderly farmer returned to see Dr. Gerson each month for three months, but then without notice ceased coming. Then after three more months, he and his wife again appeared.

"Where have you been, Mr. Kramer?" Max asked calmly yet rather sternly.

"Well, *Herr Doktor*, I have to admit that after a while on this strange diet, I thought it wasn't working for me. So I wanted to give it up."

"And yet you are here. What changed your mind?"

"It was my wife, Helga," said the farmer. "She noticed something odd."

The farmer's elderly wife continued. "When my husband was last here, he was much better, but one month later, when he was supposed to return for another examination, the *lupus* on his cheek was all swollen and red, and looked worse. Then it improved again, and a month later, it got all red and swollen again. He was very discouraged, and wanted to stop the treatment. It is so difficult, and didn't seem to be helping."

"What changed his mind?"

"I noticed that his cheek had gotten very red and swollen for a few days, then it improved, and the healing proceeded for a month. The cycle happened again, swelling and healing. I told him, 'If things follow nature, then you are having your *period* on your cheek!' So he decided to continue, and, you can see how much his face has improved." Again, Max Gerson was reminded that people who lived on the land were sensitive to the cycles of earth, sun and moon, and often made shrewd observations missed by more scientific minds or city dwellers.

The course of the farmer's healing was also of interest to Dr. Gerson. The healing did not proceed smoothly, always improving. Instead, the farmer experienced several weeks of healing, punctuated by apparent setbacks. This pattern recurred until the patient had totally recovered. Sensitized by his encounter with the elderly farmer's wife to this pattern, he began to see flare-ups in other patients as well, eventually recognizing them as healing reactions, or "healing crises." When he could warn his patient about these crises or setbacks, the patient would accept them as part of the healing process instead of thinking that the treatment was not working and becoming discouraged.

Max Gerson took such folk wisdom seriously, as his wife remarked in her memoir: "Another example of the extent to which all life is dependent on cycles in nature was given to Max when he was visiting a friend of his, who was a mayor of a coastal town. A boy rushed into the room and announced that a cow was calving. The mayor looked up on his chart and said the birth would take a while longer, for it was still two hours until high tide. Research in other coastal towns and in official books confirmed this observation: humans and animals tended to be born at flood tide."

Another time, the mother of a 14-year-old girl brought her sick daughter to Dr. Gerson. The girl had a severe case of lung tuberculosis, complete with fever, bad coughing spells, night sweats and bloody expectoration. The mother insisted on continuing to care for her daughter at home and not sending her away to some impersonal clinic. Since the woman was not wealthy, Dr. Gerson knew it would be difficult for her to stick to the dietary regime because the fresh produce would be costly and also she could not afford to pay for assistance. Impressed with the woman's perseverance, he next visited the daughter at home. He felt very sad because the girl's disease was so far advanced that he saw no chance of survival. He told the girl's mother candidly that he had never seen anyone recover from tuberculosis that serious. Why torment her with this strict diet? Why not just let her eat what she wanted until her inevitable death?

The mother refused to take his advice. "Dr. Gerson, never give up on a patient while there is still life," she said, "I will not give up on my only daughter. I will fight for her life every minute of every day. If she dies, I will at least know it won't be because I didn't do everything in my power to help her live."

To his amazement and great satisfaction, the girl recovered totally under her mother's diligent care. Never again would Dr. Gerson assume that a patient who came to him was too far gone to survive. Often in years to come the woman's words rang in his ears: "Never give up on a patient while there is still life." And often this advice was proven right by totally unexpected recoveries.

One of Dr. Gerson's patients was a middle-aged factory foreman. His wife, who provided his home care, found it nearly impossible to obtain the citrus fruits for the juices that Dr. Gerson prescribed. There was no problem with availability: the stores at the time were full of all the necessary foods. But in the galloping inflation food prices were rising so quickly and so steeply that the man's wife could not afford to buy these exotic fruits. She went to her doctor, desperate for some help.

"Dr. Gerson, my Hermann is doing very well on your diet therapy. Please don't think that I am ungrateful. Nobody else could help him, and you could. But we are not rich people, and we simply can't afford oranges and lemons for all those juices Hermann needs. I don't want to stop the therapy. Isn't there anything else that would work?"

Gerson thought for only a moment. "You have a large garden, don't you?"

"Yes, we do."

"Good," said the doctor. "Carrots and apples are easy to grow and plentiful. Here is what you do. Take carrots and apples, grate them into a large bowl together, then put the pulp into a strong cloth, such as a piece of muslin. Wring the cloth so that the juice from the carrots and apples flows out. That will do the trick, and will be much less expensive....and you can save the pulp that remains and bury it out in your garden, where it will do some good as compost."

The woman followed Dr. Gerson's new juice recipe, and he, in turn, monitored the results closely. Interestingly enough, the carrot-apple juice proved much more effective for the treatment of tuberculosis than the previously prescribed citrus juices —usually orange and grapefruit. From then on, Dr. Gerson used the carrot-apple juice recipe daily in the treatment of degenerative diseases, varying it with citrus juice. Later would come other pressed-juice mixtures, as well as gradual improvements in electrical devices that assisted making them. Seeing how powerful the combination was in the maintenance and restoration of the immune system, he also introduced it into his family.

Hard Times in Germany

While Max Gerson was immersed in his medical career and family life, he had little time to pay much attention to the political ferment and economic crisis in Germany. After the "War to End All Wars" had finally been concluded with Germany's defeat, the victorious powers —notably France, Britain and the United States — imposed harsh punitive conditions on their defeated enemy in the Versailles Treaty of 1919. The most difficult problem for Germans was paying the ruinous war reparations established in 1921 by the Allied Reparation Commission. Germany was ordered to pay a total of 132 billion gold marks to its World War enemies, even though their patched-together Weimar government had no ability to do so. One evening Dr. Gerson gave a succinct commentary to his family on the situation, blaming all the poverty, unhappiness and turmoil all around them in Germany on these ruinous reparations demands. They were only political remarks Charlotte can recall his ever making when she was a young child.

The means Germany's political leaders chose to use in attempting to pay off the monumental debt involved issuing additional currency for use as legal tender. Students of basic economics know that runaway inflation will inevitably result when a country prints money without increasing its gross national product, the total value of goods produced and labor utilized, and also creating a favorable trade balance with other nations — meanwhile failing to materially back up a portion at least of the declared values of any newly issued paper monies by storing additional internationally valued precious-metal ingots in government-owned vaults that constitute its real treasury. The early 1920s became a terrible time for the average workers, who might receive a wheelbarrow full of notes for their week's work. Hyperinflation was so rapid that salaried people learned to run to the stores and spend their earnings all on goods or services they needed, since by the next week, or even the next day, the value would fall drastically. Money ceased to have any worth. Some merchants would not accept banknotes in payment for goods, and barter became standard economic procedure. It cost millions, even billions of marks for the postage stamp to mail a single letter. Life savings were wiped out overnight. People who actually owed money, as in mortgages secured for solid purchases such as land and thriving businesses, often had a great advantage over those who had stayed debt free, since their debts were now reduced to near nothing, ironically, people and businesses that *owed* money to others could take advantage of the hyperinflation situation by paying off their original debts. Charlotte Gerson recalls how this strange economy affected her family: "My grandfather, Max Hope, owned the general store in Verl, along with a good deal of land. He was very wealthy; and among other things also acted as a 'banker', lending farmers money to buy seeds and other necessities. In one case, he had loaned a farmer the princely sum of 20,000 Gold Marks, and had a note to prove it. Not too far into the inflation, the farmer came to the store and handed my grandfather an egg that was worth 20,000 marks that day. Thus he discharged his debt." People with the means to do so invested in and held onto intrinsically valuable, readily portable wealth, such as jewelry made of precious metals and diamonds. But among the population there was a plethora of unemployment and suffering. Elderly citizens, many of whom had lost their sons in the war, committed suicide because they had nothing to live on: inflation had made their pensions worthless.

Germany had also been stripped of various territories the ambitious nation had formerly taken over in eastern Europe, such as the province of Posen, where Max Gerson had grown up. Overseas colonies in Africa and Southeast Asia were relinquished. German citizens for the most part lost faith in the Weimar Republic, the postwar, democratically elected central government, which was increasingly weakened by feuding factions. Some looked toward the new Soviet Union's energetic experiment in Marxist communism as a model to correct the country's depression in both its economy and spirit. Others, most notably the Nazis — the National Socialist party promoted by Adolf Hitler (who was imprisoned in 1923 for an attempt to overthrow the Bavaria's democratic leadership) — sought a totalitarian control over the populace even firmer than that of the autocratic Kaisers. There was a resurgence of chauvinism — angry ethnic pride intent on overcoming the nation's humiliating defeat in the Great War. Eventually, the crushing peace treaty that ended World War I, coupled with the bitter German resentment over it and the harsh reparation payments involved, was instrumental in supporting Hitler's demagoguery and incitement to violence, and the perhaps inevitable progression into World War II.

Like many of his colleagues, Dr. Gerson treated welfare patients during thee years, but he was unlike some colleagues in their tendency to crowd as many as possible into their schedules, since the state did not pay as much per patient as private patients did. Max Gerson never differentiated between his welfare and private patients. Each patient coming to him received the same careful and thorough examination and treatment. But it could not continue that way indefinitely. The combined workload of treating migraine and tuberculosis patients, processing pension applicants and conducting a large state-supported welfare practice was becoming too much for Max. He was not getting time to pursue his real goal now: conducting research, both theoretical and clinical, on the treatment of tuberculosis, encompassing not just *lupus vulgaris* but the disease when entrenched in other, interior parts of the body. Although he did it rather reluctantly, Gerson withdrew now from both his pension and welfare work so that he could focus more on his unique dietary approach to treating tuberculosis.

The First Sanatorium

Dr. Gerson might sometimes have wondered why some people were more susceptible to infection than others, why the bacillus lodged in some organs but not others, and under what conditions it would spread from one organ to another. But his research efforts were not concerned with the causes, course and spread of the disease, since these issues were already well documented. Instead, he wished to pursue the successful eradication of tuberculosis in individual sufferers and to acquaint the entire medical profession of the tactics for doing so. He was convinced that perhaps the most important factor in his dietary regimen was the intake throughout the day of fresh fruit juices, the apple and carrot mixture added to squeezed orange and grapefruit juice.

Dr. Gerson emphasized that adherence was essential in the strict diets he assigned to his patients. Migraine headaches seemed to be caused mostly by the body's inability to handle certain foods, principally meats, and his migraine diet was therefore mostly vegetarian. Since in tuberculosis the body must deal with severe organ degeneration, the diet prescribed was even more severe in its ban on salt, its meat restrictions and its frequent intake of the juices. This tuberculosis diet, with modifications, was also used later for patients suffering various other diseases because it had turned out that these also responded favorably. The diets he prescribed were often difficult for patients and their families to follow, however. Apart from sheer expense, fresh produce was often not readily available (especially when out of season), and dedicated or even adequate caretakers to shop for and prepare the daily or even hourly special foods, juices or medications were not at hand in most families. There was also the problem of compliance: some patients were inevitably tempted to eat or drink forbidden substances. Max Gerson was fully aware of how the requirements and restrictions in this regimen inevitably added extra stress within a household where one family member was seriously ill. How much better it might be to have a special place where the intensive dietary treatment could go on, at least in the crucial beginning stages of intervening in disease progression.

One day a Pastor Vogelsang telephoned Dr. Gerson, wishing to meet with him. An hour was set, and the pastor arrived.

"Dr. Gerson," the pastor began, "I have become aware of your nutritional treatment for various diseases from several of your patients who are also parishioners of mine, and have been very impressed by what I have heard. My daughter Erika has long studied nutritional healing, including Mazdaznan's methods of food preparation."

"Can you tell me something about this Mazdaznan diet?" Max asked, for he always wished to learn more about dietary principles that might be similar to his own.

"It is a wholly vegetarian food system that is connected with the religion of Zoroastrianism—the ancient Persian worship of Ahura Mazdao, the god of light, as the supreme being. It is possibly six or seven thousand years old. But I cannot give you many details about the diet. You'll need to ask Erika for them. She has heard about your therapy method and is extremely interested in it because of its similarity to the Mazdaznan diet."

"Now, Reverend, how might I assist you?"

"Actually, Doctor, I have come today to offer *our* assistance to you. We live in Herford, which as you may know is only 20 minutes from Bielefeld by train," Pastor Volgelsand explained. "We have quite a large house, but only the two of us live there. Erika has expressed a great desire to help you with your therapy while exploring nutritional healing on her own. From what my parishioners have said, we understand that your treatment, though very effective, is difficult to begin at home.

"So here is our proposal: You could send patients to stay with us for the initial period of their treatment. Erika, who understands your food requirements and preparation methods, would fix all the meals. That way, the patients could eat food that is properly prepared while they learn how the therapy should be administered. Our house can easily accommodate a dozen patients at a time. My daughter is quite enthusiastic about the idea."

After a week of discussing the idea with Gretchen, Max came to the conclusion that the pastor's idea would be very helpful to patients. He called the pastor and gave him the go-ahead.

The pastor's idea turned out to be very popular with Dr. Gerson's patients. Those who could afford the moderate charge involved were very pleased to have a place to go for a couple of weeks while they learned a new way of eating, while being cared for by the Vogelsangs. They then had a much better start when they returned home. Since Herford was so close to Bielefeld, Dr. Gerson could visit once or twice a week and see all the patients. The house was always full; the situation seemed ideal. The cost for residency was surprisingly reasonable, as it would be wherever Dr. Gerson established sanatoriums in Europe and the United States. The Gerson therapy normally does not require a lot of sophisticated, high-priced medical equipment when administered in a sanatorium: the main focus is what goes on in the kitchen, where the food and juices are prepared.

For about 10 months, the Vogelsangs cared for Gerson's patients, and all seemed well. But it appeared that some physicians in Bielefeld who were envious of Dr.

Gerson's growing reputation and success, and increasingly angered by his unorthodox methods of treating patients by dietary means, which they considered bizarre and unacceptable, devised a scheme to strike out at him. One day a 'Health Commission' formed by city officials at the urging of local physicians appeared at the door of the Vogelsangs' home. They told the pastor that they had come to inspect the conditions of the home, to make sure that it was adequate for the housing of a dozen people at a time, and contained no health or safety violations. They fanned out, inspecting the kitchen, patient rooms and bathrooms, measuring the width of doorways, stairs and halls, looking for exits and other hazards. Not once did they inquire about the patients' health or medical progress.

By the end of the inspection, the Commission had collected a few violations of the housing codes they were enforcing. But instead of giving the pastor a chance to correct the discrepancies, they prohibited any further use of the house for the lodging of Dr. Gerson's patients, over the strenuous objections of the patients themselves. Six weeks later, at the end of the summer, the highly successful experiment was closed down, to the undisguised satisfaction of Gerson's Bielefeld 'colleagues'.

Max Gerson's conflicts with the medical establishment were only just beginning.

~6~
The Diet for Tuberculosis
(1924–1927)

"Diet Gerson"

During his early years of practice in Bielefeld, Dr. Max Gerson had learned that the practice of healing, true medicine, could not consist of a collection of specialists with distinctly separate domains — just as the human organism is not simply the sum of an individual's body parts. Medical specialization tends to lead away from restoring total health because physicians are apt to focus on one particular disease symptom with the goal of eradicating its apparent single cause. This viewpoint is akin to examining a tree or a set of leaves and then deciding that one can now understand the composition and function of an entire forest, though ignoring its complex totality.

In this period Dr. Gerson also kept considering the nature of good health in all living creatures — plants and animals, as well as human beings. He sensed that all of life was somehow interconnected, and that changing some aspects of the environment, the living conditions, of one kind of creature might well affect the health of others, whether at that time or in the distant future.

Max Gerson was not a religious person in a traditional sense, but probably his philosophic position contained an element of spirituality that was grounded in the natural world. As a scientist and physician he was already searching for a unifying concept of wholeness. It was part of his deep nature as a true healer: a person dedicated to helping people get well or stay well. The groundwork may partly have come from his upbringing within a closely knit family that instilled a deep ethical concern for others' welfare. To the end of his life, Dr. Gerson was a gentle, humble and unassuming man, whose clear blue eyes looked calmly out on the world around him, confident that each day gave him new insights into both its intricate workings and its wondrously comprehensive overall design.

For Max Gerson the right approach to practicing medicine involved regarding the human being as a whole unit who should be maintained in good health, if possible; however, if sickness did occur, symptoms indicated some probable systemic weakness in the whole body. Thus Gerson's inclination as a healer was to search for ways to treat the total organism, not just address one or two of its many parts. This viewpoint led to his developing a unique nutritional and biochemical approach to curing various diseased conditions. It took a great step forward when he had early and remarkable success in treating different types of tuberculosis. But his pathway toward his real goal, alleviating as much human suffering around him as he could, was not going to be an easy one.

As was his nature, Max Gerson was unguarded in his enthusiasm for the possibilities of this new dietary approach to treating different diseases; he seemingly expected his peers to respond accordingly, without suspicion, resentment, outrage or ridicule. He wanted to share his methods and ideas, but most of his peers wanted none of them. What business did Gerson have anyway, as an internist and neurologist, to be treating *lupus vulgaris*, a disease that clearly belonged in the domain of dermatologists or to specialists who treated severe, often fatal infections like tuberculosis? Some doctors simply wouldn't believe what Dr. Gerson was claiming about some extraordinary successes with 'hopeless' patients.

Soon, Dr Gerson noticed that his fellow physicians were not referring patients to him. Dr. Gravemann, an ear, nose and throat specialist respected by Dr. Gerson as an honest and ethical physician, explained that doctors in Bielefeld had threatened him with ostracism if he continued to refer patients to Gerson. He also disclosed how some physicians now ridiculed his treatment methods, calling him "Diet Gerson." Max was no longer invited to speak to the doctors' association in Bielefeld, though he often had been in the past. The jealousy of these local physicians toward Max Gerson escalated further. Unable to strangle his practice by depriving him of referrals, they contrived other ways to harass him, hoping that he would just pack up and leave.

One ploy that his professional detractors used was the tax audit. If found guilty of hiding his earnings, Max Gerson would be fined—and possibly might even lose his license to practice medicine in their community. Many physicians took portions of their fees as cash payments, depending on what was convenient for the patient at the time. It was not very difficult to simply 'forget' to declare these payments to the tax collectors, since there was no paper trail for the money. From time to time, one or more of Gerson's enemies would assume that he was doing what some doctors did—hiding a substantial portion of his cash receipts. It was easy enough to inform the tax authorities that some doctor was hiding income from them. This complaint always resulted in an audit, time-consuming and annoying at best, as anyone who has experienced one knows.

To subject Dr. Gerson to the maximum scrutiny and subsequent punishment by fine and possible imprisonment, the resentful Bielefeld physicians complained directly to the tax authorities in Berlin. In due course, a special auditor from Berlin arrived in Bielefeld. Max provided him with a private room in which he could work undisturbed, and submitted his records and tax declarations for several of the previous years. The auditor examined the documentation closely for two days, at the end of which he declared the books completely in order. He congratulated Gerson for his well-kept records — procedures that, of course, his wife had earlier initiated and still supervised.

The other physicians had not banked upon the consequences to them of a standard practice of taxing authorities. If an informant knows about illegal practices committed by another, the authorities assume that he is probably hiding something himself. They then also audit the informer. As soon as he had completed his work on Gerson's books, the auditor from Berlin turned his attention to the physicians who had signed the complaint against Gerson. He found discrepancies in most of the records he examined, and the informers had to pay substantial back taxes and penalties. And of course the physicians resented Gerson all the more.

A Fortuitous Case

One day a patient arrived at Dr. Gerson's office from Barmen, in the Rhineland. Afflicted with serious bone tuberculosis, Fritz Lang said he had long been a patient of a prominent thoracic surgeon, Professor Ferdinand Sauerbruch, because of pulmonary tuberculosis. Sauerbruch had developed the pressure chamber for doing lung surgery, an innovation that allowed the procedure to be performed without being universally fatal. The Munich physician had been treating his lung condition with a method that he was pioneering at the time. Sauerbruch's pneumothorax treatment used air pressure to first deflate, then inflate and dry out the lung tissue in an attempt to defeat the tuberculosis infection. But the treatment did not cure Lang, and now the tuberculosis had spread to his right hip and femur. Dr. Sauerbruch had given up on saving the patient's life, advising him that the only relief that he could offer was to remove the leg, though that would only be temporarily beneficial. The man refused — preferring, he said, to die "with my leg on." He then had returned home to Barmen, weak, ill and expecting to die.

By chance, Frau Lang heard of a Dr. Gerson in Bielefeld. She urged her husband to try the treatment. He was very reluctant to consult any more doctors, since he had such poor experiences with the ones he had seen in the past, but eventually he was persuaded to visit Gerson. When Lang arrived in Bielefeld, he was in very poor condition. Dr. Gerson immediately put him into a local sanatorium to start his treatment. While he was there, his wife stayed with him, so she could ensure that the prescribed treatment would be exactly followed. She was aware that this therapy was her husband's last chance at survival, and wanted to give him the best care she possibly could.

Slowly the patient regained his appetite, then his strength. As he recovered his health, his appearance improved noticeably. They remained in Bielefeld for nearly two months, and the man's overall health constantly grew better. Then the couple returned home to Barmen, where they continued to follow Dr. Gerson's instructions. After a half-year of strict dietary treatment, it was clear that the patient was recovering. At first, he was able to get around using crutches, but later totally regained the use of his right leg. The ravages of the advanced tuberculosis left the right leg forever shorter than the left, but the man could return full time to his important work as a factory owner. He stayed on Gerson's nutritional therapy for the rest of his life.

The story of his recovery would be instrumental in furthering Gerson's career. In 1924 one of Dr. Gerson's former patients, now a friend, happened to be taking the train from Munich to Davos, Switzerland, on business. He was telling his traveling companion about the patient of his doctor friend who had been dying of lung and bone tuberculosis. He said that the doctor had discussed the case of the man from Barmen with him — telling him how, rather astonishingly, the strict dietary therapy he had prescribed had actually cured him. Moreover, the talkative traveler disclosed to his companion that this patient had earlier been treated by the eminent Professor Sauerbruch of Munich, one of the foremost surgeons in Europe. It was said that when he gave up on a patient, there was no chance for salvation by any other doctor. Yet this man was now alive, totally recovered, and running his factory again. As the two men talked animatedly about the patient's recovery, they did not notice that an elegantly dressed gentleman sitting across from them had been staring at them, dumbfounded, as their conversation unfolded. Eventually he could contain himself no longer. He jumped out of his seat, nearly cracking the foldaway table that held the men's teacups. The man balled his fist and pounded the small table. "Who is this doctor that you are talking about?" he demanded, excitedly. "I must know his name!"

"Why, it is Dr. Gerson, Max Gerson," the ex-patient replied. "He practices in Bielefeld, on Gütersloher Strasse. He has been practicing there for some years. But why are you so upset?"

"I *am* agitated," said the man. "Allow me to introduce myself. I am the very same Professor Dr. Ferdinand Sauerbruch who could not save your factory-owner friend from his lung and bone tuberculosis, despite my great efforts. I told him that the best thing I could do to temporarily relieve his pain while he was dying would be to remove his leg. I was certain that would not make much difference, since the disease was progressing rapidly and would soon claim his life. Now, if what I have overheard is correct, you are saying that the man not only is still alive, but he is cured, and has been restored to complete health. I *must* know how he did that!"

Dr. Max Gerson's name and address were duly recorded in Prof. Sauerbruch's notebook. As soon as Sauerbruch arrived in Davos, he fired off a long telegram to Gerson, asking if Gerson would be willing to come to Munich to speak at his clinic. Max and Gretchen discussed this proposal seriously. If he acceded to Sauerbruch's invitation to Munich, Max would probably then be asked to introduce the treatment at the clinic there. This, in turn, would mean a change in the practice he had laboriously built up in Bielefeld, since the train trip took 20 hours in each direction. The added time traveling to Munich and working in a clinic there would leave him with considerably less time and energy for his local patients. Nevertheless, Sauerbruch was a famous surgeon, and certainly the invitation to at least visit him in Munich could not be declined. Max cabled back that he would be honored to come, at Dr. Sauerbruch's convenience.

Both Max and Gretchen were excited, if somewhat apprehensive, over the probability that Professor Sauerbruch would wish to collaborate with him on tuberculosis treatment. That professional connection would doubtless raise Gerson's reputation with the medical community at large, and certainly also stop some of the annoying tactics used by local physicians to harass him by constantly questioning his credibility. But when the Gersons shared the exciting news about Sauerbruch's interest with an attorney friend, Robert cautioned Max sternly. "You have seen for yourself how when a professor works with a student or researcher with lesser academic stature or scientific credentials than himself, the results are published with the professor's name on the paper. If you are lucky or Professor Sauerbruch feels generous, your name will be mentioned as a contributor. But you certainly won't be given the credit you deserve for your ideas."

Robert now looked at Max sharply. "As I recall," he said, "that is what happened to you in Breslau, with your crucial modification to Professor Förster's spinal cord procedure. Förster published the paper describing the innovation under his own name. Your name was not even mentioned. I would be willing to wager that you will have the same experience with Sauerbruch."

Max studied his old friend for a long moment before he replied. "I am not interested in who gets the credit for this idea," he said quietly. "I am only concerned that it gets used by as many physicians as possible, since we have seen how much good it does for the patients."

"I still think you should have some kind of written agreement with Sauerbruch, in which he guarantees that he will acknowledge your part in developing this therapy. It is the only way to protect yourself and the work you have done from theft."

"Ach, Robert," Max said, "Thank you for your concern. But—can't you see?—you are still thinking like a lawyer. I am a physician. My job is not to sequester credit, but to heal people who are dying and in pain. I refuse to keep this method to myself, no matter the reason. Pride, wealth, glory or fear would be good reasons to do as you suggest. I ask none of these for myself. Now, please, no more talk of contracts!"

Max Gerson focused on readying himself for the time when Professor Sauerbruch would summon him to Munich for a discussion of his nutritional approach to treating tuberculosis.

Dr. Sauerbruch and Dr. Gerson

When Max Gerson made his first trip to Munich to meet with Dr. Sauerbruch, in April of 1924, Gretchen accompanied him on the long train ride, which lasted a full day and night. The two physicians, meeting at the Gersons' hotel, had an animated discussion that went on for several hours. Very interested in the highly positive results that Gerson had achieved with various diseases, especially in treating tuberculosis, he wanted to know how Max had developed these ideas. They exchanged ideas on ways of using nutritional therapy, in which Sauerbruch had already done some preliminary but as yet unproductive research.

Sauerbruch had already arranged for Dr. Gerson to give an hour-long lecture next day to a hall full of physicians at the University of Munich. Max found, to his disappointment, that no question-and-answer period followed his lecture. As Gretchen Gerson later recounted, "A discussion was not planned because up until then scientific investigation did not concern itself with questions of diet, considered beneath the dignity of the university level. After the lecture everyone left the room. Sauerbruch was very impressed and had a long discussion with Max the next day. He told him that the others held it against him to invite them to such a lecture." Apparently it was below the dignity of medical school professors to give any thought to matters of diet. Nutrition was simply not a subject worthy of scientific or clinical investigation. Furthermore, they would be asking themselves and each other: "How could an individual unaffiliated with a university possibly come up with a cure for all these different degenerative diseases on his own, and just by using food — moreover, having no government funding, no staff and no laboratory? " As Mrs. Gerson commented in her memoir, "Everything new in scientific knowledge that did not originate in the university is unpopular and fought as long as possible, until the establishment can take it over into its domain (Ignatius Servato, Copernicus, Columbus, Semmelweis, Jenner, Paul Ehrlich, Pasteur, etc.)." Doubtless Gerson's experience in Munich illustrated well how the entrenched "Old Guard" in universities and medical practice routinely dismissed the importance of dietary factors, including vitamins and other micronutrients.

Yet in Germany some rebels within the upper ranks, as well as members of the younger generation, were obviously far more open to moving research and clinical practice toward exploring and experimenting clinically with nutritional biochemistry, among them Dr. Gerson's eminent Munich host, who was surprisingly disposed toward taking nutrition seriously. "Sauerbruch was a gifted man, the top surgeon of his time in Europe," Mrs. Gerson remarked. "To a certain extent he had tried to influence his cases through changes in their nutrition, but had not got far with it. He was determined to research the problem further."

Sauerbruch asked whether he might send two of his capable associates,

Professors Schmidt and Herrmannsdorfer, to Bielefeld, where Max would show them some of his cases — "all of course with the supporting evidence," Mrs. Gerson specially noted, meaning detailed patient records, backed up by X-rays and laboratory test results. Max Gerson readily agreed, though knowing that the professors' investigative work would somewhat disrupt his own schedule in treating patients.

After their arrival, Gerson gave part of each day to presenting recovered and recovering tuberculosis patients to them. They also saw evidence of Gerson's successful treatment of various conditions besides tuberculosis. He spent additional time in preparing the supporting documentation for the visiting dignitaries, some of which they would take back to Munich. Whenever Gerson invited patients to be present for a demonstration, they happily obliged, as they were devoted to him — as he was to them. During the rest of the day, while Max saw patients, he provided a room where his visitors could work. Both made copious notes in thick black notebooks.

After a week, the two professors returned to Munich. Together with Sauerbruch they pored over the documents they had brought back. There was no question that a number of patients had been cured, for the doctors had examined each one themselves, heard their stories and found them to be in good health. The documentation, which included evidence of tests and treatments given not only by Dr. Gerson but by any physicians preceding him, was complete and convincing. It was evident to them, to Sauerbruch and some of their associates that Gerson had indeed cured tuberculosis, as well as migraine and a scattering of other diseases. Sauerbruch was eager to try the therapy on the patients in his tuberculosis ward. Not long after the professors had left Bielefeld, Gerson received another telegram from him: "PLEASE CONSIDER RETURNING TO MUNICH. I WOULD LIKE TO SET UP A CLINICAL EXPERIMENT USING YOUR DIET THERAPY. SAUERBRUCH."

Gretchen, ever the practical wife, noted that there was no mention of payment: for the time or expense it would take Max to travel to and from Munich, and for the time lost in his practice and the fees he otherwise would have earned from patients. Nor was there any word about joint authorship of any articles that might result from a collaboration. What would protect her husband from not becoming known as the originator of the therapeutic diet he had laboriously devised over the years?

Gretchen knew her husband well. He would not be concerned about protecting his own interests, both professionally and financially; instead, he would just be interested in getting the results into practice — not who got the credit for it. So Gretchen spoke privately to their attorney friend again. This time, without asking Max, Robert drew up a short but clear agreement regarding the procedures to be followed in any joint venture, including publication credit. Then he brought it to Gerson's office.

"Max, Gretchen thought it would be best for me to clarify the issues of treatment and publication before you go charging off and give it all away to Sauerbruch.

So I have prepared a simple and straightforward agreement to ensure that your rights are protected."

"Robert, I thought we had discussed this matter before. No contracts, please."

"Just read it over, Max. It is not complicated, and is fair to both parties."

Max took the document, which was ready for signing. It looked intimidating and formal, even cold, he thought. This was not the way to start a mutual and trusting relationship. He pushed the paper across his desk.

"I appreciate your concern, Robert, and the time you have spent preparing this contract. But I cannot send this to Sauerbruch and still expect to work with him. I will send a letter myself, if that makes the two of you happy. But I will not send him this contract."

Holding to his promise, Gerson wrote a gentle letter to Professor Sauerbruch, mildly suggesting that, should either of them wish to publish the results of their joint work in Munich, the paper should list both of them as authors. To Gretchen's dismay, he did not mention the issue of being reimbursed for travel or time lost from his practice. Instead, Max said that he would arrive in Munich in two weeks to help start the clinic. And he did not request a reply.

Gretchen, always a worrier, spent the next few days in great agitation. She was alarmed that her husband's stunning discoveries might now be wholly credited to someone else. By now, having seen what Gerson's fellow physicians were capable of doing—the day-to-day harassments from his Bielefeld colleagues were still occurring —Gretchen no longer believed in the goodness and generosity of human nature, particularly with a discovery of this magnitude. She could not just sit by and watch Sauerbruch take advantage of her husband. Ten days before Max's departure, she secretly sent Sauerbruch a telegram: "KINDLY REQUEST YOUR ANSWER TO PROPOSAL. GERSON." Then she waited.

The day before he was scheduled to leave, Max breezed into the kitchen where Gretchen was preparing lunch. He was holding a telegram in his hand, and beaming broadly. "Look, Gretchen," he said, "I told you Sauerbruch would treat me fairly. I never requested a reply, yet he was good enough to send me this." He handed it over.

She read: "FOR AN HONORABLE PERSON IT IS UNDERSTOOD THAT I SHALL ALSO HOLD TO YOUR PROPOSAL. SAUERBRUCH."

Gretchen didn't tell Max about her subterfuge until two years later.

Launching the Clinical Trials

Professor Sauerbruch and his two colleagues, Professor Schmidt and Privatdozent (assistant professor) Herrmannsdorfer, greeted Dr. Gerson in Munich, and together they sketched out a work plan. Afterward, Max Gerson, usually from the distance, helped decide on the many details for the clinical trial to be set up in

Munich basically under Dr. Sauerbruch's aegis. For instance, the ward would need to be renovated, the kitchen specially equipped to prepare the dietary therapy, suitable staff hired and funds allocated.

In the meantime, Drs. Sauerbruch and his two associates were working on finalizing the ambitious experiment to be conducted in Munich. He informed Dr. Gerson that he had arranged for the Bavarian regional government to put a 60-bed hospital pavilion at their disposal in a major effort to determine the value of Gerson's dietary therapy in treating tuberculosis patients. Moreover, two wealthy philanthropists from Berlin, who were friends of Gerson's, had donated the financial means to fund the initial experiment. The three Munich doctors had already selected a number of tuberculosis cases from their university clinic who would be treated only with the Gerson dietary therapy. Their progress, if any, could be compared with that of patients in similar conditions, past or present, who did not undergo this special treatment.

"We securely barred doors and windows to prevent escape," Sauerbruch recalled of the preparations in his autobiography. "A person who, over a long period, is given food with no salt at all suffers from his situation."

After going to Munich to inspect the final setup for the experiment, Gerson was shocked at the condition of the selected patients. A number of the patients were clearly dying of their diseases. The remainder were in such poor condition that he had only witnessed such human wreckage in photographs of extreme cases in medical textbooks. Not one of the patients had been said by their previous physicians to have even the slightest chance of improvement.

After introducing Gerson to the patients who would be taking part in the trial, Sauerbruch said to him privately, "Max, if you can bring about some slight improvement in even *one* of these cases, never mind healing them, I will believe your every word."

Encouraged at least by these low expectations, Gerson set to work. The first thing he had to do was to ensure that the proper tone was set, not just for the patients, but for the staff as well. He was aware from his prior experience with tuberculosis patients that the attitudes of both patients and staff made a difference in the ability to heal disease. If patients believed that a cure could be effected, they would cooperate with the treatment and not spend their time worrying. Gerson had already learned that the stress caused by fretting about the slow progress or lack of improvement *itself* generated toxic chemicals in the body that could stop the healing process. Patients had to believe that they had a chance for recovery. The way to accomplish that was to convince the staff as well. If the attending doctors and nurses went around with long faces reserved for facing the walking dead, the patients would receive and amplify their beliefs. The same negative effect was caused, of course, by patients' distraught relatives and friends.

Max Gerson knew well about the Bavarian patients' normal dietary preferences for meat, salt, sharp spices, beer and other distinctly damaging foods. He warned them in no uncertain terms that, though he was sure he could help them, they had to do their part by ensuring that there was no cheating with the food. Anyone caught smuggling food into the ward would be immediately discharged.

Gerson stayed in Munich for the first 10 days to get things off to the right start, then returned to Bielefeld. After that, he traveled to Munich every three weeks, to make sure that things were being run as he wanted them to be. During the three months of the initial experiment in Munich, with much of his time and attention diverted elsewhere, Gerson neglected his Bielefeld practice. His colleagues, jealous of his close contact with the eminent Dr. Sauerbruch, soon found out the reason and began writing numerous letters to the surgeon, making negative comments about Gerson. Some of the letters were signed, others were anonymous. When Sauerbruch showed the critical letters to Gerson, they both had a good laugh.

Dr. Gerson was very impressed with Sauerbruch's brilliant and incisive mind, with his ability to recognize the truth and even to admit his own shortcomings. Gerson considered Sauerbruch a genius, and always found it stimulating to exchange ideas with him. The admiration was clearly returned. On one of Max's visits, Prof. Sauerbruch showed him two of his newly published volumes on surgery. "Gerson, with the success that your therapy has shown, my books are already obsolete," he remarked.

One day, a telegram arrived in Bielefeld from Prof. Sauerbruch. "PLEASE DO NOT OPEN MY LETTER OF YESTERDAY. LETTER FOLLOWS. SAUERBRUCH." Shortly, the reason for this cryptic and surprising message became clear when Max received the letter mentioned and, of course, immediately read it. The progress observed while Gerson was last supervising the experiment in Munich had ceased, Sauerbruch reported. Some of the patients were experiencing relapses in their conditions. He and Herrmannsdorfer could find no explanation for the reversals, other than that the diet therapy might work only for a while, then fail. So he had regretfully decided to give up the dietary tuberculosis ward, since it was showing no further positive results.

In his autobiography, *Master Surgeon*, Sauerbruch later recounted the circumstance so long ago that caused him to reverse his decision:

> That afternoon, a nurse called me to an emergency case: a patient had a severe post-operative hemorrhage.
>
> I hastened along corridors and down stairs and did what was necessary. Pensively, I was strolling back along the corridor near the lupus ward, when I saw a nurse, the fattest nurse in the building, carrying an enormous tray loaded with sausages, bowls of cream and jugs of beer. It was four o'clock in the afternoon,

hardly the time for such a feast in a hospital. In amazement, I stopped and asked her where on earth she was going with all that food. And then the whole story came out.

"I couldn't bear it any longer, Herr Geheimrat," she explained. "Those poor patients with skin TB. The stuff they are given—no one could eat it!"

She was astonished when I dashed her tray to the ground. It was one of the occasions when I completely lost my temper.

Every day, at four o'clock, when no one was around, she had been taking the patients a nice, appetizing, well-seasoned meal.

I sent off a telegram to Dr. Gerson, asking him not to open the letter I had written him.

We were back at the beginning again, and from that moment we took extra precautions in guarding the *lupus* wing. In comparison, a prison would have been a holiday camp.

Soon, Dr. Gerson proved right. Nearly all our patients recovered; their sores disappeared almost under our very eyes.

In this experiment involving 450 patients, only four could not be cured by Dr. Gerson's saltless diet.

Although the clinical results were published in medical literature, the recollections of the principal investigators differ slightly. Dr. Sauerbruch account of this important clinical trial differs significantly from the account told by Mrs. Gerson in her unpublished memoir. For instance, Sauerbruch indicated that the only form of tuberculosis under clinical study using the Gerson diet was *lupus vulgaris*. Yet in the literature published later describing the results of the experiment, it is clear that other types of tuberculosis were represented as well. The recovery of 446 of 450 patients, however, is not disputed. A 99+ % cure rate for patients deemed "terminal" was achieved in the joint experiment. Dr. Sauerbruch also told a different story than Gretchen and Max did about how he first heard about the Gerson's cure of lupus while taking a train ride. In his tale, the cured patient himself rode with him and provided the information directly, and according to this account, he had not been a former patient of Sauerbruch.

Several possible explanations can be proposed for various discrepancies between the Gerson and Sauerbruch perspectives on their relationship, including an imperfect recall of events. Regardless of these questions, the central fact remained: Dr. Gerson's dietary therapy cured patients. And this therapy needed to be communicated to other physicians.

A Preliminary Publication

No record has yet been found of the details behind Max Gerson's co-authorship with Dr. Sauerbruch and Dr. Hermannsdorfer of a scholarly paper in early 1926 that in its English translation is called "Experiments Attempting to Influence Severe Forms of Tuberculosis through Dietetic Treatment." The paper derives from a joint lecture delivered to a conference of surgeons and physicians in Munich, in which the three men in turn described their promising preliminary work in treating lupus and then several other forms of tuberculosis. The transcript of the meeting was published by the *Münchener Medizinische Wochenschrift* (Munich Medical Weekly), about two years after their association began.

The paper is dominated by Dr. Hermannsdorfer's detailed account of his own modifications of the initial Gerson diet. Curiously, it emphasized the consumption of fats, dairy products and meats — which Gerson specifically ruled out in his own tuberculosis diet. Dr. Gerson's brief and modest contribution follows those of his Munich associates; he mentioned his intention to publish a paper about the diet in the near future, but it appears that either he did not do so or else the report appeared in an obscure, long-expired journal. The news of this intriguing dietary approach to treating lupus and other tuberculosis-caused disorders soon spread through Germany's medical community and beyond following this first publication, in related discussions and case presentations at other conferences. In 1927, several papers by other physicians were published about the diet, and from then on other papers followed, with Sauerbruch and Hermannsdorfer publishing the first of their own papers in 1929.

As for Max Gerson himself, in the late 1920s he was more interested in the challenge of applying his diet in treating patients suffering from a wide variety of illnesses than in actively pursuing a publication record of his own.

~7~
Publicity and Fame
(1926–1928)

Trying Gerson's Therapy for TB in America

In the summer of 1927, a Dr. Edgar Mayer from the Trudeau Institute in Saranac Lake, New York, sent an inquiry to Dr. Gerson to see if he could visit him in Bielefeld while he was touring many of the tuberculosis clinics in Europe, on a grant from Mr. August Hecksher of New York, investigating the latest techniques being used to treat the disease. The Trudeau Institute, a well-known clinic specializing in the treatment of tuberculosis, took great interest in learning about any new approaches to therapy. Dr. Mayer, who had already visited clinics in England, France and Switzerland, had been told everywhere about the incredible results being achieved by the Gerson diet. He had even visited Sauerbruch's clinic in Munich, but now he wished to speak with Max Gerson himself. He would like a larger demonstration than he had gotten at Munich so that he could actually study some tuberculosis cases.

Dr. Gerson invited numbers of patients to present themselves to Dr. Mayer for examination, and put a room at Mayer's disposal for examination and study of patient records. Mayer had never seen such results in tuberculosis. The therapy was especially interesting because it consisted of lifestyle changes, not technology or drugs. This was a radical concept for physicians in 1927. In the week before he had to return to the United States, Mayer asked Gerson if he could borrow an experienced diet-nurse to take with him to Saranac Lake for a few months. His request made sense. Although the Gerson therapy is quite simple in its concept, it requires an experienced doctor to devise variations on the basic treatment for individual patients. Particularly in a clinic setting, it requires a professional thoroughly versed in the food preparation to make sure that all the patients are getting the correct quantities of properly prepared, high-quality foods and juices. Mayer promised that Gerson would have co-authorship of any publication that resulted from the experiment, and even went so far as to offer Max a considerable sum of money if he would let the nurse come to Saranac Lake. He also reassured Gerson that as soon as he saw some progress, he would want him to come over and supervise the treatment himself.

The wife of a physician named Dr. Jungklaus, whom Dr. Gerson had been treating for gall bladder disease, was available and willing to go in his stead. She was grateful for all the medical help he had given her and her husband. She was not only intelligent and reliable, but also well versed in the food preparation necessary for the Gerson therapy. When Mrs. Jungklaus volunteered to travel to the United States with Dr. Mayer to supervise the application of the therapy, Gerson agreed to allow the experiment to proceed.

The ward at the Trudeau Institute in upstate New York that would be given over to the experiment with Gerson regimen had a capacity for about two dozen patients. When Mrs. Jungklaus arrived, she organized the ward and began the diet therapy with various additional mineral supplements, as Gerson had instructed Dr. Mayer. She reported to Gerson twice a week, usually by telegram.

Gerson was initially encouraged by Mrs. Jungklaus' reports. With Dr. Mayer, she seemed to be taking excellent care of the patients, who were becoming quite dependent on her. Then the tone of her letters began to change. After four weeks of administering the therapy to the tuberculosis patients, her letters began to sound more and more depressed. Some clear progress had been shown in the ward, she said. That was not the problem. The experiment was doomed to failure for two chief reasons: the doctor's inattention and the reluctance of the kitchen staff to perform their tasks. The kitchen staff had begun to balk at the sheer volume of food that needed to be purchased, stored, moved, cleaned, juiced, cooked and served. Eight ounces of fresh juice had to be prepared and served to each patient every hour. It was an enormous task. Each patient consumed between 15 and 20 pounds of fruits and vegetables every day. That meant over a *ton* of material needed to be procured and processed for 20 patients every week. Soon the kitchen staff refused to purchase enough fruits and vegetables to sustain the therapy, especially for the all-important juices.

In addition, Dr. Mayer was hardly ever present. After nine weeks of the experiment, Mrs. Jungklaus reported that she wanted to come home, but she remained for the agreed-upon three-month period.

In 1929, Dr. Mayer and a colleague, I.N. Kugelmass, published a paper, "Basic 'Vitamin' Feeding in Tuberculosis," in the *Journal of the American Medical Association* (93[24]:1856-1862, Dec. 14, 1929) describing the failure of the Gerson therapy in the Trudeau experiment. Contrary to the commitments that Mayer had given Gerson in Germany, neither did he give Gerson co-authorship credit, nor did he even tell Gerson that he had published the article. Some years later, when practicing in the United States, Dr. Gerson drafted a statement (which was never published) entitled "Dr. Mayer's Account of My Diet," in which he explained at least some probable reasons for the poor results at the Trudeau Institute. It had become clear to him from reading Mayer's statements in a publication entitled *Clinical Tuberculosis*, by a Dr. Goldberg, that Mayer had not well understood how the basic Gerson diet had to be modified for treating TB, and instead had seemingly followed Gerson's associates' instructions:

> I hold that his diet instructions are very different from mine, and that I strongly object to their being referred to as the Gerson Diet. My program and forbidden foods ... are based on precise scientific observations, in part also on clinical experience.

> For instance, he writes in *Clinical Tuberculosis*, p. 69, that my diet contains nuts, milk, puddings, white cheese, spices, alcohol, coffee. Not only are these foods "unnecessary" to my tuberculosis therapy, but they are also forbidden....
> [H]e refers in his false description to my article in the *Munich Medical Weekly* (Muenchner Medizinichen Wochenschrift), 1930, "Fundamental directions for the Gerson diet."

> However, an exact description of the method is contained in my book, "Diaettherapie der Lungentuberkulose," Deuticke, Leipzig, 1934. The article from which he draws refers to migraine, chronic arthritis and certain other chronic diseases, but nowhere to lung tuberculosis, although lupus is mentioned.

> In no way have I recommended the special diet for tuberculosis as Dr. Mayer states. Such errors about my various diets for special purposes are due to the fact that I did not state in every case for which disease each diet should be applied. At any rate, I prefer to explain some of Dr. Mayer's errors that way.

> My tuberculosis diet has been changed in the course of time through observation and experience. Even recently I have been able to make improvements.

> But it is important that nothing in his article indicated that at Saranac Lake he tested my tuberculosis diet in a somewhat changed form, as we had arranged and to which purpose he took a trained diet nurse on my recommendation from Germany, employing her there. Apparently the diet he used was the Sauerbruch-Herrmannsdorfer diet, which is quite different from mine and with which I do not agree.

> In Germany it has been conceded that the Sauerbruch-Herrmannsdorfer diet does not have as favorable results as my own diet....

> In about 600 treated tuberculosis cases I lost 42 cases. Probably 20 of these deaths could have been avoided if the present improved treatment had been applied.

Mayers' report was brought to Dr. Gerson's attention in 1944 by Professor Irving Fisher of Yale University after Max had immigrated to the United States and was practicing in New York City. Still considered one of America's foremost economists,

Professor Fisher filled in the story behind Mayer's report. Apparently, when Mayer's experiment began producing impressive initial results, other tuberculosis physicians in the area who had been using the minimally helpful Finsen Ray became more than a little afraid for their own livelihoods. They threatened Dr. Mayer that if the experiment were not terminated, they would complain that his clinic was being run under unsanitary conditions, and thus shut down his entire operation. This had been the source of the mysterious and inexplicable reversal in the application of the therapy reported by Mrs. Jungklaus. And while the Gerson diet did receive praise in March 1929 when Clarence Emerson, M.D. reported in the *Nebraska State Medical Journal* that "results of [dietary] management in both operative and non-operative cases of pulmonary tuberculosis in [the Y pavilion of the Sauerbruch clinic] and in the Lincoln General Hospital has been so favorable that further dissemination of the knowledge of this method of treating tuberculosis seems desirable," Mayer's adverse report in the most prominent American medical journal would have subsequent adverse ramifications on Dr. Gerson's professional career. Although dietary approaches to treating tuberculosis had many medical advocates in Europe by the 1930s, it was denied a foothold in America where the American Medical Association largely decided, for physicians' information and convenience, which therapeutic approaches to ameliorating disease were acceptable, and which ones were quite beyond the pale.

European Renown

In the following years the Gerson diet was often referred to as the Gerson-Sauerbruch-Herrmannsdorfer diet ("GSH" for short, as it increasingly was being called), though sometimes one or two of their names were omitted, or the sequence was changed. After their initial work with Gerson, both Sauerbruch and Herrmannsdorfer modified the diet in various ways, as did other physicians and dietitians. By the early 1930s in Europe, the diet had become the standard treatment for *lupus vulgaris*, as well as other forms of tuberculosis. The proliferation of articles on these treatments began in 1927 and peaked in the mid 1930s. This diet became widely used for treating many other immune system impairments, and was also recommended as a regular dietary regimen for health maintenance. As Max Gerson later indicated, with considerable irony, even Adolf Hitler, a near-vegetarian, was said to be following the Gerson diet.

Both Max and Gretchen Gerson loved the Alps. They escaped to them for vacations as often as they could, usually leaving the three girls behind with a trusted governess. They would take long walks, enjoying the clean air and the long vistas punctuated by permanently snow-covered peaks. These were times of refreshment, regeneration and reunion for them. As they usually did when on vacation, they had the *Vossische Zeitung* sent to them from Berlin. This newspaper had the highest national reputation—speaking with an editorial authority akin to that of today's national edition of the *New York Times* in the United States. One bright Alpine Sunday morning in 1928, Gerson opened the paper to an unpleasant surprise. Large front-page headlines proclaimed that the famous thoracic surgeon Professor Ferdinand Sauerbruch had presented a sizable number of cured tuberculosis patients in a crowded room in Berlin. The demonstration was so successful and the research so innovative that Dr. Sauerbruch had been called to the venerable Charité Hospital at the University of Berlin. There Professor August Bier, holder of the senior chair in Surgery, offered him the Second Surgery Chair. An appointment to a chair in the leading university hospital in the nation's capital would forever mark the recipient as a legitimate national leader in his field.

The Gersons noticed that all the cases that Sauerbruch had introduced to the assembled dignitaries in Berlin were the ones that he and Max had worked on together in Munich. Despite Sauerbruch's promise "as an honorable man," his idea of sharing the credit was to mention in an inconspicuous quotation in the newspaper article that he had taken the method over from a Dr. Gerson in Bielefeld. Regardless, Dr. Gerson as modest as ever, was pleased that the treatment he had originated was now receiving such attention from an internationally prominent newspaper: now the public could learn about the importance of using a special therapeutic diet in the treatment of tuberculosis.

The medical reporter of the *Vossische Zeitung*, Dr. Wolfang von Weisl cabled Dr. Gerson the next day. He had see in the headlines a perfect example of one of his pet peeves—theft of scientific ideas and methods. To explore the subject further, he requested a meeting with Dr. Gerson the next day in Munich. Both Max and Gretchen met with Weisl to work out the details of an article in response to the Sauerbruch announcement. The resulting article appeared the next Sunday, with headlines just as large as those trumpeting the Sauerbruch announcement. Max and Gretchen cut their vacation short, and immediately returned to Bielefeld, anticipating a great flurry of activity. They were not disappointed.

From that day on, there would be no more peace at the Gerson home. Because the medical consulting rooms were part of the family home, the newly famous doctor had no escape. No sooner would the telephone be placed on its cradle than it would ring again, insistently and incessantly. Telegrams and letters arrived by the bushel-baskets full. Besides the sick patients that besieged Gerson's door, consulting and employment offers arrived from tuberculosis sanatoriums, sometimes several in a week. Each of these had to be carefully considered.

As Charlotte Gerson remembers that period in her family's life, "We had a cook and a maid doing the work, since mother was tremendously busy with huge quantities of mail that arrived daily, as many as two to three hundred pieces. It was so extensive that she had to hire a secretary to help handle it all. She had little time any longer to devote to taking care of us girls. There was a great deal of talk and writing in Europe about Gerson and the Gerson therapy. One day a letter actually arrived from Turkey that was addressed only to "Dr. Gerson, Biele."

A number of the letters and telegrams were invitations for Dr. Gerson to lecture. One of the offers came from *Deutsche Rundfunk* (German Broadcasting). Would Dr. Gerson come to Berlin to do a 45-minute lecture on the radio? At first, Max felt uneasy. Getting on the radio seemed too close to advertising one's practice, and he didn't want to violate any ethical rules for physicians. The station assured him that other doctors had lectured on the medical-information program, so there was no problem in that regard. So he accepted, recognizing that a radio talk would be an excellent way to educate listeners about the importance of excellent nutrition in avoiding or overcoming illness.

The station normally had a policy requiring a script of the proposed lecture to be given to the station manager three weeks before the broadcast. This practice was new to Max, since he had never before used a prepared script; instead, he could speak easily and coherently about whatever medical topic was on the agenda, without referring to either notes or a script. He had a lot of material to cover in the forthcoming radio talk. Nonetheless, he submitted a script to Deutsche Rundfunk, and all was set for the broadcast. The title was *"Die Entstehung und Begruendung der Diaetbehandlung der Tuberkolose"* (The Development and Basis of the Dietary Treatment of Tuberculosis).

Five days before Gerson was scheduled to go on the air, a telegram arrived from Berlin. "IN THE INTEREST OF MEDICINE, I MUST REQUEST THAT YOU DECLINE THE LECTURE. SAUERBRUCH." Dr. Gerson was indignant. What on Earth could Sauerbruch mean? How could a 45-minute radio lecture threaten the "interest" of medicine? He decided that Sauerbruch's request was utter nonsense. Nonetheless, he telephoned Dr. Frank, the head physician of the radio show, who totally agreed with Gerson, saying there was no reason at all for withdrawing from the program. On the contrary, the public had already shown extraordinary interest in this coming broadcast. Also, at such a late date he would have had great difficulty filling three-quarters of an hour. Gerson cabled Sauerbruch with his decision to go ahead with the address.

The day before the lecture, another telegram arrived, saying: "IF THE LECTURE IS NOT CANCELLED, I MUST WITHDRAW MY COLLABORATION. SAUERBRUCH." This did not seem to be much of a threat, however, since by now Gerson had seen the dubious value of collaborating with Professor Sauerbruch.

Gretchen replied to the cable herself. "DR. GERSON HAS ALREADY DEPARTED FROM BIELEFELD TO GIVE THE LECTURE IN BERLIN." In fact, Max and Gretchen were going together.

When the Gersons arrived in Berlin, they met with Dr. Frank to go over the various arrangements and contractual obligations of each party. Frank was very upset. Apparently Sauerbruch had called him the evening before, to notify him that Gerson would *not* be doing the lecture. Wanting to clear up the matter, Frank told Gerson that he would call Sauerbruch again, since the two doctors knew each other.

Late in the evening, Dr. Frank called Max at his hotel. He told him that, of course, Sauerbruch had conceded that Gerson would do the broadcast, but said that he wanted to see Gerson in the morning, before he went on the radio.

By this time, Gretchen was livid at the perfidy of Gerson's former collaborator in the work with tuberculosis patients at the university hospital in Munich. She argued strongly against going to see Sauerbruch the next day. "He knows where to find you, Max. Let him come *here*. After the shoddy way that he has treated you, he can't just summon you to his offices! He violated his agreement to share credit. He has tried every trick he knows to keep you off the radio. He is a snake."

"Gretchen, please. Professor Sauerbruch is a very important man, and can't just be dismissed. He may not be terribly useful to me now, but he could be very dangerous if he is ignored. I understand your anger, but I will just stop over to his offices tomorrow to see what he wants."

"What he wants, Max, is to keep you off the air. He does not want you to get the credit you deserve for your own treatment. He wants to steal it."

"That won't happen, *Schätzchen*. I promise you that I will do the broadcast tomorrow. Come with me to the Charité tomorrow. Be my support."

At 11 o'clock the next morning, the Gersons went to Prof. Sauerbruch's new offices at the venerable Charité Hospital. This famous institution, a complex of two dozen ivy-covered brick buildings on the bank of the River Spree, had been founded over two hundred years earlier as a free hospital for the treatment of those who could not otherwise afford medical care. As most of the soldiers of that era were drawn from the ranks of the poor, the facility originally doubled as a military hospital. Having a facility of this type was an old tradition in Europe as there were Charité hospitals in many European cities. Few, however, held the reputation of Berlin's, where the Charité had become the teaching hospital of the University of Berlin.

Sauerbruch's waiting room was full, but when Dr. Gerson identified himself, he was immediately ushered into Sauerbruch's office. Gretchen remained in the waiting room, where she could hear Sauerbruch's agitated and angry voice through the office door. "Gerson, you must under no circumstances talk about lung tuberculosis! In Berlin alone there are over 250 physicians who earn a living from the practice of pneumothorax. You would be destroying their livelihood. It is unthinkable, and I forbid it." Gretchen knew that the pneumothorax procedure often used at the time in treating pulmonary tuberculosis involved collapsing the diseased lung by artificially introducing air within the thorax, with the purpose of allowing the raw edges of the lung with tubercular cavities, or *kavernen*, to come together and heal. Max had told her, however, that unfortunately the technique was generally unsuccessful, since the cavities were still filled with tubercle bacilli. But it was all that surgeons to offer at the time, so it was used anyway.

"Professor Sauerbruch," Gretchen heard her husband calmly replying, "research and scientific knowledge is honest and unarguable. Can you possibly be suggesting that we should *not* help thousands of sick people and perhaps rid the entire country of tubercle bacillus carriers ... just so that these physicians can earn a living?"

"Gerson, you realize, of course, that I can make life very difficult for you in the future. I will not tolerate your going on the air this evening. I shall not allow it!"

As for Max's own experience in Sauerbruch's inner sanctum, he watched the surgeon's face turn a deep shade of purple as he kept pounding a fist on his heavy oaken desk. And as he pounded, Sauerbruch's fist landed repeatedly on a manuscript that lay in the center of his desk blotter.

"Professor, I am sorry that you are so upset about this," Max said. "But even you cannot stop me. I have promised the radio station, Dr. Frank, my wife Gretchen and a lot of other people that I would give this lecture, and I fully intend to do just that. Now, that is settled. Is there anything interesting in that manuscript you have been punishing for the past ten minutes?"

After some embarrassed mumbling, Sauerbruch finally admitted that he wished to give the broadcast himself. Having recognized how important the address was, he had prepared his own manuscript for the lecture. The script lay on the desk in front of him. Also lying on Sauerbruch's desk, Gerson saw, was a copy of *Mein Kampf* (My Struggle). Adolf Hitler's political memoir and blueprint for future action was gaining popularity in Germany in the late 1920s. At the next opportunity, Sauerbruch downplayed Gerson's contribution in a scholarly article and said that much more study this method was needed.

Sometime later, Sauerbruch met Gerson at a medical congress in Cologne, where he apologized for his behavior in Berlin regarding the radio broadcast, and offered Gerson his hand in friendship. This personal apology was, of course, not published in any medical journal — or anywhere else.

Dr. Gerson gave the radio talk, as scheduled. His address was broadcast on the original station as well as 24 other stations throughout Germany with links to Deutsche Rundfunk. Not only did he discuss the importance of correct nutrition in preventing and curing diseases, Dr. Gerson also expressed his developing point of view about medical practice. His ideas appeared contrary to the direction that modern medical specialists were taking. Instead, he honored the physician's roots in the ancient or classical role of effecting cures by regarding and treating a patient's body as an organism whose various parts, including the mind, were interconnected and integrated:

> So far as medicine is concerned, a sign of our times is growing specialization. Each specialist is more or less exclusively active in the techniques of his

own special field, his diagnoses or his therapy. Everywhere the thinking leads away from giving attention to the body as a whole. Slowly, however, out of itself, the art of healing is changing. The new research in the areas of inner secretions, the nervous system's regulation of the internal organs, the metabolism of minerals and their interactions, presses firmly toward a new concept. The totality of functions and their dependence on each other must be understood in the healthy as well as sick body. The meaning of a sick organ and even the deficient secretion of an internal gland must be subordinated and joined together in a perspective on the entire system and all its activities. We again have to honor the remarkable assumption of Hippocrates (460–375 B.C.): "Everything in an organism is a flowing together, in one single, harmonious cooperation. Everything is directed to the totality; each little item is designed to fit together with every other one — everything is present in the combined activity."

This philosophical position, expressed in Germany as *Ganzheit*, or wholeness, was equivalent to Jan Christiaan Smuts' concurrent proposal of *holism*, which regarded systems on all levels of planetary existence, large and small, whether living or inorganic, material or immaterial, as integrated within themselves and yet interrelated with others. Notable thinkers of that period, such as Alfred North Whitehead and J.R. Haldane, had similar perspectives. So had Rudolf Steiner, the late 19th-century Austrian philosopher-educator who had taken such an interest in organic farming methods and had also founded the Waldorf Schools, which encouraged individualism and creativity in students on all levels.

The unifying concept of *Ganzheit* would return later in Dr. Gerson's life to take an important role in his attitude toward the practice of clinical medicine. He expressed it several decades later in an English word, *totality*. This point of view soon evolved into what is now called *holistic medicine*.

The Jewish Question

When Max Gerson had noticed the copy of *Mein Kampf* in Sauerbruch's office, he should have considered its presence there as prophetic. During the Nazi era, Dr. Ferdinand Sauerbruch's position as one of the leading surgeons in Europe brought him into the highest circles of the political elite, yet when Max Gerson knew him, Sauerbruch was not pro-Hitler or a National Socialist. Later, considered one of Nazi Germany's "leading lights" in medicine, Sauerbruch was said to have participated in medical experiments on inmates of the concentration camp at Dachau, though in his 1951 autobiography, *Das War Mein Leben* (translated editions, *Master Surgeon* in the U.S.A. and *A Surgeon's Life* in U.K. followed in 1953), he slides smoothly over the dark underside of his practice during the war years.

Max took little if any interest in politics, but by then his Jewish friends had told him about Adolf Hitler's book, first published in 1925. They probably drew his attention to such ranting passages as this one, in which the author declared that the generic "Jew" was not inherently a nomad, but was—

> … always only a parasite in the body of other peoples. That thereby he sometimes leaves his previous living quarters is not connected with his intention, but is the simple logic of his being thrown out from time to time by the host nation he abuses. But his spreading is the typical symptom of all parasites; he always looks for a new feeding soil for his race.
>
> But this has nothing to do with nomadism for the reason that the Jew does not think of leaving a territory he occupies, but he remains where he is sitting, and that means so 'sedentary' that he may be expelled only with force and with great difficulty. His spreading to ever new countries takes place only in the moment when certain conditions for his existence are apparent there; without that he would (like the nomad) change his previous residence. He is and remains the typical parasite, a sponger who, like a harmful bacillus, spreads out more and more if only a favorable medium invites him to do so. But the effect of his existence resembles also that of parasites; where he appears the host people die out sooner or later.

As both humanist and medical man, Max Gerson must have regarded this sort of thinking as the ravings of a madman. How could sensible people, which most German surely were, ever take such vicious thinking to heart? In time, however, he began to realize that quite a number of non-Jewish "Aryans" obviously delighted in Hitler's description of this uniform Jew as "a real blood-sucker which attaches itself to the body of the unfortunate people and which cannot be removed until the monarchs themselves again need money and in person tap the blood that he has sucked in." The monarchs had been eliminated at the end of the Great War, and now Hitler obviously believed it was time to eliminate Jews. This Austrian-born agitator, released from prison, where he had written the book that was becoming the Nazi party's blueprint and bible, had resettled in Munich and was preparing to expand his own political territory by declaring the German right to *Lebensraum* — to occupy lands stretching beyond the nation's borders.

A Sanatorium for Foxes

On one of his beloved mountain vacations, this time in Thüringen in the Harz Mountains, Max was taking his daily walk through the woods when he chanced upon a fox farm. The owner was pleased to show him his setup, which consisted of a large, circular pen built around a smaller pen. The foxes were kept in the outer pen; rabbits stayed in the inner one.

"What is the purpose of this arrangement?" asked Max.

"The foxes need exercise," replied the owner, "and, as you can see, they are constantly trying to chase the rabbits. This keeps them active, and the exercise and fresh air gives them the shiny coats that bring top prices."

"They certainly look healthy."

"Yes, they are. But would you believe that they all had tuberculosis when I acquired them?"

"Tuberculosis?" The word had, of course, piqued Gerson's interest. "But these foxes don't seem at all sick!"

"Ah, that is my secret for success, sir. In captivity, foxes often develop tuberculosis. This destroys the value of their fur, and the breeder must dispose of the animal. A few years ago, I heard about a certain doctor in Bielefeld, Dr. Gerson, who cures skin tuberculosis, and I thought, 'Why not foxes?' So I tried a little experiment. I got seven sick foxes, all with tuberculosis, and fed them only naturally grown food, rich in the minerals from good earth. Six of the seven recovered, and their coats regained their thick and shiny appearance. Now I advertise to buy foxes with tuberculosis, which are naturally quite inexpensive. I feed them good food, and later sell them at premium prices, since their coats are so handsome. I have to tell you, sir, I am making a fortune doing this. It was just like this Dr. Gerson said! He is becoming quite famous, you know."

"I am quite flattered, sir," Max said, "as I am the Gerson that you speak of. But I had no idea that my diet could be used in such a clever and enterprising way."

"You? *You* are Dr. Gerson?" the man exclaimed. "But I am honored! Please, won't you come into the house for some coffee? I have many questions that you could perhaps answer for me."

The two men spent the rest of the afternoon deep in conversation about the treatment of tuberculosis, the importance of having whole foods grown in soil that contains particular minerals, and the growing interest in restoring traditional agricultural practices. This movement, rejecting synthetic fertilizers and pesticides, would later become known as organic farming.

When Gerson finally had to leave, the farmer took out a beautiful and quite valuable pelt and gave it to him. "Please, Dr. Gerson, as a small token of appreciation for my prosperity and your excellent advice, I would like you to have one of my finest silver fox furs."

"Thank you very much," Gerson said, handing it back to his host. "Though I really appreciate the offer, I simply can't accept."

When he returned to Thüringen, Gretchen was naturally curious about the unusual length of his walk. She had grown somewhat concerned when Max hadn't returned by his usual time. He related the story of the fox farm to her.

"A beautiful silver fox fur? And you turned it down? Do you know what that is worth, Max?"

"Ach, Gretchen!" Max replied defensively. "I know. But I had just spent the whole afternoon watching these beautiful creatures happily chasing their captive rabbits. I could not constantly see the skin of one of them without seeing the animal itself in my mind. It would have made me very uncomfortable."

Gretchen didn't quite forgive Max for turning down that gift, and within the month, the grateful fox farmer sent Gretchen a fur piece made from three of his prime pelts.

The incident at the fox farm had once again demonstrated to Gerson the importance of the minerals in food, minerals that could only come from the soil. He was becoming more and more convinced that tuberculosis was a problem that might somehow be connected with food coming from deficient soil.

Treating Rheumatoid Arthritis

A noteworthy case of Dr. Gerson in this period was that of Lilli Steinhaus, the wife of a prominent cigar distributor in the neighboring town of Gütersloh. Fritz Steinhaus, who also wrote delightful books in the local dialect, had previously discussed his wife's condition with Max. Lilli's condition was grave, as she had been under treatment for almost two years for another disease (besides tuberculosis) considered "incurable" — acute rheumatoid arthritis. Steinhaus was in despair, as his wife's condition continued to deteriorate inexorably. Here again was a disease that Dr. Gerson had not yet attempted to treat. He had seen arthritic swellings and joints heal before, but only incidentally to his treatment of tuberculosis or migraine. Acute rheumatoid arthritis was a much more serious ailment.

By the time Gerson arranged to see Lilli Steinhaus, her joints were all but frozen, making her as stiff as a board. Neck, shoulders, hips, arms and legs were nearly immobile, and she was in extreme pain. Her jaws were unusable so that she could barely eat. She had become totally apathetic, not caring if she lived or died, since living was such torture. A woman friend was taking care of her.

At first, Gerson was reluctant to take on the case, but Fritz would not give up. He pleaded with Gerson to at least try to help his suffering wife. Eventually, Gerson relented and agreed to treat the arthritic woman. He cautioned her and her husband, however, that he could not possibly guarantee positive results with this disease, with which he had no prior experience.

This case presented unique problems that Dr. Gerson had not dealt with before. Lilli's rigid jaws made the administration of a dietary treatment nearly impossible. Another problem was that the patient was totally immobile and apathetic—unable to help with her own therapy. Everything would have to be done for her. Dr. Gerson realized that this patient required more than food. Two or three times a day, he would massage the swollen and locked joints all over her body. In the early stages of the treatment, she could not stand more than a few minutes of contact, but gradually the massages got extended to several minutes at a time. The sessions were very strenuous: on the patient's part due to the extreme pain involved in touching any joint; on the physician's, due to the effort expended in such intensive caregiving. At the end of each session, both were covered in perspiration.

At first, Lilli could only accept fluids fed to her in very small amounts, since every movement, every swallow, was painful. Gradually, the patient's condition improved so much that she could begin to eat and drink normally. From then on, she strictly maintained the prescribed dietary regime. The massages and the diet together were having an effect. Although the treatments took several months, both patient and physician had enough energy and will to continue. After four months of nearly daily care, the swellings in Lilli's joints had nearly completely receded, and she was able to stand by herself. Her family was delighted that she could participate in Christmas festivities, for the first time in some years. The treatment continued, with the family providing support and encouragement. After several more months, as spring was arriving in Westphalia, Lilli realized that full movement had been restored to all her joints.

Fritz Steinhaus was well known in the region as an occasional poet and raconteur whose his stories were much sought after. Naturally, the happy event of his wife's recovery from an agonizingly painful "incurable" disease became a major topic of conversation in his circle. Nobody else had yet cured rheumatoid arthritis, a disease that 70 years later is still considered incurable, though continuous high-dose treatment with corticosteroid drugs may alleviate it somewhat in a trade-off that poses risks of serious damage to other parts of the body. Mrs. Steinhaus lived another 40 years in excellent health.

First Experiences with Cancer

Occasionally Dr. Gerson made house calls to patients were unable to come to his office. Often he rode his bicycle, since he did not drive his own car. Many years later he told the story of this memorable occasion in 1928.

> One day I was called to see a lady. I asked her what was wrong with her, but on the telephone she didn't want to tell me. So I went there, a little outside of town. Then I asked her, "What's wrong?"
>
> She told me she was operated on in a big clinic nearby and they found a cancer of the bile duct. I saw the operation scar. She was running a high fever, was jaundiced. I told her, "Sorry, I can do nothing for you. I don't know how to

treat cancer. I have not seen results, especially in such an advanced case where there is no longer the possibility of operation."

So, she said, "No, doctor, I called you because I saw the results in your treatment of tuberculosis and arthritis in various cases. Now, here is a pad and you write down a treatment. On that table over there, there is a book, and in that book, you will be good enough to read to me aloud the chapter called "The Healing of Cancer." It was a big book of about 1200 pages on folk medicine and in the middle there was that chapter. I started to read. That book was edited by three schoolteachers and one physician. None of them practiced medicine, so they put together that book. I read that chapter. In it there was something about Hippocrates who gave these patients a special soup. I should like to tell you, we use that soup at the present time! That soup from that book, out of the practice of Hippocrates — 550 years before Christ! He was the greatest physician at that time, and I even think the greatest physician of all time. He had the idea that the patient has to be detoxified with the soup and with enemas and so on.

I read and read, but finally I told the lady, "Look, because of my tuberculosis treatment physicians are opposed to me. Therefore, I'd like not to treat you." Again she insisted. "I'll give you in writing that you are not responsible for the outcome of the treatment, and that I insisted that you do so." So with that signed statement, I thought, all right, let's try.

I wrote down the treatment. It was almost the same which I used for tuberculosis patients which I had worked out and used at the University Clinic in Munich with Professor Sauerbruch. After the work at the University Clinic the treatment had been established and had been found effective. I thought that maybe it would be effective in cancer too. It is always written in scientific books that tuberculosis and cancer are both degenerative diseases where the body has to be detoxified. But this latter thought was written only by Hippocrates.

I tried — and the patient was cured! Six months later she was up and around in the best condition. Then she sent me two other cancer cases. One of her family with a stomach cancer where it had been found during an attempted operation that there were metastasized glands around the stomach — also cured! And I had to cure then, against my will, a third case. I expected to have still more opposition from the medical profession. The third case was also a stomach cancer — it was also cured. Three cases were tried and all three cases were cured!

I have to tell you that up to this day, I don't know how this happened, how I stumbled into that, how this was achieved. At that time I always said that I didn't know why they were cured. I didn't know enough about cancer and it was such a difficult problem to go into. But once it was in my head and in my hands and in my heart, I could no longer separate myself from that problem. ("The Cure of Advanced Cancer by Diet Therapy: A Summary of 30 Years of Clinical

Experimentation," given at Jensen health ranch in Escondido, California, in 1956, printed by the Gerson Institute as an addendum to A *Cancer Therapy*)

When Max Gerson told this story, he usually left out a crucial part of it, which he of course shared with his wife and later, with his daughters. He had been monitoring the woman's progress for some six weeks when, on one of his house calls, Gerson finally met Mr. Schmidt. The man was a painter, a cold and hard man who was often away on business trips. Despite his wife's spectacular progress, Schmidt was very hostile to Gerson. While Gerson was examining his patient, her husband could not restrain himself from making several harsh and ugly anti-Semitic remarks. Mrs. Schmidt was horrified, and tried to divert her husband from his disastrous course, but to no avail. When it became clear that his presence was unwelcome, Dr. Gerson rose, turned to the couple, and said, "I am sorry, sir, but I refuse to have anything to do with you. I will not return to this house, *ever*. Good day, Mr. and Mrs. Schmidt!"

He regretted having to leave, because he would have liked to observe the outcome of the case that had been progressing so well until then. When she was fully recovered, Mrs. Schmidt came to see him at his office, and at first he could scarcely recognize the woman he had first visited when she was totally bedridden. She remained well as long as Gerson could follow up on her case, for several more years. She returned to Gerson's office each Christmas with small gifts from her garden that she brought her doctor out of gratitude for saving her life.

Gerson had cured all three of his first three cancer cases, including one with liver metastases—a remarkable achievement. Though an isolated instance, here was another degenerative disease that yielded to his dietary therapy. Apparently, the body had the ability to restore its own equilibrium and heal even the most serious diseases if it was only given the correct materials with which to work. Much of what Max Gerson had learned in his medical school training and from the scientific literature he read so carefully had stressed the concept of "one disease, one treatment." Yet he had now seen many degenerative diseases cured by his one, simple dietary therapy.

Having read that recipe for Hippocrates' vegetable soup in *Deutschen Gesundheit* (*German Health*), he had adapted it for his own diet. Here is Dr. Gerson's version. In his printed diet form, he prescribed an open-ended "About _____ glasses a day," since the total number and amount would be variable, depending on the patient's overall condition and circumstance.

> For 1 person use a 2-quart pot, use the following vegetables,
>   then cover with water:
> 1 medium celery knob, if not in season,
>   substitute 3-4 stalks of branch celery (pascal celery is preferable)

1 medium parsley root
2 small leeks (substitute 2 small onions)
2 medium onions
little parsley only
1/2 lbs. tomatoes or more
1 lb. potatoes

Do NOT peel any of these vegetables; just wash and scrub them well and cut them coarsely; cook them slowly for 3 hours, then put through food mill in small portions; scarcely any fibers should be left. Vary the amount of water used for cooking according to taste and desired consistency. Let soup cool off before storing.

Keep well covered in refrigerator NO LONGER than 2 days; warm up as much as needed each time.

These first three cancer cases that Max Gerson treated successfully in Bielefeld would be just the beginning of his exploration of the possibility of curing many forms of cancer through dietary means. And what other diseases might his diet also ameliorate? The potential for exploration and experimentation tantalized him.

~8~
Moving Onward
(1929–1932)

Dr. Gerson on Trial

Dr. Max Gerson continued to experience favorable results in his own practice of curing patients of tuberculosis and other degenerative or infectious diseases, and his renown spread throughout Europe as his techniques were properly applied by other physicians when treating TB. Not unreasonably, then, Max began harboring the hope that his surprisingly successful dietary approach to treating the diseased body—whether for *lupus vulgaris* alone, various other forms of tuberculosis or for many different disorders—might someday earn him the Nobel Prize in Physiology or Medicine.

Therefore it came as a shock that not everyone was impressed with his accomplishments, especially in the city he lived in. Jealousy of Max Gerson's growing fame had seemingly reached a fever pitch in Westphalia, among certain Bielefeld physicians.

In her memoir of her husband's life and medical career, Gretchen Gerson told the story this way. On a lovely day in the early spring of 1929 a letter addressed to Dr. Max Gerson arrived from the Westphalian Medical Association. It contained a summons requiring his appearance, three weeks hence, at the organization's headquarters in Münster, to answer charges of irregular medical practice. A doctor in Bielefeld, representing many of his colleagues, had lodged a professional ethics complaint against Gerson: he was accused of practicing medicine outside his declared specialty.

Max was astonished at the hostile and accusatory tone of the summons statement. The only goal he had ever pursued was the health of his patients. Gretchen was terrified that the physicians' collective resentment against her husband's way of conducting his practice had actually resulted in legal proceedings. She urged Max to get an attorney to assemble documentation to prepare his case. After all, if he were found guilty, he could be fined, have his license suspended or revoked, even be imprisoned. But Max calmly declined to engage a lawyer to handle his defense, since he had done nothing wrong.

Three days before Dr. Gerson had to board a train for Münster, the *Munich Medical Journal* arrived in the mail. Professor Albert Jesionek of the University of Giessen, who ran a special lupus ward in that town, had contributed an article to this latest issue. A dermatology specialist who pioneered the use of light therapy in treating skin disorders, he reported that some while earlier he had read a provocative article describing the successful treatment of lupus by administering the special diet initially devised by Max Gerson. Dr. Jesionek had decided to use this dietary method on some of his own patients. His just-published article described the favorable results. When Gerson boarded the train for Münster, he took nothing with him except for this latest issue of the *Munich Medical Journal*.

As Dr. Gerson entered the meeting room of the Westphalian Medical Association, a panel of no less than nine physicians motioned for him to sit in a chair situated somewhat below the dais, giving them a height advantage as well as their overwhelming numerical superiority. The chairman of the disciplinary panel began the de facto trial. "Dr. Gerson, you have been accused of a gross breach of medical ethics," he said. "As a specialist, you are only permitted to treat diseases specified on your nameplate, and none other. Your shingle unequivocally states your specialties as 'Internal and Nerve Diseases.' Yet you have openly and blatantly treated skin diseases for some years. This violation of yours goes against all the rules and regulations of the Westphalian Medical Association. If this complaint is proven, you face censure and possible revocation of your medical license. Moreover, you have even provided the board with clear evidence of your unethical behavior by publishing an article in a medical journal that specifically states that you treat *lupus vulgaris*, a skin disease that is within the special province of dermatology, and even giving details about your methods. Do you have a defense for this behavior?"

Sitting calmly in the witness chair, Dr. Gerson had been absorbing the disapproving glares of the panel. He now stood and drew himself up to his full six-foot height. His voice was calm and self-assured. "Gentlemen," he began, "I see you have done your research thoroughly, so I cannot, nor would I, deny that I have been treating *lupus vulgaris*. It would be foolish to attempt to deny that lupus is not a skin disease, for it is quite clearly that. However, you have not mentioned the contents of the article I wrote, which demonstrates that I have *cured* this disease, not just *treated* it.

"Medical literature available today in Germany states that lupus is considered an 'incurable' disease. Less than 25 years ago, the Nobel Prize was awarded to Dr. Niels Rydberg Finsen, a respected Danish physician, who treated *lupus vulgaris* with concentrated light at his Medical Light Institute in Copenhagen. Since the disease is still considered 'incurable,' this treatment obviously did not solve the problem. Yet he was given the highest honor that can be bestowed on a physician in recognition of his advances.

"Only two years later, the same committee saw fit to honor Dr. Robert Koch similarly with the Nobel Prize for identifying in 1882 the *mycobacterium* bacillus that causes *lupus vulgaris* and other tuberculosis conditions, and for devising the test that provides today's physicians with the means to diagnose exposure to the disease easily and accurately, and monitor the progression of the disease, even though they cannot cure it.

"Today I stand before this panel accused of unethical medical behavior for having succeeded where so many others have failed before me. I am fully aware of the consequences of being found guilty by the Association, yet I have no fear of your verdict. On the contrary, I would consider it a great honor to be punished or even imprisoned for being the first physician to find a successful treatment for *lupus vulgaris* — a disease that has remained incurable for over two thousand years despite the most aggressive and inventive attacks from physicians the world over.

"If perhaps you think that my work and the various published papers based on applications of my therapy are frauds, you might be interested in considering this recent follow-up article by Professor Albert Jesionek of the University of Giessen in the recent *Munich Medical Journal*. He has confirmed the results of my dietary treatment on patients in his own *lupus vulgaris* sanatorium, thus showing again that the therapy is reproducible."

Dr. Gerson now handed the chairman his copy of the *Journal*, folded open to Dr. Jesionek's article, "On the Dietary Treatment of Skin Tuberculosis." The board was not expecting such calm in the face of an accusation that could not be denied, and which could well end this particular doctor's medical career. Physicians brought before the disciplinary board were normally in fear for their professional existence. Muttering in confusion, the board members looked at each other.

The chairman glanced at the *Journal* article briefly. Then he read aloud to the others the first paragraph in it: "Under treatment by the Gerson-Sauerbruch-Herrmannsdorfer Diet, tuberculosis diseases of the skin, specifically including lupus, disappear and heal. This fact cannot be argued. However, how does the disappearance and healing occur?"

The room was silent. "A footnote says that this article is based on a lecture that Professor Jesionek gave at the Medical Group in Giessen in February of this year," the chairman said gruffly. "We will need some time to consider this new information. This meeting is adjourned for two hours. Please be so kind as to return to this room at that time, where the hearing will proceed." He banged his gavel, and the board retired to a private office.

As Max turned to leave the room, he overheard one of the spectators, a Westphalian country doctor, say to his neighbor, "If we punish Dr. Gerson, reason becomes nonsense."

The atmosphere was noticeably different when the meeting was again called to order. The nine panel members seemed more relaxed; some were even smiling.

Again the chairman spoke, this time with warm courtesy. "Dr. Gerson, the Association congratulates you for your outstanding success in treating *lupus vulgaris*. We encourage you to continue this aspect of your practice and the excellent research associated with it. The article you gave us leaves no question as to your high degree of integrity and truthfulness. You will have no further difficulty from the Westphalian Medical Association regarding medical specialty.... The hearing is adjourned."

When Dr. Gerson returned to his home in Bielefeld, his step was a little lighter, his spirits brimming with new confidence. His worried wife and little family were greeted with the good news of his total exoneration. Before he opened his office the next day, he removed the plaque announcing his specialty as a physician who dealt primarily with diseases of the nervous system and internal organs. Dr. Gerson never again advertised a specialty to the world. He had become a general practitioner — a front-line physician who receives and treats patients presenting with a wide variety of health problems.

The Sanatorium Wilhelmshöhe

Despite his honorable exoneration by the Westphalian Medical Association, Max Gerson had grown wholly weary of dealing with the envy and dislike of the Bielefeld practitioners. After 10 years of mostly unpleasant relations, he felt that changes in both scenery and professional associations were essential. So he began seeking a new place to pursue his medical work and locate his family.

Among the various facilities offered for Gerson's consideration was the Sanatorium Wilhelmshöhe. This 150-bed facility was located in the Wilhelmshöhe hills on the western outskirts of Kassel, a garrison town on the Fulda River in Northern Hesse. The town was in the mountainous country south of Bielefeld — 100 miles 'as the crow flies,' but for ground travel the route was far longer and quite circuitous, over narrow and winding roads through mountain passes. Kassel had been the home of the Brothers Grimm of fairytale fame and the of the Hessian mercenaries used by the British in their attempt to put down the American Revolution. Max agreed to take over a section of the sanatorium, to be called "Dr. Gerson's Diet Sanatorium." Additionally, a local physician, Dr. Keding, who was favorably inclined toward Gerson's approach, saw to it that 25 beds were made available to him as a staff physician in the tuberculosis department at Landeskrankenhaus, the State Hospital in Kassel.

The Wilhelmshöhe district took its name from the mountain just to the west of the city of Kassel, whose name appropriately derived from the Latin word *castrum*, meaning "stronghold." The sanatorium was located at the edge of the forested ridge, on which sat the castles and monuments of the local hereditary rulers of

Hesse, with the *Habichtswald* (Hawk Forest) just across the street. This forest likely played a large role in Max Gerson's choice of this facility, as he always found relaxation in the woods. Ludwig Hartman, an enterprising fellow married to Gretchen's sister Gertrude, not only had initially set up this connection, but also found a house in town for both the Gerson family and his own. This attractive house stood alone in the midst of fields, with a wide-open view of Wilhelmshöhe Mountain, not far from the large boulevard with a trolley line that conveniently went one way up to the sanatorium and the Wilhelmshöhe castle, the other to the downtown area. The Gersons occupied the ground floor, where Max and Gretchen had their bedroom. The Hartman family lived on the second floor. On the third floor were rooms for the three Gerson girls and a maid, as well as the girls' *Oma*. Their grandmother — Max's mother Ulricke — had now joined the family. A neighborhood convenience store was located in a portion of the basement of the large house.

The three Gerson girls — now ages 12, 11 and 8 — were enrolled in two schools. While Hanni and Trudy attended the local *gymnasium*, young Lotte went to the new Waldorfschule downtown, a short streetcar ride away from the house. The Waldorf School's educational approach, addressing the whole child as an individual, had derived from the late Austrian philosopher Rudolf Steiner, a holistic philosophy of education that closely paralleled Gerson's evolving approach to medicine and health and became popular worldwide during the 1960s and 1970s.

The family never had cats or dogs, because Gretchen would always attract any flea on a furry pet, but they had a beautiful room filled with plants, the *Wintergarten*, which held a collection of canaries the girls loved. On sunny days Gretchen would give the birds air by putting them out on the adjoining porch. One evening she forgot to bring them in and the local cats killed them, but she didn't have the heart to tell the girls what had really happened. She gave up on keeping birds as pets.

Because their mother was often so busy helping Max with professional matters — bills, writing articles, a great deal of correspondence — while also managing the family home, the Gerson girls appreciated the ready accessibility of their paternal grandmother. Many years later Charlotte Gerson vividly remembered her:

> When *Oma* lived with us, she did a lot of work, sewed, crocheted, made a carpet after a complex pattern, mended socks and kept busy doing other useful things. In general, her presence in the household was a pleasant addition. But she was very strict about keeping the Jewish Shabbat and therefore did no work then, but instead would read and say her prayers. My parents were almost wholly secular, but they did insist that we three girls get religious training at Shabbat school.
>
> My grandmother always kept a "kosher" kitchen and never mixed meat and milk products or the cookware containing them, so she was able to live

with us because we were vegetarian and had no meat in the household. However, a dietary problem always emerged during Passover. Grandma would then cook her own food for herself, using special pots and dishes. Because she found it wasteful and unreasonable, my mother got rather uncomfortable and angry when Oma followed a standard Orthodox Judaism practice at Passover time. This involves throwing out the dishware used for the past year and using a special new set, which will then be used during the next year. Like many religious traditions, this one had a basis in health practices. It derives from the old desert days of using porous plates and bowls, which soaked up food juices; a year was about the limit for hygienic usability. Also during that time of Passover when Grandma was fixing her own minimal food, she lost weight, and Gretchen worried about this.

Another issue that bothered Mother was how Max was always so involved and concerned with his patients and their problems that he paid little attention to his mother. She was a very wise and caring lady, who had saved Max's life several times when he was younger. Grandma didn't complain about his inattention to her, but she must have been hurt. Only when Gretchen sometimes reminded him to do so did he look toward his mother when he left the house and tell her goodbye.

The comforts of a close family was especially appreciated in Kassel. Little Charlotte had soon noticed that the Hessians were not as friendly as the Westphalians — quite a statement, considering the well-worn adage, "Before you call a Westphalian your friend, you must share a bushel of salt with him." Which takes a lot of meals — even if non-Gerson diet ones!

The sanatorium opened in September 1929. Starting a new enterprise of this magnitude proved an enormous task. Hospital staff needed to be retrained to administer Dr. Gerson's therapy, and the kitchen staff had to learn new food preparation techniques to prepare the Gerson diet. Dr. Gerson required that, for their own protection, nurses in the clinics where tubercular patients were being treated should eat the same food as the patients. In other tuberculosis wards in Germany, nurses were customarily rotated to other wards every three months, in the hope that the shorter exposure would help protect them, but nurses became infected, nevertheless. In Dr. Gerson's wards nurses *never* contracted tuberculosis, even though they were not rotated out of the wards — surely the best testimony possible to the immune-enhancing properties of the Gerson diet.

With a large number of patients concentrated in one facility, all receiving the same diet, people were able to compare notes about some strange effects that they experienced. Every day, each patient on the dietary therapy received six eight-ounce glasses of carrot and apple juice, plus a glass of orange juice. Some of the patients began to notice that their skin color was gradually taking on the color of carrots. Naturally, patients worried about their apparent "jaundice"—until Dr. Gerson explained that this was perfectly normal. He explained that when canaries were fed a piece or two of carrot daily, in a few weeks their yellow feathers turned completely carrot-colored. This manifestation is known today as carotenemia. Physicians routinely caution patients that drinking "too much" carrot juice will result in the condition — "which might be dangerous." But besides the skin coloration, there are no other symptoms or any adverse effects of this 'condition' associated with ingesting certain vegetables containing the beneficial phytochemicals known as carotenoids. Another natural dye caused consternation and alarm until it, too, was explained. This was the harmless tendency of the patients' stools to turn red when red beets were added to the juice or accompanied the meals; also their urine turned pinkish. When the patients understood that this rather peculiar manifestation did not come from internal bleeding and began expecting this to happen, there was no further concern.

One day, the kitchen staff called Dr. Gerson into the juice-preparation area. The freshly pressed carrot and apple juice had completely jelled. His first question was, "Is one of the pressing girls having her period today?" When one answered affirmatively, the puzzle was solved. From then on, the standard practice was to have men do the juicing. Gerson perhaps never explicitly explained the reason for this odd chemical occurrence, which must have been due to a volatile hormonal secretion or pheromone that somehow, wafting through the air or possibly carried through skin contact with the produce, activated enzymes in the juice so that it became gelatinized.

The new Diet Sanatorium was soon filled, mostly with tuberculosis and migraine patients. Max threw himself into the task with his characteristic energy, receiving tremendous satisfaction from the evident progress that his patients made. But no matter how tireless he was in his work, he saw that he would be unable to supervise each case as closely as he was accustomed to do in Bielefeld. This was a great source of concern and regret to "Diet Gerson," whose personal rapport with patients had proved so valuable. This hands-on approach was a vital consideration when other physicians attempted to replicate Gerson's results; not only did they tend to modify his specifications and allow patients to do so, some lacked Dr. Gerson's healing manner or 'presence'.

No Smoking!

Dr. Gerson was puzzled by one of the migraine patients in the sanatorium. The wife of a doctor in Budapest, she had been in residence there for weeks, but was experiencing no positive results from the regimen. It was a mystery to Dr. Gerson that her headaches did not yield quickly to his therapy, as they did for all the other patients he treated. Day after day, her migraines continued.

The problem was solved, however, when he unexpectedly walked into her room one day. He found her smoking — totally against hospital rules, and in direct contravention to the therapy he was using to help her.

"*Frau Szabo*," he said, his blue eyes turning steely, "you know there can be no smoking in the sanatorium. It is strictly forbidden. Put out that cigarette now!"

"I can't, Dr. Gerson," she pleaded. "I have been smoking for 20 years, and it is not that easy to just stop."

"Put it out. *Now!* I cannot help you if you continue to smoke."

Under the doctor's stern gaze, she reluctantly stubbed out her cigarette. Dr. Gerson picked up the pack of cigarettes that lay on the bedside table, and crumpled it in his hand. "I am going to tell the nurses to make sure there are no more cigarettes in this room."

"Please, Dr. Gerson. I've tried but I simply can't stop. It is too strong a habit. Can't you allow me to have just that one little sin?"

"No, *Frau Szabo*. I can't, and I won't. If you insist on smoking, I am afraid that I will have to discharge you. You are just wasting your time and ours, and the bed is needed for someone who truly wants to get well. It is your choice. If you wish to continue with your habit, I shall send a telegram to your husband today and ask him to come for you at once. I will not have you smoking in the sanatorium."

The wife of a respected physician, she was not used to being treated in this way. "Please, Dr. Gerson, wait just a bit before you contact my husband. I will stop, I really will. But give me two days. Please don't send me away!"

"All right. Two days, then. But you must make your decision by then."

Gerson checked her again after the two days were up. The woman had stopped smoking completely. In two more weeks her migraines had disappeared, sped by the weeks of dietary therapy she had already received.

Struck by the powerful effect of nicotine on the patient's progress, Dr. Gerson kept a careful eye on the influence smoking had on his treatment of other diseases as well. Less than two years later, in 1931, he published a paper on the subject: "Nicotine as a Deterrent Factor in the Treatment of Lupus."

Notable Visitors and Patients

Dr. Mikkel Hindhede and his wife came from Denmark to Kassel-Wilhelmshöhe as patients. During the Great War, Dr. Hindhede had supervised the Danish national nutritional program and now was the Danish Minister for Nutrition. The two doctors spent many hours exchanging scientific and medical information — a stimulating and rewarding pastime for both men. Dr. Hindhede had recently become familiar with Dr. Gerson's work, which was becoming well known throughout Europe, thanks not only to Gerson's published papers and his international lectures, but also to the growing number of papers being published by other research physicians about the Gerson diet and its variations in the Sauerbruch and Herrmannsdorfer versions. Dr Hindhede and his wife stayed at the sanatorium for about four weeks; were both helped by this intensive experience with the Gerson diet.

In July 1930 Hélène Schweitzer came to Kassel-Wilhelmshöhe with pulmonary tuberculosis. She was the wife of the famous German physician-humanitarian who, before starting a clinic in Central Africa, had been renowned throughout Europe as a musician, author and theologian. Her health had always been fragile, and repeated stays in Lambaréné, Schweitzer's jungle settlement and hospital, had aggravated a prior tuberculosis infection, so that it now flared up dangerously. She had returned to Europe to be treated again.

Hélène Schweitzer was 43 years old and seriously ill when Max first saw her. X-rays confirmed that her right lung had one or perhaps two *Kavernen* — "caverns" or holes eaten in the lung by the disease. The left lung also had a large cavern. As he did with all tuberculosis patients, Gerson put her on the dietary therapy. Mrs. Schweitzer's progress, though steady, was slow. She stayed at the sanatorium in Kassel until the middle of November. By then, the lesions in her right lung were no longer visible on X-rays, her left lung was healing, she had put on some weight, and her sputum was negative for tuberculosis.

When she was sent home, Max gave her explicit instructions to stay on the diet for another six months to complete the healing process. Yet Hélène did not adhere to the diet, and the tuberculosis recurred. She was re-admitted in serious condition, with a fever and difficulty breathing. Dr. Gerson put her on an even stricter regimen than before, and she recovered in four months, this time permanently. She lived for almost three decades longer, dying in May 1957 at the age of 70, apparently of congestive heart failure. Mrs. Schweitzer's case — No. 45: Mrs. H.M.S. — was discussed by Max Gerson in his book, *Diättherapie der Lungentuberkulose* (Diet Therapy for Lung Tuberculosis), published in 1934.

Attempting to Preserve Juices

The Gerson treatment was difficult enough for patients at the sanatorium, but it became quite onerous when they were sent home. First, there was the shopping for, storing of and careful washing of the fresh fruits and vegetables, which were supposed to originate from growers who did not use pesticides and synthetic fertilizers. Then, not only did three fresh, salt-free vegetarian meals have to be prepared daily, plus batches of the slow-cooked Hippocrates soup concocted, but near-constant juice-making activities were required as well. Six or more glasses of carrot and apple juice had to be pressed daily, to be consumed by the patient as soon after pressing as possible. The pressing of the juice, requiring a special machine, was very tedious and time-consuming. This process had to be continued day in and day out, seven days a week, for the entire course of the treatment, which often lasted many months.

Since the Gerson diet therapy was gaining quite a following in Germany and elsewhere in Europe, a commercial laboratory in Berlin spotted an entrepreneurial opportunity by easing these shopping and juice-making tasks. The lab managers approached Dr. Gerson with a proposal to develop a means of preserving the juice, either by using some chemical additive or by jellying it. The idea of a market source for ready-made juices was attractive to Gerson because of its convenience to patients undergoing the treatment at home. This would encourage them to adhere to his regimen. He was also interested in having several different types of juice tested and compared for their mineral and vitamin properties, which the company's chemists could readily do. A lifelong experimenter, Gerson constantly tinkered with the composition of his juices. For instance, he tried adding different leaves to carrot juice. At one point he even tried out nettles. In Kassel Gerson began creating the "green leaf juice," later called "green juice," a combination of dark green leafy vegetables that eventually became a mainstay in his therapy — one of the prescribed daily juices.

The Gerson home included a large garage and two extra rooms, which were offered to two professional chemists and a female assistant, whom the laboratory in Berlin sent to work out a method for preserving the juice. A cage for guinea pigs was also installed in the garden tool shed. Each day a quantity of freshly pressed juice was brought from the sanatorium kitchen to the small but well-equipped laboratory. Here the three chemists worked daily with a particular juice, analyzing its contents, then adding different preservative substances. They tested the different versions out on the guinea pigs, and finally on patients.

The chemically modified juices were given only to patients who were not seriously ill and had volunteered for the experiment. Preparation after preparation was tried, but none achieved results equal to those routinely observed with the freshly pressed juices. Nothing the chemists did resulted in juices that healed the patients in the amazing way that the wholly natural juices did.

After three months, the chemists were forced to abandon the effort. "One day the chemists, the guinea pigs and all their activities disappeared," Charlotte Gerson remembers. But before the chemists left, they gave Gerson their chemical analysis of his basic juice. Dr. Gerson took great interest in their analyses, which showed that the juice had approximately the same minerals as the healing waters from Bad Lippspringe, but at approximately 100 times the concentration. In the early 1930s laboratory assays could detect mineral contents but only a few of the vitamins (many of which had yet to be identified). Little was known then, too, about other microconstituents of plant foods, such as the natural enzymes or the essential and nonessential amino acids that were the "building blocks" of the complex protein molecules. Far in the future was the very concept of phytochemicals — those many forms of chemical substances in plants that enable the sunlight-dependent process of photosynthesis on which all life forms are essentially dependent, and that confer protection from predators and diseases, encourage growth and reproduction, fill other useful functions . . . and also may often help humans because of special nutritive or medicinal values.

Though this early experiment in preserving his uniquely therapeutic juices failed, it brought home a very important principle to Max Gerson. He had based his treatment and philosophy on the notion that beneficial changes in the body's metabolism could only be brought about by natural methods. He had originally discovered the elements of his treatment by empirical means: that is, if a change worked, he kept it; if not, he discarded it. Now the chemists had underscored his findings with exhaustive experiments that showed that any alteration to the freshly pressed living material rendered it nearly useless for healing. They had discovered nothing that contradicted his already successful methodology, while proving themselves unable to devise any techniques to make it easier to undertake.

Publications, Lectures and Notoriety

In addition to the workload that Max Gerson carried at the sanatorium, he continued his academic endeavors, constantly studying the medical literature. During the period from 1929 to 1932, he contributed many articles to medical journals. His sobriquet, "Diet Gerson," was becoming so well known, not only in the medical community but also in the general culture that his name began to surface in crossword puzzles, and eventually in the definitive *Knaur's Encyclopedic Dictionary*.

Dr. Gerson was invited to lecture at the great universities in Germany as well as in many major cities of Europe — Amsterdam, Vienna, Dresden, Budapest, Munich, Berlin, Brünn, Frankfort, Darmstadt, Wiesbaden, Bremen, Hannover, Rostock, Halle, Norderney, Copenhagen, Oslo, Bergen, Trondheim, Upsala, Stockholm and Goeteborg. In Upsala, Dr. Gerson was invited to sign Archbishop Soederbloom's Golden Book of Sweden; in it his signature followed that of Nuncio Eugenio Pacelli — who would become Pope Pius XII in 1939.

Gerson's renown drew visiting doctors from tuberculosis clinics all over Europe and the United States. He was always willing to show them the facility and share his methods with them, including the all-important kitchen organization. But not always were these efforts worthwhile to him or the furtherance of his dietary regimen. One physician, visiting from the Harz region, stayed in Kassel-Wilhelmshöhe for nearly two weeks, examining patients and medical records under Gerson's guidance. When the time came to return to his own clinic, he asked for a well-trained nurse to be allowed to accompany him to instruct his staff in the operational details of administering the Gerson diet. It so happened that such a nurse was indeed available. A well-known Swedish actress had come to the county hospital in Kassel with lung tuberculosis. Her progress was excellent, and within three months she was able to return to Sweden. She had left her private nurse, Birgid, in Kassel to learn everything she could of the food and juice preparation. Intelligent and industrious, she volunteered to go with the doctor to the Harz, and Dr. Gerson recommended her with enthusiasm. Birgid had been in the Harz clinic for only three weeks when she overheard the doctor who had brought her there instruct his head nurse, "See to it that within six weeks the patients refuse to eat their meals." Angry and discouraged, she quickly returned to Kassel and reported her experience to Gerson. It wasn't the first or the last time that Max Gerson's work was sabotaged

The German state of Prussia's Secretary of Health, Dr. Hirtsiefer, a former patient of Gerson, recognized his contributions by appointing him a consultant to the Ministry of Health. Although the appointment added further to Dr. Gerson's prestige, it also increased his workload, since he now had to attend periodic meetings of the board of directors and review various reports and proposals regarding public health issues. In his capacity as a consultant, Gerson proposed and supervised a novel experiment stemming from his lifelong interest in the health of the topsoil. He described the experiment much later in his book, A *Cancer Therapy* (published in 1958):

> While I was a consultant to the Prussian Ministry of Health in Germany during 1930–33, I had occasion to advise Dr. Hirtsiefer, State Secretary of Health, about the deplorable condition of the soil around certain large cities, especially Essen, Dortmund and Dusseldorf. I suggested the use of human manure, mostly wasted by canalization in place of chemical fertilizers. This was carried out along with the planting of vegetable gardens around these big cities. Composts, i.e., a mixture of dried manure from humans and animals plus straw and leaves, were used to cover these gardens in October and November and were allowed to remain through the winter. The soil was then ploughed in the spring; planting was done from four to six weeks later. Depending upon the original condition of the soil, it took several years or more to develop a fertile topsoil by this method. According to Dr. Hirtsiefer, the results were highly satisfactory, in that vegetables were obtained which were greatly superior in both quantity and quality to those previously obtained by the use of commercial chemical fertilizers. It is interesting that no human disease was transmitted by this type of fertilizing, due, most probably, first to the compost being exposed to sun, air, freezing and snow throughout the winter, and second to the fact that most pathogenic bacteria will not survive long in a healthy soil which normally contains much antibiotic material.
>
> This is the method of the natural cycle used for over a thousand years by the

farmers of the ancient Teutonic or Allemanic Empire, now known as Western Europe. ("Significance of the Soil to Human Disease," A *Cancer Therapy* p. 183)

The 16-year-old nephew of the chairman of the Berlin Doctors' Association, Professor Hoffmann, came to Kassel with his mother. The boy was suffering from lung tuberculosis; as usual, conventional treatments had been unsuccessful in reversing the course of his illness. Hoffmann was naturally intensely interested in the case, and he telephoned the boy's mother twice a week for progress reports — probably expecting the worst. But to his utter amazement, he kept receiving news that the boy was steadily improving. The patient's fever and expectoration had diminished, and his appetite was returning to that of a normal teenager. His slender frame had even regained some weight. Dr. Hoffmann was so astonished at the reports that he began regularly to discuss the boy's X-rays with Dr. Gerson over the telephone. Finally, Hoffmann could stand it no longer. Doctors then, as now, did not have many opportunities to see the healing of a disease considered incurable. He had to witness for himself what was going on in the hills of Northern Hesse. Hoffmann arrived in Kassel, his attitude one of curiosity and skepticism in equal measures.

Dr. Gerson greeted his eminent visitor much as he would any visiting physician with an open mind. The first order of business was a tour of the sanatorium, to meet the patients. The introduction continued with a presentation of the case histories and X-rays of the patients Hoffmann had just met. The Berlin doctor studied the plates and records with great incredulity, eventually asking Dr. Gerson if he could study the materials, alone and undisturbed. Dr. Gerson happily obliged, putting the records and the X-ray room at his disposal. Two hours later, Hoffmann emerged from the room, visibly shaken over the awesome results. "I have never seen anything like this, Dr. Gerson," he said, his voice quiet. "Are these cases typical of your patients here?"

"Yes, they are," he answered. "The cases that you have examined are neither much better nor much worse than the usual patients who check into the sanatorium."

"I can't believe it. The results you are getting are unheard of! I would very much like to bring copies of the materials you showed me to Berlin, where I can have my assistants study and evaluate them. I will be happy to pay for copying the records and X-rays, if you would allow me."

"Certainly, Professor Hoffmann. It would be an honor. I will arrange for the records administrator to copy the materials for you."

Hoffmann returned to Berlin, still having difficulty believing what he had seen. He could not possibly relay his findings to the Doctors' Association without some corroboration. He would need several unbiased evaluations. When he got back to Berlin, Hoffmann gave each of his three assistants the X-rays independently, and asked them for individually written reports containing specific descriptions on what they saw. One by one, the reports were given to him; they all contained similar comments. The assistants had never seen such pre- and post-treatment X-rays and were at a loss to describe the unique healing phenomena that clearly had taken place.

Nazism Arrives in Kassel

By the beginning of 1932, the Nazi movement had gained enough followers to become truly threatening to anyone not of their political and Aryan race-championing persuasion. People started to be more vocal with their anti-Semitic attitudes, as young Charlotte recalls:

> In Kassel, when I was about eight years old, there was a girl in my class with rather long blond hair. Her name was Hadwiga. She lived very close, just across the empty field from our house on Werraweg, and across the Wilhelmshöher Allee, in a private house. We often played together — and, for a reason I can't remember now, usually at her house, not mine. Her father was an artist. He was handicapped, with a hunched back. I remember him as a very dark, angry figure. One day, just out of the blue, he demanded that I leave. He set down the law: Hadwiga was not to play with me any more . . . because I was Jewish.

Hitler's hatred of Jews, vehemently detailed in *Mein Kampf*, was striking a sympathetic chord with disgruntled fellow Germans who needed to blame others for their own economic hardships as well as their nation's defeat in the Great War. "We are the result of the distress for which the others are responsible," Hitler told a Munich gathering in 1933. Furthermore, since German culture historically tended to respect and even venerate the military class, Hitler's National Socialist Party had shrewdly created the *Sturmabteilungen* — Storm Troopers or SA. This forceful independent militia, made up of ardent young and energetically chauvinistic hardliners, revered their chosen *Führer* (leader). Hitler's 1932 "Boxheimer Document," published in a small provincial newspaper near Kassel, laid out his plans in detail. He advocated banishing Jews from all government and academic positions, and appropriating all their property and wealth; and announced the doctrine of *Anschluss*, projecting the annexation of Czechoslovakia and other weak nations, then conquest of Poland, France, England — and finally Russia. With this accomplished, Hitler would march triumphantly to India as a modern-day Alexander the Great. This document was not printed in other newspapers, as the pan-Germans did not yet feel strong enough to declare their true intentions to the world.

Few Germans who were not Jewish, whether they were indifferent, unprincipled or fearful, protested when Hitler called Jews filthy and corrupt parasites. Newspapers and public speakers began to parrot the Nazi contentions: an international Jewish conspiracy was the cause of Germany's defeat at the hands of the

Allies; Jews, the chief source of socioeconomic and political instability in Germany and elsewhere in the world, were promoting international communism so that they could eventually control all wealth and power everywhere. Anti-Semitism spread to other nations, including the United States.

Kassel, a right-wing army town, jumped on the Nazi bandwagon early as Hitler's party aimed to take over the government. Even in the sanatorium, the mood had now turned ugly. It did not help that the owner of the sanatorium made his dislike of Jews obvious; this encouraged some employees to show disrespect for Dr. Gerson, who, after all, was a Jewish doctor. The cook, one of the worst of the group of anti-Semites, was heard to remark to a fellow kitchen worker, "Now we'll really put some salt into the Jew's food." Even with sanatorium workers who were not anti-Semitic, their friends, their families and neighbors put pressure on them to transgress Gerson's precise dietary and other rules.

Within the Gerson household itself there was little discussion between parents and the children about the growing public hatred against Jews. Possibly Max did not even talk much with Gretchen about it either, since he still considered anti-Semitism just a constant but bearable annoyance, like a low-grade headache that had to be endured while doing one's important work in the world. But as Charlotte Gerson recalls, anti-Semitism was rife in Kassel:

> Every so often a delivery boy would bring merchandise to the convenience store downstairs. And whenever he bicycled away, he would make it a point to loudly whistle the "Horst Wessel Lied," Hitler's theme song. One of the lines in the song went, ". . . und wenn das Judenblut vom Messer fliesst, dann geht's nochmal so gut!" [and when the Jews' blood drips from the knife, things go twice as well!].
>
> Of course Kassel, being a military town, was generally "Nazi"-inclined earlier than the rest of Germany. The above incident took place in April of 1931, well before we moved away — before Hitler's total rise to power.

With a strong military tradition and a burgeoning weapons industry on the outskirts of town, Kassel was fertile ground for the Nazi party.

During these years, Dr. Wolfgang von Weisl resumed his relationship with Max Gerson. Weisl had initially brought Gerson's name to the fore several years earlier in the *Vossische Zeitung*, after Ferdinand Sauerbruch had taken credit publicly for Gerson's dietary success against tuberculosis. Weisl had been a medical reporter in Vienna as well as Berlin, but later, as an ardent Zionist, he had moved to Palestine, to help with the establishment of a permanent Jewish homeland there. This fervent effort was scarcely popular with the local Arab population. There were constant clashes in the streets between armed or unarmed groups of Arabs and Jews. During one of the street brawls, Weisl was stabbed in the chest with a bayonet and suffered a punctured lung. Mrs. Gerson later remarked that the Arabs apparently thought he was Lawrence of Arabia. He was treated in a local clinic, but as soon as he had recovered sufficiently to travel, he came to Gerson's sanatorium in Kassel-Wilhelmshöhe. He responded well to treatment, and was soon in robust health.

Long a proponent of Gerson and his therapy, Weisl began working closely with Gerson, as they two co-authored several scientific articles. Later Weisl would encourage Gerson to write a book about his dietary therapy.

On to Berlin

At the beginning of February 1932, a timely letter arrived from Berlin from Professor Hoffmann with an offer for Dr. Gerson to move to Berlin and take over a tuberculosis ward. Hoffmann hoped to prove to the large medical community there, through a demonstration at a special meeting of the Berlin Doctors' Association, that the dietary method could cure even the most advanced cases of tuberculosis. This new opportunity was most welcome to Max Gerson, since he wished to leave the now-poisonous political atmosphere of Kassel. He traveled to Berlin to discuss plans with Professor Hoffmann and his associate, Professor Hermann Zondek, who was a tuberculosis specialist and director of the Urban Hospital at the University of Berlin. His brother, Dr. Bernhardt Zondek, achieved renown as the inventor of the first pregnancy test. It was agreed that Gerson would get a separate tuberculosis ward with its own special kitchen for preparing the juices and other foods essential to his therapeutic diet.

As soon as he arrived in Germany's capital city, Dr. Gerson set to work. The first thing to be done was setting up the proper clinical environment. He was given a 25-bed ward at the Urban Krankenhaus (City Hospital) with the essential kitchen attached. While Max organized his clinic, he also worked out a protocol with Drs. Hoffmann and Zondek for the tuberculosis demonstration they wanted. So much methodological doubt had been cast in the past by the therapeutic diet's adversaries that nothing could be left open to criticism. On many occasions, when Gerson had presented a cured case, other physicians would just sniff, "Well, we see cases clear up by themselves, too. That's not so unusual. A certain percentage of sick people experience 'spontaneous' cures. Your case was probably just one of them." The fact that Gerson's diet produced an extraordinary number of recoveries seemed irrelevant. For this demonstration the entire clinical trial would be set up impeccably. Patients could only be admitted to the Gerson tuberculosis ward if they brought a written statement from their previous physician — or better yet, more than one doctor — saying that the case was incurable, and that there was no treatment that could influence the downward course of the disease. Each patient was warned, in the strictest of terms, that any attempt to smuggle in foods or other forbidden substances, such as alcohol or tobacco, would result in immediate and irrevocable discharge from the unit. Dr. Gerson's gentle manner and kind approach covered a resolve of steel that did not often have to be tested.

Once the Urban ward was set up, Dr Gerson had to find a way to support himself. He refused compensation for his work at the hospital. His family was still in Kassel, so he had the further stress of having to live alone in apartment, doing without the comforts of the home that Gretchen normally provided him and the lively company of his three daughters. A friend in Berlin helped him to gain staff privileges at a clinic in Wannsee, suitable for patients with migraines, multiple sclerosis and other clinical non-infectious conditions. The owner, an elderly physician by the name of Dr. Croner, was in semi-retirement, so much of the clinic was available to Gerson's patients. Max also learned that 15 beds in a clinic in Neu-Babelsberg could be occupied by his tuberculosis patients. Making the daily rounds among these three geographically separated clinics was an additional strain, but he was healthy and energetic, so handled the task with no ill effects.

Max lived a bachelor's existence for six months while Gretchen took care of the thousand large and small details involved in moving a family from one city to another. Schools needed to be arranged for the girls, movers hired to transport furniture, the house in Kassel-Wilhelmshöhe sold and vacated. Gretchen's first order of business in Berlin was to find a suitable apartment. Berlin between the World Wars had great beauty and grace, yet its monumental architecture seemed almost secondary to the pastoral effect of its abundant and ubiquitous large, leafy trees. Berliners, the Gersons learned, were nearly obsessive in their love of trees, and during hot or dry spells would carry cans of water from their fourth or fifth floor apartments to bestow on their favorites.

Like many residents and visitors, Gretchen much admired the Kurfürstendamm, one of Berlin's most fashionable and beautiful streets. This lovely broad avenue started at the corner of the large Zoo Park and extended far westward, with its broad sidewalks passing upscale shops and cafes. It carried motor traffic in both directions, and along the forested median strip ran a streetcar line and horse path. The five rows of large trees gave the impression of living in a forest rather than the center of a cosmopolitan capital city in Europe. Gretchen managed to locate a very comfortable apartment on the "Ku'damm" only a few blocks from the Zoo Park, in a graceful old building with wide marble halls, spacious rooms and lovely views over the trees and sidewalks below. Before long, she had the apartment beautifully decorated with the many luxurious furnishings they had collected over Max's 20-year career as a doctor, which had provided some material rewards. Charlotte recalled the splendor of their new home:

> Just around the corner was the Moericke, a famous restaurant and meeting place of the "rich and famous." In our building a beautiful broad wooden

staircase led up to the apartments. The building had an elevator, which was a complicated and delicate mechanism that required a special key and the operation of gates. The managers were afraid of injury or damage to the machinery, so we children were discouraged from using it because they didn't trust us.

Our apartment was on the fifth floor. But since the count went from the street floor (*not* first floor, but "Parterre") to the first floor (really the second) and so on upwards, it was actually the sixth, so when we didn't have an adult with us to run the elevator we had quite a climb to get home. To get down fast, of course we often happily slid down the banister—as European kids even nowadays are apt to do, not overwhelmed by worries about injury and liability, which have become a byproduct of American litigiousness.

Our apartment had many rooms. Two rooms in the front, right beyond the entrance door, were set up as Max's consultation rooms, although they were rarely used by him to see patients at his home office. He had little time for that, because he was so busy traveling all over Berlin between the three clinics. He used it mostly as a study, where he could retreat from the usual family commotion. There he could concentrate on keeping up with research around the world by reading medical journals, or else review patient records.

Then came my parents' bedroom, the living room and the dining room—all holding gorgeous furnishings. Beyond it was a huge room that could be described as a "California room." It easily held our three full-sized beds, desks and night tables, as well as a large worktable and a bookcase; it even had a sewing-room area with a sewing machine. On the other side of the hallway was a large kitchen, with the cook's large room off it. Next came another bedroom where my grandmother stayed, and at the end of the hall were a full bathroom and a separate toilet stall. Near the attic was a huge laundry room, where Gretchen, along with the maid, did the *grosse Waesche* (big wash) every couple of weeks.

Our kitchen still had no refrigerator, and this meant almost daily shopping trips, since perishables could not keep for long. In those years domestic chores took a great deal more time than they do now, but that was considered just part of life and not particularly seen as an inconvenience. Housewives, as Gretchen was, just dealt with it. And it helped, of course, when one could afford to have servants, so that much of the household work primarily only needed to be directed and supervised.

Albert Schweitzer's Visit

No sooner had the Gerson family gotten settled in Berlin than Max received a note from Professor Albert Schweitzer. He was visiting the city, and would like to thank him in person for having cured his wife Hélène's pulmonary tuberculosis. He also wanted to meet Dr. Gerson, about whom he had heard so much from his wife. Dr. Schweitzer would soon be returning to Africa from one of his extensive lecture tours through Europe. He supported his hospital at Lambaréné in French Equatorial Africa on the proceeds of his organ recitals, lectures and publications. Schweitzer, an extraordinary man with doctorates in medicine, philosophy, theology and music, could write books or speak eloquently on an astounding array of topics. He was also an organ builder. Though possessing a remarkably superlative intellect, Schweitzer always maintained an aspect of simple humility that drew people of all walks of life to him.

Max naturally invited the Schweitzers to come to his new home. Gretchen found him to be "a strong, upright man, full of goodness and energy, who created a wonderful atmosphere around him." Aware of the slander that had plagued Gerson during his career, Schweitzer counseled him: "Gerson, you must develop an elephant hide, and let everything bounce off it." He related a recent experience of his in Frankfurt while attending at a medical lecture, where he had mentioned Gerson's work to some colleagues, and had been taken aback when Professors Holfelder and Vollard made highly derogatory and uncalled-for remarks about Gerson. Schweitzer, whose wife's life had been saved by that very work, stood up and left the room in protest.

Schweitzer's visit was very cordial. Thus began a friendship that would last for the rest of their lives and involve considerable correspondence. From time to time Schweitzer wrote to Gerson to discuss matters relating to diet and supplements, certain that Gerson would respond with ideas of his own. For instance, from Lambaréné came this:

> Herewith something that I think will interest you. You are using cod liver oil. But from what source are the valuable materials in the fish livers derived? From the algae! How do the algae get it? They are accumulated from the sea water, activated by the sun's radiation. On the basis of this understanding, one of my friends, a pharmacist, for many years now has conducted experiments in order to use algae as a replacement for cod liver oil. During the war, he was in the French Health Service. At that time, he was able to make good serial experiments on horses. Those who received algae recovered [from injuries] much faster than those who did not. He credits the good outcome of its activity not only to the organic iodine contained in the algae, but also to the trace minerals

contained in them. Thus, he prepared medications from algae, easy to take and equal to the best activity of cod liver oil, if not exceeding it. You may be interested in getting in contact with this intelligent man. To use algae in place of cod liver oil presents a great simplification. At Lambaréné we use doses of ground algae, which are much more effective than cod liver oil. This also can be applied to tropical ulcers. (June 12, 1936)

As Gerson replied regarding the therapeutic potential in algae:

Often, the presence of the important substances alone is not sufficient to obtain healing. The deposits of minerals in the liver also play a great role. So, it is important in order to prepare for the effectiveness to first remove the edema from the liver, as well as from the other vital organs, and to supply them with the correct minerals. This promotes the natural physiological activities which will start the healing. The fact that algae work better than simply vitamin D can also be explained by the fact that they are rich in potassium, like all plants. It is not needed to add algae to the Gerson dietary treatment, since the vegetable juices are already very rich in all the minerals.

Despite Gerson's reservations, Schweitzer's own apparently successful use of algae in Africa, following his French pharmacist friend's excellent experimental results, did indicate a future opening for the high therapeutic dietary value, in treating various conditions, of what nutritionists and supplement suppliers now commonly call blue-green algae—which are far more abundant and less costly to obtain than cod livers.

Clinical Trials

The demonstration ward was achieving results that were fully expected by Gerson, but astounding to his pleased colleagues. The collaboration with Professors Hoffmann and Zondek was proving highly satisfactory. To check on progress, both doctors visited the ward daily—just as Gerson did, of course. X-rays were taken of the patients on a monthly basis, and the plates showed that they were experiencing good progress. Professor Ferdinand Sauerbruch also took interest in this new project, but this time he stayed in the background, while being kept up-to-date on the status of the patients.

When the experiment had been in operation for about a year, the excellent results convinced the three doctors that the treatment was consistently helping pulmonary tuberculosis patients, and therefore should be shown to the medical world. Drs. Gerson, Hoffmann and Zondek arranged for a large demonstration in the spring of 1933 at the Berlin chapter of the German Medical Association. There, Max Gerson was to be acknowledged for more than a decade of research and perseverance in treating different forms of tuberculosis. Not only would the demonstration be a crown jewel for him, it would also be a springboard from which his unique dietary therapy could be launched throughout Germany and beyond to the entire world. But Max Gerson wasn't fully cognizant that another German and his regime were now positioned to impose their own system upon these same geographic entities and their inhabitants—not to heal, but to dominate and destroy.

~9~
The Exile Begins
(1933–1934)

Best Proof

At age 51, Max Gerson was about to reach the pinnacle of his medical career. The demonstration of the efficacy of his treatment for gravely ill pulmonary tuberculosis patients was scheduled for May 5, 1933. Drs. Gerson, Hoffmann and Zondek all agreed that the most important proof of results were the patients' X-rays. In previous demonstrations, Max had not foreseen the need to arm himself in advance by having objective, acknowledged authorities examine the "before-and-after" plates and attest to their validity. Now there must be no question whatsoever of fraud. In too many of Gerson's past demonstrations, physicians had questioned the authenticity of the roentgen plates shown to them. "These are from different patients," Gerson's detractors would say. "The plates have been retouched" was another common criticism—despite the fact that it is totally impossible to retouch lung X-rays, for the high-energy radiation penetrates so many different tissues that the slightest pinprick would be glaringly obvious to any trained observer.

The three doctors discussed extensively this problem of proof. Who was unquestionably the most respected authority, to be asked to examine the plates and virtually guarantee the authenticity of the X-rays of the healed patients? Four radiologists' names were proposed, including Professor Holfelder in Frankfurt am Main, often considered the top expert in Germany. But Holfelder's uninformed and highly derogatory remarks about Gerson reported by Dr. Schweitzer automatically eliminated him as an unbiased evaluator. Finally they decided to approach Professor Felix Fleischner at the University of Vienna, widely acknowledged as the most eminent radiologist in Europe. His word would stand unchallenged by all physicians.

Dr. Gerson wrote to his friend Dr. Wolfgang von Weisl, now living in Vienna, to ask him to approach Professor Fleischner with the request. Two weeks later, the response arrived: Fleischner had agreed to examine the X-rays and then authenticate them if they showed truly unusual results. Gerson had no fear on that score. He arranged to travel to Vienna on April 1, 1933, to take the X-ray plates to Professor Fleischner personally.

As Max Gerson took this last step to confirming the validity of his diet therapy, his only sorrow was that his beloved mother would not be there to share this occasion for honoring his work. Ulricke had died in the middle of February. Max and Gretchen were now pondering a remark she had made early in the year, not long before her death; at the time nobody in the family had taken it seriously.

The first month of 1933 had ended in political turmoil. On January 30, the elderly German president and hero of the Great War, Paul von Hindenburg, weary of constant feuds among the political parties and under heavy pressure from the National Socialists or Nazis, had named Adolf Hitler as the new Chancellor. The elevation of Hitler to the most powerful government position sent an immediate shock wave through the Jewish community.

"Does that mean that we will have to leave Germany?" Ulricke Gerson had asked her family when learning of Hitler's accession to power. Mercifully, she did not live to see the true magnitude of her fearful prediction.

Boycott Day

Normally Dr. Gerson traveled in second-class railway cars. European passenger carriages are generally divided into compartments, with each compartment containing two facing upholstered benches of varying size and degrees of comfort. First-class compartments were occupied by four people seated on deep plush cushions. In second-class, six people sat in somewhat less space and ease, while in third-class eight travelers were crammed together on utilitarian wooden seats. Max was not concerned with luxury, but he felt that occasion merited the expenditure for a second-class ticket, specifically a window seat because passengers in seats by the window were least likely to be disturbed each time someone entered or left the compartment. The evening before his scheduled departure, Gerson checked his things again for the last time. The X-rays to be authenticated were in his large briefcase, his small bag was packed with clothes for a four-day stay in Vienna. The train tickets were in order and safely stored next to the X-rays. All was ready for the next day's journey.

Then the telephone rang. Max was not accustomed to receiving telephone calls at night, since his long days usually started very early. It was Hermann Adler, an attorney married to Gretchen's cousin. Like most attorneys, he was attuned to the politics of the city, and since Berlin was the capital of Germany, he was also familiar with national politics. If he himself didn't yet know what was about to happen, his informants supplied the information ahead of time.

Hermann seemed agitated. "Max," he began, "I understand that you have some plans for tomorrow." He mentioned no specifics, neither the trip nor any reason for his call, as it was already widely assumed in Nazi-controlled Berlin that telephone conversations were being monitored.

"Yes, that's right," Gerson replied.

"Well, listen, Max. This is important. Do it tonight. Don't wait until tomorrow. Do you understand? *Tonight!*"

"But Hermann, what difference does it make, tonight or tomorrow morning? It's only a few hours difference."

"Max, I really can't explain. But you probably know why. I have never been more serious in my life. Trust me. *It is absolutely imperative that you carry out your plans tonight.* Do I make myself quite clear?"

After they broke the connection, Max conveyed Hermann's urgent but cryptic message to his wife. He and Gretchen looked at each other. Both well understood why Adler could not explain the purpose of his warning, out of concern for a telephone tap. Both knew Hermann Adler as a serious man, not given to panic or flights of fancy. There must be a very valid reason for him to sound such an alarm.

Gretchen rushed to get the train schedule from Max's study. There was only one more departure that night for Prague and Vienna. If Max hurried, he would just be able to make the train. They kissed each other quickly, and Gerson sped out the door. He paid a taxi driver a bonus to rush him to the *Hauptbahnhof* before the 10:30 p.m. departure time. Gerson managed to get to the platform a few minutes before the train pulled out of the station.

The train was already moving as Max searched for a seat. Of course, his normally reserved window seat was on the next day's train, and all the window seats in the second-class car were taken, so he took the only seat left in the last open compartment, the one immediately in front of the compartment's door.

This undesirable seat selection may have saved his life.

The Berlin-to-Vienna railway trip runs almost due south from Berlin, roughly parallel to and a few miles east of the Oder River. When the Oder bears sharply off to the east, the tracks continue southward to Dresden, more or less following the course of the Neisse River. The Czech frontier is just south of Dresden, about five and a half hours of train travel from Berlin. For the first two hours of the trip southward, Gerson pondered the strange and urgent telephone call from Adler, but could find no explanation. Then he fell into a light sleep.

The train glided to a halt at the border-crossing station, where many times Gerson had undergone routine passport control on his way to Prague or Vienna, or points beyond. Normally, this procedure was a simple formality. But the drowsy passengers could see that tonight something was drastically different. Though it was now four in the morning, the platform was swarming with uniformed Nazi storm troopers, and the trucks that had brought them were pulled up alongside the platform. Rifles and side arms were very much in evidence. Yet before the impact of this display of force could be made on the travelers, some of the troopers boarded the train and fanned out throughout the cars, one to a compartment.

The trooper assigned to Gerson's compartment brusquely opened the door. Since he was seated next to the door, Gerson was the first person the man saw. "You!" he said curtly. "Where are you going?"

"Vienna."

"Purpose of your trip?"

"I am a physician and am taking some X-rays to Vienna for certification."

The trooper was immediately suspicious. "Show me the X-rays," he demanded.

Extracting the X-rays from his briefcase, Max held them up for the trooper to see. His demeanor was calm yet held the same positive quality he showed when talking with other practitioners or with patients themselves. "You see, in this X-ray here the patient's lungs have big holes in them caused by tuberculosis," he explained. "Yet look at this picture, taken only six months later, where only scars remain. There is no more tuberculosis! This cure is so unusual that other physicians continually accuse me of fraud. That is why I must see Dr. Fleischner in Vienna: he can certify that these X-rays in my briefcase are taken of the same lungs, in the same patients."

Gerson's enthusiasm, which fascinated children and adults alike, had mesmerized the trooper, distracting him from his assigned mission. Deciding finally that this man's X-ray plates were of no apparent interest to the Third Reich, the young trooper now turned his attention to the next man seated in the compartment.

"You! Are you a Jew?"

"Yes, I am."

"Get off the train."

"Why? I have done nothing. I must be in Vienna tomorrow."

"You heard me! Off the train — now!"

The frightened man rose trembling from his seat, and turned to get his luggage from the rack above his seat.

"You won't be needing luggage where you're going. Leave it!"

Before the storm trooper withdrew, two more people in the compartment — who could not very well have denied their ancestry because their passports, probably newly issued, identified them as Juden — were rooted out of their seats. Prior to that day, Jews rarely denied that they were Jewish, as they assumed they were relatively safe. After all, they were citizens of Germany — war veterans, successful business people, professionals of all kinds, who could not bring themselves to believe that in cultured, scientific-minded, modern Germany they could possibly be in mortal danger.

Max could see that all along the platform people had been dragged from other compartments. They stood there, imploring the soldiers to allow them to get their possessions. Their pleas fell on the deaf ears of the troopers, who replied instead with anti-Semitic abuse. It was apparent that *all* the Jewish passengers, and *only* Jews, had been pulled from the train. Except for Max Gerson. Max watched the spectacle in utter horror as the people on the platform became more agitated. Their voices grew louder as they indignantly demanded their belongings and asserted their rights as German citizens. Without warning, the troopers began using their rifle butts to beat the passengers, knocking many of them down. What was he to do? If he protested this abuse, he would still be unable to help the hapless people on the platform, but would place his own life in jeopardy as well. Inaction at such a time is humiliating to one's conscience. Max Gerson forever felt guilty about his escape from the fate that faced his fellow Jews on the platform.

As the train resumed its trip and rolled across the Czech border, Max closed his eyes and wept. He knew that he could not return to Germany. His immediate priority was to save his wife and three young daughters from the violence and hatred that was growing uncontrollably, like an ugly cancer, in the land of his birth. And, like most cancers, its pernicious growth probably could not be stopped.

Max now realized that he might never again have the opportunity to demonstrate to the medical world the value of his dietary treatment. Instead, within a hairsbreadth of achieving universal professional acceptance, he had barely escaped with his life. As the train hurtled toward Austria, Max realized that he had suddenly become an outcast, a refugee, from his homeland. When he was learning some Hebrew in childhood, he had found out that the word *Gershom* meant "a stranger there" — from this word the surnames Gerson and Gershon were derived. It now seemed fitting, for surely he, too, was becoming a stranger, destined to wander in countries far from his homeland.

Max Gerson arrived in Vienna with only a small suitcase and his briefcase with patients' X-rays and medical records. He soon found out that within his Nazi organization Hitler had secretly declared April 1, 1933, to be "Boycott Day." He had ordered his Brownshirts to go through commercial districts all over Germany with placards that urged loyal Germans to no longer patronize Jewish business establishments. Thus encouraged, Nazi thugs beat up any man they saw out in the streets who looked even vaguely Jewish. To soothe the world's censorious public opinion, Hitler later tried to pass off this attack as an April Fool's Day joke.

No longer was the visit to *Dozent* Fleischner the paramount item on Dr. Gerson's agenda. The first thing Max needed to do was to contact Gretchen by telephone and tell her to start arranging at once to leave Germany. The Austrian newspapers were full of the brutal events in Germany, so Max knew he need not explain the urgency of the situation to his wife. He devoutly hoped that she and their daughters had all escaped any direct harm, but he knew that at least they would have witnessed a frightfully ugly spectacle. Years later, Mrs. Gerson recalled what she had beheld on Boycott Day, when looking out upon the scene below their apartment windows:

There was tremendous activity with a great number of trucks carrying uniformed Nazis. Their hoods were crossed with the red swastika banners. With meticulous planning they stopped at every corner in the city. In the front near the driver sat an officer and a trumpet player. The latter blew three times on his horn and the whole wild chorus, drunk with victory, chanted, "Christians, defend yourselves. Don't buy from Jewish shops!" and similar shouts.

Other Nazis had great piles of posters over their arms, and they went through the city accompanied by boys proudly carrying a bucket with paste and brush. They stuck the posters with their aggressive slogans wherever they saw a shop sign or professional shingle with a Jewish name. The atmosphere was terrible. With evil beastly pleasure they beat up men of Jewish appearance in the streets, homes and subway stations.

When he finally got through to his wife over the busy telephone lines, Max learned that his family was safe. He told Gretchen that she must join him now in Austria. Then he gave her the names of some of his recovered patients who worked in the relevant government agencies, saying that surely they would help her to obtain the visas and travel documents necessary for her and the girls. Many decades later, the Gersons' third daughter, Charlotte, remembered that tense and fearsome time:

When Max unexpectedly left Germany after his frightening border crossing, he would call regularly. Guardedly — since at that time it was already assumed that phone conversations were tapped—he had given orders that we follow him to Austria, leaving in the greatest possible hurry.

This left poor Gretchen, who had three minor children in schools, not only to apply for and obtain the documents for emigration demanded by the government, but also to deal somehow with all the contents of the huge apartment: the furniture, clothing, linens; exquisite porcelains, crystals and silver; and of course the grand piano, a *Blüthner*. Also very important, per Max's order, was to pack up his large book and medical-journal collection. Most of our possessions would have to be left behind us in storage, because our parents knew that any permanency in our future residence had suddenly become so uncertain.

Gretchen spent a great deal of time shuttling from one government office to another, seeking out the personal contacts that Max had provided. Still, she sometimes had to deal with minor officials who were not favorably inclined towards a prosperous Jewish family that wanted to emigrate from Germany. Partly to bolster her own courage and partly to soften the hearts of the *Beamten* (government bureaucrats), Gretchen brought her youngest daughter along with her. Eleven-year-old Lotte — pretty and with a wide, blue-eyed innocence to her appearance — often enough elicited the compassionate interest of the officials.

It took Gretchen six weeks to collect the necessary exit documents and make all the arrangements for moving the family once again. They left Germany on May 12, 1933. Gretchen had arranged for a trusted friend to pack up the whole apartment, except for a few articles of clothing they would take along with them. All possessions left behind were placed in a large shipping container, to await the Gersons' decision on their ultimate and hopefully permanent future residence. The household goods would not rejoin the Gersons until they lived in Paris in 1935. All during that time Dr. Gerson's entire medical library was unavailable to him.

Whether or not Drs. Hoffmann and Zondek continued Dr Gerson's work at the Berling clinic is not known. Charlotte Gerson does not know whether her father had any correspondence or further clinical research connections with them. They worked now in Nazi Germany, and communication by letter, telephone or telegram with refugee Jews was neither encouraged nor safe. Probably it would not be considered safe, either, to practice and promote a therapy closely connected with a Jewish fugitive.

Interlude in Palestine

Fortunately, Dr. Wolfgang von Weisl, who had already collaborated with Gerson on several published articles, took Max under his wing as soon as he arrived in Vienna. He invited him to stay in his home and assured him that his family could join him there when they got to the city. He also began introducing Max to various Viennese physicians. Gerson wanted to determine whether he might conduct his special tuberculosis therapy there, under another doctor's auspices, since his medical license would not be valid outside of Germany. And Dr. Gerson kept the appointment with Professor Fleischner. He showed him the X-rays that he had brought to be authenticated for the Berlin meeting, even though it was certain that the presentation would never take place. Fleischner, duly impressed with Gerson's results, promised to support any arrangement he might make for providing treatment in Vienna.

After Gretchen arrived safely in Vienna with the girls, a large issue remained to be settled. During his six weeks in Vienna, Max had gathered enough information from the newspapers and friends to believe that Austria would eventually join Germany and come under Nazi domination. Both Max and Gretchen realized that Austria could provide only a temporary solution to their living situation. So what should they do now about the many elegant household furnishings and goods that Gretchen had in left Berlin, in the care of the friend who had helped pack them up for storage? As an ardent Zionist, Weisl held firmly to the opinion that the only safe place for Jews in the long run was Palestine. He convinced his friend that he would eventually end up there, so Max directed that the large container with all their household goods be sent to Hamburg and then loaded on a ship bound for Palestine.

Before Gretchen's arrival with the girls, Weisl had made a significant effort to help Gerson recover from his depression and the shock of the events of Boycott Day. He convinced Max to begin writing an authoritative book on his treatment regimen, offering to collaborate with him on the manuscript as well as work on several papers. This productive distraction from constant worry seemed to help raise Max's spirits. Several months later, with his wife and daughters now settled in Vienna and the tuberculosis book well under way, Gerson decided to travel to Palestine. He traveled by train to Trieste, where he received the required vaccinations. Though these made him temporarily very sick, he boarded the ship to Haifa. Several members of his family were already settled in Palestine, including his Aunt Betty Abraham, on his mother's side of the family. His aunt, a lovely lady who lived in Tel Aviv, welcomed Max warmly. Several members of her family lived close by, and her apartment had become a social hub. Every afternoon she gave a *Kaffee Klatsch* (coffee party) for relatives as well as friends and neighbors. She baked continuously, producing a variety of cakes, pies and cookies to serve to her guests. Max enjoyed tremendously these afternoon get-togethers with members of his mother's family, even though he normally avoided drinking coffee and eating desserts that were sugary and rich with butterfat, as German pastries tended to be.

Gerson's relatives graciously took him to visit some Jewish settlements. Wherever he went, he looked carefully around him and made many inquiries. Despite his idealistic nature, Max had to become a realist now. He learned that many German-Jewish doctors had already emigrated to Palestine, so there were far too many physicians for him to be able to build up a practice successful enough to support his family. Many of these emigré doctors had in fact become chicken farmers, just to make ends meet. Max at length decided — to his deep disappointment and that of his maternal relatives — that Palestine simply was not the place for him to settle permanently. Instead he would return to Vienna, to complete the book he was working on, with Weisl's encouragement and assistance, and to seek some way of resuming his medical and research work.

Aunt Betty came to the ship to see Max off on the boat heading for Europe. As he stood on the deck, he was filled with lovely memories of the times spent with his family in this ancient land that had once belonged to distant ancestors — and might someday belong to their descendants. Then he cupped his hands around his mouth and shouted down to his aunt waving from the dock below, "Don't drink so much coffee!"

Max Gerson's best immediate prospects for practicing medicine still lay in Vienna, where at least he had a foothold. But the problem remained of obtaining a medical license, since his German one was not valid in Austria — or anywhere else, for that matter. Dr. Gerson's professional reputation internationally and Weisl's connections in Vienna helped Max establish working relationships with some prominent physicians, so that he could at least work as a consultant on cases. Under this arrangement, Dr. Gerson was called in to treat some relatives of Austrian Chancellor Engelbert Dollfuss, who was so pleased with the results that he personally intervened directly with the medical board to obtain a license for Max. In the autumn of 1933, Dr. Gerson became the first refugee physician to be granted an Austrian medical license.

Invitations to lecture abroad continued to arrive, and Gerson accepted many of them. He made it clear that he did not intend ever to return to Germany, even to lecture. However, since Max's passport was German, and Germany was making ever more belligerent noises, many European border police had become jittery about allowing German nationals to cross their borders, including those who declared themselves to be refugees. Chancellor Dollfuss himself assured Gerson that, if he ever encountered trouble when trying to return across the Austrian border, he should telegraph him directly for clearance. This invitation proved useful when Max was coming back home from a lecture in Bruenn, Czechoslovakia. An Austrian border guard refused him reentry to Austria and even threatened to arrest him. Max cleared up the situation by firmly requesting the captain of the guards to call or wire Chancellor Dollfuss immediately and obtain his authorization for reentering the country where he now lived. The astonished officer quickly changed his mind about detaining or arresting Dr Gerson.

The Westend Sanatorium

Max Gerson began to immerse himself again in the medical treatment and research he so enjoyed. He had arranged to use the facilities at the Westend Sanatorium in Purkersdorf bei Wien for the new patients that he was acquiring, but he also saw patients in their own homes. The sanatorium was easy to reach from Vienna by the *Westbahn* rail line. The train continued on to Purkersdorf, from which it was easy for people to get to a popular Viennese ski area. Since Westend was the medical facility closest to the ski area, many ski-related injuries ended up in its emergency room. The constant stream of serious injuries he witnessed caused Gerson to forbid his children from participating in the sport, though as a young man he had been an avid skier in the Carpathian Mountains near Breslau.

The Gerson family conveniently was provided with a house on the grounds of the sanatorium. Much later, Charlotte Gerson recalled that period in their life together there:

The sanatorium was a huge complex of extensive villa-style buildings in a park-like setting. I remember with great pleasure the huge chestnut trees that lined the road into the park. But our living quarters, in one of the villas, were now very modest compared with those in the past. We had two bedrooms — one for the parents, one for the three girls — and a small workroom with desks and a table.

We ate the sanatorium food in the common dining room in the main building, and also had access to the social rooms there. In one room stood a billiard table, on which I played many games with a boy somewhat older than I, whose parents were co-owners of the sanatorium. (He later became renowned as an evolutionary biologist, and for some years Dr. Emile Zuckerkandl was the president and director of the Linus Pauling Institute of Science and Medicine in Palo Alto, Calif.)

I often looked out the window at the spacious grounds beyond the villas and below the steep, heavily wooded hill, and especially enjoyed seeing the deer come down close to our house in the wintertime, when they could not easily find food. But because of the economic depression and the need for money, the owners of the sanatorium complex sold some of the wooded area for lumber. So we were then treated to the sad spectacle of seeing the beautiful trees being felled and the lower part of the hill being denuded.

In the midst of his busy new life, Dr. Gerson had managed to finish the ambitious *Diättherapy der Lungentuberkulose* (Dietetic Therapy for Lung Tuberculosis), with some assistance from Dr. Weisl—a facile medical writer as well as newspaper columnist, who was already the author of several published volumes. Despite his close professional association with Max Gerson for several years, Wolfgang von Weisl never became a good friend, since Max felt he essentially had a cold demeanor and tough character. Later, in fact, he parted company with Weisl, who for his own gain chose to bend the terms of an agreement between them to the breaking point.

Gerson's book introduced many patient cases and discussed much of the accumulated experience that he had planned to present to the Berlin meeting. Published by Franz Deuticke of Leipzig and Vienna in 1934, the title page contains not only Max Gerson's name but also acknowledges "the X-ray findings and a chapter about X-rays by Dr. Felix Fleischner."

As soon as Gerson's book was in print, he sent a copy to his friend Albert Schweitzer at his clinic in Africa, pointing out that Hélène Schweitzer's recovery was included in the book as case study number 45. Dr. Schweitzer was so impressed with Gerson's book that he made it required reading for any physician who ended up working with him at Lambaréné. Among various praises he wrote about it over the years was this one:

I read each day in your *Diättherapie*. I have picked up the book again and am enjoying it bit by bit, like a bee sips nectar from a bloom. I find your presentation excellent. Your statement of the whole problem is also wonderful. I have ordered a copy of the book just to lend it to an Alsatian doctor.

Several of Dr. Gerson's cases in Austria were quite noteworthy — some for their influence on his later cancer work, some for their unusual nature. A woman from the south of France came to Dr. Gerson's clinic at the sanatorium with her four-year-old grandson, Pierre, since both were suffering from lung tuberculosis. The two stayed at the sanatorium for about a month, then returned home to continue the treatment, which had worked well for them.

About a year later, when the boy was ready to begin school, he was given a required routine physical examination by the school doctor. Aware of Pierre's history of pulmonary tuberculosis, the physician did the usual test for the bacillus to see if the disease was still active. Normally, when patients have been ill with tuberculosis, their tuberculin skin test will always register slightly positive, as the tubercle bacilli are never fully removed from the body. The only time that people's tuberculosis tests are completely negative is when their immune systems have been completely overwhelmed and the tubercle bacilli are attacking the vital organs. With a tuberculosis sufferer, this phenomenon only occurs in the last few hours of life. The school physician therefore was very surprised to detect a negative reaction to the boy's skin test. Since his experience and education indicated that the child was in the end stage of this terrible disease, he immediately sent the boy home and informed the family that he would be dead in less than 24 hours.

The family had been told that the Gerson therapy had cured the child. The father immediately called Gerson in Vienna. "Dr. Gerson, we are in shock! We have just been informed that Pierre has less than a day to live. How can that be? You sent him home and said he was making good progress."

"Calm down, please, Monsieur LeBlanc. Let me just ask you a few simple questions."

"Certainly, Dr. Gerson. We are just extremely upset. Everything seemed to be going so well with Pierre until now. Is there any hope at all?"

"Of course there is. How is the boy now? Is he active?"

"Yes, he appears fine. That is what is so puzzling. He has rosy cheeks and a good appetite, just as he should."

"How about sputum? Does he have any?"

"No. What are you getting at, Doctor?"

"In a moment. How about his energy? Is Pierre running about and playing normally?"

"Yes. He *seems* quite healthy. What can the problem be?"

"Sir, your child is healthier than even I could have imagined. What has happened is that his immune system has taken care of the tuberculosis so thoroughly that it has completely eliminated all bacilli from his system. This is unheard of in normal methods of treating the disease. But that is why you sent him and your wife to Vienna in the first place, isn't it? You wanted something better."

Indeed, young Pierre was quite healthy, and of course did not fulfill the school doctor's dire prediction of an imminent death.

Another time, Dr. Gerson was called to treat a Mrs. Lederer for tuberculosis as an outpatient. Arriving at the residence, he felt overwhelmed by its opulence. The stately villa stood in the midst of a vast, manicured park. When the butler ushered Dr. Gerson into the entryway, the doctor was impressed with the white and pink Greek marble floors, the graceful staircases and the fine art that hung on the walls. It looked like a magnificent museum. A thoroughbred greyhound with a silver gray coat was at Mrs. Lederer's side — as it often would be during Max's regular checkup sessions with its owner. Dr. Gerson became very familiar with the high-strung, stunning greyhound, and developed a deep affection for the animal. Upon arriving, he always expected to see Prinz bounding around the fenced area in front of the villa, sometimes even trying to jump the high fence of his enclosure so as to greet him with proper enthusiasm.

One day, Dr. Gerson didn't see his dog friend as he approached the house. He was surprised this time to be met with an empty pen and no barking. "Where is Prinz today, Frau Lederer?" he asked his patient. "I missed his greeting."

"Oh, Dr. Gerson," she began, her eyes beginning to glisten with tears. "He was in his pen last week when the postman came. He actually jumped over the fence this time, but broke his forepaw when he landed on the other side. We had the veterinarian out to examine the dog, but he told us that the leg will never heal, so we will need to have him destroyed. Of course, we are devastated. Prinz is a part of our family."

Gerson, who also loved this graceful and elegant dog, thought for a moment. "Perhaps we can save him," he said. "Since the veterinarian says he can't do anything, what is there to lose?"

"Oh, Doctor, if there is anything at all that we can do to help him, please tell me."

"I suggest that we put a splint on the leg, and keep Prinz suspended in a sling, so that he cannot put any weight on the injured foot. But give him the same food and juices that you are taking. One small variation is in order: grind up raw liver with some carrots so that he gets used to the taste. And let us hope that he, too, will heal from my diet!"

The dog was duly put on almost the same dietary regimen as his mistress. At first, he balked at the strange food, but eventually aversion was overcome by hunger and thirst, and the dog became accustomed to the new diet. After three weeks, the dog's leg had totally healed, to the everlasting gratitude of the entire family. There was only one small aesthetic consequence: Prinz's beautiful silver-gray coat had acquired carrot-colored spots running right down the middle of his back.

On another occasion, the Lederers' young married daughter, who was pregnant, developed eclampsia and Cushing's syndrome. This notorious hypertensive condition in pregnancy threatened the baby's life, and possibly the mother's, too. Tests had shown that her blood had abnormally low levels of sodium. Her physicians attempted to rectify the deficiency by giving her high intravenous doses of sodium. Subsequent blood tests showed temporary improvement in the sodium level; but then the level would suddenly and inexplicably drop. Urinalysis, moreover, showed that the young woman was not eliminating the sodium in her urine. The cramping continued.

Mrs. Lederer, very worried about the survival of both her daughter and grandchild, finally told Dr. Gerson about what was happening — and asked for his help. He immediately discontinued the high sodium supplementation, and prescribed high doses of potassium instead. The other physicians were incredulous. The girl was suffering from an extreme deficiency in blood sodium, and now Gerson was prescribing high levels of its chemical opposite, potassium! They predicted disaster. The patient and her mother, however, had faith in Dr. Gerson and stuck with his approach.

Within a few days the young woman's blood sodium level rose to normal levels. Her urine tests showed that she was now eliminating great quantities of sodium. Soon the cramping stopped, and the pregnancy proceeded normally, to the immense gratitude of the Lederer family.

Patiently, Gerson had explained his reasoning to his shocked Viennese colleagues. The sodium that they had been giving their patient had not been eliminated, nor did it show up in the serum. It was being stored instead in the cells, where it caused even more water retention and higher blood pressure. An imbalance in body fluids due to a lack of potassium had caused the cell walls to become porous and let in sodium; it began being imported in great doses, along with water. That is why the sodium disappeared from the blood serum and why the edema was increasing dangerously. Sodium belongs in the serum, he explained, as it is properly an *extracellular* mineral, whereas potassium belongs inside the cells as an *intracellular* mineral. Gerson's solution, therefore, had been to give the woman high doses of potassium — the deficient mineral that the cells urgently required, to restore the intracellular fluid to its correct mineral balance. Thus supplied, cells no longer sequestered sodium and H_2O, and instead pushed them both back into the bloodstream, where were eliminated in the urine.

This case underscored Dr. Gerson's growing interest in the electrochemical factor in physiology. Based on current research studies he was reading as well as on his own observations of patients' recoveries over the years, he knew that it was crucial to determine the sodium (Na), or negative ion, and potassium (K), or positive ion, levels in the body, measuring their presence and ratios in different fluids, organs and systems. Because in those days there was no effective way to test cell chemistry, only blood chemistry, this patient's high intracellular sodium level had gone unnoticed. This ratio or balance issue would be increasingly perceived by Dr. Gerson to be a crucial factor in maintaining or regaining health, but not until he practiced in New York, a decade later, did he add potassium supplements to his regular dietary regimen. Instead, his diet featured foods that were rich sources of natural potassium and other potassium-group elements, along with eliminating or restricting intake from sodium-group sources.

During his exile in Austria Dr. Gerson resumed his interest in treating cancer, since he had been encouraged by his success with those first three patients in Bielefeld, but he had less ability now to control the outcome. As he recalled much later, "There in Vienna I tried six cases and in all six cases, no results — all failures. That was shocking. The sanatorium where I treated my patients was not so well organized for dietary treatments. They treated other diseases by other methods and didn't pay much attention to diet. So, I attributed the failures to that" (from the lecture given at the Jensen Health Ranch, 1956). Despite this discouragement, he hoped that in the future he could again use his dietary therapy on cancer patients — with far better success than in Vienna.

Moe Erstein, a wealthy American who had been living in Paris since the 1929 stock market crash, came to visit Dr. Gerson in Vienna because he was suffering from severe rheumatoid arthritis. He had been hearing about the Gerson therapy for years, but he had refused to visit him in Germany. He wanted nothing to do with Germans; he thought they were all cheats. But his arthritis kept getting worse, despite the best efforts of a legion of physicians. Erstein had even gone as far as Egypt to seek relief from a highly regarded doctor there. Now that Dr. Gerson was no longer in Germany, he decided to undergo his stringent dietary therapy on the chance that it might alleviate his pain and disabilities.

Erstein brought an entourage with him: his wife and daughter as well as a servant. His arthritis had become so severe he could hardly move, dress himself or eat without help. Along with the food requirements and restrictions Dr Gerson prescribed, Erstein's joints had to be massaged twice a day—as in the earlier case of Lilli Steinhaus in Gütersloh. The massage sessions were excruciatingly painful for the patient. They were exhausting for Dr. Gerson as well. Seeing this, Erstein wanted Gerson to train a professional masseur to provide these daily massages, but Gerson turned him down. Massaging the swollen joints is not the same as massaging muscle tissue, he explained. Arthritic bones and joints are very fragile from decalcification, and twice before he had seen professional massage therapists break bones while massaging them. At first, the treatment made little progress. But both patient and physician persisted, and with the daily massage and healing diet, the swollen and immobilized joints slowly began to recover mobility. Erstein stayed at the Westend Sanatorium for six months; when he returned to Paris, he was restored to health.

Shortly after Moe Erstein returned home, he recommended Dr. Gerson to former French Premier Paul Painlevé, who suffered from severe kidney disease. Max was summoned to Paris. This journey was not easily undertaken before commercial air travel, since the train trip, including passport formalities at the various borders, lasted 24 hours in each direction. To get there, Max understandably chose to travel through Switzerland, not Germany. The official policy surrounding an ex-Premier required that all Painlevé's doctors be present for each examination, and that any treatment prescribed by Gerson had to be submitted in writing, then signed by the attending physician.

Painlevé was suffering badly. His abdomen was swollen and filled with fluid that had to be tapped every 10 days. Depressed and in great pain, he could neither walk nor lie down, and had great difficulty in breathing. He had poor appetite and was not sleeping well. Dr. Gerson examined Painlevé thoroughly, then discussed the course of treatment with him and with the other physicians present. He gained the patient's total confidence. The chef was called in and given detailed instructions regarding the diet to be followed—in writing, naturally. As in the case of the pregnant young Viennese woman, this illustrious patient had serious edema, which in his circumstance was caused by cardiorenal dysfunction related to heart failure and overmedication. That, among other things, was affecting his kidneys' ability to regulate blood pressure and maintain his electrolytes in the optimal Na/K ratio.

The next day, Dr. Gerson urgently requested his colleagues on the case *not* to tap the fluid in Painlevé's belly again. With the treatment he prescribed, he assured them, the fluid would gradually disappear on its own. Moreover, under *no* circumstances were they to give the patient any pain-numbing drugs. Because of prior adverse experiences in patients of his who were given potent analgesics, Gerson had concluded that anyone suffering from a degenerative disease and undertaking his detoxifying, nutritionally intense therapy should never be given pain killers, sedatives and other drugs, since they were apt to stress an already overtaxed liver and immune system.

Dr. Gerson then left for Vienna, promising to return in 10 days to check on the patient's progress. On his return Paris, Dr. Gerson saw enormous improvement in Painlevé. The fluid was largely gone from his abdomen, and he was able to lie down and sleep well again. Very pleased with the patient's current prognosis, Dr. Gerson made some minor adjustments in the treatment, and arranged for a return visit in three more weeks. When he next came to Paris, the patient was feeling so well that he had already resumed his normal activities, but his French physicians had spread the rumor that Dr. Gerson had given the cook a secret remedy to slip into the patient's food.

Several weeks after Dr. Gerson's last visit to Paris, there was a general election in France in which Jean Painlevé, the patient's nephew, was actively involved. In support of his nephew, the popular former Premier had taken part in some of the campaign controversies. His health, though not as tenuous as when Gerson had first seen him, was not yet ready for the strain he placed on it. One day, to help him overcome his constant feelings of illness, Painlevé's physicians gave him a shot of morphine. The next morning, Dr. Gerson received a telephone call from Paris: Painlevé had fallen into a coma. Before he could leave Vienna, Dr Gerson received the sad news that Painlevé had died without ever having regained consciousness. In his mind, he knew that Painlevé's death was caused by the morphine, which was administered against his absolute prohibition against any drug use. Along with other interesting information about the application of the Gerson diet to various cardiovascular diseases, Dr Gerson discussed this case in a paper he published with Dr. Wolfgang von Weisl in April 1935 in the Munich Weekly Medical Journal: "Flüussigkeitsreiche Kalidiät als Therapie bei cardiorenaler Insuffizienz" (High Fluid Content Potassium-Diet as Therapy for Cardiorenal Insufficiency).

Lainzer Hospital

Professor Noorden, Director of the Lainzer Hospital in Vienna, a large facility with several hundred beds, offered to put at Dr. Gerson's disposal 10 beds at the hospital and a nurse to care for patients. Gerson took him up on the offer. Noorden wanted to see some of Gerson's original patient files, so Gerson brought along several of his best prior cases to show to him, including that of the Swedish actress who had come to the Kassel sanatorium. When Gerson was finished explaining them, he was asked to leave the records "for a few days" for further study by the hospital staff. When Gerson requested the return of the files, he was given some delaying excuse. Several more requests were deflected. Finally, after a week of witnessing her husband's frustration, Gretchen herself went to the offices to demand the return of the records. Though usually a gentle and unassuming woman, she had enough Germanic steel in her makeup to convince almost anyone not to trifle with her. The files were quickly collected, but when she checked them, the file on the Swedish actress wsa missing. Nobody would accept responsibility for having removed it.

The arrangement at Lainzer Hospital soon proved to be unsuitable for Dr. Gerson. Due to its distance from the Westend sanatorium, it took several hours for him to make his rounds there. Since he visited the patients almost every day, it became a terrible strain — besides which the patients there were not improving at all. Once again, he sent Gretchen to ferret out the reason, since by now his own face was well known in the hospital corridors. When she visited the kitchen, she discovered that. all the food for the hospital was being prepared in large vats. Then, before salt, fat or spices were added, the kitchen staff would ladle some of the food into smaller pots for Gerson's tuberculosis patients. This resulted in totally unappetizing and barely edible food. Tuberculosis patients usually have poor appetites to begin with. The hospital staff was obviously not committed to helping his patients, a problem he had faced twice before — with Dr. Mayer in Saranac Lake, and again in the Harz clinic in Germany, which the Swedish actress's nurse had tried to help set up. He withdrew from the ward.

Lotte Contracts Tuberculosis

In 1934 Charlotte began complaining about a pain in her right knee. At first, Max assumed it was growing pains, but became concerned when the pains persisted. If both knees had been affected, he would not have been worried, but it was only on the right side.

Max took his daughter to Professor Fleischner, the eminent radiologist at the University of Vienna who had verified the X-rays of his patients and contributed a 24-page section to Diet Therapy of Lung Tuberculosis. They took X-rays of Lotte's right knee from several angles, then examined the film. Not seeing an abnormality in the structures or any other reason for the pain she was experiencing, they almost shrugged off the difficulty again as growing pains. But then Dr. Gerson noticed an almost invisible shadow on the image of the bone at the bottom margin of the film. Just to be on the safe side, Fleischner took another X-ray six inches farther down her shin. This time, the film confirmed their worst fears. There was a hole in the right tibia that measured 2.5 cm high and nearly 2 cm wide. Lotte had contracted bone tuberculosis. Before the availability of powerful antibiotics, bone tuberculosis could be a death sentence. Max immediately put his daughter on the strict dietary therapy.

Since her father was in daily contact with tuberculosis patients, it was possible that Charlotte had contracted the disease from bacilli carried by him. The stress over the move from Berlin to Vienna had disrupted the regular dietary regime of the family. Living in residence hotels and eating at restaurants and in the sanatorium's dining hall had taken its toll on the growing girl's immune system. Fortunately, by the time the diagnosis was made, the Gersons had moved into an apartment of their own, where they were able to prepare their own food. Lotte always fixed her own juices, using a hand-grinder and press — not an easy task for a 12-year-old. Since she had lived most of her life eating healthy foods, the treatment took effect rapidly, and she was soon well again.

Nazi Rule Draws Closer

Max and Gretchen Gerson were disturbed to watch Nazism making inroads in Austrian politics and the everyday life around them, but they were not really surprised. By the mid 1930s Nazi sympathizers were carving swastikas in the heels of their shoes. Then dipping them in red paint, they walked the streets of Vienna, stamping little red swastikas on the pavement. The atmosphere was starting to feel disturbingly like Germany before Boycott Day. Rumors persisted of an *Anschluss* — a lightning-strike invasion and immediate annexation of Austria by Nazi Germany. On July 25, 1934, Austrian Nazis tried to speed up the process of unification with Germany by invading the Austrian Chancellery. Taking Chancellor Dollfuss prisoner, they attempted to declare a National Socialist government. During the ensuing suppression of the abortive coup, the Nazi insurgents murdered Chancellor Dollfuss — Dr. Gerson's benefactor.

In early 1935, Max Gerson received a telephone call from an intermediary who said that a very important German personage, who was not named, wished to undergo his dietary treatment, and requested that Dr. Gerson travel to Passau immediately. Normally, Gerson would have responded with enthusiasm, but then he considered the location. Passau, at the confluence of the Inn and Danube rivers, straddles the border between Germany and Austria; in fact, only the Inn River separates Germany and Austria at Passau. Gretchen had heard from several sources within the German-Jewish refugee community in Vienna the Nazis were using various subterfuges to lure Jewish emigrés to areas near Germany, where they would be arrested and sent to German prison camps or otherwise permanently detained in Germany — if they had skills or knowledge perceived to be useful to the Nazi leadership. Next morning, another call was received: Dr. Gerson was urgently needed. This time, Max politely but firmly declined the invitation.

Max Gerson and his family sometimes speculated about the identity of this eminent would-be patient, figuring that if was not just a trick to take the doctor captive, it may even have been Adolf Hitler himself who wished to confer with him, since the Führer was known for his ardent health-diet interests and ate largely vegetarian fare. Later on, Hitler ordered that organic farms be established in various concentration camps. There natural foods were grown without the use of chemical fertilizers and pesticides by the inmates — not intended for their own consumption, of course, but for the Nazi elite.

Even young Lotte was becoming aware that a more pervasive malaise was going on around her in Vienna. As she commented later about this period in her childhood: "In the general depression of the '30s, due to the economic hard times in Austria, a great deal of political agitation was started there by both the German and Austrian Nazis. During hard times, it is easy to 'sell' the idea that it is time for 'a change.' My father was becoming quite sure that it would not be safe for him and his family to continue to live in Austria in the future." Knowing that their haven in Austria was definitely imperiled, the Gersons worried over where the next round of events would take them.

~10~
On the Move Again
(1935–1936)

Settling in Paris

In the spring of 1935, Moe Erstein returned to Vienna for a visit, bringing with him a young Frenchman, Dr. Gutmann. Erstein soon made his mission clear: he was eager to convince Dr. Gerson to move to Paris, since he wanted Gerson nearby as his physician and did not want to give up his Parisian residence. Erstein had an incentive to offer as well. Horace Finali, another grateful Gerson patient who was now president of the Banque de Paris, had purchased a lovely hotel near Paris, and he wanted Dr. Gerson to put it to use as a clinic. Each room had its own bath, and there was a fine kitchen, plus plenty of space for relaxation and recreation. The plan was to have Dr. Gutmann serve as medical director, since Gerson was not a citizen and could not officially practice medicine in France unless and until he obtained a medical license —which would take time, along with acquiring some knowledge of French.

With the political situation in Austria deteriorating rapidly, Max Gerson accepted the offer without delay. The nomadic Gersons pulled up stakes to move to another country, joining many other refugees from Hitler's Germany who found their way to France, where they formed émigré communities — as had been done earlier by White Russians and other dissenters from Communist Russia, as well as American expatriates who relished the bohemian lifestyle for which Paris was renowned.

The Hôtel du Parc in Ville D'Avray had belonged to a consortium of English investors that recently had gone bankrupt. The graceful, 35-room hotel was surrounded by tall trees, lawns and a beautiful garden, an appealing setting for Dr. Gerson and a pleasant atmosphere to promote healing for the patients under his care. Gretchen found a comfortable *pension de famille* near the sanatorium-clinic, and in May of 1935 the Gerson family settled into their new environment. Ville D'Avray is on the road from Sèvres to Versailles, about 10 miles west of Paris, so the city's culture and comforts were accessible but not intrusive. Max Gerson especially enjoyed the close access to the beautiful Bois de Boulogne, where he could indulge his love for the woods. Every Sunday afternoon, just as his own father had done, Max made it a practice to take his family for a long walk outdoors. The children particularly loved their frequent visits to the exquisite formal gardens of nearby Versailles. There they explored the palace grounds and visited Le Petit Trianon and other outbuildings.

As agreed, young Dr. Gutmann was the titular medical director, since Max lacked the requisite French medical license. Because of Gretchen's fluency in French, communication did not pose a great problem. Mr. Erstein had a large circle of friends in Paris, and his enthusiastic recommendation of Dr. Gerson as a physician soon filled the rooms at the sanatorium with both French and English patients. With his constant close supervision, the patients experienced good results, and the family enjoyed the overall atmosphere in this new location.

Cancer and Fats

In Paris, Dr. Gerson found himself asked to treat cancer patients. Three of his first Parisian cancer patients were treated at home: one of the three cancer patients did not respond, a second showed marked improvement, and a third presented a special problem. Dr. Gerson always found a home-based therapy course more difficult and unreliable for patients than treatment at a sanatorium because he had no way of telling whether the patient was properly following the therapy, but a problem even more difficult was having a patient with family members or friends who were medical practitioners. The third cancer patient in Paris was an Armenian woman in her late 50s who had breast cancer. Her brother and two friends were all physicians, and they insisted on being present at each consultation Dr. Gerson had with the woman. They second-guessed his directions, objecting to the food, despite the fact that the cook made all possible efforts to prepare appetizing and attractive dishes adhering to Gerson's diet. According to their experience, they did not believe that the Gerson diet was sufficient to sustain, much less heal her. When she lost weight (expected in the initial stages of the diet), they began to demand she be allowed to have butter, eggs and meat. Dr. Gerson struggled to keep these foods out of her diet because he suspected certain substances in them, particularly fats, were harmful to cancer patients. But he could not hold out forever against the three family physicians. After three weeks of arguments, Dr. Gerson gave in to the other doctors, and allowed her a half egg yolk twice a week. He noticed that the effect on the breast with the tumor was almost immediate: it got redder and looked more aggressive. He immediately excluded egg yolk from the woman's diet, and the tumor regressed again.

Several weeks later, the doctors began agitating to give the woman some raw, chopped meat. Once again, the tumor re-grew, and once again Dr. Gerson had to reverse course to avoid new damage. Then the doctors insisted that he give the woman oil, and when he did so, again the cancer showed signs of advancing. For the third time, Dr. Gerson had to pull the patient back from the family physicians' requests.

Quite passive throughout all these battles, the patient simply took what she was given; she did not complain either about what she *wasn't* being fed. In a few more months, the tumor had completely disappeared, and she recovered her health.

In this notable cancer case in Paris, which inadvertently became an experimental study, Gerson observed the adverse effect of adding fat to the diet of a patient too early during the recovery phase. He saw the malignant tumor respond quickly to the intake of fat, as if it needed fat to live. Time and time again, as Dr. Gerson searched over the years for some kind of fat that might be safe to give to a cancer patient, he would see the same phenomenon.

Prominent Patients

Among the patients recommended to Dr. Gerson by Moe Erstein were some with specific health problems that he felt confident of curing; others just appeared to need a 'rest cure' achieved by a stress-free stay at the elegant Hôtel du Parc while being served simple and nutritious foods and juices that gave their digestive tract a needed vegetarian respite from the usual rich gourmet fare heavy with meats and fats.

Phillipe Jean Bunau-Varilla came to Ville D'Avray with his son for treatment. Bunau-Varilla was the engineer who had achieved fame for building the Suez Canal; then under Ferdinand DeLesseps he had directed the abortive French attempt to build a canal across the Isthmus of Panama in Central America which was plagued by malaria-carrying mosquitos, landslides and volcanic instability — and the loss of thousands of workers' lives. Bunau-Varilla later incited the rebellion that separated Panama from Colombia and became Panama's first Foreign Minister Plenipotentiary to the United States. Among other patients were Mrs. Mowinckel, wife of the Norwegian Ambassador to France; Marquis Chasselou Lobat; Mme. Clemenceau, the sister-in-law of the late Georges Clemenceau, who had been Premier of France during and after the First World War; the German theatrical producer/director Erwin Piscator and film actress Marlene Dietrich; American actor Anthony Quinn; the Russian bass singer Fyodor Chaliapin; and Dr. Max Bircher-Benner of Switzerland. Dr. Bircher-Benner ran a famous Swiss clinic that also featured a vegetarian diet. During the Gersons' sojourn in Paris, their second daughter, Gertrude, was sent to the Bircher-Benner clinic in Zurich to learn clinic management. While there, she ate the food served to patients, which included heavy cream, butter and salted foods — far removed indeed from the Gerson therapy. Trudi developed acute boils, or furuncles, in various places on her body. Only when she resumed her father's diet did her skin clear up. While renowned musician Joseph Szigety was at the sanatorium, he would often practice his violin in his room. The glorious music attracted the other patients, who collected in the hallway outside his room to listen to his playing. He was being treated by Dr. Gerson for an arthritic condition, which through the dietary therapy was wholly alleviated.

A delightful story made the rounds at the sanatorium. Dr. Gerson alternated night duty with his assistant, Dr. Gutmann. One night when Gerson was on duty, a female patient, an attractive Greek countess, came into his office where he was working. She sat on his desk and started to chat. Dr. Gerson, never comfortable with small talk, gently tried to get her to leave, since he was working.

"Ah, *mon Docteur*," the countess said in her most seductive manner, "I am so lonesome. Wouldn't you like to come to my room for a while?"

Max Gerson understood her suggestion all too well. "But I am a married man," he demurred. The countess found this response so amusing that she often repeated the story among her cosmopolitan friends.

When a Mr. Kraemer came from the Hague with excruciating pain, he brought along his sister and brother-in-law. He had consulted many physicians seeking relief from his pain, with no success. Kraemer had been offered an operation, but was told that the problem could be kidney stones, in which case the operation would provide no relief. He declined the operation. As soon as Kraemer arrived at Ville D'Avray, Gerson prescribed strict bed rest and put him on the juice of 30 lemons a day, mixed with oatmeal. After two days of this treatment, the patient passed his kidney stones, which his body had broken down into sandy particles. In the absence of pain, Kraemer's appetite quickly returned, and he was discharged in another week.

Due to his position as president of the Banque de Paris, Horace Finali, the owner of the Hôtel du Parc, was involved in many charitable organizations. One of the activities he supported was a tuberculosis camp for children in Berck-Plage, on the English Channel south of Calais. On a visit to Versailles, Finali told Dr. Gerson about a five-year-old boy with bone tuberculosis and many open, scrofulous wounds all over his body. Dr. Gerson agreed to examine the boy. Fortunately, the boy's family lived in Paris, near enough to Ville D'Avray for Gerson to treat him at home. The parents followed the treatment plan carefully. Every day for two weeks they brought the boy with his nurse to Ville D'Avray, until the reactions to the treatment were fully under control. Gradually, the boy's wounds dried up, and granulation tissue began to form. Within three months, all the wounds were covered with scar tissue.

Mr. Finali was elated at the prospect of a way to cure all the children at Berck-Plage. He encouraged its director and one of the senior doctors to visit Dr. Gerson's sanatorium for a demonstration. The two physicians duly arrived in Ville D'Avray for a few days' stay. They spent the entire time examining patients, medical records and X-ray films. They made extensive notes, especially of the kitchen organization. Before they left, they met again with Dr. Gerson to discuss how extensively his treatment could be applied in their sanatorium. The discussion ended on a very discouraging note. "Dr. Gerson," the director said, "your therapy is most interesting and, apparently, quite effective. However, if we heal the tubercular children at the camp, what will there be for us to do? We would go out of business!"

Nothing further was heard from them. Dr. Gerson was always shocked at physicians who would put their pocketbooks before the health of their patients.

War Clouds over France

France had been so hospitable to the Gersons for nearly a year and a half that Max decided to become a French citizen. Through some prominent patients who held posts in the French government, he had arranged to have all the papers put through for his five family members to acquire French citizenship. But then propaganda from Nazi Germany began seeping into the French media, and the latent anti-Semitism of the French was being revived into open hostility. On three separate occasions, the Gersons were required to come to the Préfecture de Police and identify themselves—showing the increasing official harassment of Jewish refugees in France.

Hitler had already succeeded in stirring up widespread persecution of the Jews. The Austrian population had been subverted and looked to Hitler for leadership: Max had seen for himself the German-sponsored unrest there. Gathering up more like-minded allies, Hitler supported the aggressive dictatorship of Italy's Il Duce, Benito Mussolini, who had invaded Africa and grabbed Ethiopia as a late-acquired colony. He would also soon send weapons and troops to Spain, to ensure fascist General Francisco Franco's victory over the Loyalist republican forces during that nation's Civil War. In the summer of 1936, Hitler unilaterally decided to rearm the Rhineland, in direct contravention of the Treaty of Versailles that had ended the Great War, and sent his troops in to reoccupy the Saar. None of the other signatories to the Treaty raised a finger in protest, thus encouraging Hitler in his next adventures.

Hitler's unchecked depredations understandably alarmed the French, who over the centuries had seen far too many invasions by German armies from the east. In late summer of 1936 Dr. Gutmann was drafted into the French Army, leaving Gerson's sanatorium to begin his national military service. The French were caught up in a frenzy of preparations to deal with the looming German threat. Anything German was seen as perilous to French defensive integrity. Germans became distinctly unwelcome. Even Jews who had fled Hitler were still basically regarded as Germans, thus receiving a double rejection. As the atmosphere began to shift more rapidly, the French began to voice their hostility openly, and the watchword became "La France pour les Français!" —France for the French! At the Hôtel du Parc, Dr. Gerson began to receive anonymous letters, saying, "Donnez vos jus de légumes aux autres!" —Give your vegetable juices to someone else!

When Gutmann returned later from his tour of duty, he no longer wished to be involved with the sanatorium at Ville D'Avray. Though other arrangements could have been made to continue the work there, Dr. Gerson saw the writing on the wall. It was time to leave France. Max considered the possibility of eventually immigrating to the United States. While still in Paris, he transferred some capital assets to a brokerage house in New York City, which would enable the Gersons to enter the United States without needing either a sponsor or guarantor of financial support. He knew that his wife's knowledge of the English language would be very helpful to him there, since he spoke no English. Also, Gretchen would be able to handle all day-to-day affairs of the family while he focused, as always, on the practice of medicine.

While awaiting an appropriate time to apply for permanent visas to live in America, the Gersons moved in early autumn 1936, for a time at least, to England. There they could put more distance between them and the Nazis, as well as escape the corrosive combination of anti-German and anti-Jewish sentiment among the French citizenry.

On to London

A rriving in London in mid-October can be a cold and miserable experience, and the weather gave no special favors for the Gerson family as a greeting. Indoors, too, it seemed perpetually cold and damp. The Gersons had rented a furnished flat in St. John's Wood, which was decorated in the typical London style of the '30s. The flat had no central heating, and the only relief from the damp chill—winter arrived early in England, it seemed—was a fireplace in the living room. The family had to get used to roasting in front and freezing behind. The other rooms were even worse: cold and clammy. The outer bathroom wall had a permanent slit instead of a window to provide constant ventilation. As Charlotte Gerson recalls her school days in London:

> Since I was 14 years old, of course I was expected to continue my schooling. My mother already knew from our experience in France that the easiest way for children to learn a new language was to attend school, so she enrolled me in a British school. As I would be unable to follow the regular course of instruction without speaking the language, the headmaster, Mr. Strong, put me in a class of 11-year-olds.
>
> The class assembled in a large theater-style room with a tall ceiling, and suspended high up on the wall the schoolmaster kept a thermometer, which he periodically consulted. On the rare occasions when the mercury in that thermometer reached 65° F, the teacher immediately threw open the windows to let the damp, cold fog into the "overheated" classroom. Apparently he believed that the British brain simply couldn't function whenever it became slightly warm.

Each time the Gersons moved, their refugee status became more precarious, Max's income more uncertain, their lodgings less spacious and comfortable. Max now had to present himself at a government office to register his presence and whereabouts. The office was overwhelmed with refugees and émigrés from various central European countries fleeing the Nazi presence. Each time Max went, he had to wait in one or another queue for hours, which took him away from his medical work.

By this time, several of the patients from the Ville D'Avray sanatorium, including Moe Erstein, and were very happy to have their doctor living nearby. However, since immigrant physicians could not practice medicine in England or open an office without a license, but he consulted with his old patients whenever they wished. Through one of his former patients, Dr. Gerson was introduced to the Chief Consultant at St. George's Hospital in London, who turned out to be very congenial. Soon Dr. Gerson was invited to doctors' meetings, as the staff valued the opinions of this internationally recognized tuberculosis expert. He was delighted to be treated with respect and deference. His new colleagues suggested that he take a staff position at St. George's, but Gretchen urged him to prolong the negotiations, as she did not feel that they should stay in England much longer. One country after another in which her little family sought refuge had fallen under Nazi hegemony, and she feared the small island of Great Britain, separated from the Continent by only a narrow channel, would fall, too.

Although England had no history of organized persecution of its Jewish population, a definite undertone of anti-Semitism was mixed in with its tight social-class structure. During the mid 1930s, a number of prominent people were openly expressing admiration for the new German culture. England's Crown Prince Edward supported Hitler's opposition to Soviet communism. This vocal approval, probably even more than his desire to wed the American divorcée Wallis Simpson, would lead to his being forced to abdicate soon after he became the new monarch, following the death of his father, King George V, on January 20, 1936. He reigned as King Edward VIII at the time the Gersons moved to England.

The time had come for Jews to leave Europe—*if* they could. Gretchen and Max were looking for the first opportunity, which might be their best and even only one.

Another Transition

After several weeks of suffering the dismal London autumn, Dr. Gerson received a telephone call from Lady Greville, née Grace, a member of the American family that owned the W.R. Grace Company, a world power in steamships, energy, railroads and other related enterprises, who had been very happy with the results of the treatment she had received from him while staying at Ville D'Avray. She explained that her sister was seriously ill with rheumatoid arthritis. Several doctors at the Abington Hospital in Philadelphia had been treating her, with no success. Lady Greville proposed that Dr Gerson travel to the United States, at her expense, to consult with these doctors. Here was the chance for an escape to America that the Gersons were seeking. With Lady Greville's intercession — she was a personal friend of the American ambassador in London — a visitor visa as processed for Dr. Gerson and he was booked for passage on the French passenger ship the Normandie, leaving from Southampton in two days. Max and Gretchen agreed that he would have to go alone while she applied for permanent entry papers for the whole family. Max hastily took his leave of the staff at St. George's Hospital and packed his things.

Two days later, Gretchen and the girls took Max to the London-Southampton train station. After the three girls kissed their father goodbye, he boarded the train and took his seat beside a personable young German, Otto Berndt, who was also sailing to America on the Normandie. This ship was a showcase for French style in luxury liners and the fastest ocean liner on the North Atlantic route, having won the coveted Blue Ribbon.

After Max's departure, Gretchen and the girls applied at the American Embassy in London for immigration visas. Among various requirements, the process involved obtaining police papers from their country of origin that would prove their good character and verify that they had no police record. This itself was not a simple matter, since they were Jewish refugees who had fled from the very regime that now had to certify their character. They were given physical examinations to ensure that they were healthy and not afflicted with any communicable disease which might endanger the citizenry of the United States. Amazingly, the application process was completed quickly, and Gretchen and the girls had all their papers together by December 15. At that time, the flow of Jewish refugees from Europe to the United States was rather thin, so it was still possible to immigrate. Later on, when the applications for entry increased to a torrent, it became much more difficult, almost impossible, to obtain such visas. Six weeks after Dr. Gerson had crossed the Atlantic to New York, Gretchen and the girls were booked for their passage to America.

Charlotte informed the headmaster of her school that December 10 would be her last day there. Calling a meeting of the entire student body on that day, Headmaster Strong delivered two weighty announcements:

> Students, you should recall that Queen Victoria, in honor of her beloved consort Albert, decreed that there is never to be a king of England by the name of Albert. Therefore, King Edward's brother Albert is hereafter to be known by one of his middle names, George. That is because our present king is leaving us today, to follow the woman of his heart. The king's younger brother now will assume his throne, as George the Sixth.
>
> Also leaving us today is Charlotte Gerson.

Charlotte's departure from school happened to occur on the same day that King Edward VIII announced his abdication from the throne of England, so that he might marry the woman whom the monarchy's rigid nuptial rules had deemed unacceptable to be an English queen, since she was a divorcée. As the Duke of Windsor, in the following year he married Mrs. Simpson; together they would spend the rest of their lives in virtual exile.

Another form of lifetime exile had already begun for Dr. Max Gerson in America.

Dr. Max Gerson, 1911

Gretchen Hope and Max Gerson, Wedding Portrait, 1916

Captain Max Gerson Medical Corps, Breslau, circa 1916 (front row seated, third from left)

Charlotte, Gretchen, Trudi, Max, and Johanna Gerson, Bielefeld, 1927

Trudi, Johanna, Charlotte Gerson, Purkersdorf/Vienna, 1934

Max Gerson with Charlotte, Vienna, 1935

Dr. Albert Schweitzer, Lambarene

Hélène and Rhena Schweitzer,
circa 1938

Max Gerson (left), unknown, Otto
Berndt, Johanna Gerson, North
Atlantic Crossing, *Normandie*, 1936

Dr. Max Gerson with friends at his
clinic, Wannsee/Berlin, 1932.

Dr Max Gerson with young patient,
Nanuet, New York Clinic, 1949

The American Years

Forest Hills, New York, 1949

~11~
Starting Out in New York
(1936–1941)

Landing in America

Crossing the Atlantic Ocean on the *Normandie* gave Max Gerson a time to relax while pondering what the future might hold for him if he could settle his family in the United States, far from the threat of Hitler and the Nazis. During the trip, Gerson spent much of his time with the affable young Otto Berndt, a stockbroker and a partner in the Wall Street firm of Weed, Hall and Berndt. A German émigré but not Jewish, he had been living in the United States for several years, and was returning now from Germany after visiting relatives. Since Max Gerson spoke very little English as yet, he was grateful for Berndt's company, for he could easily converse with him, and doubtless Berndt taught him some basic American lingo to prepare him for what lay ahead. When they arrived in New York City on November 10, 1936, Otto Berndt helped his new friend Max Gerson find hotel accommodations and arrange for his first order of professional business: making the medical call that had brought him to America.

The day after his arrival, Dr. Gerson traveled by train to Philadelphia, to visit Lady Greville's sister at the Abington Memorial Hospital. Her physicians, alerted to Dr. Gerson's being brought in as a case consultant, were obviously ill-pleased when he came into the hospital: he was not even permitted to see the patient. He tried again the next day. This time he was allowed into her room, but not to examine her. Discouraged at this hostile reception, Dr. Gerson wrote out his therapy regimen for rheumatoid arthritis—the patient's diagnosis seemed quite accurate to him—and presented it to the woman's physicians. He also recorded his description of how the healing would progress, including his estimate of how long it would be until the patient was healed, if the patient followed exactly his recommended course of treatment.

The other doctors requested a private meeting with Dr. Gerson. In the conference room, he told them, through a translator, that his therapy had worked very well with similarly afflicted patients of his in Europe — as their patient's sister, Lady

Greville, well knew. Then the German physician clarified all he could about his special methods, including massage as well as diet, which would lead to the patient's complete recovery. The physicians decided against using such unorthodox treatments. Dr. Gerson could see that there was no chance of helping the woman he had come all the way from England to heal. He returned to New York in sadness, and soon wrote a full report to Lady Greville. He would hear nothing further about the patient he had come to America to cure of a painful and disabling ailment.

Back in New York, Max went about getting settled there. Otto Berndt helped him find a hotel with a restaurant. Since Max had eaten a salt-free diet for years, he paid the headwaiter of the restaurant an extra tip to make sure that his food would be specially prepared, without any salt added. The headwaiter was not very conscientious, though: Gerson's food was routinely salted—even oversalted, like other people's. The language difficulty proved to be a major obstacle in simply accomplishing various tasks necessary for Max in setting himself up financially. To ease at least this important aspect of life, he asked Berndt and his brokerage firm to manage the money that he had earlier transferred from Paris to another New York firm. This was money he and Gretchen had luckily been able to salvage from Nazi Germany, and was added to later from Max's earnings while practicing in Vienna and Paris.

Max also needed to obtain a medical license as soon as possible. During his time in Vienna, he had met several physicians who practiced in New York and they had assured him that his German medical license plus his international reputation and publications would be more than sufficient credentials in obtaining a license to practice in New York State. But to his great dismay he learned that a new law had taken effect on October 15, 1936, three weeks before his arrival. Now all immigrant physicians, no matter how prestigious their backgrounds, had to take the New York State Medical Board examinations, just like all new medical-school graduates. So Max Gerson would have to learn the English language *and* American medicine at the same time. By now 55 years old, at first he felt overwhelmed by the challenge.

It was mid-December when Gretchen and the girls crossed the Atlantic on the *Normandie*, in some of the worst weather conditions the ship had ever experienced, according to the crew. Most of the adult passengers, severely seasick, spent the voyage in their staterooms—leaving the lavish entertainment facilities empty and available for the enjoyment of the children and teenagers on board, including the three Gerson girls. They had a wonderful time playing games, seeing all the movies and dancing, with no adult interference, as Charlotte recalls:

> One afternoon, the social room was set up for showing a movie by covering the large dance floor with a big carpet and chairs. The audience, as usual, consisted mostly of young people. We were deeply involved in the movie plot when suddenly the entire group — carpet, chairs and people — gave a serious

lurch forward as the ship rolled on a particularly heavy wave. Though we were quickly jolted back into reality, no damage was done.

On the last day of the trip, since the weather had become still worse and the ocean more agitated, the chairs in the dining room were bolted to the floor. All the plates and glasses on the table were set into a metal frame attached to both sides of the table, which kept them from sliding onto laps or the floor. We were quite impressed.

Since the voyage had been slowed due to the bad weather, we arrived in New York harbor in the evening — too late for the immigration authorities to check the passengers through. Also, because of the late hour and the nasty weather outside, we couldn't go up on deck to fully enjoy the sights of arrival. Thus as we sailed in, we missed seeing the impressive first view of the immigrants' huge icon, the Statue of Liberty, and the approach toward the Manhattan skyline with its famous skyscrapers.

Early next morning, before we were up, the ship moved into its dock at the French Line's 48th Street pier. At this point, with the ship anchored, the passengers had overcome their seasickness, and the *Normandie*'s dining room offered a huge breakfast, literally from soup to nuts. Next came Customs and the visa-checking process for immigrants, which elicited nothing memorable.

The *Normandie* docked in New York just before Christmas 1936. As the family disembarked, the wintry weather continued its savage assault, and a freezing rain was falling. Lotte saw her father waiting for them on the pier, and in her eagerness to greet him, ran down the steeply sloped gangplank. The walkway was lightly coated with ice, and near the bottom of the plank she slipped and fell. She would forever remember sliding into the United States on her cold, wet rump.

After the family was joyfully reunited, they set off for their new home, as Charlotte's recollects:

> Now it was time for us to look around. Regrettably, from the pier on the Hudson River my first impression of New York City was not very favorable. The elevated streetcar line made terrifying noises and shook the ground whenever a train passed along its tracks above us. The streets, dirty and slushy from the melting snow, were lined with ugly little shops, diners and bars and afforded no view of the downtown skyline. I was particularly fascinated to notice a number of Negroes around us — walking, working, just living in this city. Strange to say, before the end of World War II there were few if any black people living in Europe; the only time I had ever seen one before was in a circus.

Gretchen was shocked when she took her first look at her husband. Max's face had broken out in an angry rash, and he told her that the skin was red and raw all over his body, a condition caused by eating in restaurants. Gretchen set to work at once to remedy the situation. She had to get him back on his own strict and healthful dietary regimen—and quickly. Once Max again began eating the foods so essential to his good health, while avoiding the salt and the foods that were bad for him, the nasty skin outbreak disappeared within a week.

Otto Berndt had already found the family a furnished apartment at 1040 Park Avenue, in a very pleasant and upscale neighborhood in Manhattan. The spacious apartment was on the ninth floor, "higher than we had ever lived before," and Lotte was impressed with its four bedrooms — quite a contrast to the close quarters the family had shared in the past few refugee years in Vienna, Paris and London. "It even had a separate pantry next to the kitchen. And the electric refrigerator was something entirely new to us."

Back in Practice

Before he could begin studying medicine, Dr. Gerson had to pass an English-proficiency examination. The government of the United States was very generous in providing help for immigrants who had succeeded in entering the country. English-language classes were given free of charge. When duly enrolled in one, Max felt no age discrimination, even though he was in a class with young adults, teenagers and six-year-old children. He gamely participated in the group activities, including singing songs, learning children's poems and even taking excursions. His favorite trip was to Bear Mountain State Park, a large wooded area on the Hudson River, north of the city. In three months, he passed the English-proficiency test, and then began to study for his medical license. Again, special courses were being given for physicians in just his situation. Despite the discomfort of having to study in the high humidity of a New York City summer, he passed the New York State medical examination and received his license to practice medicine in January 1938. He had been in the program for almost all of 1937.

Meanwhile, the Gersons' three daughters were making their own adjustments to American life, or at least life in New York City. The older girls were 18 and 19, beyond the age of compulsory education. Trudy, a gifted seamstress, fond a job at Hattie Carnegie, and later she worked for Lily Daché — both very elegant fashion salons. Johanna began taking shorthand classes — which, as it turned out, she would never use. Lotte had begun attending the local public school, Julia Richman High School. As she recalls:

> My English language skills were rather minimal, though during my stay in England I had thought that I had mastered enough of the language to understand it well when spoken. But now I was struggling again, before my ears grew

accustomed the very different American form of speaking English.

Nevertheless, in January of 1937 I started school with the new semester. The people in the admissions office were quite familiar with girls arriving from Europe; they automatically gave me credit for three years of both German and French, since I spoke both fluently. I was put one semester down in English, but was placed in other classes with my age group and managed to catch up rather quickly, since I was way ahead in all the subjects except for American history.

My mother's English, learned in England when staying with relatives before her marriage, proved very helpful. Unlike Max, she never needed to take English classes. My sisters quickly picked up whatever English they needed — Trudy at her job and Johanna in secretarial school.

After a semester, Lotte was placed in a special "country school" group for students who maintained grades over 90 points. During her two years at JRHS, through her classroom window Lotte often observed a very high building under construction a block away. Only later did she find out that she was watching the construction of the Memorial Sloan-Kettering Hospital — an institutional cancer research and treatment center that would become a significant adversary of her father's own medical work.

To celebrate his passing the New York State's medical board examination, Max and Gretchen took a three-week cruise through the Caribbean. Arranged by their friend Otto Berndt, the trip provided a welcome respite before Max launched his new American medical practice. After Max rented an office, he began to realize that it might be difficult to acquire patients because of the kind of therapy he customarily provided. At first he depended on getting referrals from a circle of acquaintances and from friends of other patients who had been helped by his unusual approach to treating a variety of chronic conditions. Occasionally, he got a patient through the doctor with whom he shared an office. But Dr. Gerson was finding that diet therapy — probably not just his, but anyone's — somehow seemed more difficult for Americans than for Europeans. One of his first patients in New York, however, proved otherwise.

Mrs. Albert Schweitzer came to the United States on a fundraising tour on behalf of her husband's clinic in Africa. Hélène stopped in New York to ask for Dr. Gerson's help, hoping that her former physician, who had cured her tuberculosis, could now cure her daughter's mysterious ailment. From the age of 13, Rhena had suffered from a strange skin disease that no specialist as yet had been able to treat successfully. Small and large ulcerations opened up on her skin and oozed pus for a while. Though these abscesses eventually closed, others had by then opened, so there were always some open sores. Over the past four years, the problem had increased in intensity, so that by 1938 the ulcers covered her body. Fortunately for this teenager, at least there was no scarring on her face from this intolerable condition.

Rhena's disease was so rare that the malady had only been described in the medical literature four or five times: it had not been named, nor had an etiology been proposed, much less a treatment. Dr. Gerson could not diagnose it, either. Since the disease process was unknown, it was difficult to tell whether it might be infectious. Since Rhena's mother had had tuberculosis for some years in the past, thereby exposing her daughter to it, Gerson thought a connection might be possible, though this was definitely not *lupus vulgaris*.

Hélène Schweitzer temporarily rented an apartment in New York City, where she could make sure that her daughter would receive exactly the right foods that Dr. Gerson prescribed. Lotte often visited, spending time with Rhena, who was about two years older than she was. Gerson relied upon letting Rhena's bodily functions do their healing work, once his dietary therapy began to be administered; he felt confident that her immune system could take care of the problem if restored to full functioning. He put Rhena on the same regimen he used for tuberculosis and cancer patients. She had so many lesions that she had to be wrapped in bandages from top to toe daily—a time-consuming, painful process. After a few months, however, the disorder disappeared, and now she could take up a normal 17-year-old's life — or as normal as it could be if Dr. Albert Schweitzer was one's father. Rhena eventually would marry an organ builder, and they had five healthy children.

Financial Disaster

One day in June 1938, less than a half-year after obtaining his medical license, Max Gerson called his friend Otto Berndt to ask about an investment. He was told by the desk clerk at the residential hotel where Berndt lived that the stockbroker had shot and killed himself. With a terrible foreboding, Max rushed over to the hotel. He remembered that a few months earlier, Berndt had requested a signed blank check from him so that he might transfer funds from one account to another. And Max, of course, had trusted him implicitly.

The facts, when Max learned them, confirmed his worst fears about his check's disposition. Before his suicide, Berndt had embezzled the funds from accounts that he controlled at his brokerage house — including Gerson's. Using his investors' money, he had been speculating in stocks. The savings the Gersons had brought from Europe were wiped out. Ironically, though, only about a week after Berndt's suicide, the market turned around, so he might well have recovered his losses. Much later, it was discovered that Berndt had initially fled Germany because he had embezzled funds there as well. Apparently, when he was made a member-partner of the New York brokerage house, his past record hadn't been thoroughly investigated.

Max and Gretchen found themselves in dire personal straits. Now they had no financial cushion to carry them through the lean times normally associated with starting a new medical practice. They had to survive on what Max could earn by using his brand-new medical license. Added to their stress was the predicament of having three daughters, two already of marriageable age and expecting, in the German-Jewish (as well as American) tradition, to have lovely weddings and generous dowries. The youngest almost certainly would expect to go to college. Gretchen sadly wrote to their good friend Albert Schweitzer in Africa about this latest blow in their life. Quite unexpectedly, and with the nobility of a true friend, Dr. Schweitzer immediately wired the Gersons $500—a princely sum at the time. This most welcome assistance helped them cope with their immediate problems.

The Gersons were forced to ask the landlord of their comfortable Park Avenue apartment to release them from their rental contract, since they no longer had funds to cover the monthly payments. Fortunately, he did so, and the Gersons moved to a much smaller residence just two blocks from Max's office. Since the previous apartment had been furnished, they bought secondhand furniture at minimal cost. The apartment was located at Lexington Avenue and 85th Street, at the boundary of "Yorkville," the German section of New York City. Unfortunately, the apartment was located directly across the street from the German-American Bund meeting hall, where the family again heard a full repertoire of Nazi songs being noisily sung, including the *Horst Wessel Lied*.

> *Die Fahne hoch die Reihen fest geschlossen*
> *S. A. marschiert mit ruhig festem Schritt*
> *Kam'raden die Rotfront und Reaktion erschossen*
> *Marschier'n im Geist in unsern Reihen mit*
>
> *Die Strasse frei den braunen Batallionen*
> *Die Strasse frei dem Sturmabteilungsmann*
> *Es schau'n auf's Hakenkreuz voll Hoffnung schon Millionen*
> *Der Tag fur Freiheit und fur Brot bricht an*
>
> *Zum letzen Mal wird nun Appell geblasen*
> *Zum Kampfe steh'n wir alle schon bereit*
> *Bald flattern Hitler-fahnen ü*
> *ber allen Strassen*
> *Die Knechtschaft dauert nur mehr kurze Zeit*
>
> *Die Fahne hoch die Reihen fest geschlossen*
> *S. A. marschiert mit ruhig festem Schritt*
> *Kam'raden die Rotfront und Reaktion erschossen*
> *Marschier'n im Geist in unsern Reihen mit*

(Flag high, ranks closed,
the S.A. marches with silent solid steps.
Comrades shot by the Red Front and reactionaries
march in spirit with us in our ranks.

The street free for the brown battalion,
the street free for the Storm Troopers.
Millions, full of hope, look up at the swastika;
the day breaks for freedom and for bread.

For the last time the call will now be blown;
for the struggle now we all stand ready.
Soon Hitler-flags will fly over every street;
slavery will last only a short time longer.)

Dr. Heinrich F. Wolf, the physician whose office space Max Gerson was sharing, was sympathetic about Max's financial situation and did not add to the strain by demanding the rent payments precisely on time. He trusted instead that Max would eventually pay him — which he did, of course. Within weeks, several wealthy former patients cabled Dr. Gerson to request consultations in London, Paris and Nice. Though Max had to spend four weeks in traveling and working in Europe, this trip proved to be quite lucrative. He returned with enough funds to shore up their shattered finances.

And as strange as Dr. Gerson's methods initially seemed to Americans accustomed to pills and operations, his practice grew steadily due to his reputation for achieving consistently good results with patients who adhered faithfully to his regimen. Max Gerson usually generated fierce loyalty from his patients, especially since he could usually help them when no other doctors of theirs had been able to. His manner with patients — firm but not arrogant, compassionate, attentive, "a good listener" as well as explainer, gentle and considerate in trying to minimize pain — worked much in his favor as well, especially in contrast to many other physicians who treated patients in a remote, condescending, autocratic style that they believed would ensure respect and compliance. Some of Max's early patients were suffering from tuberculosis. After benefiting from Dr. Gerson's regimen and on the way to recovery, they shared their experiences with other patients they knew and naturally recommended Dr. Gerson. He also treated many other ailments successfully. His practice soon became quite busy.

A Microscopic Oddity

The New York City Department of Health encountered a small but baffling problem with some of Dr. Gerson's recovering patients. Tuberculosis, a highly contagious disease, threatened the public health of any densely populated area, and as a result TB patients were required by law to report regularly to New York Department of Health examiners, who tracked the progress of their disease. When patients began to use Gerson's therapy, the microscopic picture of their blood and sputum changed in a way that puzzled and alarmed the examiners.

The normal microscopic slide preparation for tuberculosis tests involves three steps that demonstrate the presence and density of tubercle bacilli. The first step is to stain the entire sample red with an oil-based dye. Tubercle bacilli have a waxy coating that permits the organism to be dyed red. Then the slide is bleached with acid, and stained again with a blue water-based dye. The entire sample becomes blue under the microscope, except for the tubercle bacilli. The waxy coating of the tubercle bacilli prevents the acid from bleaching the red color out. The bacillus, as first demonstrated by Robert Koch, is "acid fast": when only the tubercle bacilli are red on a background of blue, they stand out brilliantly in the microscope's field.

The specimens taken from patients undergoing the Gerson treatment, however, behaved quite differently. When subjected to microscopic examination after the normal preparation of the slides, the active tubercle bacilli had a very unexpected appearance. The examiners saw light pink bacilli under their microscopes, and some bacilli that were dyed blue like other cells. The bacilli no longer assumed their normal shapes, either. Instead, they had taken on bizarre and tortured shapes, showing a lack of structural integrity that the examiners had never seen before.

The New York City Department of Health examiners, not knowing how to interpret this odd phenomenon, in their efforts to understand what they were seeing urgently consulted with Dr. Gerson. He was able to assure them that they were witnessing true healing, probably for the first time in their lives, and the anomalies indicated that the patients were healing as expected. This was because his patients' revitalized immune systems had attacked and dissolved the waxy coating of the bacilli.

Most of these patients eventually recovered. In fact, because of their awareness of Dr. Gerson's unusually favorable results, the Health Department officials allowed his TB patients to resume their working lives three to five months after the disappearance of symptoms, whereas patients of other physicians were not permitted to return to jobs for 18 months. The Health Department found this significant. Text in an extant, handwritten draft of a proposal to the Russell Sage Foundation for a funding grant, specifically to study the methodology and results of the Gerson diet for tuberculosis and compare them with outcomes of conventional TB therapies of that period, asserts that—

[In] the publication of such findings by the Tuberculosis Committee and general acceptance by the medical profession, this saving of twelve to fifteen months working time of tuberculosis patients would mean a vast improvement in living conditions. This improvement is exclusive of the fact that any treatment which secures such results would also shorten the period of complete recovery by sometimes years. Also, recovery might not be achieved at all through other and older methods. These economic savings would be equally important, per patient, in the case of cancer, arthritis and some other chronic diseases. (from Gerson manuscript collection belonging to Charlotte Gerson Straus)

Treating tuberculosis through dietary means, as Dr. Gerson had done successfully in Europe since the 1920s, seemed during the early 1940s a stepping stone toward applying similar tactics to overcoming cancer and other degenerative diseases in a natural, noninvasive way. However, the introduction at this time of antibiotics in the rapid, easy and cost-effective treatment of tuberculosis, which was a bacterial infection, basically eliminated the possibility of serious consideration by the American medical profession. When Max Gerson launched a concerted effort to address the curing of cancer by dietary means, he would find both professional acceptance and accessibility to funding unwelcoming, to say the least.

Adding Liver Juice

In the course of his practice over the years, Dr. Gerson received many patients who were already considered terminal. One reason for this was that until they reached the end stage, most physicians tried to influence the course of the disease by trying various treatments that might at least extend their patients' lives. However, once the disease had progressed to the point where death seemed inevitable, the primary physicians would tell patients and their families to "get your affairs in order" in preparation for death. Many cancer patients did just that — and still do today. But some refused to give up, and sought out less conventional therapies in the frantic hope of securing a few more days or even hours of life. Dr. Gerson was always amazed that a simple change in diet was considered so radical that it was the *last* resort of the desperate cancer patient, not the *first*, before mutilating surgery, damaging radiation or potentially toxic medication. He often said, "People are not willing to change their diets until the knife is at their throats."

One new patient of Dr. Gerson, a 19-year-old woman at Beth David Hospital (later renamed Gotham Hospital), was suffering from the end stages of leukemia. Her body had deteriorated to the point where her mouth was one big sore. With her tongue swollen and red and her gums inflamed, she was totally unable to eat. Dr. Gerson, thinking about the problem on his way home, recognized that her liver needed to be supported in a more effective way than he had been able to accomplish thus far.

When he arrived back at the apartment, his youngest daughter, Charlotte, was there, home from a day at her high school. "Lotte," he said, "I need some liver juice."

"Liver juice?" she repeated in a questioning tone, puzzled. As a child, she had been cured of her tuberculosis by the hourly-consumed pressed fruit and vegetable juices. But liver juice was totally new. "Pappa, what do I do? How can I make liver juice?"

"Please run down to the butcher store and buy me a pound of calf's liver. Now remember, it must be from a young beef animal, a calf. So be sure you tell the butcher of this. And of course I expect to pay more for it."

"But why so young?"

"Well, I am sure you remember that the liver, among many other functions that it performs, is the filter device for the bloodstream. So it tends to accumulate toxins over the years. The liver from a full-grown cow or steer has accumulated pesticides and other problem chemicals over its lifetime. A newborn calf's liver is still relatively pure and untainted."

"But when I bring it home, what will you do with it?"

"I am going to give it to a patient who is very, very ill. But first I need for you to grind it up and press it for me. Just the way you do the other kinds of juices." Lotte had now become the family's main juice maker, a job that also entailed the laborious clean-up stage afterwards.

Lotte followed her father's instructions. Bringing the liver from the butcher shop, she ran it through the grinder to make it ready for the next step. She was very familiar with the operation of the juicer — a two-stage appliance that had been built to Dr. Gerson's specifications by a machine shop in Manhattan, for about $125, a goodly sum at the time. It consisted of a motor-driven flat blade, about 6 inches in diameter, with zigzag cutting edges. The housing had an opening in the front, and the vegetables and fruit were fed diagonally into the grinder, which emitted the pulp out of a 3- or 4-inch tube.

After Lotte ground up the fresh liver, she spooned the gooey, brownish pulp into a muslin filter bag, and inserted into the second stage of the juicer: the press. The press portion of the device looked like a winepress, with a stainless steel cylindrical pail with perforations for the juice to exit. It was operated by rotating a 9- or 10-inch wheel at the top that turned a screw press drive. The press exerted high pressure on the filter and pulp, so that the juice would be expressed through the holes in the cylinder. This time-consuming procedure was a crude forerunner of the dual operation of today's Norwalk electric grinder and hydraulic press.

She now began pressing the filter bag with a hand-operated hydraulic jack. But no matter how much pressure Lotte applied, no juice came out of the press. She went to her father. "Could you please come to the kitchen? I'm not getting any juice from the liver."

Max saw that the thick, gummy ground liver was not yielding any of its fluids. He usually found solutions to any problems that threatened to interfere with carrying out his innovative plans. "Mix it half and half with ground carrots, and try it again," he instructed.

Lotte processed a pound of fresh carrots through the grinding machine, then stirred the viscous ground liver together with the carrot pulp. She put the mixture into the press bag, and this time a thick, brown liquid flowed out of the press.

There were much easier ways to produce juice from solid foods, but Dr. Gerson had discovered, after trying out some of the new electrical devices that more readily made juices from fruits and vegetables, that the therapeutic effects on patients given such juices were ineffectual. After conferring with physicists and reasoning through the various explanations, he better understood why, and concluded that it was essential in his therapy to use a two-stage juicer. In a one-stage liquifier or centrifugal device, a "dynamo" effect is created by the spinning pulp, causing electricity (negative ions) to flow through the very conductive pulp and juice, virtually killing the essential enzymes. The centrifugal juicers cause an additional problem. They extract only 5 to 10 percent of the minerals and vitamins from the pulp. Furthermore, the blades turn so rapidly and the teeth are so small that the abrasion heats the surface of the vegetable or fruit, damaging the very active oxidation enzymes. Dr. Gerson therefore insisted that patients undertaking his therapy use a two-stage juicer; subsequent and repeated experimentation have confirmed his observation that juice prepared in the other kinds of juicers *do not reduce cancer.*

As soon as Lotte produced the first glass of juice, Dr. Gerson put it in a jar and carried the precious fluid over to the hospital. When he gave it to the girl, she was able to drink it. To his great joy, she responded very positively. In the succeeding hours, he gave her more. The swelling in her mouth came down so that she was able to drink the other juices. As she started to improve, Dr. Gerson decided to incorporate the extra liver support from the raw liver juice into his program for all cancer patients. The raw calf's liver juice proved to be a very valuable addition to the regimen, and remained a part of the dietary therapy for many years after Dr. Gerson's death. Others after him would find additional or substitute ways to introduce potent and therapeutic enzymes and other substances removed from the livers of young animals into ailing human bodies whose own failing livers lacked them.

Dr. Gerson's therapy also began to incorporate crude liver injections and other liver-derived dietary products. He always attributed the origin of this innovation to the work of several American medical researchers in the early 1930s. Unfortunately, nowadays it is ill advised to use raw liver, even from young animals, in the Gerson therapy, since too often it contains microorganisms that cause serious food-borne illnesses, as well as toxins coming from prenatal or postnatal exposure. The crude liver injections, however, are still considered safe and therefore are standard.

Evolving Family Life

Max Gerson's 'old world' habits were a constant source of curiosity to his daughters, notably his manner of dressing. He showed no interest in conforming to the American custom of casual attire. In winter, he would wear a long coat and scarf, as he had in Europe. In his office in summertime, he could always be found in his jacket and tie, even on the hottest and most humid days. He would no more think of removing these formal articles of clothing in front of patients than to present himself to them naked. In such oppressive weather, Max might unbend a bit and wear short-sleeved, open-necked shirts, at home. His standards extended to his daughters, who were forbidden to wear slacks.

As the Nazi war program accelerated and broke out in most of Europe, the finest artists, whether Jewish or not, were fleeing the continent, usually to take up residence in the United States. When the European émigré artists converged in New York City, culture—literature, music, the visual arts, ballet and theater—flourished as never before. Max Gerson appreciated this unintended benefit from Hitler's assumption of power. He attended concerts and operas whenever his wife could lure him away from his medical reading in the evening. Gretchen especially loved the opera, so the Gersons had seasons tickets to the Metropolitan Opera, but often Max's seat was taken by a friend or other family member.

The Gerson household was changing. After finishing high school, Lotte, the youngest daughter, enrolled at Smith College in Northampton, Massachusetts. Trudy was still creating beautiful hats for fashion salons. Johanna, the eldest, now lived in Philadelphia with her husband, Samuel Cohen, whom she had married at the end of 1938, thinking that she would help her family by giving them "one less mouth to feed." A year later she had one more mouth of her own to feed. This early marriage proved unfortunate and ended in divorce.

On August 23, 1939, Dr. Gerson was alone at home. Gretchen had gone to Philadelphia to be with her daughter at the birth, two days earlier, of their first grandchild, Suzanne. Max had spent a long day seeing patients, but there was still plenty of daylight, so he decided to take a refreshing walk in Central Park, about four blocks from the Lexington Avenue apartment. As he was crossing Fifth Avenue — then a four-lane, two-way street — on a green light, an old jalopy came hurtling down the middle of the street and hit Max. Thrown all the way back to the sidewalk, he was knocked unconscious. The car careened into another vehicle and finally came to a halt. The driver was unable to stop because the brakes had failed.

A police officer was on the scene almost immediately. He grabbed the vehicle's driver. "Look, you've killed this man!" he shouted. Leaving the culprit for a moment, he stopped a taxicab. With the help of a pedestrian, the policeman slid Max onto the floor of the vehicle. "Take this man to the morgue," he ordered the shocked cabby.

Mount Sinai Hospital was only a few blocks away, and the cab headed north on Fifth Avenue toward the hospital. In the middle of the ride, Max regained consciousness. He sat up and looked around.

"Where are you taking me?" he asked the understandably shaken driver.

"To the morgue."

"No, don't do that. I'm not dead. Please take me to my apartment." Max gave his address. The cabby, relieved, drove Dr. Gerson home. Instead of having a corpse in his taxi, he had a passenger who would pay the fare for the trip.

Gerson never remembered how he got into his fifth floor apartment. He was alone in the apartment, in bed, when Trudy returned from work late in the afternoon. He was in severe pain, with three cracked ribs and a hairline fracture of his right tibia, his whole right side black and blue. Nonetheless, after only three days of rest Gerson became so impatient to get back to work that he could not be kept in bed, and returned to seeing patients.

Not long after, Trudy decided to marry Fred Selten, the owner of a fine New York City candy shop, the Cosmopolitan Confiserie (which the Gersons' grandchildren would later love to visit). The entire family attended the 1940 civil marriage in lower Manhattan. The girls all noticed that the justice of the peace was chewing gum, and braced themselves for the expected explosion. One American habit Max Gerson could not tolerate was the widespread practice of chewing gum. If a patient would come into his office masticating, Dr. Gerson would insist that the patient leave the room to discard his wad of chicle, telling him in no uncertain terms, "Seeing someone chewing gum makes me want to throw up!" Before Gerson could spot the offensive behavior, however, the justice had parked the gum in his cheek, where it remained, thankfully undetected, during the ceremony. When the wedding was over, the man resumed his chewing, but by then, fortunately, Dr. Gerson's attention was drawn elsewhere.

Almost immediately after his flight from Germany in 1933, Max had sent money from Austria to his relatives in Germany so that they, too, might escape from the Nazis. He often wrote letters to his remaining seven siblings, urging them to flee Germany because of the brutal anti-Semitism he had personally witnessed and he knew was getting even worse. On more than one occasion, he sent money for tickets out of Germany, but to Max's frustration, none of his brothers or sisters took his desperate warnings seriously. "It's not that bad," they would write back; "Hitler can't possibly do the things he said in *Mein Kampf*. Germans wouldn't allow it. We are a cultured and civilized people in this land of Goethe, Schiller and Beethoven."

The money that Max sent his family members was spent instead on food or clothing, as their incomes dropped. One by one, his brothers and sisters stopped responding to his letters as the Nazis gathered them up and they disappeared into the dark horror of Hitler's Holocaust.

A few of Max's siblings' children, however, did manage to get away. In 1938 Max's older brother Gustav's two boys, by then in their early 20s, emigrated. Hans went to Israel, while Günther left for South America. On the boat, Günther met a young man who gave him an introduction to a wealthy coffee plantation owner in Brazil and suggested that he look him up and ask for a job. Günther wasted no time in approaching the man when he got to Brazil.

"Sir," he said, "I have just arrived from Germany, and am looking for employment. An acquaintance of yours on the ship said you might have work for me. I am hardworking and learn quickly. I would be willing to accept any kind of job you might have available."

"I am sorry that you wasted your time, young man. I am not in need of extra help right now. But if you leave your name and a place where I can get in touch with you, I will be happy to call you when a position opens up."

"Thank you, sir. I appreciate your consideration." Günther wrote his name and contact information on a card, which the man accepted.

As Günther walked toward the door, the man looked at the card. "Just a moment, young man," he said. "I see your name is Gerson. Would you, by any chance, know a Dr. Max Gerson?"

"Why, yes, I do. He is my uncle — my father's brother."

The plantation owner became very excited. "Dr. Gerson saved my life!" he said. "Since you are part of his family, you can have a job here right now. You may work for me as long as you wish."

A long and happy relationship followed, and Günther worked at the coffee plantation for many years. Some years ago Günther wrote to Charlotte Gerson, his cousin, and told her his story. She believes that her father may never have known about what happened to his nephew.

In May 1939 Gerson received a welcome communication. His youngest sister, Hilde Levin, and her three daughters — Inge, Ilse and Miriam — had booked passage on the SS *St. Louis* of the Hamburg-American Line. They were bound for Cuba with 928 other Jewish refugees to join her husband, who had taken an earlier vessel bound for the U.S. Like the other refugees, she had received immigration papers for Cuba when paying for her passage. Because of the long and uncertain wait for documents for an American entry visa, they realized they had little chance of evading "relocation" by the Nazis if they remained. All were greatly relieved to have grasped what seemed like their last hope for escape.

Hilde had been badly shaken by the events of a half-year earlier, epitomizing the massive, coordinated attack on Jews throughout the German Reich. The night of November 9, 1938, extending into the next day, has come to be known as *Kristallnacht* (Crystal Night) or "The Night of Broken Glass." All over Germany, Austria and other Nazi-controlled areas, synagogues, Jewish shops and department stores had their windows smashed and contents destroyed. The Levin family finally decided to leave a Germany that was being turned into a killing ground for Jews, Communists, mental defectives, homosexuals, gypsies and other people deemed undesirable.

The St. Louis left Hamburg on Saturday, May 13, 1939, with passengers eager to begin a new life far away from Germany. More than a few passengers had already spent time in forced-labor camps (along with over 25,000 other Jews) after Kristallnacht, so they had witnessed firsthand the barbarity that would grow ever worse as the Nazis applied their "Final Solution" to the problem of the Jews. The refugees' hopes were cruelly dashed, as is revealed in detail in the book *The Voyage of the Damned*. After the ship had left Europe, Cuba passed a measure making all the Jews' visas invalid, despite the fact that each had paid dearly for visas as part of the price of their passage. Personal corruption, attempts by shadowy intermediaries to squeeze every last penny from the desperate passengers, and actions by Cuba's pro-Fascist President Frederico Laredo Bru combined to prevent all but 30 of the passengers from leaving the ship. The rest of the refugees were within a few hundred yards of salvation, but could not reach land.

Then German Propaganda Minister Joseph Goebbels saw an opportunity to use the *St. Louis* as part of his master propaganda plan. He instructed agents in Cuba to stir up anti-Semitism, stressing the vicious nature of the passengers about to disembark. The thought of nearly a thousand "criminal" Jews suddenly being dumped on the small country's resources sealed the refugees' fate. No more passengers were allowed to disembark. On June 6, 1939, ten days after the *St. Louis* had arrived, the Cuban navy chased the ship out of the harbor at gunpoint. Appeals were made to other Caribbean countries and to the United States government to accept the refugees, who faced certain internment and death in Germany's concentration camps if forced to return. The pleas for sanctuary were refused. Running out of food and water, and under pressure from the Hamburg-American Line, the *St. Louis* turned its bow once more to Europe. The passengers became so desperate that they even attempted to seize the ship by inciting a mutiny, but it was quickly put down.

Through miraculous negotiations, a committee of passengers managed to get several European countries to each accept some of the refugees: 181 went to Holland, 224 to France, 228 to Great Britain and 214 to Belgium. For most, this meant only a short reprieve. As the countries of Europe fell, one by one, to Hitler's advancing *Wehrmacht*, the returned refugees would be collected and shipped east to waiting concentration camps, where most perished. Only those in Britain remained safe, unless they later died, as many people in England did, in German bombing raids and rocket attacks.

The rejection of the refugees aboard the SS *St. Louis* was, for Adolf Hitler, a clear signal that no nation would do much of anything to help the Jews, though it was clear they were in imminent danger of being slaughtered. Even the President of the United States, Franklin D. Roosevelt, by adhering to a strict refugee policy, had been willing to send a shipload of helpless men, women and children to their deaths. The SS *St. Louis* incident made a dark blot on the history of the United States. Encouraged in his genocidal endeavor, Hitler shifted his extermination program into high gear. The rest of the world turned a blind eye, as he had expected.

Hilde Levin and the three girls were in the group sent to Holland. Put ashore at Brussels and shipped to Holland, they were immediately placed in a refugee camp in Rotterdam. As refugees were not permitted to work in the general economy, along with all other displaced persons they were given jobs maintaining the camp.

Meanwhile, the Gerson family helped Hilde's husband make strenuous attempts to complete immigration papers for Hilde and the girls to enter the United States. Trying to get certifications of good character from the Nazi government was difficult enough, without the extra complication of being shifted from camp to camp. The family finally landed in another refugee camp, at Westerborg. Their papers were nearly completed when Germany invaded Holland, capturing the refugees already interned in the camps. After falling in the hands of the Nazis, Hilde and her daughters were shipped to the infamous extermination camp at Bergen-Belsen.

Max's sister Hilde and the three girls miraculously survived malnutrition, typhus, tuberculosis and the brutal camp regime at Bergen-Belsen, but two weeks before the camp was liberated by American troops, Hilde died. Somehow she had managed to keep her daughters alive throughout the entire war. When the camp was liberated, the girls, sick with tuberculosis and typhus, were taken in by Swedish relief workers and nursed back to health. They could then search for their father; after locating him in New York City, they joined him there. Two of Hilde's daughters, Ilse and Inge, are now living in Tucson, Arizona. In a note to her cousin Lotte, Ilse recollects: "Your father was my mother's favorite brother. My mother always followed your father's 'Rohkost' [raw foods diet]. She made sure we ate carrots, cabbage, etc. and made carrot juice and spinach juice — all these from scratch. Maybe this kept us alive in the concentration camp for 16 months."

Though some of Max Gerson's other nieces and nephews escaped to Israel, the United States and South America, none of his siblings survived the Holocaust. Most of Gretchen Gerson's relatives, sent to a variety of concentration camps around Eastern Europe, were also exterminated. Though Gretchen's two brothers died in the Holocaust, her sister Gertrude and her family immigrated to the United States after the war.

The Military Diet

Max Gerson was greatly concerned over Hitler's rapid advances after the fall of France, having enslaved almost all of Europe by then. He deeply feared that England was in a most precarious position. He expressed this to a friend, Professor Irving Fischer, referring to "My friends the Russians" — because the Russians were the only ones effectively fighting Hitler at the time. It appeared that only after the United States itself suffered some unanticipated, grievous attack, similar to the World War I sinking of the *Lusitania* and other submarine assaults, would the nation join the fight against vicious despotisms.

The American press began portraying the German soldiers as supermen and the German war machine as invincible. In response, Dr. Gerson wrote "Feeding the Germany Army," an informative article published in early 1942 in the *New York State Medical Journal*. Interestingly, he put to good use his knowledge of Nazi Germany's application of the findings of nutritional science, drawing his insights from various research papers and published reports on the physical status of military-service recruits in Germany in the years after World War I, and on different facets of an optimal diet for different categories of work in terms of need for calories, meat protein, fat, carbohydrates, specific vitamins (notably A and D) and minerals. At least several people had told Dr. Gerson that Hitler and a number of his advisors tried to follow the main elements of the Gerson diet — which he took as a backhanded compliment. It was clear to Dr. Gerson that for overall health maintenance of their fighting forces and food-storage convenience, not for economical reasons, the Nazi administrators favored a low-meat consumption and vegetarian-leaning diet. He also discussed preferred methods of cooking in order to retain micronutrients. Though he pointed out the superior nutritional care the German took of their troops, Dr. Gerson also noted some of the dietary weaknesses in the general population, which contributed to the large number of unsatisfactory recruits.

In writing the paper, Dr. Gerson obviously hoped that his suggestions might persuade American military dietitians to consider taking a similar nutritional approach in designing meals for the armed forces, in what surely would be a future war engagement against German "soldiers nourished with the help of this knowledge." As he concluded, "One moral remains to be added: it is a terrible tragedy and paradox that the accomplishments of the new technic in the science of nutrition should now be used without limitation for the demolition of human life. Far better fields could be found for putting this progress to work than causing death and destruction."

Max Gerson's paper had been written just prior to the bombing of Pearl Harbor and the declaration of war against the Axis Powers — Germany, Italy and Japan — on December 7, 1941.

~12~

New Focus on Cancer
(1941–1944)

At Home During the War

By the early 1940s, Dr. Max Gerson had built a very active general practice in New York City away from the forum of World War II — that giant, violent convulsion which in its formative stages had driven the Gerson family from Europe. Much of the time during the first two years of the war, Max and Gretchen lived by themselves, having moved toward the end of 1941 from their Lexington Avenue flat to a nicer apartment at 40 West 55th Street, just off Fifth Avenue. Trudy lived close by with her husband, so she could visit often.

By now all three of the Gerson daughters were married. Among their spouses, only Irwin Straus, Lotte's husband, was in the military service, having enlisted in the Army right after Japan's surprise bombing of Pearl Harbor on December 7, 1941. At first he was sent to Texas to be trained as a tank driver, but when his young wife found out that men in this position under combat conditions had very short life expectancies, she went at once to Irwin's commanding officer to request that the Army make better use of her husband's skills as a professional photographer. The C.O. must have been impressed with the audacity of this very young woman (Lotte was 20 years old) with a heavy German accent, for he soon got Irwin transferred to Kansas, where he worked as an X-ray technician. Later, because he was fluent in German, Irwin was sent overseas to participate in the invasion of Europe as an aide in "psychological operations." During the Battle of the Bulge, he was almost shot as a spy; sentries, hearing his German accent, at first decided he was an enemy infiltrator posing as an American G.I.

With her husband away during the war, Lotte came to live with her parents at their apartment on 55th Street. There, in May 1943, Dr. Gerson delivered his second grandchild and first grandson, Howard Straus (the author). It was a home birth.

Electrochemistry

In the United States, as in Europe, Dr. Gerson prescribed his nutritional therapy — a saltless, no-fat, vegetarian diet and hourly juices made from ground and pressed fruits and vegetables — to heal serious conditions in patients other physicians considered beyond medical rescue. Over the years Dr. Gerson had been fine-tuning his diet by trying out different foods and experimenting with various supplements. Some of his innovations came from reading he had done or talks he had heard about research done by other physicians and health practitioners, as, for example, when he read studies of the effects of injections of crude liver extracts in boosting patient vitality — a procedure that had originated with some American doctors in the 1930s. He was also interested in the possibility that particular vitamins, notably B_3 (niacin) and B_{12}, contributed additional potency to key activities in the body if given in higher doses than were available in foods. Dr. Gerson was creating a rationale within his dietary therapy that could be classified as electrochemistry: he had come to believe that much of the body's metabolism, physiology and consequently overall health depended upon maintaining the correct balance of positive and negative charges — ions, or electrolytes — within cells of body tissue, nerves, muscle, bone marrow and the various organs, but also surrounding them in the blood and other extracellular fluids. The appropriate amounts and presence in their designated sites of particular minerals in the body — certain elements and elemental compounds derived from inorganic earth materials — determined the appropriate effects of these positive and negative charges.

Toward the conclusion of his paper "Feeding the German Army," written in 1941, Dr. Gerson displayed his continuing belief in the importance of maintaining the right sodium:potassium (Na:K) ratio in the body, to make sure that the two minerals dominated the correct fluids, tissues and organs.

> Keller [Keller, R.: Med. Klin. 11: 38 (1934); Die elektrischen Gruppen in Biologie und Medizin, Sperber-Verlag, Zürich, 1938] has developed the classification of mineral salts into potassium and sodium groups within the animal and vegetable kingdom and found their electrical transformation in "biologic milieu." Of course, they are not the only powerful biologic forces, but their great significance for practical usefulness has been demonstrated, among others, by the increased efficiency of the soldiers nourished with the help of this knowledge

Gerson referred to the important research work in this area that had been conducted in the early 1930s by Rudolph Keller. Keller's research had fascinated Gerson while he was in Vienna, where first he began to apply it in his clinical practice there, most notably when successfully intervening in the case of the pregnant young woman with life-threatening pre-eclampsia by administering high doses of potassium. (Today, of course, health practitioners are far more knowledgeable about and attentive to balancing the electrolytes in body fluids.) Now Rudolph Keller was living in New York City. Like Max, he was a transplanted European — but a Czech, and not Jewish. Their professional association became quite close. They exchanged research information, read each other's papers being prepared for submission to medical and scientific journals, and also collaborated on pursuing projects of mutual interest in the realm of biochemistry, nutrition and health.

In his paper on the optimal army diet, Dr. Gerson had concentrated on the need to avoid or treat fatigue brought on by physical exertion or psychological stress in military training and combat by ensuring a diet high in potassium and moderate in salt and sodium usage. But he was clearly interested in the wider implications of regulating this Na/K balance, as discussed later in his book, A *Cancer Therapy*:

> K has to be predominant chiefly within the cells (called, therefore, intracellular) while Na has to stay outside the cells in serum, lymph, connective tissue (therefore called extracellular). Later observations led to the opinion that the minerals do not react singly but in groups. As a consequence, Dr. Rudolph Keller established the doctrine of two mineral groups, the intracellular (potassium) or anodic group traveling to the anode, and the extracellular (sodium) or cathodic group traveling to the cathode under biological conditions. A further consequence was the discovery that hormones, vitamins and enzymes obey the same rule as the two mineral groups; this means that their function depends upon the prevalence of the K-group within the cells of the organs and tissues such as the liver, muscles, brain, heart, kidney cortex, etc., whereas the Na-group remains outside of them. The Na-group is stationed in fluids and tissues: serum, lymph, connective tissue, thyroid, bile ducts, etc. Here are also the cathodic or negative vitamins and enzymes, of which the main functions, metabolism and storage, are confined to this extracellular group....
>
> To the K-group belong about 60 per cent of body tissues and to the Na-group 30 per cent; 10 per cent are on the borderline. All of them are kept in their proper place, probably by means of their electrical potentials. During the day, some Na penetrates the potassium tissues, and this is followed by chloride and water, a process which brings on fatigue, a little heaviness or swelling. At night, it is reabsorbed and in the morning it is eliminated in urine, and the person feels refreshed.
>
> These biological rules are vital for the maintenance of health inasmuch as a deficiency, defect or change means sickness. Almost all acute and chronic sicknesses begin with an invasion by Na, chloride and water of the anodic organs, causing the so-called edema produced by poisons, infections, trauma, etc.

If the potassium level becomes low within cells throughout the body, the capillary walls begin to leak out protein-laden fluid into intercellular areas; this reduces efficient blood flow in transporting oxygen to cells and removing waste products. The cells' protective membranes, weakened, become permeable and permit sodium, water and chloride to pass through and flood the cells' interiors, to impede overall metabolism. The swelling in edema and inflammation of body tissue, as in collagen, muscles and vital organs, are symptomatic of this condition. (pp. 24-25)

Dr. Gerson suspected that sodium overload and a corresponding potassium deficiency were implicated in a number of degenerative diseases. Some minerals, such as sodium, chlorine, iodine and (sometimes) calcium, assumed a negative charge, with atoms or molecules taking on an extra electron or more (anions). Others, such as potassium, magnesium and phosphorus, would lose an electron and then become positive ions (cations). In electrochemical cells to which electrolyzed minerals are introduced in solution, anions migrate to the positive pole or anode, whereas cations are attracted to the negative pole or cathode. Within the body, however, a similar yet opposite electrolytic phenomenon appeared to take place biologically. Negatively charged minerals gravitate toward negatively charged organs or tissues, and positively charged minerals move toward positively charged organs or tissues, as if drawn in to reinforce the particular normal polarity of that unit in the body.

Dr. Gerson's interest in the electrochemistry of metabolism and physiology, pertaining especially to the cause and manifestation of disease, became an integral part of his dietary therapy, as he explains in A *Cancer Therapy*:

> The general approach to the treatment of patients with degenerative diseases should have as its purpose the overcoming of the biochemical abnormalities which are more or less responsible for the development of the disease. I am convinced that the problem of chronic disease is not one of biochemistry, chemistry or the symptoms we observe in and on the body. Rather, it is produced by deeper-lying forces which cause "deficiency of energies." Physicians observe biological symptoms and work only with them. The real acting forces behind the visible chemical changes are physical energies, expressed by Einstein as the "electro-magnetic field." To a certain degree, this is closely connected with the electrical potentials which are lowered in cancer, according to almost all investigators (about 30) and also according to the observations of Dr. Rudolf Keller. (p. 89)

If the sodium and chlorine in excessively used table salt had an adverse effect on many people's well-being, as Dr. Gerson had proven by eliminating salt from the diet, could one restore health by introducing more of some oppositely-charged counterpart minerals, notably potassium, phosphorus and magnesium? And what beneficial functions might iodine perform, preferentially to having sodium and chlorine lodged in particular positively-charged organs, especially the thyroid gland? Dr. Gerson was seeking a theoretical basis to encompass the empirical results he had discovered while treating seriously ill patients. The diet he was perfecting had proven efficacious in treating such diverse disorders as migraine headaches, tuberculosis, diabetes, cardiovascular disease, multiple sclerosis, rheumatoid arthritis and even cancer. But how? Dr. Gerson needed to find medical professionals who would take interest in his work and help him develop it to the point that he could publish and publicize his therapeutic approach, to make it available to physicians throughout the United States and elsewhere in the world.

Professor Irving Fisher

Sometime in 1940 or 1941 Max Gerson acquired an important new ally, a noted professor of economics at Yale University. Initially, Irving Fisher may have met Dr. Gerson when he helped restore his brother's health, then he began to learn more about him, hearing from Dr. Gerson how other physicians ignored or scorned his work, even though he often achieved extraordinary results with patients who had severe chronic illnesses or were on the verge of death.

Irving Fisher had long taken a keen interest in health issues. Born in 1869, Fisher he had been afflicted with pulmonary tuberculosis as a child. He credited his recovery to the "fresh air cure," which was not widely used on patients until around the turn of the century, even though in the early 1800s a small-town practitioner in England, a Dr. Bodington, had announced his success with this treatment. For decades the medical journal *Lancet* and England's TB specialists had ridiculed the very notion of such a therapy, but after German doctors rediscovered this often effective therapeutic technique, it was exported to back to England and then on to America's Trudeau Institute, where it became the standard residential treatment — until Gerson's diet therapy was shown to be even more effective. As Professor Fisher noted, "I was one of the millions of victims of this typical delay in the acceptance of new ideas. Naturally I have never forgotten the history of Bodington; and it is primarily because I now see history repeating itself that I am doing what I can to shorten the time when Gerson's methods will be adopted as fully as were Bodington's."

Professor Fisher's knowledge of Dr. Gerson's therapy was recorded in an article he wrote in 1943-44 — primarily, it seems, to be used in his effort to convince military health authorities to hire Dr. Gerson as a consultant. (The document was initially typeset, changes were made in Max Gerson's own writing, and deep cuts were made in the text, but it seems never to have been actually published, though probably it had some limited circulation.) Dr. Gerson could advise the military on the best diet for the armed forces (as he had done in the early 1930s with the Prussian Army) and improve the health of men who had enlisted or been drafted but subsequently were rejected from service because of health problems. In the early 1900s, Professor Fisher had assisted physiological chemist Russell Chittenden in conducting important clinical studies demonstrating that humans could maintain good health while greatly reducing animal protein in the diet, and during World War I he had published a paper on the influence of diet on physical endurance, so crucial for training and combat conditions. Fisher knew the potential reparative value of the Gerson diet. "Dr. Gerson has had 11 cases of rejects from the Army," Fisher wrote in his report. "Over half of them were restored and Dr. Gerson expects all of the others to be. The restorations have, I understand, all occurred in a relatively short time. Thus there already exists striking evidence that Dr. Gerson could be of use in restoring man-power now lost to the armed forces."

Professor Fisher became Dr. Gerson's advocate, presenting his credentials and defending him against his detractors:

> In spite of all opposition . . . Dr. Gerson rose in Germany to the highest standing in his profession. His methods were followed in many places, both inside and outside Germany, including Norway and Switzerland. In Switzerland, Davos-Platz and St. Moritz had been great health resorts, chiefly for tuberculosis. They are now chiefly sports resorts, and the change was largely due to Dr. Gerson's demonstration that in the cure of tuberculosis, the most important factor (in addition to rest) is not climate but diet.

When Irving Fisher first met Max Gerson, the doctor had few TB patients. Realizing that he needed assistance in making connections with New York hospitals where he could treat patients by using his special diet, not just for tuberculosis (which in this pre-antibiotic period had no sure cure) but other serious and chronic diseases as well, Professor Fisher set out to convince representatives of the American medical establishment to explore the Gerson diet therapy. For instance, Irving Fisher undertook to persuade physicians of his acquaintance (and he knew many) to visit Dr. Gerson's office and learn more about patient outcomes in his practice. Positive impressions, if passed on to others, might eliminate the reluctance to accept his unusual methods or a downright prejudice against him based on professional hearsay. "The medical profession seems peculiarly prone to gossip and to be taken in by gossip," the professor remarked. And in another context, he remarked, "The medical profession is not entirely free of rogues. In fact, as is well known, it contains so many quacks and swindlers, sometimes M.D.s with fake 'cure' for everything, that the average honest physician is always more or less suspicious of his colleagues." As he continued, "the worst species of a medical rogue is that (of which I have seen several specimens) which has managed through 'medical politics' to attain respectability and power in the profession and to capitalize their alleged services to it in the fighting of other quacks, real or alleged. . . .

Professor Fisher was dismayed that Edgar Mayer's two papers, published a decade earlier, had cast such an unfavorable light on the Gerson diet that American doctors refrained from using it. Fisher attributed a considerable part of Gerson's problems in America to the machinations of an unidentified physician, "Dr. B," who like Max had earlier practiced in Germany, where, years before, Dr. Gerson had brought a lawsuit against him—and won. After coming to the United States well ahead of Dr. Gerson, this man had gained considerable professional power. Rankled by the past legal defeat, he succeeded in 'blackballing' Dr. Gerson from obtaining a staff position or hospital privileges in New York City. Thus when Dr. Gerson offered to try out his treatment on 34 patients confined at "N" Hospital with bilateral tuberculosis of the kidney—at that time considered a hopeless condition—his help was turned down. The refusal was traceable to this physician's objection, which Fisher called "the most revolting experience with medical practice in my forty years of close contact with medicine." Fisher elaborated on this position:

> I cannot imagine any legitimate reason for such an inhuman act. Even if Dr. Gerson were the most deep-dyed villain, any friend of humanity would, we would suppose, have welcomed the faintest chance not only to save some of those 34 lives, but to prove that this "incurable" disease is curable.
>
> That Dr. Gerson's diet has apparently cured such cases has been amply proved for all who are willing to examine proof. I myself, in Dr. Gerson's office, have seen and talked with a woman who had one kidney removed because of tuberculosis, after which the other was attacked by the disease. She was, therefore, even a more hopeless case than if she had had both kidneys diseased in the first place. After getting nowhere with any other physician, she heard of Dr. Gerson and, when I saw her, she had been apparently cured. At this writing, which is a year later, Dr. Gerson informs me that she is doing her housework and continues to be healthy.

Professor Fisher took obvious delight in writing about what had happened when patients at this hospital, after learning about Dr. Gerson's success in treating tuberculosis, which accommodated charity cases, began defecting to Gerson's practice:

> The medical authorities there have tried, and in many ways, to stop this exodus. If Dr. Gerson had hospital facilities of his own, probably almost all the inmates of this hospital would leave if we may judge by what the enthusiastic patients say. The only things which prevent such an emptying out are the inability of Dr. Gerson to handle so many, the inability of many poor patients to change from free food and free lodging to meeting food and lodging bills themselves. They would not, apparently, be greatly restrained by the efforts of the hospital physicians to persuade them not to go to Dr. Gerson. I could tell some amusing stories about

these efforts and their futility, if it were possible to do so without making trouble for the patients and for some employees of the hospital. I have personally talked confidentially with some of these thoroughly altruistic people who know, and are profoundly sorry for, the terrible mistake to which their superiors have committed themselves in not letting Dr. Gerson introduce his methods there, and, instead, fighting their use even by Dr. Gerson himself.

The physicians have, over and over, pled with patients not to go to Dr. Gerson, casting aspersions on him and his methods, only to create resentment and lose the respect of the patients. They have even requested ex-patients who were satisfied with Dr. Gerson's success where the hospital had failed, not to write letters to their fellow sufferers at the hospital! They have sent doctors and nurses to the homes of their deserters only to find reports that they were doing better than they had done at the hospital. In one case, the patient's mother received a N Hospital physician with a nurse; but when she learned who they were and what they wanted, she became enraged and ordered the physician to leave, crying excitedly, "You made my boy a cripple by cutting out his ribs; but Dr. Gerson is curing him of his tuberculosis. You shan't see him, but the nurse may." The nurse did and was astonished at the improvement she saw.

These physicians have tried to get the cooperation of the New York City Department of Health. Some of the Department physicians at first "fell" for this....

Thus Dr. Gerson has now over 100 tubercular patients living at home and trying to meet the expenses involved in their troubles rather than accept free of charge all the facilities of a hospital for rest, etc.

This is certainly an acid test of Dr. Gerson's diet. For he can give these patients *only* his diet, not rest, not nursing, not freedom from financial worry. V [a patient] and many others have not sufficient money to buy all the foods necessary or the additional minerals, etc.

Dr. Gerson charges the poor patients nothing, merely saying if and when they get jobs and can afford to pay they may if they choose. Many have gone back to work already and are proud to pay what they can.

To gain support for Dr. Gerson, Professor Fisher had solicited letters from some physicians who were impressed with his work, despite their awareness of the medical establishment's disapproval of Max Gerson personally, apart from his diet therapy. Speculating on the reasons for the medical establishment's distrust and dislike of Max Gerson, Professor Fisher he enumerated a dozen partial explanations:

There is a reluctance to let a foreign doctor reach the top. One physician at the top said of Gerson, "We'll put these refugees in their places."

Dr. Gerson's personality lacks tact. He is so direct, honest and naive as to be sometimes offensive. He is incapable of finesse and would be a very poor politician, medical or other. I have myself painfully witnessed his making an enemy unconsciously and unnecessarily.

Gerson is a pioneer and should therefore be expected to get some of the cold reception which most pioneers get. Pioneers simply cannot at first be understood. The gap between them and their contemporaries is too great. Their claims seem so fantastic that they are, at first, mistaken for cranks, charlatans, insane people. Before this gap is bridged they have to lead a lonely, neglected or even persecuted life.

Professor Fisher then named various notable physicians, scientists and artists who were rejected by their peers or society itself during their lifetimes, then pointed out that elements in Max Gerson's therapeutic diet were based on respected research:

The ideas for which Dr. Gerson is famous and for which he is also fiercely opposed are not, in the main, discoveries of his. His great achievement consists of studying, sifting, absorbing, and combining the work of others. Chittenden at Yale, for instance, famous for lowering the protein requirement, has harped on that one string all his life. Gerson owes much to Chittenden, but he has combined Chittenden's low protein with low fat, and for good reason. So, also, all he knows as to the individual vitamins has (recently at least) become common knowledge. But he has found that, to be most effective, the vitamins must be properly combined not only with each other but with minerals, which latter are still greatly neglected even by those who insist on the vitamins. The vitamins and minerals seem to form a chain in which every link is needed for its strength. Gerson has found how, by proper cooking, to get the best mineral supply out of vegetables and how to increase this supply by means of vegetable juice. . . .

Professor Fisher nevertheless recognized Dr Gerson as a pioneer in the study of nutrition, which oddly had been ignored as a legitimate field of medical research.

It must not be forgotten that nutrition is a very new field, and one almost entirely neglected in the medical schools until recently. Practically all physicians now practicing are ill educated on this subject, except in the case of a few who had made special efforts to study it up since leaving medical school. Even these few have largely confined their study to insulin and vitamins, topics which smack of the laboratory.

Ordinary food smacks not of scientific laboratories but of the kitchen, and the ordinary physician knows little more about the ordinary foods than the layman.

He was taught to prescribe "medicine" (drugs), not food.

Until recently, laymen like Sylvester Graham, have contributed more toward improving eating habits than physicians....

[E]ven today the subject [nutrition] is foreign to ordinary medical thought and is a ticklish one for the ordinary physician to discuss with his patients. They still expect a prescription of pills not of apples. Their food habits they regard as their own private concern.

Recently at a National Research Council Conference it was disclosed that workmen in war plants were much more willing to be experimented on by drugs than by foods. . . .

The curious fact is that most of the knowledge utilized by Dr. Gerson, though known by many other physicians, is not utilized by them but is being commercialized by industry, particularly by the "health food stores" who incidentally have gotten their knowledge from others than Gerson.

I see the medical profession losing a great opportunity. They realize that an improved nutrition is a newly available resource. Yet they do not generally avail themselves of it, or do so half-heartedly. They do not take their profession seriously enough. Modern nutrition offers them an opportunity which they do not yet appreciate.

"I am not trying to induce any hero-worship of Dr. Gerson," Professor Fisher claimed. "I'm trying to help make every physician into an equivalent. ... I am seeking to convince [people in the medical field] regarding the importance of Dr. Gerson's message to the world." Max Gerson needed just such a friend and apostle.

Resuming Cancer Therapy

Dr. Gerson had been fascinated with the challenge of treating cancer ever since his first three cancer cases in Bielefeld, during the late 1920s, had experienced full recoveries, but he encountered mostly disappointing results treating this disease condition during his later practices in Kassel, Berlin, Vienna and Paris in the 1930s, though he could count several patients in France as successes. When some cancer patients had followed his dietary regimen, their tumors disappeared without surgical or X-ray intervention; even some seemingly intractable malignancies, including metastasized cancers, had yielded to his unique therapeutic approach. But these empirical results resisted easy scientific explanations.

Dr. Gerson began to explore in depth the medical literature about cancer, but he was dissatisfied with most of the published information in books or medical journals, finding it often confusing, contradictory and pessimistic. Charlotte Gerson remembers her father showing her the first sentence in a book written by the most famous stomach cancer specialist in France: "By the time stomach cancer is discovered, it is too late to overcome the disease."

Cancer specialists at the time focused narrowly on the site of the tumor or cellular abnormality, neglecting the overarching questions Dr Gerson posed: How did the immune system deteriorate so profoundly that it could no longer stop the development of cancer? Could the process be halted or reversed? Dr. Gerson knew that experiments by the European surgeon Dr. J. L. Alibert in 1808 had shown that it was very difficult, if not impossible, to induce cancer by inoculating a healthy person with tumor tissue. Later other researchers theorized that the recipient's immune system created a severe inflammation that in the process destroyed the errant cancer cells and no further damage resulted. The phenomenon of a possible resistance to cancer mounted by the immune system in response to an acute infection was repeated toward the end of the 19th century in the United States, after a young surgeon, William B. Coley, while studying records of cancer patients, concluded that acute infections might eradicate neoplastic tumors. He developed an infectious brew known later as "Coley's toxins," and variants on it have, over the years, resulted in some surprising cancer cures. This microbial-injection tactic in treating cancer is now usually known as mixed bacterial vaccine, or MBV. Dr. Gerson's own observation in treating disease showed that patients undergoing his strict dietary regimen would begin experiencing a "healing reaction," involving a fever, rapid increase in leukocytes (white blood cells) and an overall feeling of malaise. This health state was actually promising, because it indicated that the immune system had become revitalized and was now working to destroy potentially harmful cells in the body, whether these were invasive and infectious ones (such as bacteria or viruses), allergens that could induce detrimental immune reactions, or the body's own cells that were abnormal and defective, as in cancer.

Dr. Gerson now took great interest in reading whatever was written about the immune system, whose complexities were beginning to be analyzed by research scientists. He believed that the biochemistry and biophysiology of cancer were connected with immune dysfunction or failure and with adverse aspects of diet. He also suspected that liver debility and the sodium/potassium balance might be involved with the inception of cancer, thus indicating routes toward its possible eradication.

Another area of cancer research that intrigued Dr. Gerson was the biochemistry of the blood. For instance, one paper he read had noted that the higher the blood cholesterol level was in cancer patients prior to surgery, the more quickly they died. He read this article with a shock of recognition, recalling the Armenian woman in Paris with breast cancer who had the three physicians in her family. When he had acceded to the demands of the other doctors and given her egg yolks, her tumor immediately started to grow. This process had been repeated: three times he had allowed the patient to be given fats, meat and egg yolk, and three times the cancer had resumed until these food substances were withdrawn. Egg yolk is very high in cholesterol. He also remembered Frau Schmidt in Bielefeld, whose anti-Semitic husband had caused him to terminate her treatment. Dr. Gerson had been about to give the woman egg yolk — just as he did to fatten up his tuberculosis patients, with no ill effects. The fact that he had stopped treating the woman before putting her on egg yolks had probably saved her life!

Dr Gerson continued to question what caused cancer. Evidence was mounting that some cancers might be caused by viruses or by some special susceptibility coming from defective genes passed from parent to child. Then there were already identified environmental hazards. Dr. Gerson knew well that people who had worked with radioactive substances, such as radium, and with X-rays, especially using minimal protection, were far more likely than the general population to suffer from particular cancers, such as skin cancer, leukemia and bone sarcoma. He was also aware that epidemiological studies were proving that the incidence of certain cancers, as of the lungs and liver, greatly increased in occupations that involved sustained or heavy exposures to substances such as lead, asbestos, radon gas, benzene and carbon tetrachloride. The organ involved in cleansing the body of these toxic substances was the liver.

The Toxic Liver

While he explored the medical literature on cancer, Dr. Gerson maintained his practice, taking in more and more patients suffering from terminal cancer. A number of his patients recovered, but some died earlier than normally would be expected in cancer progression — which in itself was baffling. He was administering treatment he knew to be healing, yet somehow it had seemingly accelerated their demise As Gerson often did in terminal cases, he had autopsies performed. The results of these postmortem examinations revealed that the patients had died of *coma hepaticum*, or hepatic (liver) coma — their livers had simply ceased working. Postmortem examinations revealed that the livers were not only badly deteriorated, as he had expected from his previous dissections of cancerous cadavers, but they were also overwhelmed by an extra load of toxins expelled from the rest of the body.

Dr. Gerson was aware that the metabolism of cancer cells produces toxic byproducts, and these are added to the customary noxious substances the body accumulates during normal metabolism, to detoxify and then eliminate. He recognized that as his dietary therapy began to stimulate immune function, the cancer cells in tumors were actually being rapidly killed. Apparently the bodies of patients with cancer had become so deficient in essential nutrients that their normal immune system "policing" functions could no longer prevent the formation and proliferation of abnormal cells. But now, when the micronutrients, minerals and plant enzymes he was giving the patients entered the body and bloodstream, the immune system was revived and undesirable chemical imbalances were also being corrected, so that necrotic tumor cells and accumulated poisons were released into the bloodstream, where they would be transported to the liver for processing and then expulsion. The liver, the organ with the primary job of cleansing the blood of toxic substances formed in metabolism or absorbed during digestion and inhalation, was simply overtaxed by the amount of poison suddenly dumped onto it. Its multiple basic functions came to a halt, causing death.

Dr. Gerson theorized that these cancer patients' bodies apparently had a far more toxic overload than those of the tuberculosis patients because they had the additional burden of dead tumor masses to eliminate. Probably the very cleanup and elimination of toxins, then, were overwhelming the liver and causing its collapse. The initial toxic buildup had caused the appearance of cancer, which was actually the disease symptom. But it did not cause the rapid death that Gerson was witnessing. It was actually the healing process itself that had killed these patients, as it was proceeding too rapidly for an already weakened liver. (Some of the most recent techniques that kill tumor tissue, such as direct ozone injection into the tumor and cell-specific cancer treatment, have to be slowed or stopped when the patient begins to exhibit toxic symptoms from the rapid absorption of the dead tumor tissue. The problem is that these tactics by themselves do not help the liver to detoxify.)

This removal by the liver of poisons from the body was highly desirable and necessary — a process that Gerson did not wish to halt. But he had not anticipated such a volume of toxins or the rapid rate at which the body was trying to get rid of them. What he was witnessing was not only the breakdown and removal of necrotic cancer tissue, but also probably the elimination of long-accumulated toxins coming from the environment and from food. The challenge now was to find a way to keep this massive self-intoxication buildup from overpowering the liver and destroying it. Since he did not want to hinder the vital detoxification process itself, he had to find a way to assist the liver in clearing itself of the toxic overload. Otherwise, many of his cancer patients in the future might actually die of the byproducts of their healing process — as seemed to have occurred in some previous cases. This was a major puzzle, since he knew of no medical means of flushing the liver of poisons quickly enough.

The Coffee Enema

One of the habits that Max Gerson had developed over the years was to place a small writing tablet and pencil on his bedside table to record ideas. Often he awoke in the middle of the night with the solution to a particularly vexing problem, but he would then be unable to remember it in the light of next morning. One morning he found the notation "Coffee enema — Göttingen" on his notepad. This was the liver detoxification method he urgently needed now for his cancer patients. Like so many other discoveries of note, this had came part by necessity, part by accident.

Max recalled how during the Great War, when the Allied Powers were trying to deprive Germany of its external sources of war material, they blockaded the Kaiser's sea lanes, successfully preventing imported oil, rubber, ores and other vital supplies used in conducting the war from reaching German factories. This blockade prevented morphine, at the time the most effective and commonly used analgesic, from reaching Germany as well. Only a small amount of morphine was available for each surgery, but there was not enough to relieve patients of postoperative pain. With tens of thousands of battle casualties being operated upon daily, the nurses at the front lines and in military hospitals were desperate for any means of relieving the agonies of their recuperating charges.

The suffering was so great that at times nothing seemed too strange to try. In some cases, the surgeons ordered enemas for the patients. The most readily available and aseptic material available for this purpose was the ever-present coffee that the overworked surgeons drank. Now and then a large pot of coffee was left over, and the nurses poured the now tepid coffee into the enema buckets. To their amazement, the soldiers reported tremendous pain relief from these coffee enemas. Though they had no idea of why this procedure helped, the nurses — practical people who wanted results, not theories — were grateful that they had at least found *something* to relieve their patients' suffering. The technique spread quickly throughout the post-op wards. Soon, the coffee enema was the German Army's treatment of choice for reducing postoperative pain.

After the war was over, Professors Meyer and Huebner of the University of Göttingen were curious about the analgesic effect of these coffee enemas. They set up a series of animal experiments that revealed the connection. When coffee was given rectally, the hemorrhoidal vein in the colon absorbed the caffeine in solution and transported it to the liver through the portal venous system. On arriving at the liver, the caffeine stimulated the opening of the bile ducts to increase the flow of bile, which removes toxins from the liver and deposits them in the small intestine, for eventual elimination in the feces. The unburdened liver is then free to remove more toxins from the bloodstream — one of the organ's most crucial normal functions. The toxins, after having been flushed from the liver into the upper intestinal tract, have some 10 meters more to travel before they exit the body. While traversing that long distance, unfortunately they can be largely reabsorbed by the natural processes of the gut. Therefore, when a patient's large tumor load is being released into the bloodstream, the correspondingly large amount of toxicity present needs to be rapidly moved along and out with the feces, to prevent it from being recycled through the liver.

The German researchers had also discovered that any toxins in the bloodstream irritated the nerve endings in the body, especially those in tissues that were damaged.

Swelling, cell deterioration and nerve irritation all act together, thus causing pain. But pain is quite diffuse when the cause is toxicity. Removing the toxins from the blood through administering coffee enemas therefore removed the source of the pain, rather than simply blocking the pain impulses from reaching or registering with the brain, as did most analgesics. Strangely, drinking coffee did *not* have the same beneficial effect, and in fact was forbidden in the Gerson diet except under extraordinary circumstances, as when used as a needed stimulant or cathartic.

Max Gerson had been struck by these findings about coffee enemas when he had read the research article some years earlier. Here was a powerful means of assisting the liver by rapidly flushing out its toxic contents, at the same time diminishing pain. He had first used enemas at Ville D'Avray, where the patients would jocularly refer to the nurses who brought them as *les pompiers* (the fire brigade). The enemas were a regular but not a central part of the tuberculosis therapy. In that period, distilled water with caffeine drops added, not brewed coffee, was used. Now, instead of using caffeine drops, he prescribed brewed coffee since it contained the requisite substance without having to be refined and concentrated. This may have made a difference in the degree of relief or healing. Today, we know that many other beneficial substances in coffee are not present in the water/caffeine combination. For instance, potassium, kahweol and cafestol all play important and therapeutic roles in detoxification.

At first, Dr. Gerson administered two or three enemas daily, which eliminated the problem of hepatic coma. He could see under close observation, however, that the effects of the enemas often faded before the next scheduled treatment, so he gradually increased the frequency of enemas for his cancer patients to five a day—one every four hours, starting at 6 a.m. When he started using them with his cancer patients, Dr. Gerson found that the coffee enemas assisted considerably in both discharging the toxins accumulating in the liver and alleviating pain. Sometimes patients did not get enough relief even with an enema every four hours. For these patients Dr. Gerson temporarily increased the frequency to every two hours. He noticed that when the patients, especially those who were absorbing large tumor masses, woke after eight hours of uninterrupted sleep, they were sometimes dazed and semiconscious in the morning. It had been too long since their last enema, and they were starting to go into hepatic coma. He required these patients to wake in the middle of the night for an enema.

Once Dr. Gerson was convinced that no harm would come of it, he urged his patients to do a treatment whenever they felt toxic—a feeling that they quickly came to recognize as irritable, depressed, achey, dopey, slow or low-energy. During some healing-reaction periods, patients were known to take coffee enemas round the clock for stretches of 24 to 36 hours at a time. These measures were required to keep the patients from poisoning themselves with the products of their own healing process.

When even the coffee enemas failed to keep up with the rapid dumping of toxins into the bloodstream, Dr. Gerson began to use castor oil as well. Castor oil also stimulates bile flow, helping the liver to clear its toxic load. He introduced the "castor oil day" to the treatment regimen. Every other day, patients in the early stages of the treatment were given oral castor oil before their first coffee enema of the day. After five hours, when the castor oil had reached the lower intestines, a castor oil and coffee enema was given. This one-two punch flushed the intestinal tract powerfully and rapidly, removing enormous amounts of toxic mass. By lunch time, patients were ravenous, because the digestive enzymes were restored to normal levels. An alternative substance often used in enemas in Gerson therapy was, and still is, an infusion made from the chamomile herb.

Dr. Gerson also began using the coffee enema to replace morphine as a pain killer. He could see that there was a basic contradiction in doing his best to detoxify the patient on one hand while giving highly toxic narcotics on the other. From then on, he used the coffee enemas as pain relief almost exclusively — with stunning effects. Patients who had been on frequent morphine injections were often free of pain in a few days, even without the morphine. Because the entire volume of blood in the human body is filtered through the liver approximately every three minutes, the blood can be quickly cleared of toxins, giving the patient rapid and fundamental pain relief by removing the cause of the pain rather than temporarily masking it with morphine or other toxic drugs.

Protecting and Regenerating the Liver

With his new understanding of the importance of liver protection, Dr. Gerson had a powerful basis from which to treat *all* degenerative diseases. He realized that a healthy liver, the seat of all the body's biochemical functions, has vastly more capacity than it is normally called upon to use. A partially functioning liver can keep a person virtually symptom-free, even if down to 30% of its full capacity. If we are born with a fully functioning liver, we can spend years drawing down the treasure of our liver's ability to keep us healthy before we notice that there is a problem — as happens with some forms of viral hepatitis. Thus, the majority of the population blithely ignores the probable ill effects of some of the food they eat because there are no *immediate* effects. The process of liver destruction is slow but constant in most people, unless they contract a serious liver infection or ingest a potent poison, such as poisonous mushrooms or a significant amount of the deadly aflatoxin B in moldy peanuts or grains (which has been proven to initiate liver cancer).

Rebuilding the liver is less difficult than one might imagine, since liver cells are completely regenerated every six weeks. Dr. Gerson calculated that it took between 12 and 15 generations of new cells to repair and rebuild a severely damaged liver.

Thus he calculated that a cancer patient needed to remain on the therapy for 12 times six weeks, 72 weeks, or about a year and a half. (With today's more micronutrient-deficient and toxin-contaminated soil, water and food, and the increased use of drugs, antibiotics and hormones, Gerson patients now require closer to two years for the same liver healing to take place, longer yet if they have been treated with chemotherapy.) That is a long haul, demanding dedication and hard work from patients and their families. The progress is not always steady, but comes in fits and starts, and it is easy to become discouraged — as many of Dr. Gerson's patients did. But he reassured them that perseverance usually paid off in recovery, often even for far-advanced cases. It always resulted in a better quality of life during the treatment, even for those patients who ultimately failed to survive.

In this period Dr. Gerson was also using calf liver juice, crude liver injections and other substances, such as lecithin, derived from the livers of young animals, to boost the detoxifying and immune-enhancing functions of failing livers in patients with cancer and other degenerative diseases. (Because of past problems with contaminated raw liver, the use of liver juice has had to be discontinued in Gerson therapy.) He found that regular doses of niacin (vitamin B_3) had a liver-supportive effect.

An Organic Diet

In keeping with his discovery of the need to detoxify and regenerate the liver, Dr. Gerson returned attention to the quality of the food his patients were consuming,. From the earliest years of his medical training, he had been interested in ingredients in the normal diet, such as sodium chloride (table salt) or fat, that could have deleterious effects on their consumers — whether individuals hypersensitive or allergic to certain substances, or a general population that favored certain types of foods. He also was intrigued with the apparent differences in micronutrient content among different forms of a particular food, especially in produce — fruits and vegetables — and grew concerned about their implications to health. His failed experiments in Kassel, when attempting to preserve the therapeutic value of his fresh-pressed juices, were valuable at least in showing that ingredients crucial to the healing process had been transformed, depleted or lost during the process of handling them. Since deficiencies can cause a wide range of degenerative diseases, he reasoned that his therapy should be effective against many of these ailments.

Dr. Gerson had long considered the degree to which the different cooking and food-preserving techniques depleted or completely destroyed micronutrients. He studied the elaborate charts that the U.S. Department of Agriculture and other agencies assembled for the purpose of comparing different types of foods, such as the grains, dairy products, animal flesh (meat, poultry, fish), vegetables and fruits (including their raw and cooked forms). The charts gave the widely varying food values for protein, carbohydrate, fat, mineral and vitamin contents.

Dr. Gerson also conducted his own tests, working closely with biochemist Rudolf Keller, frequently trying new additions to patients' diets so he could observe the possible benefits or drawbacks from one or another particular dietary element. Some substances appeared to be excellent additions; others seemed to be neutral in value. And sometimes his observations of patients' negative responses led him to conclude that the food should be restricted or even banned from the Gerson therapeutic diet. Some types of fruits and vegetables were favored over others. Based on either his close observations of patients' responses to them or on research from other sources, Dr. Gerson banned a few vegetables and fruits from his prescribed menus because of observed adverse effects on patients' digestion and metabolism —mushrooms, dried beans, soybeans, avocados, berries, pineapple, for example. He also declared that some fruits should be eaten in a stewed form, not raw. To this list of prohibited foods, he added alcoholic beverages in any form; coffee and regular tea; commercial soda drinks; most spices; chocolate; refined flour and sugar. For perfectly healthy persons, an occasional indulgence was considered permissible, if not desirable, but to be consumed in utter moderation.

Dr. Gerson insisted that patients and their caregivers should *only* purchase for use food known to be untainted by chemicals, an edict that added to the difficulties of following his diet. Max Gerson was a very early advocate of "organic foods," which in cities were usually only available in small health-food stores; in the countryside it might still be possible to locate produce that had not been sprayed or treated with pesticides and fungicides, or grown using the chemical fertilizers commonly used in growing crops. If denatured, processed and refined foods were causing nutritional deficiencies, the reason the Gerson diet's fresh juices and plentiful foods helped patients was due to their ability to replenish the body's depleted reserves and reactivate the immune system and essential organs. But there was also the major problem of toxicity that inevitably came from foods in the modern diet, in which food coloring, chemical preservatives, salt and all forms of sodium (as in baking soda and powder), artificial sweeteners and other substances are added with little regard for their effect, positive or negative, on the human body.

Thus Dr. Gerson believed that the combination of two adverse factors, nutritional deficiency and toxicity, is the root cause of *all* the diseases that can be cured using his dietary and detoxification methods. Many of the foods people generally ate were not just empty of nutrients, but they had also been severely poisoned during the processing, storage and preserving operations. To maintain or regain their health, people had to take extraordinary — indeed revolutionary — measures to reform the way they regularly ate.

The more Dr. Gerson developed this theme, the more powerful the implications of his therapeutic approach became. In that postwar time period, much more had become known about the minerals' functions in the body, and about the various vitamins and their crucial function as coenzymes or cofactors. Without their constant presence in tissue and fluids, different enzymes and enzyme systems essential in initiating and carrying out a vast number of intricate digestive, physiological and metabolic tasks to take place in the body became disabled, defective, even defunct. Also, it was apparent that as the body aged, the gastrointestinal tract was less capable of absorbing needed micronutrients, and some intricate enzyme-producing systems simply shut down, causing food allergies and intolerances.

What was not known but had begun to be suspected by nutritional biochemists and dietitians was the possibility that plant foods contained some compounds that could not be classified as vitamins or minerals, or even active plant enzymes (which Dr. Gerson believed could be consumed best in freshly pressed juice but also in raw plant foods). Over time, discoveries were made of the various "phytochemicals"(special types of biochemical constituents in plant foods such as the bioflavonoids, polyphenols, carotenoids, sulforophanes whose identities and biophysical actions were exactly analyzed and delineated after Dr. Gerson's time. Abundant research in recent years, in laboratories as well as in clinical and epidemiological studies, has demonstrated that specific phytochemicals often have potent preventive and curative properties in specific health conditions. These compounds exist in plants not to benefit human health, of course, but as defense mechanisms against predators, aids in photosynthesis or protection from sunburn, hormones and reproductive inducements (as with aromatic or color attractants for pollinators).

A Case History

By the mid 1940s Dr. Max Gerson was accumulating an impressive group of recovering and apparently fully recovered cancer patients. He routinely kept detailed files on his patients, making technical notes during and after each contact, obtaining reports on their histories directly from physicians, hospitals and laboratories. In various cancers he ordered X-rays taken before his treatment regimen was undertaken, then at different stages of recovery. Thus he preserved valuable records of the effects of his therapy on individual cases.

Among Dr. Gerson's patients was a woman named Beatrice Sharpe, who lived on Long Island in New York. She had undergone a number of cancer treatments before she came under his care, but all of them had proved futile and even damaging. Her trouble had begun six years earlier, when it was found that she had a cancerous tumor on her left breast. It was removed in a mastectomy operation in September at the St. Francis Hospital in Jersey City. The discharge report stated:

The above named was admitted to this institution 9/19/40 for a mass in the left breast. An X-ray report was taken 9/19/40 of ribs and dorsal spine: Examination of the ribs and dorsal spine did not reveal any evidence of bone metastases.

Preoperative diagnosis and Postoperative diagnosis — carcinoma of left breast; Hard irregular mass in left breast, left of nipple mid-plane; skin hard over the mass — underlying mass attached to the skin.

Pathological examination — <u>Micro</u>: Sections taken thru the tumor area are infiltrated by intact skin. The underlying areolar tissue is fibrous and contains numerous groups of small papillary cells which are fairly uniform and somewhat hyperchromatic. There is a moderately active scirrhous process throughout the breast accompanied by a moderate degree of inflammatory reaction. The remainder of the breast tissue is similarly fibrous and diffusely infiltrated by tumor growth.

Sections of axillary lymph nodes are enveloped by a diffuse capsule. Most of the lymphatics are filled with tumor emboli. There is widespread tumor metastases throughout.

Diagnosis: Duct cell carcinoma. Grade IV, scirrhous type with metastases to axillary lymph nodes.

Patient discharged in good condition, 10/16/40; Wound cleaned and well healed.

A year later, the patient experienced a tumor recurrence, and she was sent to the Memorial Hospital in New York City for X-ray treatments to subdue the cancerous lesions that were appearing elsewhere, which was scarcely unexpected, given the prior evidence of metastases. Three series of radiation treatments over several years still hadn't solved the problem. As Beatrice recalled at this stage in her treatment, "they told me I couldn't take any more treatments, and that was all they could do for me. I heard of Dr. Gerson through a chiropractor. He gave me Dr. Gerson's name and I thought I had nothing to lose. My head was stiff. I could not move my neck."

At Dr. Gerson's request, Memorial Hospital forwarded to him this new patient's records of treatment given there:

Admitted: To O.P.D. September 8, 1941. Discharged.
Diagnosis: Recurrent Inoperable Carcinoma of left breast.
Remarks: Patient first examined in Breast Clinic on September 8, 1941, at which time it was noted that she had no local recurrence but had bulky left supraclavicular mass. This was treated with radium element pack in September, 1941, patient having received 60,000 mghrs — 8,000 mghrs having been given every other day, with excellent regression of mass. Node discovered in left cervical region in September, 1942. This was also treated with radium element pack for a total of 64,000 mghrs with complete regression of disease.

Disease remained quiescent until July, 1943, when patient developed multiple skin nodules over left chest wall in region of scar and medial to it. Low voltage X-ray therapy given to these regions, patient having received 1,500 r (500 r X 3) to left chest wall anterior and left chest wall lateral. At completion of this cycle, two additional treatments (400 r X 2) were given to left chest wall anterior, remained under control until July, 1944, when it was noted coming active as well as the mass in the cervical area. It was felt that these areas could not be treated because of proximity to previously irradiated skin.

Dr. Gerson's own treatment record stated:

On July 24, 1944, the patient was first seen by us. She didn't complain much, there was no loss of weight, no pain, she had a good appetite, slept well, but the turning of her head was painful at this time and she was able to lift it with difficulty. There was at the base of the left sternocleidomastoidaeus a hard tumor in the supraclavicular region, attached to the underlying tissue, approximately 10 x 10 x 4 cm in size. A smaller irregular hard enlarged gland was felt at the upper end of the left sternocleidomastoidaeus. The skin above and around the tumor first mentioned was red, very thin and hypersensitive. In the left infraclavicular region there were multiple hard skin nodules, the majority as large as split peas, some a little larger and some a little smaller, as well as a few nodules of similar size in the right infraclavicular area. At this time she was started on the combined low salt, low fat, high potassium diet and liver therapy.

When seen again after five weeks, the patient reported that the tumor had apparently disappeared slowly within three to four weeks. The smaller gland, however, was still present, though it decreased in size markedly in two to three months, at which time the patient was able to move her head freely and without pain. Urine and blood examinations were normal. The patient stated that she never missed a day's work. Her weight remained stationary between 116 to 118 pounds, and no fever was observed at any time.

Physical examination on May 5, 1945 revealed the following: all swelling of the hard tumor of the left sternocleidomastoidaeus had disappeared and the tumor itself was no longer palpable; all but two of the multiple skin nodules in the infraclavicular area were no longer visible within the two apparently receding. The skin was no longer red, but had fine red lines, nor sensitive any longer, was movable and thicker. The heart was normal. The lungs did not show dullness nor any abnormality in breathing. The left sternocleido muscle, formerly as hard as stone, was definitely softer and more easily movable.

The patient's general condition remained good.

In July of 1946 Beatrice Sharpe volunteered to appear in person before a Senate subcommittee and talk about her experiences in receiving cancer treatments from Dr. Max Gerson. During her testimony, Dr. Gerson showed contrasting X-rays of her thoracic area taken before and after her undertaking his dietary and detoxification therapy. When asked by the senators whether she attributed her recovery entirely to the treatment that she had received from Dr. Gerson, Mrs. Sharpe simply replied, "Oh, absolutely."

And as Dr. Max Gerson commented at the time about metastatic cases such as this one: "It is known in medicine that they cannot be influenced." But with this cancer case and a growing number of others he had certainly showed that his therapy could do this very thing: reduce, even eliminate, metastasized cancer cells that had grown into tumors.

Surely the medical community would be interested in that phenomenon, he thought.

~13~
A Growing Cancer Practice
(1945–1946)

Credibility

B y the mid 1940s, Dr. Gerson was gaining a reputation among cancer sufferers for being able to reverse cancer progression; in fact, about 90 percent of his patient population consisted of people who had been diagnosed with cancer and classified as terminal. Dr. Gerson's patient load grew by word of mouth, even though other physicians ridiculed and ostracized him due to his "bizarre" dietary methods. As Gerson later wrote to Albert Schweitzer: "If a cancer patient comes into my care, sent home from a large hospital to die, and I heal him after the orthodox methods failed, then disfavor and enmity [from my colleagues] increase." While many physicians of repute in Europe, Asia and the United States had duplicated Gerson's success in the dietary treatment of tuberculosis and other diseases during the 1920s and '30s, publishing their results in the most respected medical journals of the time, these endorsements had failed to impress most of Dr. Gerson's American peers. Doctors refused to even consider trying out Gerson's techniques for treating TB, despite hundreds of published clinical confirmations of his therapeutic protocols. Then when they heard that he was using dietary means, with the coffee-enema tactic added, on patients with cancer, this regimen of his seemed even more peculiar to them, even laughable or outrageous. ("How do you take your coffee enema? Black, or with cream or sugar?" was a typical sardonic joke among doctors.) Some physicians told their patients when asked for a referral to Dr. Gerson that "He is terribly expensive. He charges $2,000 for the first visit, and thousands for his treatment." Patients desperate enough to come to Dr. Gerson anyway often found that their first office visit, involving his taking a detailed history and giving a thorough examination, cost a moderate $25, or even less. Remaining the same kind-hearted doctor he had been during his years as a young physician in Germany, Max sometimes treated at a considerably reduced price, or even free, patients who could not afford to pay his basic fee for a consultation, examination or treatment session. And he might lend them money or even cover the cost of their transportation to and from his office.

Max Gerson must have been puzzled by this response from his American peers, especially since his work had been well-received over a decade ago by European and American medical bodies and journals. By this time, he had published several dozen articles in the peer-reviewed literature, his first one in 1910; by the late 1920s he had written numerous papers and a book about his therapeutic diet. The results of his dietary cure for *lupus vulgaris* and other forms of tuberculosis were confirmed in scores of other articles written by other researchers and physicians. A number of respectable American medical journals had positively appraised Gerson's methods in whole or in part. Most notable — and indeed most amazing of all in light of the subsequent behavior of the long-reigning editor of this medical journal as well as the powerful organization behind it — had been the publication in July 1929 of a favorable article on the Gerson therapy in *Journal of the American Medical Association* (JAMA for short) — as it name implies, the official voice of the American Medical Association (AMA). Dr. Gerson was credited for "the curative value of a base-forming dietary low in sodium chloride, protein and carbohydrate, and rich in fats and vitamins" for treating tuberculosis:

> Recent studies from Sauerbruch's surgical clinic in Munich urge the curative value of a base-forming dietary low in sodium chloride, protein and carbohydrate, and rich in fats and vitamins. This regimen, devised empirically by Gerson, is particularly worthy of critical consideration, coming as it does from a clinic which made distinctive contribution to thoracic surgery in tuberculosis....
>
> One of us [E.M.] has been privileged under the auspices of Mr. August Heckscher to visit Sauerbruch's and Gerson's clinic and to observe the dietary methods applied to their tuberculous patients in pavilion Y at the Munich clinic and at Bielefeld, Germany. Definite healing was observed in advanced cases of lupus vulgaris on the face and mucous membranes that had previously been resistant to all other accepted forms of treatment....
>
> This visit and observation of cases stimulated sufficient interest on our part to lead us to subject a group of patients at Saranac Lake (NY) to the diet. ... Thirty patients with far advanced pulmonary tuberculosis were selected who had previously undergone all of the accepted therapies for two or three years but had failed to respond. Each patient was given a complete study, including physical examination, roentgenograms of the lungs and intestine, and blood and urine studies before and after the six months period of investigation....

The group studied showed a substantial gain in weight which it had been impossible to attain by previous procedures. Many of the disturbances, which had persisted on other diets, cleared up rapidly with this regimen. The diet was well tolerated except in two instances. It was effective in diminishing fatigue and induced a sense of well-being. . . . Physical and roentgen examinations of the chest showed definite clearing in about one third of the cases.

In *The Nebraska State Medical Journal*, March 1929, Dr. Gerson was likewise acknowledged for his treatment:

It may be stated further that the Gerson diet has become in the Lincoln General Hospital almost the routine medical management of tuberculosis by members of staff. Dr. J. M. Mayhew, chief of staff and head of the Department of Internal Medicine, and others in the department, report very favorably on it. . . . The consensus of opinion is that the Gerson diet distinctly favors improvement in tuberculosis.

Again in the U.S. *Veterans' Bureau Medical Bulletin*, January 1930, Dr. Gerson was acknowledged :

In this country, C. Emerson of Lincoln, Nebraska, has used the Gerson therapy in a number of cases of pulmonary tuberculosis with very favorable results. . . . Both in the operative and nonoperative cases of pulmonary tuberculosis, this dietetic regimen has proven very satisfactory."

The American Review of Tuberculosis, May 1931, reported:

Considering the fact that 82 percent of our pulmonary cases had far-advanced tuberculosis, with serious complications in many instances, we feel that the beneficial results found justify the further application of the Sauerbruch-Herrmannsdorfer-Gerson diet in the treatment of tuberculosis.

Then in the *Proceedings of the Staff Meetings of the Mayo Clinic*, February 10, 1932:

It must be conceded that good clinical results have been obtained by the Gerson diet.

After he had established a successful private practice in America, Dr. Gerson began writing articles in English that described his techniques and results and in using dietary therapy to treat cancer and diabetes, rheumatoid arthritis and tuberculosis, heart disease and stroke, submitting them to peer-reviewed medical journals across the country. In 1941 Gerson's "Feeding the German Army" was published in the *New York State Journal of Medicine*, though it had been previously declined by the *Journal of the American Medical Association*, as having insufficient interest for the medical profession.

Two years later, "Some Aspects of the Problem of Fatigue" appeared in *The Medical Record, New York*. And in 1945 the *Review of Gastroenterology* published "Dietary Considerations in Malignant Neoplastic Disease" after it, too, had been rejected earlier by JAMA. Gerson rightly figured that editors of a journal directed at specialists of the digestive apparatus might be more responsive than JAMA. The article was subtitled "A Preliminary Report" because clearly Max Gerson was going to have a great deal more to say about his special therapy. He gave essential information about the Gerson diet, as he had modified it for the purpose of treating cancer patients. But before providing details, he wrote in his introduction to physicians:

> It is a fact that many patients with malignancy are treated by surgery and/or irradiation for the malignancy without systematic treatment of the patient as a whole. Among many things that can be done for patients with malignancy to build them up physically and maintain comparative physical well-being along with a good mental outlook is attention to the diet.
>
> In the consideration of diet various subdivisions may be made: (1) Can the origin of cancer be influenced by diet? (2) Can the course of a cancer already established be specifically influenced? (3) Can diet influence the patient as a whole favorably so that the consequences of malignancy can be staved off even temporarily or so that the patient can be rendered fit for further treatment?
>
> With the first of these subdivisions we have nothing to say, nor do we feel that there is as yet, conclusive evidence on the second in our work, but on the third we shall concentrate and give a regime which has proved satisfactory in many cases as a supportive measure.
>
> A modification of the low salt and low fat but high potassium diet originally used about twenty years ago to control skin tuberculosis (Gerson, Sauerbruch and others) has come to be known as the Gerson diet. We have now used it in a large number of cases of malignancy and a preliminary report is the purpose of this communication.

The tone of Gerson's statements was measured. He did not making claims for permanently curing patients, though the 10 case history abstracts at the end of the article provided a promising aspect. He left a door open for questions and rebuttals, or at least for further research and clinical application by others, when he stated in his summary:

> In all of these patients, while no actual cure has occurred, nevertheless improvement was manifested not only in general bodily health but also in many cases the tumors themselves diminished in size. It is possible, as stated, to marshal evidence on both sides of the question of the efficacy of the sodium-poor, potassium-rich diet. Theoretical considerations lead into many directions

but there is lacking conclusive evidence which will settle many of the moot questions.

This communication is therefore offered to again emphasize that (a) intelligent general care of the cancer patient often produces marked amelioration of symptoms and improved general health even to the point of being able to resume work, and (b) that the high-potassium, low-sodium, fatless diet combined with liver therapy tends to inhibit the rate of growth of malignancies and in some cases even to cause the individual nodules and metastases to become smaller.

To Gerson's disappointment, however, most articles he had written since his arrival in the United States were rejected by the journals to which they were submitted. The rejection letters were polite but firm:

New York State Journal of Medicine, February 9, 1943: "I regret to inform you that the [Journal] is unable to avail itself of your article entitled 'Cancer: A Deficiency Disease' for publication."

Medical Record, December 7, 1944: "We are returning, herewith, your paper on 'Dietetic Treatment of Malignant Tumors' as we cannot see our way clear to publish it. I would suggest that you send it to one of the journals devoted to the subject of cancer, as it is more in their field than in ours."

The Ohio State Medical Journal, June 18, 1947: "I have enjoyed reading your manuscript entitled 'An Outline of the Mineral Metabolism Theory in Malignancies.' Unfortunately, The Journal is not designed to present original works of this sort ….Our function is to refresh and bring up-to-date the minds of the physicians in Ohio in matters already established."

Despite these rejections, Dr. Gerson persisted in his desire to share his clinical findings. He began sending some articles, written in his native language, to European medical journals, where they were published readily. After their publication, he had the articles translated from German into English and reprinted at his own expense, so that he could send them to physicians in the United States who had inquired about his work or to ones he believed should be interested in it. In December 1945, Dr. Gerson sent five copies of the translated papers directly to Dr. Morris Fishbein at the Journal of the American Medical Association. Fishbein never acknowledged receipt of these articles. He would become Dr. Gerson's most influential adversary in years to come.

And despite this tepid response to his articles by the American medical establishment some doctors were ready to champion Dr. Gerson's work. Heinrich F. Wolf, M.D., an immigrant himself, shared his Manhattan office with Max Gerson. They were not just co-tenants. "The friendship was very precious to both of them, pleasant

and harmonious," Mrs. Gerson recorded in her memoir. In July 1946 Dr Wolf recorded his observations of the effectiveness of Dr. Gerson's treatment his testimony to a
Senate subcommittee investigating Dr. Gerson:

> For the last seven years I have shared the same office with Dr. Max Gerson,
> and in that time I have had the opportunity, not only to observe nearly all the
> cases treated by Dr. Gerson with his diet, but I have used the latter on my own
> patients.
>
> The results in some chronic skin diseases, in some types of heart diseases and
> in some dangerous cases of high blood pressure, were astonishing. In some of my
> patients the blood pressure that had been up to 170 and 180, went down to 130 per-
> manently, and the symptoms of headaches and dizziness disappeared entirely.
>
> During the last three or four years, since Dr. Gerson paid particular atten-
> tion to the effect of his dietary regimen on benign and malignant tumors, I
> observed practically all of the tumor cases which he treated. I observed and
> supervised their X rays and saw the patients at nearly every visit.
>
> One of the first cases of malignant tumors was a Mr. Baldry who, after sur-
> gical removal of a mixed tumor of the left side of the neck, developed a
> metastatic tumor of the right lung which was diagnosed by X ray and broncho-
> scope. During this treatment, the tumor disappeared and there was no recur-
> rence when we last heard from the patient about one year ago.
>
> In 1942, I saw one of his patients who had been operated on for cancer of
> the tonsils and subsequently treated by radium and X ray which resulted in an
> X-ray ulcer about two inches in diameter. There were several metastases in the
> glands of the neck. Under the dietary treatment the ulcer healed, and the
> glands became very much smaller. After a year the patient left New York. Later
> I read in the papers that the patient died, two months ago.
>
> Since then I have observed many cases of primary and metastatic cancer. I
> saw two patients, each with a colostomy which had been performed because
> the cancer had completely obstructed the lumen of the sigmoid and rectum. I
> verified this personally by barium enemas carried out through the colostomy
> opening and the rectum. In one case the colostomy wound closed, and normal
> passage of the bowels was established. The other patient, treated for about nine
> months, has gained weight. I had no opportunity to re-examine him as far as the
> local condition was concerned. I saw him last three weeks ago.
>
> One of my own patients whom I referred to Dr. Gerson because she had
> been suffering from cancer of the stomach for half a year is doing well. I saw
> her four weeks ago.
>
> One of Dr. Gerson's patients, who, upon a laminectomy, was found to suf-
> fer from an inoperable malignant intramedullary glioma tumor, has regained

the use of her arm which was paralyzed when I first saw her seven months ago. I saw her last two weeks ago.

Among his patients I saw four cases of malignant brain tumor, one of them metastatic. Two seem to be now perfectly well; both of the others had their failing eyesight partly restored; the progress was arrested.

I saw three women who had been operated on for breast tumors, malignant and verified by biopsy, and who had experienced a recurrence. In all three the metastatic tumors in the lymph glands disappeared, in one of them, also, a local recurrence.

There were quite a number of failures also, but they were, in my opinion, due to the fact that Dr. Gerson accepted for treatment patients who were so far gone that they were absolutely hopeless, even for the most optimistic observer.

I wish to mention that the dietary treatment is equally effective in benign tumors.

In one of two cases of goiter, the goiter disappeared. In the other the tumor shrunk to about one-third its size. In the first-mentioned case, the diagnosis of malignancy was made in the Memorial Hospital, but the method used is not accepted as reliable.

In a case of Recklinghausen, the neurofibromas in the face have practically disappeared.

In a case of myoma of the uterus of the size of a small watermelon, clearly outlined by X-ray films, the tumor has become much smaller.

This statement is not intended to give exhaustive summary of Dr. Gerson's work. It is not a copy of his records but a simple report of my personal observations for which I can vouch.

I am intentionally refraining from entering into the question of the theoretical foundation of this method but only report my personal observation of the facts.

Experiments with Potassium

Dr. Gerson had often observed that patients who had cancer, or indeed any serious degenerative disease, showed a marked deficiency of potassium in their tissues and organs. Sometimes this anomaly was matched by a surplus of potassium in their serum. High serum potassium, he knew from experience, signaled a rapid loss of potassium from its appropriate intracellular sites, indicating an ongoing disease process. At the same time, high levels of sodium — potassium's ionic antithesis and counterpart in the crucial serum/cell mineral balance — had to be rapidly reversed before the disease process could be halted.

Since many of Gerson's cancer patients were in the last stages of the disease, there was never time to waste. Removal of all sodium from the patient's internal and external environment was essential, since the smallest amount of sodium can have drastic effects on a patient with cancer. Nutrition is one means of absorbing sodium through ingesting salted foods and baked goods made with baking soda (sodium bicarbonate) or baking powder as a leavening agent. But absorption can come, too, through the oral cavity, as when using baking-soda toothpaste or gargling with salt water; also through skin contact, as when swimming in seawater or having a salt rub. A worse sodium ingestion and transdermal-absorption problem comes from sodium fluoride, used in the fluoridated water now prevalent in many city water systems with the intention of reducing dental cavities in children. This is a rather dubious tradeoff since sodium fluoride is a poison when ingested in high doses or accumulated in the body over years of drinking it in water.

To build up potassium in intracellular storage and counteract any overwhelming presence of sodium in the body, especially in tissues where it was detrimental, regularly eating foods rich in potassium, such as apples and potatoes, became crucial to the Gerson therapy. The large amounts of fruits and vegetables, particularly in juice form, already contained significant amounts of potassium, but the deficiency was usually so great that Dr. Gerson felt dietary supplementation was probably essential to restoring the proper sodium-potassium balance. He puzzled over the problem of how to increase the levels of cellular potassium safely and quickly.

As a young medical student, he had witnessed the standard experiment where a beating frog's heart was exposed to a high dose of potassium, which sent it into a fatal fibrillation. However, it was later determined that the problem came not from the potassium but from the chloride ion in potassium chloride, the mineral salt used for the experiment. Dr. Gerson certainly did not want to cause cardiac fibrillation in his already weakened patients, yet he needed to boost the potassium levels rapidly to help the healing. He undertook extensive experiments to find a potassium salt or combination of salts that would not be harmful to patients.

Dr. Gerson had learned to be a keen and cautious experimentalist and careful clinical observer. He put little stock in arcane and complex theories unless they resulted in positive results for his patients. His operative philosophy echoed Professor Kussmaul: "The result at the sickbed is decisive." This rule translated into Dr. Gerson's method for determining whether a substance was helping or hindering the healing process. He gave a patient small trial doses of a substance in question and watched the results carefully. If there was no positive result after a short time, the substance would be discontinued. Even if the result was positive, the substance would be withdrawn after a month or two, and the patient carefully observed for any changes in his condition. Only after he determined that there had been no adverse effects from the substance would it be reintroduced into the patient's regimen. Doses might be varied, or different substances tried, but always with close observation of the results.

Dr. Gerson now carefully used his methodology with different potassium compounds, attempting to find one that would boost the cellular potassium level without causing problems to the patient, particularly cardiac fibrillation. The compounds he introduced and then rejected are lost to the record, but not the number of experiments. After over 300 experiments, he settled on a combination of potassium gluconate, potassium acetate and potassium phosphate (monobasic) in equal weights, dissolved in water at an 0.1 molar concentration and added to most of the 13 daily fruit and vegetable juices. This total dosage might seem like an excessive, even dangerous daily intake of potassium to many physicians drilled in the dangers of excess potassium. In fact, many Gerson therapy patients have accidentally overdosed themselves by factors of 10 or more, yet suffered no ill effects. In the 60 years since Dr. Gerson developed the compound, no patient has suffered ill effects from this precise combination.

Of course, he avoided any potassium compound that contained the element chlorine, knowing it had been proven the malefactor in the frog experiment. Dr. Gerson's combination of three potassium salts contain no chloride ions. In the Gerson lexicon, chlorine as an element or in a compound is to be sedulously avoided, since it has been increasingly recognized as toxic to the body. People usually do not realize that it daily enters their bodies in abundance: through ingestion, especially in table salt and chlorinated water in urban water supplies; through breathing and absorption via the skin, when cleaning oneself with chlorinated tap water, using household bleaches and — far more potently — in entering swimming pools and hot tubs or spas, where chlorine is commonly used as a disinfectant. Chlorine's adverse effects on the thyroid gland are considerable, as its molecules displace those of iodine, which belong there.

A New Facility and a New Threat

Dr. Gerson had physician's hospital privileges at a few Manhattan hospitals, but applying his special dietary and detoxifying therapy properly was proving impossible in a hospital setting with a standard kitchen. Treating most patients on an outpatient basis was more effective, for they could rely on relatives and friends to assist in the produce shopping and the arduous hourly pressing of the fresh juices and frequent small, nourishing meals prepared under strict restrictions and using special cooking methods. In 1945 Gerson-referred patients began staying at a facility run by Mrs. Margaret Seeley in a classic old townhouse in Manhattan's East 60s, between 2nd and 3rd Avenues. Having been a Gerson patient herself who had recovered from pancreatic cancer, she now provided a valuable service because she believed in the Gerson therapy, understood well its requirements and was able to operate an excellent kitchen to help others with health afflictions. Some Gerson patients resided there; others came by her place daily only for their juices and meals.

Throughout the Second World War, Gerson mourned the deaths not only of the combatants, but even more so of the innocents — who are always the first and most plentiful casualties of war: the children, the mothers and, this time, millions of his fellow Jews who had disappeared into the mass burial pits and ovens at Hitler's concentration camps. Max never forgot that he had been perilously close to the hatred that killed off Europe's Jewish population, including all his brothers and sisters and most of the rest of his extended family. But for Max the most shocking event of the war did not happen until the combat in Europe had already ended.

Max's workday would end before supper with an hour of reading the newspaper. So unconcerned was he about money that he often had to ask Gretchen for a nickel so he could walk down to the newsstand on the corner and buy a paper. Reading the daily news had not always been relaxing, especially during the dark early days of the war, when blow-by-blow reports of the Nazi victories in Eastern Europe, the Low Countries, Denmark and Norway, North Africa and France, the Dunkirk debacle and the bombardment of Britain dominated the news. But at least after Pearl Harbor in December of 1941, when the United States brought its industrial might to bear and added millions of young soldiers to those of the few remaining Allies, the tide of the war began slowly turning against the Axis powers, then became decisively favorable following the D-Day landing at Normandy beach. Germany surrendered on May 8, 1945, ending Europe's long nightmare — temporarily at least, as it turned out. Allied troops in the Pacific were finally overwhelming the Japanese emperor's forces. Though Japan fought on, there was little doubt that it would only be a matter of time before the war ended.

On August 9, 1945, Dr. Gerson opened the newspaper and read the headlines. "Atom Bomb Destroys Hiroshima!" the three-inch high letters shouted. As he read the rest of the story, the color drained out of his face.

Gretchen glanced over at him. Seeing her husband in shock, she became alarmed. "What is wrong, Max? Are you all right?"

At first, he was too stunned even to speak, but eventually found his voice. "Look at this, Gretchen," Max said, holding the paper out to her. "We struggle with all our might to save lives, one at a time. You know only too well how much work it takes to pull even *one* person back from the brink of death, when we can do it at all. And in the past few days, our Army Air Force has dropped two bombs on Japanese cities that together have killed hundreds of thousands of people in the blink of an eye. Old women, schoolchildren, babies, factory workers alike: all died in seconds. I understand the necessity of it. But still, it is unthinkable."

Max put the paper down, unable to read further. The nuclear age had dawned.

~14~
Progress in Curing Cancer
(1946–1947)

The Cancer Ward at Gotham Hospital

Throughout his career, in both Europe and America, Max Gerson made devoted new friends who became good companions, correspondents, advocates and even financial supporters because he had cured them or their relatives or acquaintances of chronic conditions or life-threatening illnesses. Famed Yale economist Professor Irving Fisher often solicited support for his friend's research. Professor Fisher was on the board of directors of the Robinson Foundation, a nonprofit organization founded in 1941 by two industrial corporations, which contributed a portion of their profits to worthy causes. In charge of health education, Professor Fisher somehow persuaded the foundation's other directors to help further Dr. Gerson's work. After all, he himself had seen it in action and admired it for its simplicity and effectiveness. By 1945 it was known that one of the first antibiotic drugs, called streptomycin, was effective in treating tuberculosis cases, and more were being developed. By then, too, it had become clear to Irving Fisher that Dr. Gerson's recent and amazing success with cancer patients was the breakthrough needed to persuade the medical establishment of the value of the Gerson diet cure.

Fisher wasn't surprised to frequently encounter rude rebuffs to his efforts, as he knew well from Max's own stories. As he told it:

> When the distinguished head of a cancer hospital, after hearing of Dr. Gerson's work, asked his board, in all seriousness, if they would favor some dietetic experiments, their response was merely to laugh! One physician, in conversing with Dr. Gerson, said sententiously, "You mustn't think I'm such a fool as to imagine that what sort of food I put into my stomach will make any great difference to my health or disease."
>
> Eating is commonly regarded not as a hygienic procedure but as merely

one of the pleasures of life. Seldom are any others than seriously ill people willing to eat by prescription. And even Dr. Gerson (who has probably written more such prescriptions and succeeded better in having them followed than any other private physician who ever lived) constantly meets with resistance. Too often the patients want to compromise....

In short, physicians are almost universally prejudiced in favor of the food habits with which they are familiar and prejudiced against the idea that any changes such as Dr. Gerson prescribes ... can have any great effect toward curing hitherto incurable diseases.

But now at least, doubtless thanks to Professor Fisher's unceasing efforts, the Robinson Foundation decided to support Dr. Gerson's special cancer research. In January of 1946, directors arranged for a 20-bed ward at the Gotham Hospital in New York City to be made available to Gerson. Set aside for a group of his cancer patients, it would be devoted to what the hospital declared would be a "controlled study," involving observation of Gerson's therapy by other physicians on the Gotham staff.

Naturally, this new ward had to have its own kitchen facilities. The hospital management assigned Dr. George Miley as the administrator who would supervise the work in this special ward, and also report directly to Dr. Stanley Reimann, the head of oncology and pathology. Prior to coming to Gotham Hospital in August of 1945, Dr. Miley had been on the staff at the Hahnemann Medical College and Hospital of Philadelphia. (Samuel Hahnemann had founded the medical practice of homeopathy in Germany in the late 18th century, and Philadelphia became a center of homeopathic activity in the United States.) Miley had worked in medical research as clinical professor of pharmacology and director of the Blood Irradiation Clinic at the latter institution.

Dr. Miley had first met Dr. Gerson in 1943, when he visited his office with Dr. Charles Bailey, a well-known chest surgeon. Interested in learning about Gerson's diet therapy for tuberculosis, they talked with several of the TB patients who had made remarkable recoveries. Miley wrote this to Prof. Fisher two days afterwards:

As a result of my visit to Dr. Gerson's office I am convinced that Dr. Gerson has uncovered the fundamental basic principle which warrants a much more thorough and careful investigation than I was able to give the subject in a single day. The possibilities of the Gerson diet properly prepared and given are almost unlimited in scope.

It is my opinion that Dr. Gerson is a man of good character and unquestionable sincerity and requires the aid of a large medical center, plus an endowment to bring his subject in its proper perspective to the attention of the leading men of science and medicine in the country.

During this visit, Dr. Gerson had also mentioned the potential use of his diet in cancer — "an idea which then seemed rather fantastic to me, but no longer does," Dr. Miley said later.

At the start of the professional association, both Max and Gretchen regarded Dr. Miley as a shrewd businessman, but not a dedicated medical researcher. They realized, however, that not everyone has the same interests. Some people gravitate towards administration, even though their degrees may be in medicine or science. Every hospital activity needs a manager or supervisor, and Max Gerson of course had no desire to oversee the day-to-day operations of the nurses, the kitchen, admissions and finances. He readily agreed to Dr. Miley's participation on a coequal basis. Ethical sometimes to the point of punctiliousness, Dr. Gerson did not ask for or receive a salary from the Robinson Foundation or Gotham Hospital. Dr. Miley was already on the hospital payroll, and the hospital itself received funding for the project from the Robinson Foundation.

The Gotham Hospital setup seemed ideal for Dr. Gerson, for he could easily visit his patients there daily since his apartment was nearby. The patients were getting good results from the dietary treatment — always Gerson's goal. Furthermore, the special ward enabled him to take on some deserving patients who were financially unable to stay at Mrs. Seeley's sanatorium in the East 60s or else could not, for whatever reasons, undergo the special therapy at home.

Dr. Gerson always kept careful records of his patients, including copies of original medical reports, written by physicians or hospital staff at different stages of examination and treatments well as laboratory tests and X-rays done prior to his taking over their care and during the course of his own therapy. Nevertheless, his primary focus was on curing each patient, not on seeing them as individual 'cases' for data collection, with the aim of proving statistically the efficacy of his methodology. While such statistical proof has become a major concern in clinical studies for medical researchers seeking to qualify for funding in recent years, during the 1940s there was not the same rigid insistence on conducting double-blind or other control studies, in which neither physician nor patient knows whether the treatment course is in fact being given. Moreover, it would be difficult, if not impossible, to administer "placebos" to hide the identity of the Gerson method, and Dr Gerson was not willing to withhold his therapy, whether knowingly or unknowingly, from a seriously ill patient willing to try it. The Gotham Hospital study appeared to offer the only possible way of judging the merits of the Gerson therapy, by comparing the progression of particular types of cancer (as had been done earlier in Europe with tuberculosis) among patients undergoing the regimen with that of others who were still receiving different forms of treatment. Objective outcomes could be compared, such as survival time, shrinkage or disappearance of tumors, absence of pain, improvement in test results, remission of disease symptoms or the ability to return to a normally functioning life, whether this meant being employed at an outside job or resuming housework and child care.

Despite Dr. Gerson's satisfaction with most of the initial results of patient treatments at Gotham Hospital using his therapeutic methods, he increasingly felt uncomfortable. The atmosphere seemed chilly whenever he was there, reminding him of the years of social ostracism in Bielefeld, when his unusual ideas and treatment practices, coupled with surprising patient successes, alarmed and annoyed his medical colleagues. This atmosphere would soon spread beyond the wards of Gotham Hospital to the halls of the United States Senate.

Senate Hearings on Cancer

Among Dr. Gerson's patients was Samuel Markel of Richmond, Virginia, who had suffered from serious osteoarthritis, which had been pronounced incurable, but was healed by the Gerson therapy. In the past, he had lost his wife to cancer and now saw the promise for treating this disease in the Gerson therapy. A good friend of former Virginia Governor Harry F. Byrd, Samuel Markel used his influence bring Dr. Gerson's work to the attention of Senator Claude Pepper of Florida, who had a special interest in natinal health questions, especially the treatment of cancer.

In early 1946, Senator Pepper, intrigued by the information that he had received from Markel via Governor Byrd, wrote to Dr. Gerson and asked for his permission to send two investigators from his Senate office, a doctor and an attorney, to observe his practice in New York. Senator Pepper's investigators asked to examine records and see X-ray plates and photographs, which Dr. Gerson readily supplied. They asked to speak with and examine some of the patients themselves. Because of the amount of negative information about the Gerson therapy they had heard from other physicians, they were extraordinarily thorough. After concluding their examinations, they had a long meeting with Gerson, so that he might thoroughly explain what they had seen and answer any remaining questions. Returning to Washington, they told Senator Pepper that they were favorably impressed with Dr. Gerson's work.

Shortly thereafter, Senator Claude Pepper (D-Florida) and Congressman Matthew Neely (D-West Virginia) introduced a Congressional Bill, S. 1875; sponsored by a subcommittee of the Senate Committee on Foreign Relations, in which Senator Pepper was a powerful member, it was intended to "authorize and request the President to undertake to mobilize at some convenient place in the United States an adequate number of the world's outstanding experts, and coordinate and utilize their services in a supreme endeavor to discover means of curing and preventing cancer." The bill, if passed by both the Senate and the House of Representatives, would appropriate $100 million to fund this proposed cancer research center.

Apparently, Senator Pepper intended that a considerable portion of the cancer center's interest would be on exploring the use of Dr. Max Gerson's nutritional approach for both preventing and treating cancer. Hearings on S. 1875 were scheduled for July 1-3, 1946, and Dr. Gerson was invited to testify about his methods. He understood that several physicians would precede him, to lay the groundwork for his presentation by discussing the growing medical problem of cancer within the nation.

By now, Max Gerson was in his mid 60s — retirement age. Yet he still had so much work to accomplish. He was hopeful that by participating in the presentations in favor of S. 1875 he would be far better positioned to change the way cancer patients received treatment, not just in the United States but around the world. He carefully gathered the records of 10 of his best cancer cases as he wished to use them in demonstrating his methods and their favorable outcomes. He wrote a concluding commentary about them and arranged to have the document printed so that it could be distributed to the various subcommittee members and other interested persons. (This was long before the convenient invention of the photocopier machine.) Moreover, he invited five of these recovering patients to come to Washington, D.C., and arranged for their stay there at his own expense.

On the First of July in 1946, seated in the gallery above the Senate chambers, waiting to be called to testify on behalf of S. 1875, were Dr. Max Gerson, Mrs. Gerson, Samuel Markel, Dr. George Miley from Gotham Hospital, and five Gerson patients. After Gerson made his presentation, he planned to introduce his patients to the Pepper-Neely subcommittee members, who could then talk with them personally. They would be the first cured or recovering cancer patients ever presented to the United States Senate.

A few other physicians and other cancer-research treatment spokesmen had been scheduled to testify before Dr. Gerson. They described in detail the number and types of biomedical researchers, operating rooms, laboratories and state-of-the-art equipment needed for the proposed cancer research and treatment center— with the requisite budgets involved. Most of them also read and then submitted documents intended for scrutiny by the legislators and their aides, intended for ultimate publication by the Government Printing Office as permanent records of the hearing event. There were frequent rhetorical comparisons between the recently ended war with the Axis foes and this new medical battlefront. As a spokesman for the American Cancer Society declaimed: "When it comes to war against a particular disease, different tactics are essential. Total strength must be massed, surely and quickly. I think the men in charge should be free to 'get there first with the mostest.' That's the way our military material was assembled to fight World War II. Imagine the confusion and inadequacy of planning production for war except on the principle of 'Where can we, with a nod of course to the costs, get what is needed as quickly as possible?' — and thus save the most men from death and end the war quickly." Parallels were drawn between the wartime's urgent development of nuclear weapons in the Manhattan

Project, which had cost two billion dollars and succeeded in dropping two atomic bombs on Japan, and this new attack upon the dread disease called cancer. After all, the amount being requested by Senate Bill 1875, one hundred million dollars, was a mere drop in the bucket of government expenditures. But what triumphant victories it should bring to suffering Americans.

By the end of the first day, Gerson had not yet been called. The next day Dr. Cornelius Rhoads came forth to give his testimony. Rhoads could be said to represent a considerable portion of the medical-science community because he was dual director of New York City's Sloan-Kettering Institute and the Memorial Hospital — the first dedicated to cancer research, and the second to its treatment — as well as professor of pathology at Cornell University Medical College. He had been delegated by the National Research Council to deliver its extensive report based on the results of a survey of hundreds of noted researchers and of select panels of experts in different areas of biomedical research, who had been assembled to discuss the frontiers of cancer research. These members of the growing cancer establishment included charitable organizations such as the American Cancer Society and the National Cancer Foundation; the generous Rockefeller Foundation (the petroleum-revenue endowed Croesus that was taking such interest in developing chemotoxins for killing cancer cells, and provided ample operating funds to the well-endowed Rockefeller Institute for Medical Research in New York); and many corporations interested in supplying cancer-treatment needs that were creating and manufacturing a wide variety of pharmaceutical drugs, including injectable radioactive isotopes, or high-technology medical hardware, such as radiological equipment. There were also the off-campus research grants emanating from the National Cancer Institute, which had become a large, semi-autonomous division within the rapidly growing, federally regulated and generously funded National Institutes of Health (NIH).

But Dr. Rhoads sounded more interested in professional teamwork than in getting much money for his own endeavors:

> Unfortunately the factor of money has been so overemphasized that many have come to believe that it is the only important one. We tend to forget that money without the qualified and devoted scientific men and women, working in a proper organization, is worse than useless. Without personnel, equipment and policy based on scientific experience, only bitter disillusionment can result from an effort as extensive as the one proposed.
>
> Recall that there exist at this moment upward of 500,000 individuals who actually have cancer, and think of those who are near and dear to them who are awaiting with vital interest the course of this bill. I do not believe that we can dismiss these responsibilities lightly.

That afternoon Senator Pepper interrupted the proceedings to request that Dr. Gerson and his patients be heard. Max Gerson and his patients filed up to the witness table in the hearing room. The testimony began with a statement from Samuel Markel:

> My only interest in this matter is a humanitarian one, having lost my wife with this dreaded disease, and I feel that the least I can do is to add my voice and such funds as I am able to the eradication of cancer, and I have therefore given freely to various campaigns for research....
>
> I can readily understand that when results so fantastic [as Dr. Gerson's] are obtained that such claims can hardly be believable. My quarrel with these gentlemen is the fact that they will immediately say such things are impossible, or the doctor is a fake, without even stopping to inquire what is being done. I have had the same experience with my own doctors, who merely throw up their hands and say that anyone claiming to cure cancer is a fake....
>
> The very fact that the patients treated by Dr. Gerson are living today when they were destined to die three or four years ago, according to the statements of these good doctors who treated them, I say is a sensational result and the least that can be said for it is that Dr. Gerson has accomplished something that no one else in the medical profession has accomplished with respect to the treatment of cancer, so far as I am able to ascertain.
>
> I would hate to think that the antipathy to Dr. Gerson would be in any manner associated with the fact that his treatments are dietary and are not surgical. He does not use surgery or recommend surgery, as I understand it, unless there may be some remote cases. Therefore, if this treatment is effective, as I believe it to be, the public would be relieved of millions of dollars of surgical fees, and I repeat, I would hate to think that such possibilities should incense any of our surgeons, who after all are presumed to be humanitarians as well. Dr. Gerson has no doubt made enemies as the result of his dietary therapy, wherein he does not permit patients to smoke or to drink intoxicating liquors or to consume canned goods and other items which could materially affect trade in that respect if it became universal, and of course it was not designed for Dr. Gerson to "make friends" but rather to treat cancer as the result of the many years of his experience.
>
> I think this new approach is very important since apparently cancer research and the cancer research dollar has been traveling for many years down the same avenue of conventional orthodox research, and apparently those good scientists are unwilling to look at or give credence to anything new. In any event, the discoveries of Dr. Gerson should be carried further, as, in my humble opinion, he has unlocked the door to an avenue of approach to

this problem from which a solution will be found.

To my mind it is of outstanding importance that facilities be provided in some manner, so that Dr. Gerson may train other doctors in his technique and that hundreds of thousands may be treated rather than the limited number that he is able to personally attend. It would be a calamity if anything happened to Dr. Gerson with no one left to carry on in this particular field, and I hope that the committee will see to it that in the development of cancer research, dietary therapy will have an important part....

I want to say at the outset that I am here in favor of S. 1875. At first I was constrained to oppose that bill like a lot of other people. There was a general apathy ... a feeling that after 50 or more years, millions and millions of dollars spent, with the helpless feeling upon the part of these victims, that out of it grew nothing that they could lean on, not even a hope, and that it would just be another hundred million dollars down the same rat hole, at the cost of thousands of dollars per "rat." I feel, however, that we ought to do something.

The only assurance that I would like to see is that the commission, as constituted, would be absolutely independent, that it would be willing to do a job of research as the name implies — every avenue of research that lends promise of a solution to this problem. There should not be a closed corporation or a gentleman's club where nothing would be heard from it.

We have present here cancer victims, citizens of the United States, and I do not know who would have a greater right, Mr. Chairman, to express their opinion about the expenditures of public money for this purpose than those people. As far as I know, they are in favor of this bill, but I feel truly that research ought to be what it implies.

Since we have been here 50 people have died of cancer, while we are in this hearing. Money, as stated here, means nothing. We spent billions to destroy people, and probably we can spend a few hundred million dollars for the recapture of life. That is what this bill is designed to do, if it will do it; but I am not in favor, Mr. Chairman, of making the commission the tail to any existing kite. Let them decide what they want to do. Let them adopt their own rules. All they need to be is honest scientists and honest Americans.

Now, what bothered me was, as I said before, millions are being spent for research. We are still researching with animals, while here, an unassuming scientist in New York — and I hope the medical profession will pardon me for using the word "cure" — is curing cancer today.

Now I understand that a patient must have been free of a recurrence of disease for five years before an ethical doctor would be permitted to say the patient was "cured." Well, fortunately, nobody can take my license away, because I am an ordinary layman. I am not a scientist, I am not a doctor — and I will not cloud the results on account of six months: I say when the patient has lived 4¹/₂ years longer than the time allotted by reputable doctors, I am willing to say he was cured. At least, he has not been buried when he was designed to be by the hospitals that sent him home to die, Mr. Chairman. They were told that they could not live but a few months. That is four years ago. Something has been done for them. It has not been surgery. It has not been radium. It has not been X-ray — and those are the only three things, if my information is correct, that the millions of dollars had been spent upon. I say, if there is another avenue, a nutritional avenue — which this is — or anything else which gives promise of the cure for cancer, these research artists at least should be willing to condescend to look at it, Mr. Chairman. In this case there have been outstanding scientists, I am told, who have been told of this, and they do not even want to look at it. I do not ask them to admit that it is true. At least take a look.

Senator Pepper then began questioning Dr. Gerson and his patients. Dr. Gerson was reasoned, precise and straightforward in his testimony. He didn't try to build castles in the sky regarding how many researchers he needed or how many millions of dollars were necessary. To substantiate what he was saying, he gave each of the committee members a pamphlet entitled "Dietary Considerations in Malignant Neoplastic Disease" and his specially printed document entitled "Case History of Ten Cancer Patients: Clinical Observations, Theoretical Considerations, and Summary." And he provided an overall description of his therapy and the rationale behind it:

> The dietetic treatment, which has for many years been known as the "Gerson diet," was developed first to relieve my own severe migraine condition. Then it was successfully applied to patients with allergic conditions such as asthma, as well as diseases of the intestinal tract and the liver-pancreas apparatus. By chance a patient with *lupus vulgaris* (skin tuberculosis) was cured following the use of the diet. After this success the dietetic treatment was used in all other kinds of tuberculosis — bones, kidneys, eyes, lungs, and so forth. It, too, was highly favorable in many other chronic diseases, such as arthritis, heart disease, chronic sinusitis, chronic ulcers, including colitis, high blood pressure, psoriasis, sclerosis multiplex, and so forth. The most striking results were seen in the restoration of various kinds of liver and gall bladder diseases which could not be influenced by other methods up to the present.
>
> The great number of chronic diseases which responded to the dietetic treatment showed clearly that the human body lost part of its resistance and healing power, as it left the way of natural nutrition for generations.
>
> The fundamental damage starts with the use of artificial fertilizer for vegetables and fruits as well as for fodder. Thus, the chemically transformed vegetarian

and meat nourishment, increasing through generations, transforms the organs and functions of the human body in the wrong direction.

Another basic defect lies in the waste of excrements of the cities. Instead of returning the natural manure to the fruit-bearing soil, it is led into the rivers, killing underwater life. The natural cycle is interrupted and mankind has to suffer dearly for the violation. Life in forest and wilderness should teach us the lesson.

But we can regain the lost defense and healing power if we return as close as possible to the laws of nature as they are created. Highly concentrated for speedy reaction, they are laid down in the dietetic treatment....

As Dr. Gerson continued, he cited the results of his clinical studies:

> The treatment is ineffective in cases with less than 10 lymphocytes in the differential blood count; when the phosphorus cannot be brought back into the red blood cells and other tissues; it is also ineffective in patients with advanced liver damage, and, of course, in those who are in extremis.
>
> Since the end of January, 1946, I treat my patients in a hospital in New York, a number of them without charge, and never refuse any patients, irrespective of their condition, in order to see what this treatment can do for them. Up to the present all practical and research work in cancer, as well as other chronic diseases, including tuberculosis, was financed by myself, and I will not ask for money here. This limits the progress of the method.
>
> My experience leads me to believe that the liver is the center of the restoration process in those patients who improve strikingly. If the liver is too far destroyed, then the treatment cannot be effective.
>
> Aware of the imperfection of this as well as any other theory, I shall try, nevertheless, to explain the end results of the Gerson diet. It is condensed in three surpassing components:
>
> (1) The elimination of toxins and poisons and returning of the displaced "extracellular" Na [sodium] group, connected with toxins, poisons, edema, destructive inflammation from the tissues, tumors, and organs where it does not belong, into the serum and tissues where it belongs — gall bladder with the bile ducts, connective tissue, thyroid, stomach mucosa, kidney medulla, tumors, and so forth.
>
> (2) Bringing back the lost intracellular K [potassium] group combined with vitamins, enzymes, ferments, sugar, and so forth, into the tissues and organs where it belongs: liver, muscles, heart, brain, kidney cortex, and so forth; on this basis, iodine, ineffective before, is made effective, continuously added in new amounts.
>
> (3) Restoring the differentiation, tonus, tension, oxidation, and so forth, by activated iodine, where there were before growing tumors and metastases with dedifferentiation, loss of tension, oxidation, loss of resistance, and healing power.

As the senators first questioned Dr. Gerson and then interviewed his five patients, documents showed that all five patients had been diagnosed as "terminal" before coming to Gerson. They now willingly and ably spoke freely with the senators about their treatment. The five patients accompanying Dr. Gerson to the hearing were young Alice Hirsch, who had recovered from an inoperable spinal cord tumor diagnosed three years earlier, when she was 14 years old, which had destroyed her ability to walk, but now she was walking again; Mrs. Beatrice Sharpe, who had had metastatic breast cancer that doctors considered terminal (see Chapter 12); Mrs. Anna Hanna, a colon cancer patient with a colostomy, whose extreme abdominal problems were now resolved; Mrs. Katherine Fleming, well after a severe bout with lymphatic sarcoma and myeloma; and George Gimson, a longshoreman from New Jersey, who had come to Gerson's office in late 1945 with a growth at the base of his skull that was growing into his brain. Each of the five patients in turn talked about their bouts with cancer and their experience with Dr. Gerson's curative treatment. This is how the ensuing dialogue with Mr. Gimson was recorded in the published transcript of the hearing:

SENATOR PEPPER: Let us take the next case, here. What is your name?

MR. GIMSON: George Gimson.

SENATOR PEPPER: Where do you live?

MR. GIMSON: 729 Thirty-second Street, Union City, N.J.

SENATOR PEPPER: Dr. Gerson, tell us about Mr. Gimson.

DR. GERSON: Mr. Gimson came with a big tumor that was arrested. He was operated first when he was a soldier and was in camp.

MR. GIMSON: Fort Riley, Kansas.

DR. GERSON: And then they operated, but they could not remove the basal cell carcinoma, because it was grown up into the skull, so they sent him for deep X-ray therapy to . . . to Fitzsimmons Hospital, at Denver, Colo., for deep X-ray therapy, but there they decided that deep X-ray therapy is very dangerous to the brain, and the specialists there refused.

MR. GIMSON: They did not give me any treatment at all, so they discharged me.

DR. GERSON: They discharged him and sent him out and told him, "Sorry, we can't do anything!" Then it grew further, and the whole face was swollen. His left eye was entirely closed, he could see very little with the right one.

MR. GIMSON: This one is still swollen. You can see the crack.

DR. GERSON: And I sent the case also to Professor Howe, the neurologist, and he saw it was growing into the brain, and caused all these disturbances; and I have some X-rays and all other things, there, but I do not know whether to put them on the table.

SENATOR PEPPER: He came to you, and you treated him?

DR. GERSON: Yes.

SENATOR PEPPER: And you applied your diet?

DR. GERSON: Yes.

SENATOR PEPPER: And did you give him any liver injections?

DR. GERSON: Yes, daily, at home. I think his wife gave them to him.

MR. GIMSON: Yes; that is right. . . .

SENATOR PEPPER: Now, Mr. Gimson, you tell us about the case. What was your condition, and what treatment did you get from the Army? When did you go to Dr. Gerson, and what did he do? And what relief have you had?

MR. GIMSON: I went to Fort Riley, Kansas, and I had something like an ingrown hair, you might say, on my neck. I went down to the hospital, and the doctor, the major, looked at me, and he told me, "Have it off — it wouldn't take long" and I could be back with the troop, and I wouldn't lose any time, I would be back in a day or two.

SENATOR PEPPER: How long were you off?

MR. GIMSON: I was off 4½ or 5 months. Two days I had marching — to keep us busy, out of trouble. Then I went to the hospital. Down there they told me I would be back with the troop in two or three days. I went down and had the operation the next morning, and I wound up in bed, and I could not move my head or anything — pulled away over on the side. They came in for inspection. This captain came in one morning and told me it was about time I had my head straightened out. I told him I could not move my head, because from the operation it pulled me all over on the side, so he just straightened it up, and he opened it all up again; and when he ripped it open like that, I told him, "I can't feel anything; I can't hear anything," so he looked at me, and he checked me, and he gave me an examination; then he told me, "We are going to send you," he says, "to Fitzsimmons, Denver, Hospital." I asked him, "Why should I go there? Why couldn't I go east? He said, "Well, we haven't got the right equipment here for what your trouble is, so we are going to send you out there."

SENATOR PEPPER: Where were you?

MR. GIMSON: I was in the regional hospital in Kansas; and from Kansas they shipped me out to Denver, Colo., to Fitzsimmons, and when I went to Fitzsimmons they gave me an examination and took a hypodermic needle and stuck me in the head with it to see if my feeling was there, so I did not have any feeling whatsoever, and they were going to give me this deep X-ray therapy, and they did not give me any. I put in for a Christmas furlough, and that was refused to me, so then they gave me a discharge the following week, and when I came home the tumor was coming up. Half my white shirt is all worn on one side from where this tumor swelled up behind my ear, where the scar was. It had started to come up again, so I went to the Red Cross about it, and I told them I could not sleep at nights, and I had pains; I could not even do a day's work. I would have to quit as soon as I put any pressure on myself; so she sent me down to Lyons, N.J.; so I went down there, and they told me they had lost all my papers and records. I guess they did not want to tell me what was wrong; so they told me the only thing they could do for me was to send me to the Bronx, N.Y., and get a specimen; so I asked them, "You mean a specimen by operation?" He says, "Yes." I says, "there is no more operating on me," and I refused all operation, so I came home, and my wife told me I was going over to see Dr. Gerson.

DR. GERSON: Why did you refuse an operation?

MR. GIMSON: Well, they did not do me any good the first time, and my condition was worse; so I went over to Dr. Gerson, and he gave me this book, and that is what I am to do. There is no more tumor.

SENATOR PEPPER: Now, tell us this. Did you stay in the hospital for any length of time?

MR. GIMSON: No.

DR. GERSON: That was before the hospital [cancer ward at Gotham] was established.

SENATOR PEPPER: He gave you this book, to tell you what to eat and what not to eat?

MR. GIMSON: Yes; what to eat and what to drink and everything.

SENATOR PEPPER: And you went by this diet?

MR. GIMSON: Whatever is in that book, that is what I took.

SENATOR PEPPER: And you followed strictly, this diet?

MR. GIMSON: 100 percent. I gave away my last pack of cigarettes just before I went up to his office, and from that day to this, I never smoked a cigarette.

SENATOR PEPPER: You quit smoking?

MR. GIMSON: I quit smoking, and drinking, too. Last night I was best man at my brother's wedding, and I couldn't even drink.

SENATOR PEPPER: How long, now, did you take this diet before you began to notice any improvement in your condition?

MR. GIMSON: Well, I would say about, oh, a month, two months, a month and a half to six weeks.

SENATOR PEPPER: You took no medicine, or had no other treatment?

MR. GIMSON: No. Liver injections. Everything I am supposed to take and eat, everything is right there (referring to the little book).

DR. GERSON: Here is the medication book.

SENATOR PEPPER: So you are satisfied the treatment Dr. Gerson gave you has been responsible for the improvement in your condition?

MR. GIMSON: Every bit of it.

SENATOR PEPPER: All right. Thank you.

MR. MARKEL: May I ask Dr. Miley to talk about this case?

SENATOR PEPPER: Dr. Miley.

DR. MILEY: I saw this patient when he had already recovered to a great extent. I saw him after he had been under the treatment three or four months. I have been watching him, seeing him once a month since. There is no sign of recurrence, certainly, and this particular patient has had a lapse, establishing it as a basal carcinoma, which is sometimes inimical to other treatments, but usually when it involves the bone as it did in this case it has gone pretty far. He had actual bone involvement, and apparently there are no signs of that at present.

SENATOR PEPPER: Was the tumor that he had what we call a real tumor?

DR. MILEY: Yes, it was a tumor, starting with a hair follicle.

SENATOR PEPPER: Was it malignant?

DR. MILEY: Yes. . . .

SENATOR PEPPER: Thank you, Mr. Gimson. We appreciate your coming.

(George Gimson's clinical record appears as Mr. G. G., Case No. 35 in Max Gerson's *A Cancer Therapy: Results of Fifty Cases* [1958]. I first met an active and robust Mr. Gimson in San Diego in 1981. When I again contacted Gimson in New Jersey in 1993, he was suffering from heart disease; he had returned to smoking and eating meat after his recovery from "terminal" cancer in 1946, some 47 years earlier. Mr. Gimson died shortly thereafter.)

As Dr. Gerson's own testimony period was winding down, Senator Pepper posed more questions:

SENATOR PEPPER: How many people have you treated for cancer who have favorably responded to your treatment, would you say?

DR GERSON: I might say 30 percent, but all the most hopeless cases. When we get skin cancers, or beginning cancers, they are easy to treat! Even skin cancer growing into the bones as basal cell carcinoma, which are known in medical science that they cannot be influenced — as Mr. Gimson's whose X-rays show how far it had grown into the skull. Professor Howe was very much influenced when he saw this. This was growing through the bones, and now what is left is only a scar. . . .

SENATOR PEPPER: Let me ask you, Doctor, do you favor the appropriation of public money?

DR. GERSON: I would be for it — not for myself, personally, but for research.

SENATOR PEPPER: I do not mean for yourself. Do you favor generally the objectives of this bill?

DR. GERSON: All physicians must have money for research. The most important thing in medicine is research. I am in favor of the bill, of course.

At the Senate subcommittee hearing on July 2, 1946, Dr. George Miley further testified in a very positive vein about his impressions of Dr. Gerson and his work at the Gotham Hospital. "In the last four years I have found Dr. Max Gerson to be an honest and ethical practitioner of medicine, interested in bettering methods of treatment, as the result of many years of clinical study of the effects of diet on various disease processes," he said. "Since January, 1946, we have extended facilities to Dr. Gerson, for a controlled study and observation of his work by physicians. The results are, in my opinion, most encouraging." He even presented several letters he had received from other physicians bearing witness to the efficacy of Gerson's therapy.

Dr. Miley also gave a fairly detailed description of the Gerson diet, which Gerson himself had not done. And he summarized the major advantages of this dietary approach to cancer treatment.

> It is reasonable to assume that the closer one's diet is to nature and the soil, with fresh fruit from the trees and fresh vegetables directly from the garden, the nearer one is to normal health.
>
> Primary biochemical investigations by Dr. Rudolph Keller indicate that the use of the diet is soon followed by certain definite electrochemical changes, notably shifts toward normal or markedly unbalanced sodium, potassium and phosphorus ratios in the blood serum and the body tissues. Dr. Keller, as a result of his investigation of the diet, believes that this type of electrochemical reaction can very well change the entire metabolism of the body in cancer patients.
>
> A preliminary paper by Dr. Gerson describes the diet in detail and cites 10 cases of cancer in which it appeared that the Gerson dietary regimen favorably influenced the course and symptoms of the disease. This new approach to the cancer problem is of fundamental importance because it is the first promising method which treats cancer as a systemic disease, that is, a disease of abnormal chemistry of the whole body. Heretofore, all efforts to treat cancer have been based upon the theory that eradication of the cancer growth must be performed by surgery, X-ray, or radium without regard for abnormal body chemistry which permits the growth to occur. The reason that surgery, X-ray, and radium have not been a real success in the treatment of cancer is that cancer is primarily a disease of abnormal body chemistry, chemistry which is controlled by organs far distant from the site of the cancer. The Gerson dietary regimen is an encouraging attempt to return such abnormal body chemistry to normal.

There are certain definite problems to be overcome before any type of treatment of cancer can be considered partially or wholly successful, problems which are not solved by surgery, radium, or X-ray.

A survey made of cancer cases in Pennsylvania over a long period of time showed that those who received no treatment lived longer than those who received surgery, radium, or X-ray! The exceptions were those patients who had received electrosurgery — in other words, the surgery with an electrical knife — and lived approximately as long as those who received no treatment whatsoever. The survey also showed that following the use of radium and X-ray, much more harm than good was done to the average cancer patient. This is a conclusion which is not generally accepted and is highly controversial among leading cancer workers. It would appear that none of the routine measures employed today to combat cancer is as effective as their proponents would have us believe.

We have made two new approaches to the solution of the chief problems which have to do with the cancer patient, itself. In other words, we are trying to do the best we can for all types of cancer patients or propose something which can be studied over a long time, of some significance.

(1) The abolition of pain has been possible only by the use of narcotics, which are deleterious to any patient's general health when administered over a long period of time. This problem, in my opinion, has been solved more by the Gerson diet than by any other method today. We have observed marked relief of pain in approximately 90 percent of the patients who started the treatment with severe types of pain due to cancer.

(2) The further spread of cancer processes has been apparently retarded by the use of the Gerson dietary regimen.

(3) A reduction in the size of the original malignant growth has been observed to occur in certain instances following the use of the Gerson diet.

(4) The reduction of metastases or secondarily disseminated cancers from the original growth has been observed in certain patients where there was an apparent disappearance of metastatic nodules.

(5) The control of acute pyrogenic (pus-forming) infections in areas eroded by cancer, which is one of the chief causes of death in a cancer patient. These so-called secondary infections are eliminated by the treatment itself and by mild medication.

(6) The acute toxic symptoms, such as nausea and vomiting, which are commonly observed in a considerable number of cancer patients may be alleviated by mild medication.

(7) Hemorrhage due to erosion by cancer masses is a frequent cause of death. Its control is only possible if there is no spread from an original cancer or

there is a reduction in the original tumor or its metastases. To date the Gerson diet is of value in the control of hemorrhage only to the extent to which it limits directly the encroachment of cancer masses upon important blood vessels.

(8) General debility, and especially loss of weight, have been frequently overcome by the Gerson dietary regimen. As a result, many formerly debilitated patients were able to do normal work again.... The diet, although very low in animal protein, seems to be followed at first by a temporary loss of weight, which is usually due to loss of fluid due to the restriction of salt. I think this salt-free diet plays a big part in the reduction of jell around cancer masses. This is a rather well-known finding, and it is one of the many things which Dr. Gerson has used, which is known to influence such swelling.

(9) The maintenance of the morale of the cancer patient is of primary importance at all times. When any one or any combination of the previously mentioned eight problems are solved for the individual cancer patient, his or her morale is enormously improved so that the practical solution of one or more of these problems must be accomplished wherever possible regardless of whether the patient is considered a hopeless case of cancer or not. That is a humane way to look at that....

There have been many approaches to determine the causes of cancer. From clinical observations on cancer patients, the Gerson dietary regimen, for example, provides a most promising lead. In order to profit from this knowledge, an enormous amount of collateral biochemistry must be carried out intensively on both cancer patients and cancer animals by competent workers who are equipped with science's most up-to-date tools for such work....At present, there are no special cancer hospitals doing this highly specialized work in biology and biochemistry to any appreciable degree, though they should be encouraged to do this fundamental work in close relation to their carrying out the well-known and often not too successful routine treatment of cancer by surgery, radium, and X-ray.

The history of medicine is filled with tragic errors which allow such a long time to elapse between the time of discovery of a basic principle and the actual medical application of the discovery for the good of mankind. . . .

It is obvious that the many potentialities inherent in the Gerson dietary regimen for cancer patients should be explored and exploited to the fullest extent for the common good. In order that this new and highly encouraging approach to the problem of cancer cure and prevention be utilized on a statistically significant scale by both laboratory and clinical workers alike, sufficient funds must be made available for this work....Therefore, it is my carefully considered opinion that in view of the success so far and the excellent future promise of the Gerson dietary regimen, it would be unthinkable not to give major consideration to these new avenues of approach to the cancer problem in the research program contemplated by bill S. 1875.

Eloquent and explicit as Dr. George Miley was in his testimony in favor of Dr Gerson, he was also seeking funds from the federal government for the Robinson Foundation and the Gotham Hospital.

Press Conference

As the final witness of the day, Senator Pepper called on Raymond Gram Swing — who was recognized by everyone, he said, as "one of our distinguished radio commentators in this country." Mr. Swing obliged the assembled group with his support of the bill and his support of Dr. Gerson: " I think this bill is one of the most encouraging expressions of intelligent democracy. I hope that it gets the full approval of Congress. It has an inspired work to do, and I want to say in particular that before I came here today I have seen some of the cancer patients of Dr. Gerson, and I believe that research along these lines is so necessary and so hopeful that I am delighted that you, Senator, have had the heart and the courage to bring the doctor here, and some of his patients; and I thank you for it." Mr. Swing had been treated by Dr Gerson for a cardiovascular condition, intermittent claudication causing leg pain, not for cancer, but he had become quite familiar with Gerson's work with the disease. When Raymond Swing wrote his autobiography, *Good Evening: A Professional Memoir*, he described of his initial association with Max Gerson:

> It was in 1946 that my health began to fail, not precipitately, but sufficiently to force me to cut down my work. I had trouble with circulation in my legs and was subject to severe cramps, which sometimes set in after I had walked as far as fifty feet. I received first-class medical care and went under prolonged treatments, but the condition did not improve. . . . It was after a long siege of ineffective treatments that my attention was attracted to a German refugee physician, Dr. Max Gerson, who undertook the treatment of a number of major illnesses by a stern protein-vegetarian dietary regime. Dr. Gerson had had the dietary supervision of the postwar [WWI] Prussian army and was also a friend of Dr. Albert Schweitzer. . . .
>
> I responded to the treatment. My cramps ceased within six weeks after I went on the Gerson diet. I continued faithfully to follow the regime for nine months, and became well enough to count on doing three months of lecturing. I hoped to earn enough income by lecturing for two or three months a year to forgo broadcasting altogether and so spare myself its exacting requirements. (pp. 250-251)

Senator Pepper then directed Dr. Gerson and his entourage to the pressroom, where he had called a news conference, fully expecting an electrified press corps to question Gerson at length. The story that could be told was a blockbuster: the first known "cures" for advanced cancer ever presented to members of the United States Senate. This news would be front-page material for any reporter. Gerson and his healed patients eagerly went to tell their story to the assembled reporters, knowing that this would make a tremendous impact.

Others not so pleased with the Gerson testimony realized the impact that such a press conference would have on the print and broadcast media. Lobbyists for the organizations that would be most financially hurt by a therapy such as Gerson's had quickly spread the word among the press corps that immediately following the hearing there would be a lavish open house for reporters, with plenty of food and an open, unlimited bar. How many could resist such a distracting invitation?

When Gerson and the five patients he had presented entered the conference room, they expected an excited crush of questions. The room was empty but for one reporter, who seemed rather indifferent to the information that had been presented. He asked a few perfunctory questions, then left in a few minutes. The short article that he later wrote about the hearings themselves was neutral.

The only favorable public-news attention that would be given to Dr. Gerson's presentation to the Senate subcommittee came a day later from radio commentator Raymond Gram Swing. He happened know the virtues of Gerson and his therapy, since he himself was a patient of his who had been successfully treated.

The repercussions from Swing's statements on his nationally syndicated radio program underscored the probability that the American medical establishment and the pharmaceutical industry were indeed organizing a fierce but largely undercover opposition to a single physician and his remarkable ability to care cancer. If necessary, they would even fight against Senate Bill 1875 to prevent Dr. Gerson's therapy from gaining recognition.

~15~
Mounting Opposition
(1946–1947)

The Firing of Raymond Gram Swing

On the 3rd of July, 1946, a strong call for the cancer establishment to research and make use of the astounding curative properties in Dr. Max Gerson's dietary therapy was voiced over a nationally syndicated radio program. Based in New York at WOR, Raymond Gram Swing was a popular news commentator heard in the evening over the ABC (American Broadcasting Company) network who had resumed his radio job at the end of the Second World War after having served his nation as a war correspondent. Radio programs like his complemented printed news in newspapers and newsmagazines as the public's main source of current-events knowledge — until largely replaced by the widespread introduction of television in the late 1940s and early 1950s. They also often provided not only in-depth analyses of recent happenings in the nation and world, but also reports on important scientific and medical discoveries. When he attended the Senate subcommittee hearings on the Pepper-Neely Bill, S. 1875, in Washington, D.C., Swing spoke on behalf of Dr. Gerson on July 2, and the next day took his message to the nation in a report on the proceedings:

> I hope I have my values right if, instead of talking tonight about the agreement reached on Trieste by the Foreign Minister in Paris, or the continuing crisis of the OPA [Office of Price Administration] in Washington, or President Truman's signing the Hobbs antiracketeering bill, I talk about a remarkable hearing before a Senate subcommittee in Washington yesterday on cancer and the need for cancer research in new fields.
>
> Let me first say that I well appreciate that one of the basic virtues of the modern medical profession is its conservatism. For without the most scrupulous conservatism in the statement and application of medical knowledge, there can be no confidence in the integrity of medical science. But for the very reason

that the practice of medicine must be conservative, medical science must be bold and unceasingly challenging. Otherwise, medical science will not progress as it can and must, and will lose its integrity.

A bill is before Congress, the Pepper-Neely bill, to appropriate a hundred million dollars for cancer research under Federal control. It proposes that the government go in for cancer research with something like the zeal and bigness with which it went for the release of atomic energy, turning the job over to the scientists with resources generous enough to solve the problem. This alone would make a good theme for a broadcast, just as an example of the use a great democracy can make of its intelligence and wealth. But the subject has been made peculiarly gripping by unprecedented happenings yesterday before the subcommittee which is holding hearings on this bill, and of which Senator Pepper is chairman. He invited as a witness a refugee scientist, now a resident of New York, Dr. Max Gerson, and Dr. Gerson placed on the stand, in quick succession, five patients. They were chosen to represent the principal prevailing types of cancer, and in each instance they showed that the Gerson treatment had demonstrated what is conservatively called "favorable effect on the course of the disease." That in itself is remarkable, but it is all the more so because Dr. Gerson's treatment consists mainly of a diet which he has evolved after a lifetime of research and experimentation. To say that Dr. Gerson has been curing cancer by a dietary treatment is medically impermissible, for the reason that there must be five years without recurrence before such a statement is allowed. Dr. Gerson has cured tuberculosis and other illnesses with his diet, but he has only been working on cancer for four and a half years.

Let me say right away that I am not discussing this Gerson diet as a cancer cure-all. It has produced remarkable results. It also has the failures in its records, which anything as yet unperfected is bound to show. It is not something that offers release from the most rigorous and conservative medical observance in its acceptance and application. Whenever something new and promising comes up in medicine, the temptation of the outsider and even some physicians is to run to glowing superlatives and expect too much from it. But anything that offers even a possibility of treating successfully at least some of the 400,000 existing cancer cases in this country is stirring news, no matter how conservatively it is formulated.

There would be no Pepper-Neely bill to appropriate $100,000,000 for cancer research if the existing research were coping with the need.

I have spoken about this carefully and abstractly, which is to lose some of the shock and delight of the experience yesterday at the hearing of the Pepper Committee. It is one thing to talk abstractly about chemistry and diet and vitamins and other factors in medical science. It is another to see, as the Committee yesterday saw, a seventeen-year-old girl, who had suffered from a tumor at the base of the brain, which was inoperable, and which had paralyzed her. Yesterday, she walked without assistance to the witness chair, and told clearly about her case and her treatment. There was a sturdy man, who had been a sergeant in the army, who had suffered from a malignant tumor, also at the base of the brain, which had been operated on but needed deep X-ray treatment, and this he could not receive because of the danger to the brain. Yesterday he was the picture of health as he testified, and quite naturally he was proud of his remarkable recovery. There was a woman who had suffered from cancer of the breast, which had spread. Yesterday she was well and testified with poise and confidence. A few cases showing such improvement cannot, of themselves, affect the outlook of the medical profession. But they are attested facts and not flukes, and as such they have to be accounted for. And there are many, many more cases which could have been cited. It would seem to be the business of medical research to leap on such facts and carry every hopeful indication to a final, conservative conclusion.

So the advocates of the Pepper-Neely bill can argue that unless we learn now how to deal successfully with cancer, many millions of persons now living in this country are condemned to die from cancer. A hundred million dollars is little more than a token payment for America to make to avert such a sweep of death, and they can then point to the Gerson dietary approach as a most promising field for research. Already it has achieved results which, while relatively few, are astounding and challenging.

Dr. Gerson was an eminent if controversial figure in pre-Hitler Germany. He was bound to be controversial because he was challenging established practice in healing illnesses such as tuberculosis by diet. He has been assistant to Förster, the great neurologist of Breslau, and for years assistant to Sauerbruch, one of the great physicians on the Continent. The Sauerbruch-Gerson diet for skin tuberculosis is well-known to European medicine and the account of it is part of accepted medical literature. Dr. Gerson told the Pepper Committee that he had first come upon his dietary therapy in trying to cure himself of migraine headaches. Later he treated others, among them a man with skin tuberculosis as well. Dr. Gerson was an acknowledged dietary authority in Weimar, Germany, and was responsible for the German army of his time being placed on dehydrated rather than canned foods.

Apparently innocuous, this broadcast provoked many threatening letters from disgruntled physicians, which Mr. Swing passed on to Dr. Gerson to read. Here is an excerpt from one telling sample, written by a Dr. William Seaman Bainbridge of New York City, which appears to be part of a concerted campaign to discredit both Swing and Gerson:

I was one of thousands who listen to your radio broadcasts by which you have gained an enviable reputation. Such a reputation brings with it great responsibility. I believe that in your broadcast of Wednesday July 3, 1946 you did not live up to that responsibility.

As one who had been actively at work in the cancer field both at home and abroad, who created and for a number of years directed the research department of one of our large hospitals, whose book on the subject is published in six languages, I am dismayed by your broadcast, a copy of which I have before me....

In various centers over the world millions of dollars are being spent and countless animals and human beings are giving their lives, all in a struggle to solve the mystery that is called cancer. Until the solution is reached, conscientious doctors and surgeons must utilize every accepted present-day means to help their patients suffering with the disease. We try to give them hope and courage and faith in our desire and efforts to cure them. As I reread your broadcast I do not find one iota of good — only misery — that can result from it. You cast doubt and distrust upon the medical profession, you give a very fatal misquotation, you condemn to a hopeless future thousands of unfortunate victims. The claims of the medical profession are based on available statistics regarding the prevention and cure of a multitude of cases of malignant disease taken in time by the employment of means now at our disposal. All these you ignore to push the claims of one man with a theory not yet proved.

Frankly, I do not believe that you had a moral right to discuss a subject so fraught with danger of which it is apparent you know absolutely nothing as demonstrated by the statements and sentiments you expressed.

I feel duty bound to write to you because already some of my patients upon whom I have operated for cancer, and who have every chance to be cured, have expressed their fear and mental suffering since hearing your broadcast.

A copy of this letter is being sent to Mr. Mark Woods, President of the American Broadcasting Company.

Two weeks after the broadcast, the ABC network fired Raymond Gram Swing in a stunning display of censorship by commercial interests, for apparently a number of companies, pressured by various professional associations, notified network executives that unless measures were taken to counteract the effect of Swing's broadcast, advertising contracts would be jeopardized. Millions of dollars budgeted for pharmaceutical, tobacco, alcohol and food commercials over its radio-station affiliates could be withdrawn. The entire episode indicates the depth of the malevolence of an entrenched medical establishment determined to threaten Dr. Max Gerson's practice and damage his reputation because of his highly promising therapy.

Raymond Swing had told Gerson that physicians themselves had complained to him "that Gerson will break our heads and bones, will finish off our research work, so that we will have to go into an entirely different field." To his great credit, Swing refused to knuckle under when the network management insisted that unless he retracted his favorable words about Gerson's work and submitted future statements to their scrutiny and censorship, he would never be permitted to speak again over the radio. He, like the doctor he admired, had great personal integrity and courage. Raymond Swing maintained a cordial relationship with Max Gerson and sometimes he referred patients to him, the most notable one being Johnny Gunther (whose story is told in Chapter 16). Swing also was on the board of directors of the Madison Foundation (see Chapter 17).

Defeating S. 1875

Four congressmen who were also doctors now launched a massive and well-funded lobbying effort to block Bill S. 1875, which had passed from the Senate subcommittee for consideration in the House of Representatives. Behind them, vocal and standing solidly, were the American Medical Association and its influential journal, as well as numerous state and local medical societies. Many of these professional organizations received financial handouts or substantial advertising revenues from the medical-equipment and pharmaceutical industries; they urged their members to take immediate action and call or mail in instructions to their legislators in Congress and the Senate to cast their votes against the passage of what had now become known as the "Cancer Bill."

On July 29, Senator Claude Pepper described the gist of S. 1875 on the Senate floor itself:

> This is the so-called cancer bill. The bill authorizes the President to assemble experts from all over the world and to follow the course that he deems best in correlating public and private research in the United States in an effort to discover the cause and find the cure for cancer, and to correlate and to coordinate research in that field among the nations of the world.
>
> When Senators reflect that 175,000 men, women and children in the United States, according to past history, will die this year of cancer, I think I am justified in saying that if it is felt that the bill should require further consideration than it is now possible, I shall give notice that I will move at the earliest opportunity to bring the bill before the attention of the Senate.

Senator Pepper by then was feeling deflated about any possibility of getting the hoped-for appropriations bill passed through both of the nation's legislative bodies. He knew that the House of Representatives had already tabled it because of insufficient support (though actually only several votes short of acceptance) for considering the bill "on its merits." The senators then agreed to "pass the bill over": that is, they decided to skip over it when they got to its place on the Senate calendar for formal consideration. The senators, too, had been courted by the bill's adversaries. So, for all intents and purposes, the Pepper-Neely Bill was dead. This bill enjoys a unique distinction: S. 1875 is probably the only big-money appropriation for medical research that the American Medical Association has ever lobbied against. A renewed great 'War on Cancer', to be launched with considerable fanfare by the U.S. government and President Richard M. Nixon in 1971, had to wait in the wings for a quarter of a century. And this war, involving fierce competition among researchers and physicians throughout the land for federal, foundation, association and corporate funds, plods on while cancer mortality statistics grow ever higher. After expenditures of over a trillion dollars, after three decades of focused effort, the medical establishment is no closer to a true cure for or a viable means of preventing cancer.

An effective treatment for cancer that combines nutritional and detoxifying tactics, requiring effort and compliance from patients and their caregivers, appears to have no appeal to most people — especially when their physicians advise them against undertaking it, if they are even alerted to this possible alternative. After all, doctors have more "state of the art" (i.e., far costlier as well as damaging and toxic) treatment modes to offer — and most of them are at least partially covered under health-insurance policies. Apparently a majority of Americans believe that pharmaceutical and technological medicine will be the source of a cancer cure: that it will come from a pharmaceutical drug, an operation, a shot or some cutting-edge technology derived from molecular biology — not from food.

Yet significantly and ironically, the, the American Cancer Society and the National Cancer Institute both recommend diets similar to Dr. Gerson's for cancer prevention, if not for treatment. These stress the desirability of considerable daily consumption of fresh fruits and vegetables and whole grains, and recommend limiting the intake of fat and animal proteins. Salt, refined flour and sugar are also to be closely restricted. Furthermore, clinical research projects are being undertaken to determine whether dietary factors may be able to halt cancer progression. For example, a current study using dietary measures to treat prostate cancer patients is being conducted by Dr. Dean Ornish (famous for prescribing a strict diet for preventing or ameliorating cardiovascular disease) jointly with Memorial Sloan-Kettering Cancer Center and the medical school at University of California–San Francisco.

Chemotherapy

The medical establishment's investment in defeating S. 1875 and preventing any funding for the Gerson therapy paid off financially, however. Funds were soon being directed to cancer research involving chemotherapy as the most desirable new tactic. The pharmaceutical industry by the late 1940s it was busily developing a vast array of new toxic drugs designed to destroy cancer cells — its destructive wake also killing or maiming normal cells as well as burdening the already compromised liver with deadly substances. Chemotherapy also utilizes expensive diagnostic and treatment hardware; the medical-pharmaceutical-equipment manufacturing complex has thrived over the intervening half-century. Cancer today is a $100 billion annual industry in the United States alone. No matter that the revenue comes at the annual toll of over a million cancer diagnoses made and some 600,000 deaths.

Physicians who treated cancerous conditions in patients traditionally attempted to remove tumors by cutting them out — through surgery. When a growth seemed self-contained and on visual inspection had not invaded surrounding tissue, it was easier to regard it as a 'clean' removal, in which the surgeons 'got it all'. Over time, however, the tumor often reappeared, because perhaps only a few abnormal cells on the periphery of the tumor had remained, to start a rampant growth anew. Or cancerous growths might appear elsewhere in the body, with their cells, when histologically examined, resembling those at the original site, thus indicating that abnormal cells had migrated into the bloodstream or lymph and moved to tissues elsewhere in the body, lodging in other places, such as vulnerable organs like the liver and lungs.

Increasingly in the early half of the 20th century radioactive materials and X-radiation had been used to kill cancerous tumors, always risking burns of surrounding tissue, radiation sickness from overexposure (similar to occurred with victims of the atomic bombs dropped on Japan, or in nuclear accidents in laboratories) or, over a long period, mutations in body cells that might lead to other forms of cancer.

While Max Gerson was trying to persuade the medical establishment to look at the results of his new dietary therapy for cancer patients, a new treatment possibility was being introduced: chemical agents designed to target cancer cells so as to disrupt and kill them. The first notable use was of "mustard" — basically nitrogen-mustard gas, the same poisonous gas that had been used to such blinding, skin-burning and lung-destroying effect during World War I by both sides of the combat. Fortunately, it was not used during World War II because the Allies and Axis powers all respected the international agreement, made in 1926 for humanitarian reasons, to prohibit the use of poisonous gas in warfare. Still, lethal gas had continued to be developed further — manufactured and held in readiness by the United States Army just in case it was needed to retaliate for a violation by the enemy.

Thus a considerable supply of nitrogen-mustard gas had come a war surplus item; it was readily available and inexpensive as a raw material for making the early chemotherapeutic agents, chiefly dichlorodiethyl sulfide. Eventually it evolved into some much-used chemotherapeutic agents, such as 5-FU. (For many years, the American Cancer Society owned 50% of the royalties to 5-FU — a financial linkage that might help explain its promotion for widespread use by oncologists.)

This research came about not by sheer happenstance. During World War II, Dr. Cornelius P. Rhoads (who earlier had conducted grossly unethical medical experiments using full-body radiation and chemical agents proving that both could cause cancer in humans) had been in charge of three large U.S. Army Chemical, Biological and Atomic Warfare laboratories, so had access to the knowledge and materials through his old sources. In his report made at the July 2, 1946, Senate subcommittee hearing where Dr. Gerson gave his testimony, Dr. Rhoads presented some of the background, research rationale and treatment potential for this substance, as revealed by the Panel on the Clinical Physiology of the Blood and Blood-forming Organs:

> During the war, under a heavy veil of secrecy, extensive investigations into the biochemical and biophysical properties of a series of poisonous substances known as nitrogen-mustard gases were conducted under the auspices of the Chemical Warfare Service of the Army. It was found that an outstanding characteristic of these substances is their ability to destroy the white corpuscles of the blood and the lymphoid tissues of the animal body. This discovery suggested their cautious use in human diseases of the blood and lymphoid tissue in which there is an overgrowth of the cells concerned. A series of carefully conducted experiments indicated that under some circumstances the nitrogen-mustard compounds, though not curative, may be a useful adjunct to X-ray treatment — heretofore standard therapy in the amelioration of these diseases. The potentialities from the point of view of the clinical investigation of the substances have not been fully explored and this panel will undertake their further investigation, with especial inquiry into the fundamental mechanisms of their actions in man.

One could expect from this statement delivered by the most powerful physician in the domain of oncology that other uses in cancer treatment for these and other toxic substances, gaseous or liquid or radioactive, would soon be devised.

In 1952, Dr. Rhoads would become the director of the newly formed merger of two renowned clinical and research entities: the Memorial Hospital and the Sloan-Kettering Cancer Research Institute, to be known as the Memorial Sloan-Kettering Cancer Center. For four decades MSKCC has been a major recipient of funds from the Rockefeller Foundation, the National Institutes of Health and the National Cancer Institute, as well as vast subsidies from the international pharmaceutical industry and innumerable grants from foundations that support cancer research. During his tenure there, Rhoads virtually controlled the direction of U.S. cancer research through his enormous influence over funding until he died in 1959.

As a young physician Cornelius Rhoads had spent 1926 as a patient at the Trudeau Institute at Saranac Lake, New York, where he was being treated for pulmonary tuberculosis which he had contracted as a surgical resident at a hospital in Boston. It was in the summer of 1927 that the Trudeau Institute's Dr. Mayer visited Dr. Gerson in Bielefeld to study his regimen, so probably Dr. Rhoads at the time was aware of the tuberculosis-curing work of the then-eminent Dr. Max Gerson. Rhoads went on to establish U.S. Army Biological Warfare facilities in Maryland, Utah and Panama. He then became involved with the recently revealed radiation experiments that had been performed on prisoners, hospital patients and soldiers during the Second World War, and was appointed to serve on the U.S. Atomic Energy Commission (AEC). Then in the 1950s, from his position at MSKCC, Rhoads engaged in large-scale full-body, deep-radiation experiments. During his tenure at Memorial Hospital and Sloan-Kettering, Dr. Rhoads boasted that he would be the one to cure cancer. A zealous proponent of chemotherapy, through his positions of great influence he ruthlessly tried to crush any therapy that appeared to be a viable competitor, such as Royal Rife's and Max Gerson's. And his associates, impressed or cowed by his power, followed his lead.

Journal of the American Medical Association

Dr. Rhoads as not the only powerful physician in the medical establishment who impeded spread of the knowledge of Dr. Gerson's therapy. Dr. Morris Fishbein, for 25 years editor-in-chief of the Journal of the American Medical Association (JAMA) composed an editorial against Dr. Gerson that was scheduled for publication in the issue dated November 16, 1946. Max first heard of this editorial from a friend and was deeply concerned. On November 15, he sent off a telegram message to Fishbein implying a threat of legal action:

IT HAS JUST BEEN REPORTED TO ME THAT YOU CONTEMPLATE PUBLICATION OF AN ARTICLE IN WHICH MY WORK IS DISCUSSED. YOU ARE HEREBY ADVISED THAT IF YOU PUBLISH ANY FALSE DEROGATORY OR MISLEADING STATEMENTS CONCERNING ME OR MY WORK I SHALL HOLD YOU FULLY RESPONSIBLE FOR ALL CONSEQUENCES.

After receiving this admonitory wire, the JAMA editorial board decided to stop the presses. Below a copy of the message in his telegram, Gerson subsequently wrote a notation:

In consequence of this warning the first page (645) of the EDITORIALS: Gerson's Cancer Treatment, has been left unprinted, blank, in the rest of the editions, not passed the press yet.
Edition: November 16, 1946. Volume 132 No 11.

Only a portion of the printed journals going out to subscribers contained the defamatory article, but the copy Dr. Gerson received featured the editorial:

Some years ago a technic called the Gerson-Sauerbruch-Hermannsdorfer diet was claimed to be a notable advance in the treatment of tuberculosis. Gerson proposed, by the use of these diets, to change the nature of the soil in which the tubercle bacillus lives. . . . The good results in many types of tuberculosis reported by Gerson were apparently not susceptible to duplication by most other observers. . . .

For several years now The JOURNAL has been receiving requests from people all over the United States for information about Dr. Max Gerson, who is said to be using a dietary and salt controlled method for treating cancer patients at the Gotham Hospital in New York. The JOURNAL on several occasions requested Dr. Gerson to supply information as to the details of his method of treatment but has thus far received no satisfactory reply. . . .

In the last session of Congress hearings were held on a bill to appropriate $100,000,000 of federal money for research on cancer. Dr. Gerson is said to have presented 5 of his patients to these public hearings. Fortunately for the American people, this presentation received little, if any, newspaper publicity. However, Raymond Swing, radio commentator, in a broadcast over A.B.C. July 3, 1946 told the world that the Gerson cancer treatment was producing remarkable results. People who sent for a copy of the broadcast were referred to Dr. George Wiley [sic] at the Gotham Hospital.

Now there has come to hand through a prospective patient of Dr. Max Gerson a schedule of diets alleged to be beneficial in such cases. The patient was a man aged 83, with cancer of the stomach and multiple metastases, whom Dr. Gerson had never seen. Nevertheless he provided a complete diet for a period of four weeks, given in minute detail.

Fishbein then detailed the main features of the Gerson diet for cancer patients (both the forbidden and prescribed foods and condiments), plus the various supplements and injections:

Basis of the diet was a special soup, of which the unfortunate victim is supposed to take 1 quart a day. . . . The formula says that there should be no other medication because it can be harmful and dangerous, and it warns particularly against the use of anesthesia, because it says that the body becomes highly hypersensitive through this diet and the usual anesthesia might become fatal. As part of the routine, Dr. Gerson insists that a patient have at least one copious bowel movement a day, preferably two, and he has provided a formula for an enema to secure this activity.

Fishbein concluded:

> Indeed, [the Gerson Therapy] admits lack of any actual cure, claiming only that patients seemed improved in health and that some tumors were delayed in growth or became smaller. ("Gerson's Cancer Treatment," M. Fishbein, J. Am. Med. Assn., 132:11:645)

Another way for Fishbein to cast suspicion upon the Gerson therapy was to question the motivation of Dr. Gerson's sponsor, the Robinson Foundation. Fishbein located its origins in a nonprofit, charitable organization set up in conjunction with the operation of several industrial corporations — apparently, he implied, as a way of evading the payment of income tax for profits made from the conduct of a business enterprise. He did not point out that huge medical-research donors such as the Rockefeller Foundation were somewhat similarly devised.

Outraged at Fishbein's attack, Max Gerson immediately began drafting different versions of a letter of protest (copies of which are extant). Assisted, it seems, by several other people (perhaps Drs. Wolf and Dr. Keller), he composed a series of remarks for possible inclusion in his letter of rebuttal to the JAMA editorial. One of the sections that he left out of the final version was this one, which notably shows that Gerson scarcely claimed, whether privately or publicly, to have total success in treating cancerous cases, as his detractors obviously accused him of doing when making him out to be a charlatan or quack:

> The statement that I treat my patients without seeing them is a lie: the publicity of my methods and the periodicals I chose for them is my business alone, the soup of Hippocrates is a ridiculous mistake to ascribe it to me. But all these things are not the decisive point of the discussion. Of interest for the reader is only: Is my method an improvement or not? My adversaries know quite well that my results are better than those of the orthodox methods and the tactics to criticize the soup or my method of publicity are attempts to evade the real point.
>
> Which are the results of my treatment? At the time of my last publication I had in malignant tumor cases 30% good successes, no palpable tumors, no complaints, further 40 percent were better with less pains without morphium and 30% were failures. At present the favorable and painless cases are each better by 10% and the failures are reduced to 20%. With tuberculosis patients the success is better.

I do not claim to have special cures for tumors and other chronic diseases. Perhaps I am on the right track to raise the resistance power of weak people and that my results are a little better than those of the orthodox method. This fact is very well known to my adversaries. The small but incontestable success arouses a bitter opposition in certain circles of the organized X ray trade and among a certain category of surgeons whose motives I cannot guess.

Of course I am prepared to submit to all controls which anybody could demand to show my patients and their improvement.

The final version of the letter, cool and factual, was sent off to Fishbein on November 22. Dr. Gerson pointed out examples of European physicians' successes with his dietary treatment of tuberculosis. He said that his records showed that "the one and only request made" by JAMA for information, sent in October of 1944, was answered by stating that no information was available at that time because it had not been published yet. In the following year, the journal had been sent several reprints of Gerson's article, "Dietary Considerations in Neoplastic Disease," which recently appeared in Review of Gastroenterology. As for the "special soup," Gerson commented that the editorial had failed to note "that the soup is hardly a new idea but was first prescribed by Hippocrates" — the patron saint of physicians. As he continued:

In regard to the allegation that a patient was given dietary instructions without my having seen him I can say that our records show dietary instructions were sent only after a request has been made for the details of the treatment by a physician. Correspondence from the Gotham Hospital stressed the fact that the treatment could only be given after the patient's diagnosis and condition was definitely established and then only under the care of a physician. The details in such instances were sent directly to the family physician if requested. This was done originally because so little information was available on the dietary regime for cancer patients, and has now been mostly discontinued.

The clinician wants to know finally if the method helps the cancer patient or not. It is my personal opinion from long experience that it definitely does. A startling and favorable reversal of the course and symptoms of advanced malignant neoplastic disease including patients with metastases, following the institution of the dietary regime, has been observed in too many individuals to disregard the method now.

Time alone will tell the complete story and let me express the hope that most criticism in the future will be more constructive than destructive.

Max Gerson obviously wanted his letter to be printed in a forthcoming issue of the journal, perhaps as an indirect apology for this assault on his reputation, but, not surprisingly, this did not happen. On January 16, 1947, Dr. Gerson wrote again to Dr. Fishbein again:

> Inasmuch as I have not heard from you further concerning the letter written by me Nov. 22nd and confirmed by your office Nov. 27th, in regard to your editorial on the Gerson dietary regime in cancer patients, I wish to call your attention to this letter, since you may not have seen it personally.
>
> In justice to your readers, myself and to your position of a journal of high standing — and your position takes it for granted that you are interested in doing justice — the publication of my answer without further delay would seem essential, so that both viewpoints may be presented.

There is no indication that Dr. Fishbein ever deigned to reply. Max Gerson's letter never appeared in the *Journal of the American Medical Association*. Dr. Morris Fishbein was among Gerson's most virulent critics. He occupied the best possible position to influence the American medical establishment, whether for good or for bad.

The Gotham Study Ends

Despite these attacks on the Gerson therapy from the medical profession, Raymond Swing's broadcast had made so favorable an impression on the listening public that ABC received a deluge of letters from cancer sufferers desperate to get in touch with Dr Gerson. WABC in New York referred all inquiries not to Dr. Gerson directly but to a Dr. Wiley [sic] at Gotham, a 'typographical error', since the doctor they really meant was Dr. George Miley. However, Dr. Miley was very unlikely by then to supply information, let alone encouragement. His attitude had changed noticeably since the Senate hearings, where he had spoken so favorably and at length about Dr. Gerson and his therapy. From the time of the Washington hearings onward, Dr. Miley seemed to make a career of undermining Gerson's therapy — as Max Gerson would unhappily discover.

Gerson began to question the wisdom of continuing on with the Gotham Hospital experiment when he realized that he was not seeing the kind of patient results to which he had been accustomed in past. When he asked patients about the quality of their care and the foods and special drinks served to them, he realized that Dr. Miley was no longer ensuring that the staff, either nurses or kitchen staff, followed his therapy to the letter. Since a striking change in Miley's attitude started right after their return from the Senate hearings, Max could only surmise that someone, an individual working for some organization, had 'gotten' to Miley, making it clear that any further positive association with Gerson would affect his career negatively. For a time, Max tried to work around the awkward problem of

Miley's withdrawn support of his ward at Gotham Hospital, since at the time he had no other facility into which to put patients for closely supervised therapy. But he could not effectively fight the constant opposition and sabotage of his therapy, especially since it put his patients at risk.

The JAMA attack on Gerson's dietary therapy in mid November of 1946 had also put under suspicious scrutiny his association with the Robinson Foundation, tainting both their names. Gerson's threat of legal action had succeeded in getting the main part of the editorial removed from at least some of the issues distributed. Nevertheless, the Gotham Hospital administrators and physicians would have been fully aware of the damaging editorial and regarded any continuing connection to be detrimental to their reputation. Very early in 1947, Dr. Gerson told the board of directors of the Robinson Foundation that the attempt to treat patients at Gotham Hospital had failed, due to obstruction by the hospital and its staff physicians. His close ally within the foundation, Professor Irving Fisher, died not long after, at the age of 78. The Gerson cancer ward closed down. Max then busied himself with new plans for publicizing his work since the normal scientific channels of publication, making such information available to the medical profession, were now shut tight now to Gerson.

When Max Gerson was living in Europe, medical schools and universities, medical gatherings and conventions had vied for him to lecture at their institutions, but few invitations to speak had ever been extended to him in the United States. One event in the late 1940s in which he participated as an honored speaker was a symposium on "The Jew and Health," sponsored by the Jewish Forum Association. In his talk on "The Jewish Physician throughout the Ages," Dr. Gerson combined his knowledge of the history of medicine with his acquaintance with Judaic lore, including the Jewish sacred books and their prescribed (and proscribed) dietary practices. The address was full of scholarly information that would be provocative and even inspirational to Jews whose careers were, or someday might be, connected with health care. As he commented,

> The classical book about dietetics of the Middle Ages was written by Isaak ben Salomon Israeli, who lived in Egypt about 850 C.E. In Oxford and other medieval universities, his book on fever was included in the medical curriculum.... When the Popes worried about their own person or their own diet, they preferred to take Jewish physicians, as they were of the opinion that Jewish medicine and especially the Jewish diet was superior to the Italian diet of that time, with its excess of condiments, salt and meat. In the Middle Ages, and even centuries later, it was the general custom of the rich people to eat great quantities of meat and to drink heavy wine and a variety of liquors. The Jewish physicians, following the doctrine of the Bible and the Talmud, in the main were

dietitians and propagandists for moderation in meat and alcohol. This doctrine gave them a great number of laws of cleanliness, moderation and prescriptions on how to live a healthy life and to increase health and to live long.

In America, Dr. Gerson had long been accustomed to presenting cases and discussing them under fire, obligated to prove to some investigators from the county medical society that what he was doing with patients was quite effective in many cases, even ones that initially had been declared hopeless. Shortly after severing his connection with Gotham Hospital, Gerson arranged to rent a conference room at a convenient New York City venue. On February 5, 1947, Gerson sent the following invitation to two dozen physicians prominent in treating cancer cases:

Dear Doctor:

An informal demonstration will be held on Tuesday, February 18th at 3:00 o'clock at the Hotel Carlyle, Madison Avenue and 76th St. in the Victorian Suite, 2nd floor — for the purpose of viewing some cancer patients who are under my care.

You are hereby cordially invited to attend this demonstration which will be followed by an open discussion.

Sincerely yours,
Max Gerson, M.D.

Here are excerpts from typical responses to Gerson's invitation from his colleagues:

From H. M. Zimmerman, M.D., Chief, Lab. Division, Montefiore Hospital for Chronic Diseases: "Unfortunately, a prior appointment will prevent my being present at this demonstration."

From Dr. Alex L. Louria, Brooklyn, N.Y.: "I regret that your invitation to attend your demonstration at the Hotel Carlyle came too late for me to avail myself of the opportunity."

From Stanley P. Reimann, M.D., Director, Research Institute, The Lankenau Hospital, Philadelphia: "Very sorry but I'll not be able to be in New York on February 18th."

From Samuel Standard, M.D., New York City: "I am sorry that a previously arranged meeting of the Committee on the Study of Hospital Internships and Residencies will make it impossible for me to attend your meeting."

From Cornelius P. Rhoads, M.D., Director, Memorial Hospital for the Treatment of Cancer and Allied Diseases, New York City: "[I] wish you to know that I shall be unable to attend your demonstration on February 18th."

Only one physician out of the 20 specially invited came to see a demonstration of several healed or recovering cancer patients, but Dr. Gerson still managed to bring in enough interested participants to partially fill the room. One of the patients presented that day was young Johnny Gunther, whose treatment would become the subject of a bestselling memoir written by his father, *Death Be Not Proud*, an American classic.

~16~
Johnny Gunther's Tragedy
(1946–1947)

Gerson's Heterodoxy

During 1946, John Gunther, the best-selling author of *Inside Europe*, was already hard at work on his next book, *Inside U.S.A.* At the same time he was intensively researching various cancer treatments in order to find some therapy to save, or even just extend, the life of his brilliant and beloved 16-year-old son. Johnny Gunther had glioblastoma, a brain tumor said by physicians and medical literature to be invariably fatal. Gunther once had an unshakable faith in the medical "team" of the best-known and most famous surgeons and oncologists in the country he had assembled to treat Johnny. He had followed their methods and recommendations to the letter, sparing no effort or expense to save his son, but all to no avail — the boy was failing fast and so was his father's faith in the cancer establishment.

Johnny had been undergoing conventional treatment for five months, including surgery, X-ray therapy, even direct injection of nitrogen-mustard gas, or dichloro-diethyl sulfide. None of the conventional therapies had any beneficial effect on Johnny, nor did these experimental injections. Eventually Gunther was told that his son was not going to survive, but he refused to give up. Along with other treatment possibilities, he had begun checking into Dr. Gerson and his therapy, which his good friend Raymond Swing was strongly recommending, as Gunther explained in his memoir, *Death Be Not Proud:*

> Early in the summer Raymond Swing told me astonishing stories about a doc-
> tor named Max Gerson who had achieved remarkable arrestations of cancer and
> other illnesses by a therapy based on diet. Gerson was, and is, a perfectly authentic
> M.D., but unorthodox. He had been attacked by the *Journal of the American Medical
> Association* and others of the massive vested interests in medicine; Swing himself had
> been under bitter criticism for a broadcast describing and praising highly Gerson's
> philosophy and methods of dietary cure. My own first reaction was skeptical. . . .

Then I learned that Gerson had long experience actually in brain tumor cases, having been associated for years with a famous German neurosurgeon, Foerster, in a tumor clinic at Breslau before the war. I went to see Gerson. He showed me his records of tumors — even gliomas — apparently cured. But I was still doubtful because it seemed to me inconceivable that anything so serious as a glioma could be cleared up by anything so simple as a diet. He impressed me greatly as a human being, however. This was a man full of idiosyncrasy but also one who knew much, who had suffered much, and who had a sublime faith in his own ideas. (pp 65-66)

Gunther and Johnny's mother, Frances Gunther (John's ex-wife), now began to consider Dr. Gerson's method. They discussed this possibility with their family physician, Dr. Traeger, who had misgivings, as Gunther recalls:

At first he violently opposed the Gerson claims, but then he swung over on the ground that, after all, Johnny was deteriorating very fast and in any case the diet could do no harm. I stayed at Madison [Frances' home in central New York state, where Johnny was living] one weekend and Frances went into New York, visited Gerson herself, and looked over his nursing home. She was impressed, too. We made a sudden decision over the telephone. We had tried orthodoxy, both static and advanced, and so now we would give heterodoxy a chance. If only we could stave Death off a little longer! And — once more — there was absolutely nothing to lose.

On September 7, 1946, during a heat wave, Johnny Gunther entered the nursing home run by Margaret Seeley and Johanna Cohn, Gerson's oldest and now-divorced daughter — beginning a "new long chapter in his indomitable struggle," to cite his father's words. A decade later, Max Gerson vividly remembered this patient:

Johnny was a wonderful boy. When he was 14 years old he developed a brain tumor. He was operated on as a decompression procedure, in which surgeons took some bone from the skull so that the tumor could expand outside. When he first came to me, a large mass was there outside of his skull. He was very weak and bleeding from the skin, gums, et cetera. I put him on my diet.... (from MG's talk with Long John Nebel, 1957)

And Johnny's father later described the boy's early days at Mrs. Seeley's small sanatorium in the townhouse in Manhattan's East 60s:

Gerson's sanatorium, operated by his daughter and Mr. and Mrs. Seeley, was run with the utmost loving care. I cannot possibly pay tribute enough to Mrs. Seeley and to Miss Gerson for what they did for Johnny. Also I saw, month after month, a number of Gerson's cases. One patient, it happened, was an acquaintance of mine of twenty years' standing whom I altogether trusted. I did not know whether or not Gerson could cure, or even check, a malignant glioblastoma. I did learn beyond reasonable doubt that his diet did effect other cures. Gerson himself, zealot that he is, has never claimed that his diet will "cure anything," as his enemies sometimes charge. But some of his results have been astonishing.

One of our doctors (hostile to Gerson at first) said one evening that September, "If this thing works, we can chuck millions of dollars worth of equipment in the river, and get rid of cancer by cooking carrots in a pot.

And according to Gunther, the effectiveness of the Gerson therapy in treating his son made this projection valid:

> Those September days were grim at first. Johnny lay there pale and panting with misery. His blood count slipped lower and lower, and great bruises appeared on his arms and chest, caused by breakdown of the capillaries. We had been warned that the blood would go very low, and perhaps we were needlessly alarmed — it might well have come back of itself. But anyway we were worried sick. One doctor told us that the reason he had seemed so casual when Johnny entered the Gerson nursing home was his conviction that he couldn't possibly outlast the week anyway. In particular what is known as the polymorphonuclear count of Johnny's blood (I will not go into the technical details) was staggeringly low — down to 3 per cent, and the red cells showed a profound anemia. One specialist told us later that he has never known of a recovery with such a blood condition.
>
> Within a week, Johnny was feeling, not worse, but much better! The blood count rose steadily, the bruises were absorbed with extraordinary speed, the wound in the bulge healed, and, miracle of miracles, the bump on the skull was going down!
>
> Traeger had walked down the street with me to meet Gerson. He was deeply pessimistic. He said, "We'll move Johnny to a hospital and try massive transfusions — nothing else can save him." The two doctors retired into the kitchen , and came out after half an hour. Then Traeger looked Johnny over slowly and said, "Never mind about the transfusions. Let's do it Gerson's way for another twenty-four hours."
>
> First, Gerson took Johnny off penicillin. This we thought to be a very grave risk, but, he insisted, penicillin could irritate a tumor. Second, he refused to permit any transfusions or other emergency measures whatsoever. What a terrible chance we thought he was taking! Third, he demanded that for some weeks at least Johnny should have rest, absolute rest, nothing but rest, rest, rest.
>
> The Gerson diet is saltless and fatless, and for a long time proteins are excluded or held to an extreme minimum. The theory behind this is simple

enough. Give nature opportunity, and nature herself will heal. It is the silliest thing in the world to attempt to arrest cancer of the tongue, say, by cutting off the tongue. What the physician should strive for, if he gets a case in time, is to change the metabolism of the body so that the cancer (or another affliction) dies of itself. The whole theory is erected on the basis that the chemistry of the body can be so altered as to eliminate disease. Perhaps this may sound far-fetched. But that diet, any special diet, can markedly influence bodily behavior is, of course, well known. Consider inversely how a milligram or so of a poisonous substance, like potassium cyanide, can almost instantly kill a body.

How Gerson decided what foods helped to create new healthy cells, as the diseased cells sloughed off, is not altogether clear to me. At any rate the first principle is to make the diet potassium-rich and sodium-free. Gerson took the line that the body spends an absurdly disproportionate share of its energy getting rid of waste, and that therefore, when the body is ill, it will be much freer to combat illness and build healthy cells if the amount of waste is drastically cut down. Hence, as a patient enters upon the Gerson diet, not only does he subsist largely on specially prepared fruit juices and fresh vegetables that burn down to a minimum of ash, but he has enema after enema — in the beginning as many as four or five a day, till the system is totally washed out and cleansed.

Gunther detailed the dietary regimen imposed on his adolescent son:

This is what Johnny had to eat during the next months. For breakfast, a pint of fruit juice, oatmeal, an apple-carrot mash, and a special soup made of fresh vegetables—parsley root, celery knob, leek, tomatoes. This soup [Gerson's basic "Hippocrates Soup"] he continued to take at intervals throughout the day, until he had a quart or a quart and a half. For lunch, heaping portions of cooked vegetables, a salad, fresh fruit, the soup and mash, and a baked potato. For dinner, the same. Later he was permitted pot cheese, skimmed milk, and dry pumpernickel. Nothing canned. Nothing seasoned, smoked, or frozen. Above all nothing salted. No meat, eggs, or fish. No cream, butter, or other fats. No sugar except honey and maple sugar. No candy, sausages, ice cream, pickles, spices, preserved foods, white flour, condiments, cakes, or any of the multitude of small things a child loves. Very little water. All the vegetables had to be cooked with no added water or steam, after being washed, not scraped, and without using pressure cookers or anything with aluminum, and the fruits had to be squeezed in a nonmetallic squeezer. Back to nature!

Do not think this was starvation. Some patients gain rather than lose on the Gerson diet. The meals are enormous in size and, as Mrs. Seeley prepared them, exquisitely composed. Then to compensate for the lack of minerals there are injections of crude liver extract every day, and multitudinous pills. These were assembled in a glass dish every morning, in various colors to denote what minerals and vitamins they contained — thirty or more in all. Johnny took niacin, liver powder, lubile (dried powdered bile), vitamins A and D, iron, dicalcium phosphate with viosterol, and lugol. Iodine — in a precisely calculated amount — is essential to the cure.

Johnny's attitude to all this — he was a youngster with a vigorous, healthy appetite—can readily be imagined. He loathed the diet, but he held onto it with the utmost scrupulous fidelity. Carefully he checked off in his notebook the pills he took each day. Once the reason for the thing was explained to him, he faithfully accepted it. The jokes and protests he made were to let off steam, or provide wry humor to the occasion. One evening I asked him if he wanted something, and he replied instantly, "A dose of bichloride of mercury." Once he said that the husks of vegetable in the Gerson soup were deliberately left there as "abrasive to scour out the stomach" and he announced that he had discovered a cure for tapeworm. "Put the patient on the Gerson diet and the tapeworm will evacuate itself in despair."

Johnny's blood and urine tests improved slowly, to the utter disbelief of the physicians who had sent him home to die. They had expected him to expire on Gerson's watch, both absolving them of responsibility and giving them more ammunition against Gerson.

Despite his extreme relief over the positive improvement in his son's condition under Dr. Gerson's care, John Gunther still listened to nay-saying physicians, who tried to persuade him that the other treatments that Johnny had undergone and suffered through, such as radiation and mustard-gas injection, finally were influencing the shrinkage of the brain tumor. But it was clear that they were unwilling to take responsibility for taking Johnny off the diet, either.

Although Johnny's tumor was shrinking and he was clearly much improved, several weeks into the treatment Johnny began to feel unwell. He was running a fever and could not keep up with the schoolwork that he had been determined to pursue even in his sickbed. Dr. Gerson was certain that the tumor tissue was being killed and turned into pus, whereas the other physicians were just as convinced that the fever indicated an infection that had to be stopped before it could spread. Here was a critical juncture. Dr. Gerson was adamant that the healing process should be left to its natural course, whereas the many other physicians that Gunther had hired insisted on an operation, in spite of Gerson's protests that even anesthesia could kill the boy.

Dr. Gerson had often seen the process that Johnny was going through. Part of the healing that occurs in cancer entails an inflammation. This is the body's means of destroying tumor tissue — a healthy sign. Fluid from inflammatory processes — involving various facets of the complex immune system, such as macrophages, lymphocytes and complement — kills tumor tissue; what is left is pus, containing the dead cancer cells and leukocytes. Often the lesion erupts on its own, draining the necrotic fluid externally. In other cases, the body will absorb and eliminate the dead cells by its own means, primarily through the intestinal tract. In the Gerson therapy, frequent and regular coffee enemas become a major aid.

Nonetheless, Johnny was taken to the Harkness Pavilion at the Medical Center. The surgeon compromised only on the type of anesthesia he used, agreeing not to use a general anesthetic but to numb the cranial site simply by freezing it. While Johnny was being prepared for the operation, the lump opened spontaneously, as Dr. Gerson had predicted, and the surgeon drained more than a cup of pus from an abscess that extended nearly two inches into Johnny's brain. The pus was subjected to over 100 cultures, during which Johnny's other physicians attempted to find evidence of infection. The fluid that had been drained from Johnny's head was sterile, with no sign of infectious material or viable cancer cells. Despite this confirmation of previous Dr. Gerson's assertions, John Gunther credited the surgeon, Dr. Mount, with the improvement made by the removal of the pus from Johnny's brain.

An extant carbon copy of a note that Dr. Gerson sent to Raymond Gram Swing on November 21 mentions this episode:

> Johnny made very good progress in the last several days. About ten days ago the tumor started again to transform itself into a kind of abscess formation, caused not by infections but by the decaying of dead tissue. When it broke through, all this matter was eliminated and the tumor became reduced and is shrinking now. Dr. Traeger is very much pleased with this course. His mental capacity after this improved immediately.

Reversal of Fortune

Then came another crisis: Johnny began experiencing a type of eczema, possibly caused by the massive doses of penicillin he had received in preparation for his surgery. This particular kind of rash was usually successfully treated by giving a pituitary hormone extract. Dr. Gerson objected, knowing that it was extremely dangerous to give hormone therapy to cancer patients. As he later wrote in his book, *A Cancer Therapy*:

> In the development of the therapy 15 years ago, I had several . . . setbacks: the worst was the loss of 25 patients out of 31 who were just a few months symptom-free and to whom I had administered the opposite sex hormones to give them strength — in accordance with the initial findings of Dr. Charles Huggins. The first five patients felt so much better within a few weeks, and this misled me. (p. 210)

From this experience Dr. Gerson had learned to resist the impulse to relieve a local or temporary problem by using some drug known to be problematic, only to cause a far greater problem in the future. The other physicians, however, had no such constraint. They continued to press Dr. Gerson to give Johnny the hormone regularly prescribed for eczema sufferers. Additionally, it was suspected that Johnny might have Frohlich's syndrome, caused by a hormonal dysfunction, in which some adolescent boys' testicles remain underdeveloped and their muscles may be weak.

Dr. Gerson finally gave in to the pressure of the other physicians. With great misgivings, he gave Johnny the pituitary hormone. Sure enough, Johnny's eczema improved rapidly; moreover, his tumor was almost completely disappearing. Then, since his recovery appeared to be going well, Johnny went off the Gerson diet to some degree; he began eating meat and other "forbidden" foods containing fat and salt. Everybody involved was patting himself on the back. Even Dr. Gerson felt so confident of the outcome of his treatment that he persuaded Johnny to allow himself to be introduced, and his case discussed, at the patient-demonstration program he gave at the Hotel Carlisle on February 18, 1947.

Then the reversal in Johnny's condition began, as Dr. Gerson had feared might happen. This time, the tumor returned with a vengeance, and quickly grew out of the skull again. An operation performed as a last-ditch effort to help Johnny showed that his brain was filled with tendrils of cancer, like the roots of crabgrass. There was no hope of excising it.

Dr. Gerson was greatly disturbed by this turn of events, as he reflected in his book:

> This disaster threw me into a deep depression. I almost lost the strength to continue this cancer work, as the worst blow of all was the loss of my young hopeful friend [Johnny Gunther] who was treated by more than fifteen cancer authorities and given up with a prognosis for a few weeks. However, after a recovery within eight months, I agreed to let him have some sex hormones. Six weeks later the brain tumor regrew, histologically an astrocytoma. He was returned to the former treatment and died. (p. 211)

Johnny Gunther's death came on June 30, 1947. Ever afterwards, Max Gerson would become emotional whenever the subject of Johnny Gunther was brought up. As he told a group of listeners years later:

> I will tell you why this poor boy died. He had a terrible brain tumor growing out of the skull, larger than my fist. I cured that. It's written in the book [Death Be Not Proud]. But later than that, the boy had an eczema and this eczema was of special type which can usually be cured by giving the anterior lobe pituitary extract, a hormone. The family doctor, Dr. Traeger, said, "Why don't you

give it to him?" But I told him that this is a terrible risk and I don't like to take such a risk with the life of that boy. When we give the pituitary, like many other hormones we may kill. But finally I gave in and it was my fault. And for a long time after that I couldn't sleep nights. I gave him the hormone and the tumor regrew.

I can add to that, that more than 12 years ago now, there appeared an article by a professor in Chicago that cancer patients benefit from administration of contrary (sex) hormones. I gave it first to three patients, then to five. They reacted well for the first two to three months. Then I gave it to 25 more. They all reacted well for three to four months, but after five months they went downhill. I lost 25 of my best cancer cases. Only six I could save again. That was the disaster from the hormone treatment. The Gunther boy was another disaster. That was not necessary. I want to reemphasize that we must not give the cancer patient "a little something" for temporary relief. I learned that the hard way. (from "The Cure of Advanced Cancer by Diet Therapy: A Summary of 30 Years of Clinical Experimentation," talk given in Escondido in 1956, p. 37)

A Tale Told to the World

John Gunther's memoir of his brilliant son's valiant struggle with glioblastoma, *Death Be Not Proud*, was published in February 1949, less than two years after Johnny's death. A sizable portion of the book is devoted to the treatment Johnny received from Dr. Gerson. Gunther's friend, Raymond Swing, who had recommended Dr. Gerson to begin with, later told Dr. Gerson that Gunther had written even more complimentary words and passages about his treatment of Johnny, but his publisher, Cass Canfield of Harper & Row, was concerned about the effect that praise might have on prospective medical writers who would be warned away from the publisher and on already-published writers who might abandon the house for beings too radical. Management also feared potential lawsuits. On the advice of the publisher's three attorneys, as well as out of his own trepidation, Canfield excised many positive remarks that John Gunther had written concerning the Gerson cancer therapy. Still, John Gunther felt deeply grateful to Dr. Gerson, and was convinced of the benefits of his therapy. The Gersons were told by Raymond Swing that Gunther had wanted to donate the proceeds from the book's publication to Dr. Gerson, for the purpose of expanding his research and treatment capabilities, but his publisher also vetoed that idea, insisting instead that a portion of the book-sales royalties go to the American Cancer Society.

In his memoir *Good Evening*, published in 1964, Swing briefly mentioned this entire drama, without revealing his own key role in Johnny's story or his strong belief at that time in the efficacy of the Gerson therapy:

[Gerson's] primary, and indeed obsessive, interest was to prove that cancer could be controlled and cured through his special dietary treatment. A good many of his cancer patients undoubtedly benefited for a time. John Gunther's son, who died of a brain tumor, and about whom he wrote his deeply moving *Death Be Not Proud*, was a Gerson patient for some time and actually improved to the point that he could go back to his preparatory school and graduate, though his physicians refused to attribute the improvement to the Gerson treatment. (pp 250-251)

For years, *Death Be Not Proud* has been required reading for many high-school students in English literature classes. It is a deeply touching story of a father's desperate love for his brilliant son, the various attempts he made to save the boy's life, and his grief at the terrible loss both he and Johnny's mother suffered. The book also includes Frances Gunther's account of the ordeal and her eloquent tribute to the stalwart Johnny, who often managed to be good humored, even ebullient during his severe illness. The book was made into a television special, shown on February 4, 1975, as an ABC-TV Movie of the Week. Dr. Gerson appears only briefly. Some Gerson family members held their breath as the Max Gerson character came on the scene. Accustomed over the years to incidences of scurrilous treatment of his reputation, they fully expected a portrayal of a two-headed monster. In fact, Dr. Gerson was portrayed in a rather neutral way — neither as a brilliant physician, nor as a raving quack, but as the serious, quiet, dedicated man that he was.

~17~
The Work Goes On
(1947–1951)

The Madison Foundation

For the 10 years after he had first opened his medical practice in New York City in 1937, Dr. Max Gerson had rented three rooms for his offices from Dr. Heinrich Wolf at Madison Avenue and 60th Street. An older-vintage office building, it had a rattling old elevator that transported his patients to and from its upper floors whenever they visited him. The two physicians had become good friends, but in early 1947, Dr. Wolf needed the rooms for his own expanding practice. With regret he told Max that he would have to find some space of his own. Fortunately, it happened that his friend, Samuel A. Markel, had been looking for some material way to help the extraordinary physician who had earlier rescued him from a painful osteoarthritic condition. Markel had been responsible for initiating the contact with Senator Pepper, leading to the Senate Subcommittee hearings in the previous year.

Sam Markel organized a group of Dr. Gerson's former patients who wanted to promote his work with cancer and other diseases. Aware of Dr. Gerson's increasing dissatisfaction with the Gotham Hospital arrangement through the Robinson Foundation, they had formed a new nonprofit, charitable organization, then collected a sum of money sufficient to purchase a building in Manhattan for Gerson's clinical and research use. The five-story brownstone building was located at 11 East 74th Street, between Fifth Avenue and Madison Avenue. Thus the Madison Foundation for Biochemical Research, Inc. began.

The building acquired by the foundation had enough rooms to provide sanatorium facilities for 15 to 20 patients, depending on how the rooms were configured. There was space too for doctors' offices, examination rooms and meeting rooms. In the basement a laboratory would be installed, so that Dr. Gerson could have his tests processed on the premises. The building would also feature X-ray equipment for taking roentgenograms necessary for diagnosis and monitoring tumor changes.

However, in the midst of the Madison Foundation's bustling preparations for the new medical facility, a serious oversight was committed in the planning stage. The directors had neglected to check into the zoning regulations for the neighborhood — which, it turned out, forbade the building's use for housing patients. This setback wasn't fatal because the building could still house all the other facilities needed in treating outpatients. In the meantime, he investigated the possibility of setting up a Gerson-therapy sanatorium outside of New York City.

Dr. Gerson was surprised and perhaps even shocked when he learned that the Madison Foundation board of directors had selected Dr. George Miley as the medical director and thus his "collaborator" in providing medical services. However, he probably made no objection to this at the time. Dr. Gerson was doubtless pleased that a colleague and friend of his, the prominent biochemical researcher Rudolph Keller, was now connected with the Madison Foundation. So was Mrs. Margaret Seeley, whose home had been converted into a small city-based sanatorium and dining facility for Gerson patients. Mrs. Seeley even served on the board of directors and had an officer's rank as secretary of the organization.

In spite of any misgivings Dr. Gerson might have had in dealing with Dr. Miley in administrative and supervisory functions, his practice initially thrived at the Madison Foundation location. The space for medical offices was ample. The convenient on-site laboratory with its expert personnel provided quick test results, and the X-ray lab, run by Dr. Deutschberger, a radiologist brought in by Dr. Miley, could conduct thorough the organ- and bone-scanning examinations that were especially important in cancer and osteoarthritis cases. Income for these services, which were available to outside physicians and clinics as well, helped sustain the foundation's other projects.

West Point Farms

For patients who needed to receive round-the-clock, residential treatment, Dr. Gerson needed a sanatorium larger and more focused than the Seeleys' room-and-board facility. Mrs. Seeley's house in the middle of Manhattan was operated more as a way-station for outpatients to get soup, food and juices while they were doing the therapy or consulting Dr. Gerson in New York. It was not a particularly restful environment for recuperating patients.

After hearing the bad news denying inpatient residence within the Madison Foundation building, Mr. and Mrs. Appison came to the rescue. Like Sam Markel and Margaret Seeley, they were former patients of Dr, Gerson. Now they offered him the use of their large stone farmhouse as a sanatorium. This 50-acre property was comprised of a large farmhouse, open fields, and woods, as well as well as pigsties, chicken coops, and apple orchards. Called West Point Farms, the property was located in Central Valley, less than 10 miles west of the Hudson River town of Mohegan Lake. The farmhouse could accommodate up to 30 patients, without any fear of violating the zoning code. The large stone house commanded a sweeping view of wide lawns and wooded paths, with apple orchards stretching beyond the stone walls.. Across the valley were the tank-practice grounds used by cadets of the nearby West Point Military Reservation. On a pleasant summer day, patients could sit out on lawn chairs and watch the tanks maneuvering on the opposite hillside, as if in a giant amphitheater.

Another unusual feature of this sanatorium was the working pig farm on the property. The pigs, fed the huge volumes of organic waste materials from the kitchens, grew fat and healthy. What was ultimately done with the pigs was not Dr. Gerson's concern, but they were certainly not slaughtered and consumed on the property. There only vegetarian fare was served, in accordance with the early, intensive-therapy phases of the Gerson diet.The house had a large kitchen with an additional crucial advantage — since both the Appisons were former Gerson patients, they were experienced in the food preparation and juicing required by the therapy. They could be counted on to feed the patients properly. The large dining area was a long covered porch which ran the length of the building, and the living room doubled as a recreation room for reading and card playing. Here, too, on weekend afternoons Dr. Gerson gave his "chats" and patient presentations. Now Gerson patients could be lodged in the bucolic atmosphere of Central Valley. The facility was especially suited for those who were very sick and required specialized 24-hour care during the initial period of intensive treatment, which usually lasted for a minimum of a month but sometimes required a much longer stay.

This farm was close enough to New York City to be readily accessible to Dr. Gerson on weekends — about 55 miles from his office. The drive took about an hour and a quarter to an hour and a half. To get there, his patients had to arrange for personal transportation. Dr. Gerson normally went there every weekend, and his wife went with him. A regular taxi service picked them up and then brought them back home on those weekends when nobody else could provide a ride. On their weekends at Central Valley, Max and Gretchen took long walks in the woods behind the large farmhouse, often accompanied by one or more of their visiting grandchildren. Just as he had done years earlier with his own children, now on excursions with his young grandchildren Max pointed out the interesting life processes of the forest.

Gerson sometimes invited other patients, especially if they were particularly interesting people, to take walks with him. However, since the cancer patients were required to have total rest, using whatever energy they had for the healing process, he discouraged them from walking at all until they were almost back to normal good health.

At West Point Farms, Dr. Gerson took considerable care to educate his patients about his therapy and its results. He held patient demonstrations, eagerly anticipated weekly chats that took place after lunch or dinner on weekends when he was there. Having chosen three or four of the resident patients to be his subjects, or welcoming the presence of recovered patients as visitors, he would give brief case histories, which included discussing their improvements since they began treatment with him. It was a happy time for doctor, participants and onlookers. Patients who had been on the therapy for some weeks were eager to be on display, since they were proud of the progress they had made. And patients just starting the regimen were naturally encouraged by this evidence of improvement and renewed well-being.

Physicians often visited the sanatorium. Most apparently hoped to see confirmation of the negative views published in JAMA or mentioned elsewhere, as when promulgated by the American Cancer Society with their newly issued "Unproven Therapies" list. They would attend the demonstrations of healing patients, then usually leave without any comment at all, their expectations of charlatanism disappointed. However, on occasion, some young doctor, impressed with what he had seen and heard, would approach Dr. Gerson and ask to be trained in his method. Ever desirous of imparting his long-garnered treatment wisdom, Dr. Gerson wanted nothing more than a chance to mentor others, so he would eagerly begin to instruct the physician in his empirically derived protocols. But these learning experiences usually ended within a very few weeks as these physicians began to feel uncomfortable about veering away from orthodoxy. Some erstwhile protegés told Dr. Gerson of being threatened with ostracism by the medical establishment; they could not risk their careers by associating with him any longer.

The AMA Crusade against Dr. Gerson

In January 1949, The Journal of the American Medical Association and its editor-in-chief, Dr. Morris Fishbein, resumed their crusade against Dr. Gerson. An article within the January 8 issue, in the section "Council on Pharmacy and Chemistry: Report of the Council," displayed the title CANCER AND THE NEED FOR FACTS, and under the subheading "Frauds and Fables," covered the topic of "Dietary 'Treatment,'" citing the work of Dr. Max Gerson:

> Another 'treatment' for cancer involving dietary restrictions is that of a Dr. Max B. Gerson of New York City, who has been reported by The JOURNAL to be using a dietary and salt-controlled method that is said to be supported by a Robinson Foundation for cancer research located at 14 Wall Street, New York. The JOURNAL pointed out [referring in a footnote to its November 15, 1946 editorial] that Gerson had been previously connected with a diet method falsely

proposed as an advance in the treatment of tuberculosis and that the research "foundation" for cancer was actually financed by two business enterprises.... The detailed "diet" proposed by Gerson consisted essentially in restriction of all foods other than uncanned fresh fruits and vegetables and oatmeal and forbade the use of aluminum utensils and pressure cookers in preparation of food and the use of such items as salt, spices, sodium bicarbonate, alcohol and tobacco. His "treatment" also included the internal administration of iodine, liver, iron and various vitamins (apparently to supplement a diet lacking in essential proteins and fat) and the use of an enema formula to produce copious daily bowel movements. The diet was said to make the body highly hypersensitive, so that ordinary anesthesia might be fatal, a conjecture that is wholly unfounded and apparently designed to appeal to the cancer victim already fearful of a surgical operation which might offer the only effective means for eradication of the disease. However, there is no scientific evidence whatsoever to indicate that modifications in the dietary intake of food or other nutritional essentials are of any specific value in the control of cancer. (1949:139:2, pp. 93-96)

The malice involved in this attack by the AMA on one of its own members is evident in the omission of any reference to previously published material, including its own favorable 1929 review of Dr. Gerson's work, that might have led a researcher on his own quest for truth. Even a minimally diligent search of medical archives would have turned up two books written in German and published in Europe, plus many papers, which would culminate a decade later in his description of his dietary and detoxifying approach to healing in the book, A Cancer Therapy. Additionally, there have been several hundred articles, both domestic and foreign, written about the Gerson diet and therapy by other researchers in the over-70-year span between 1929 and 1999. These articles confirm the therapeutic value of Dr. Gerson's method and its effectiveness against tuberculosis, diabetes and other degenerative diseases.

It was invidious for the American Medical Association to dismiss Dr. Gerson's work and sully his reputation in this manner. Fortunately for Dr. Gerson, Morris Fishbein's long tenure as editor-in-chief ended soon after that issue of JAMA came out in early 1949, but taking its cue from the American Medical Association, the American Cancer Society put the Gerson's therapy on its dreaded "Unproven Therapies" blacklist, which is circulated among all medical schools and centers, health delivery-connected organizations, charitable foundations, physicians' associations and the inquiring public. (It is also available now, of course, on Internet.) This action guaranteed the rejection of the Gerson therapy by insurance companies as an acceptable treatment deserving of their financial compensation. It also discouraged any physicians from associating themselves with it in any way, such as monitoring patients who have chosen to follow it. Without support from their health insurance policies and health providers, cancer patients usually lack the ability to pursue any but the "approved" treatments. In effect, all but the more affluent people are cut off from those therapies the AMA wishes to suppress, unless determined individuals are willing to pursue particular ones at their own expense, which usually they can ill afford to do. The therapy remains on this virtual blacklist today, though the list has been renamed "Alternative and Complementary Therapies," with a euphemistic nod toward the increasing interest in unorthodox treatments shown by Americans during the 1990s.

Missing Files

Although Samuel Markel had made tremendous efforts on the behalf of the Madison Foundation and Dr. Gerson, he was not always free to oversee operations or defend the Gerson therapy because he was engaged in his own business enterprises. Dr. George Miley, in his role as medical director, supervised the day-to-day operation of the medical facility itself, and his command over its whole scope kept increasing. Dr. Miley persuaded the board of directors to appoint a group of physicians to serve as a "Medical Review Board." Paid for their participation in this deliberative body, the members were empowered to evaluate all medical documents and results of patient treatment provided by the Madison Foundation. The influence of this review board on Dr. Gerson's research became troublesome. Max began to complain to his family and friends that he could no longer get a single medical test done, and that Dr. Miley blocked every move he made — interfering with every peripheral activity of the practice, from needed tests to professional cooperation, from publication to secretarial help.

In 1950 Dr. Gerson was working on a report to be published by the Madison Foundation, about some of his most important recent case histories. He began to notice that the folders on these patients, kept in his unlocked offices, were not in his file cabinets. At first he thought they were only temporarily gone — borrowed for some reason. Now the documentation seemed permanently removed: details of laboratory test results, records of past treatment, X-rays, follow-ups, everything.

When he asked his secretary about these missing patient files, she said she would try to locate them. She instead reported this problem to Dr. Miley's secretary, who in turn informed Dr. Gerson that the files were the legal property of the foundation and that he could not have them back. No matter what was said, Dr. Gerson knew that the patients' medical records did not rightly belong to the foundation. They may have belonged to the patient, or to physicians who had prepared them, but never to the foundation itself.

When he scolded his own secretary for having permitted the files to be removed and then demanded their return, she became intransigent and hostile. After he fired her on the spot for insubordination, Dr. Miley rehired her the next day. Max now realized that the amicable "collaboration" between the two physicians that Samual Markel had intended, was over. Gerson could see well enough that the Madison Foundation was no longer, by any stretch of the imagination, a vehicle for encouraging his medical work. He immediately tendered his resignation from the organization.

Since Dr. Miley still held onto Dr. Gerson's case history files, he wrote to the New York Academy of Medicine to complain and to appeal for their help in retrieving these very important patient records. The Academy in turn passed Dr. Gerson's letter on to the Medical Society of the County of New York, whose presiding councilor, Reed B. Dawson, wrote to him:

> I confirm herewith receipt of your letter and copy of the letter of May 7th addressed to the Academy of Medicine.
>
> In your letter, you request an official judgement (or declaration) from the Medical Society of the County of New York about the right of ownership of certain X-ray plates which are described in your letter.
>
> Although I am not permitted by my contract with my employers to give an official opinion, except to the officials and Censors of the committee, the Comitia Minora, I believe that I can unofficially express that, as far as I know, there has been no precedent decision on the ownership of X-rays. Cases in other courts, Michigan, Massachusetts, Ohio, seem to indicate that films or plates belong to the radiologists, technicians or to the person who made the X-rays. The precedent case on the matter was McGarry vs. J.A. Mercer Co. (Michigan) 262 N.W. 296. The decision of the Supreme Court in this case is very well supported and I would be surprised if the N.Y. Court did not follow it.
>
> I am sure that your lawyer is quite familiar with McGarry and other cases of this kind, and that he will give you good advice about the X-rays you mention in your letter.

A casualty of Dr. Gerson's rupture with the Madison Foundation was his once-good relationship with Margaret Seeley, one of its directors and officers. Now her Manhattan nursing home would no longer be available to Gerson's patients.

In some respects the worst harm ever done to Dr. Gerson's reputation came when Dr. Miley and his colleagues on the review board at the Madison Foundation cancelled plans to send out an impressive selection of Gerson's favorable case histories (his original project) to a large list of medical establishment-connected institutions and publications across the United States, and instead substituted a report stating that the Medical Review Board had determined that no significant improvements had occurred in patients who had received the Gerson therapy through the Madison Foundation. Any Gerson detractor, then or later, could use this widely circulated letter to discredit the Gerson therapy.

Several years after this incident, Max Gerson was still rankled about it. As he wrote in a letter to his good friend Henry Schaefer-Simmern :

> The greatest damage against my work was done by that criminal Dr. Miley when he succeeded to get out of the Evaluation Committee of the Foundation a paper stating that they could not find that I had results in any case. That statement signed by the secretary of the Madison Foundation, Mrs. Seeley, was sent all over the country, to universities, medical colleges, scientific research laboratories, archives, etc., and wherever they thought they could wipe out my work once and for all. It was a funny occasion when they did it because just a half a year before that Dr. Miley [s]elected out of 30 cured cancer cases six for publication. These cases were accepted for publication by a friend of Dr. Rudolph Keller and the president of the Foundation, Markel, ordered that 3,000 copies be printed and sent to the above mentioned places. The reprints were destroyed or disappeared and instead of that he sent the statement of the Evaluation Committee. I think you would have to know these facts as they may not be so vivid in your memory and one or another may refer to them. I think you will now be able to clear this question up.

Almost certainly the nasty internal politics within the Madison Foundation as well as the negative external publicity connected with Gerson's therapeutic methods in this acrimonious 1949-50 period caused the once loyal Raymond Swing, who initially had been pleased to serve on the Madison Foundation's board of directors, to pull away from his previous close association with his former physician. As someone still much in the public eye through his lectures and writings, Swing doubtless realized that he could not afford to sully his reputation by defending further someone who was again being widely portrayed as a charlatan by the American Medical Association and its close ally, the American Cancer Society. He ended his memoir mention of his association with Max Gerson by saying:

> As to Dr. Gerson, I regret that he later came into disagreement with his medical associates in New York by claiming actual cancer cures in cases in which orthodox medical controls had been neglected, perhaps largely through his impatience. I shall always thankfully acknowledge my debt to him as a physician, but I had to disassociate myself from any assurance by him that he could cure cancer. (p. 251)

The Madison Foundation collapsed as a viable entity not long after Max Gerson's departure. But Max Gerson's own work went on. As he told Henry Schaefer-Simmern:

> I had to work harder last year to make good all inferences and disasters I had from the Madison Foundation, Miley and Seeley, but I was glad to overcome all

those troubles and I am now on the upward trend again.

At the moment half of the patients in Central Valley are from California and a few more are coming after having had several outstanding results there. (7/31/51)

Family Comforts

Despite the best — or worst — efforts of the medical profession, including the unfortunate problems caused by the Madison Foundation's management, Dr. Gerson's practice prospered in the late 1940s and early 1950s. Many patients will eventually find a doctor who has the reputation of effecting cancer cures and other seemingly intractable conditions. No matter how much power organized medicine brings to bear on the media, word of mouth cannot be stopped. The Central Valley sanatorium was always filled to capacity, as was Gerson's own waiting room, daily.

Dr. Gerson's perseverance in the face of constant opposition and active subversion within the entire medical community was remarkable indeed. He could have caved in to save his skin, stepped into line with the rest of the profession, stopped his determined efforts to heal people given up by their own doctors, and simply gone through the motions of giving treatments he knew to be ineffectual.

Max Gerson's patients were loyal to him because he was loyal to them. Their doctor put *their* recovery and health foremost in his mind and heart, and they knew it. Dr. Gerson had infinite patience with his patients because he realized that they were ill and their comprehension was impaired, that most had little or no understanding of nutrition, physiology or chemistry, and that they were toxic. However, he had no patience for perpetual incomprehension or repeated foolish mistakes in the administration of the therapy, so would raise his voice and intimidate such patients. As it is said, "Beware the temper of a patient man."

The largest percentage of his patients over the years were "terminal" cancer patients; lesser numbers were cancer cases with more hopeful prognoses, as well as people with other diseases. Now and again, a celebrity might be among them, perhaps requiring nothing more than a detoxifying tune-up and a course in healthful eating — movie actress Gloria Swanson, a notorious organic-foods proselytizer, was a notable one.

After Max Gerson moved out of his medical offices at the Madison Foundation in 1950, he also changed his apartment residence from 40 West 55th Street to a building located at 815 Park Avenue, off 75th Street — a very fashionable neighborhood in Manhattan. This larger apartment had an office and waiting room attached to it, so the doctor now had a convenient consultation office within the family's apartment on the seventh floor. His office was elegantly furnished with comfortable leather armchairs and a large, handsome wooden desk. Two different carved ebony chairs, one inlaid with ivory, were also part of the office decoration, as well as a large bookshelf with many volumes. The floor was covered by a real Persian rug.

The family's living room was next to Max's office, so shared a wall with it. A prime place in the room was occupied by the medium-sized grand piano made by Blüthner of Leipzig. Like most of their original European possessions, this wedding gift from Gretchen's parents had traveled with the family furniture in a large shipping container, sent from Berlin to Palestine to Paris — finally ending up in New York. Gretchen treasured the piano and often played it. However, since it was right next to the consultation office, she refrained from playing while her husband was seeing patients.

From the 1940s through the mid 1950s, the three Gerson daughters were not much involved directly with their father's medical practice. Busy with their own adult lives, they were often unaware of his challenges, including his difficulties with the Robinson and Madison foundations, the periodic attacks on his practice by medical associations, his ongoing feud with the AMA and by the American Cancer Society, and his frustrations over rejected papers he had submitted for publication. In his later years, though, his two older daughters would have important roles in his work, while his third daughter was destined to perpetuate his therapy after his death.

The oldest daughter, Johanna Cohn, had come back from Philadelphia to her parents' home in 1944 after a divorce, bringing with her a five-year-old daughter, Suzanne. For several years in the late '40s, Johanna had worked with Mrs. Seeley in providing the Gerson diet therapy to patients at the nursing home, and her second wedding, to Arnold Oberlander, even took place at the Seeleys' house. Johanna then moved with her new husband to Hamburg, Germany, where Arnold worked in his father's business. In the next few years she would have two more children, Michael and Paula, before returning to the New York area.

After her wartime marriage, Gertrude (always called Trudy), had left her work in millinery design and sales to help her husband, Fred Selten, run his upscale candy store, Cosmopolitan Confiserie, in the East 50s, as well as a second candy store that shipped gifts of candy and other "goodies" to U.S. Armed Forces personnel during the war years. In 1949 the couple's only child, Peter, was born.

As for Charlotte, or Lotte, she and her infant son Howard spent the later war years living with her parents while her husband, Irwin Straus, served in the Army. In 1947 the Strauses' second child, Margaret (Peggy), arrived. In 1949 Lotte worked for two months at the West Point Farms sanatorium; there she did hands-on care of patients, made the rounds with her father on weekends, shopped and generally helped run the place. This was her first intensive experience in Gerson clinic management. The Strauses then started their own business, an import brokerage office that dealt with raw materials shipped from foreign lands.

In September of 1950, I went to live with my grandparents at their Park Avenue apartment so that I could attend school in their neighborhood. Much in agreement with her father's liking for the Waldorf education methods, my mother now enrolled me in the private Rudolf Steiner School, but the school was too far from her own home on Long Island for daily commuting. At first I went home to my parents only weekends and during school vacations, except for those times when I accompanied my grandparents on their weekly trip to West Point Farms. I attended the Rudolf Steiner School through high school, except for a brief period spent in another school, and continued to live with my grandparents during the week, until old enough to travel to school on my own, usually taking the long trip via the subway. Inevitably, Max and Gretchen significantly influenced my evolution throughout boyhood. Six years my junior, my cousin Peter Selten followed a similar schedule of spending the week at our grandparents' home while attending the same Waldorf school. My cousin Suzie Oberlander also occasionally boarded with our grandparents.

One of the things that I knew for certain by age 9 or 10 was that if you got cancer, you went on my Grandpa's diet and got well. There was never was a question about it, because I saw these people, spent time with them, attended the weekend presentations, ate with them. I grew up on the Hippocrates soup, carrot juice, even for a time the liver juice for my anemia. At supper we gathered around the table, eating mostly the foods that would have been served at the clinic. Occasionally had some meat, but not often. The problems came when we had to eat sourgrass or fennel, one of the occasional dreaded meals that all the kids hated. We would sit there for hours, not being allowed to get up from the table until it was bedtime. If we hadn't finished it by then, well, we would just get it for breakfast. It didn't take too many of those lessons before we learned there was no compromising with our grandparents. Not a total vegetarian, my grandfather loved fish, and ate it probably twice a month. Since he didn't trust his own sense of smell, which had been damaged by the iodine poisoning in Breslau, Gretchen had to make sure the fish was fresh and edible. Once a week he would eat a patty of the very finest steak tartare — freshly and finely ground raw beef combined with raw onion.

My grandfather was a very quiet man, only really coming out of his thoughts when we were in the woods — he *loved* the woods — and he could explain nature to us. The cycle of birth, life, death — recycling of the dead materials to give birth again. But he was not a very warm or personal man. My grandmother occasionally had issues with him and would yell at him. When she used the name "Marcus" to address him, we knew there was trouble. There was a lot of love for the children in the house — but the kind of German love where the kids are seen and not heard. We were expected to be disciplined and to be hard-working (mostly on schoolwork). We did dishes, but mostly had the time to ourselves.

My grandmother often read us German children's stories, many of them fairly violent or bloody. *Struwwelpeter* was one of them. It was about a kid who doesn't allow his hair or fingernails to be cut, and won't eat his soup ("*Ich esse meine Suppe nicht! Nein! Meine Suppe ess ich nicht!*") Eventually he gets so skinny with long hair and nails that the tailor comes with huge shears and cuts off his thumbs. The illustration of this scene? The boy with blood spurting from his amputated thumbs. She seemed to love these stories. Our grandmother occasionally dragged us to the Metropolitan Opera, which was an ordeal. It seemed like a lot of fat people yelling at each other for hours. But Gretchen played the piano like an angel. During her daily exercises, I would lie underneath the Blüthner baby grand piano, getting the full impact of Mozart, Chopin and Schubert directly from the instrument's sounding board, a foot from my nose. A large part of my love of classical music comes from that experience of letting the sound just pour onto me.

Gretchen was shy, reticent, and it took a long time for her to warm up to people. This is apparently a Westphalian trait; they are proud to say "before you can call a Westphalian [the familiar] *du*, you have to share a peck of salt with them." She was very strong, very capable, educated and multilingual, and was able to do what needed to be done. But she worried a lot about money and business. Since her husband usually was almost wholly lacking in giving attention to those areas vital to family survival, the total responsibility fell upon her shoulders. She was not trained in any aspect of business and finance, so always worried that she was inadequate. Other reasons caused her to get into anxious states. She had lost most of her family to the Holocaust, and during the war years one never knew which side would ultimately prevail. It was very clear to her what would happen to our family if the Nazis and their confederates won the war — a situation that looked eminently possible during the early part of the war, what with the Nazis marching all over Europe and Africa, and the Japanese attacking American territory in Hawaii, as well as controlling the entire western Pacific. There were also, of course, the near-constant attacks against her husband throughout his professional life. Though Max could shrug these attacks off, Gretchen was both frightened and angered by them.

Although he may never have said so—certainly not in our earshot—Max Gerson was comforted by his wife Gretchen and family of children and grandchildren living with him from time to time.

~18~
Health Ecology
(1949–1952)

Dr. Schweitzer and Type 2 Diabetes

By the late 1940s and early 1950s the science of ecology, focusing on the interactions among living creatures and their connections with the physical environment around them, was beginning to gain attention from researchers, educators and members of the lay public concerned about human and planetary health. A growing number of people no longer felt that all was well in the natural world, whose mostly pristine or at least renewable existence had largely been taken for granted. Mortal challenges to nature, traceable to centuries of headlong human incursions, were intensified as new forms of human invention, industry and warfare spread across the planet. As if under some new insidious attack, species of animals and plants were diminishing, disappearing, dying out, far more rapidly than in the past. Even humans were being affected — developing baffling new infectious and degenerative diseases, while cardiovascular disease and cancer rates were rising alarmingly—even as, or perhaps partially because, the population numbers increased geometrically in most countries.

But Dr. Max Gerson had been interested in such issues for a long time. And so had a physician friend of his who ran a clinic in a remote part of West Africa. In the spring of 1949 Dr. Gerson got a call from Dr. Albert Schweitzer, his old friend and admirer. Schweitzer, then 75 years old, said that he would be coming to the United States, for the first time (and, it turned out, the only time), to accept an honorary doctorate from the University of Chicago and to participate in a bicentennial celebration—arranged by the University's president, Robert M. Hutchins—of the birth of the great German writer Goethe, to be held at Aspen, Colorado. He had plans to be in New York City twice during this trip, at the beginning and at the end. So he hoped to see again the esteemed physician who much earlier had cured his wife of tuberculosis and then his daughter of a baffling skin ailment.

There was another reason for Dr. Schweitzer's desire to meet with Max. He now requested absolute confidentiality about what he wished to tell him. Assured of that, he said that he had recently discovered that he was suffering from diabetes. He had lived a long, full and active life, which had placed enormous strain on his mind and body. But now diabetes was starting to rob him of his energy. Unable to work effectively, Schweitzer hoped that Max might provide advice about changing his diet in a way that would permit him to regain his strength and also avoid using regular insulin injections — which would be a nuisance, especially when at his clinic at Lambaréné. He had discreetly consulted a few diabetes specialists in Europe, who had put him on a special diet. But his health was still deteriorating, and he was concerned that he might not be able to continue his humanitarian medical work in the middle of Africa.

Many people at that stage in life might have just lightened up their work load altogether, especially if satisfied with some record of accomplishment, though only a fraction of the one Schweitzer had amassed over the years. He had doctorates in several diverse fields — theology, music, philosophy and medicine — and was an acknowledged leader in them all. Not only was he a physician who worked for much of his life at the jungle missionary clinic he established in French Equatorial Africa, but as an accomplished organist he raised money for the clinic by giving organ concerts throughout Europe. Schweitzer had a reputation for not wishing to play on organs in less than excellent shape. Before he played a concert, he would often give the organ an overhaul, as he was also an organ builder. One of the world's leading authorities on Johann Sebastian Bach, he wrote learned books on this giant composer of the Baroque period. Also a clergyman and theologian, he wrote books on the life of Christ and other religious themes. In his spare time, he wrote books on philosophy, built the organ in his hometown of Günsbach in the Alsace-Lorraine and taught Sunday school.

Dr. Schweitzer knew that the Gerson therapy worked in part by correcting the body's metabolism—which meant that it might ameliorate his diabetes as well. Dr. Gerson told Schweitzer over the telephone that age-onset diabetes could usually be healed through his therapeutic techniques. He had already had ample experience with patients suffering from type 2 diabetes, whether by itself or in conjunction with other degenerative diseases, both in his European clinics and more recently in his American practice, to know that it responded rapidly and predictably to his nutritional therapy. Thus assured, Albert said he would set aside a time to see Max during his busy schedule. He was going to have a series of visitors come to see him privately at the apartment of Dr. Ross, where he would be staying — away from the usual fanfare that surrounded him in public places. So when Max came to visit him there, they could spend some time alone together, to confer about the dietary changes that Gerson knew were crucial in controlling diabetes.

When the two German-born doctors finally got together, Dr. Gerson examined his old friend and studied the results of various tests taken earlier of his bodily fluids, especially for glucose levels and the presence of natural insulin. He concluded, in German, "You do seem to have a simple case of type 2 diabetes, Albert." Since Dr. Schweitzer's bloodstream contained adequate amounts of insulin, his problem apparently came from his body cells' inability to properly assimilate and metabolize it.

"Yes, Max," he agreed. "And I know that type 2 diabetes should respond readily to treatment. But though I asked several different European physicians for help, they were unable to offer me any form of dietary treatment that seems to work well enough. I have been following the advice that they gave me: to avoid eating carbohydrates and sugar, and to eat plenty of protein. Still, the diabetes keeps getting worse, regardless of what I do."

"What kind of protein have you been eating?"

"Well, whatever animal proteins are available to me, wherever I am. These are much more restricted, of course, at Lambaréné than in Europe. The usual ones: pork, chicken, goat, fish, eggs — and beef when I can get it. And I am forbidden to eat fruits, bread and potatoes, because of their high carbohydrate contents."

"My good friend, please don't be alarmed, but you should do almost the opposite." Then Max explained his understanding of diabetes to Schweitzer. "The problem with the conventional approach to treatment, staying with a protein-rich diet, is that animal protein is also high in animal fat, which *worsens* the problem instead of easing it. You must bring your entire metabolism back into balance. The best way to do that is to take food and drink juices that are easy to digest, as opposed to animal fat and protein, which are not. Also, of course, your diet should contain carbohydrates that are complex rather than simple — cutting down on the intake of any foods that rapidly convert to glucose during digestion, before entering the bloodstream. Try to drink vegetable juices far more than fruit juices, because there will be less sugar in them, and for the same reason eat far more vegetables than fruit. Otherwise, there is little difference between the diet I gave Hélène and Rhena and the one you should be following."

Max handed his new patient a printed booklet containing his basic diet-therapy regimen. "Other than the diabetes, you are in good shape for your age, and that should help to give you a full recovery," he commented.

"Do you think, then, that I will be able eventually to stop using insulin? It hadn't done much for me, and it is a real inconvenience."

"Just maintain a close watch on your blood picture, Albert," Max now assured him. "And if you want to keep your condition a secret from everyone around you, and therefore the world at large, do the glucose tests yourself. I know you haven't forgotten how to do that simple procedure, so don't turn them over to your assistants. If you follow the diet plan as closely as possible, after a while you may never need to take insulin injections. And soon, I think, you will be able to resume your regular duties at Lambaréné, without anyone having noticed that anything was amiss with your state of health."

Albert Schweitzer began following Max Gerson's dietary instructions as best he could. When he later returned to Lambaréné , he felt ready again to undertake the challenges of running a clinic in the middle of an African jungle, as well as the inevitable travel of his busy life connected with lecturing and fundraising activities in Europe. A highly private and stoic man, he kept his diabetes-prone condition a secret from everyone, managing to keep it under control through very careful eating. Even his daughter Rhena did not learn he had suffered from type 2 diabetes until 10 years after his very discreet consultation with Dr. Max Gerson in New York. Perhaps not surprisingly, then, in all Schweitzer's writings, including letters, and in biographies of him, no mention has yet been found of this diabetic episode or of his consultation with Max Gerson in New York City in 1949. Apparently only a few members of the Gerson family ever knew of this event, and they scarcely broadcast it to others, then or later. And knowing that any letter he wrote to anyone, including Dr. Gerson, was apt to be read by others, Schweitzer avoided discussing the matter in their subsequent correspondence.

Three years after his trip to America, Dr. Albert Schweitzer was awarded the 1952 Nobel Peace Prize for his years of humanitarian work in Africa. He lived and worked productively until his death in 1965 at age 90 — a full 15 years after he had come to Dr. Gerson, to get his advice about treating diabetes by following his diet-therapy principles.

Recent research by Nathan Pritikin has confirmed Gerson's dietary approach by showing that in type 2 diabetes the body cannot use available insulin because the insulin receptors on muscle and other tissue cells become blocked by cholesterol, thus preventing the insulin molecules from activating special portals that allow glucose to enter the cell, where blood sugar is normally metabolized. This insulin-resistant form of diabetes, therefore, may be due to excessive dietary fat intake and fat metabolism, not insulin shortage as such. The conventional diet prescribed to diabetics is rich in protein. Unfortunately, meat protein comes mostly in foods containing very high levels of fat and cholesterol, exacerbating the underlying problem. Patients deteriorate further as their arterial vessels clog with cholesterol and block circulation, causing neuropathy and even gangrene of the extremities as well as loss of energy, eyesight, kidney function and eventually life itself.

Type 2 diabetes patients are, nevertheless, still using insulin and other pharmaceuticals, indicating that Pritikin's findings have been widely ignored — certainly not put much into practice. After all, glucose-level test kits and drugs for diabetics are a lucrative business. And many type 2 diabetics, like other people afflicted with degenerative diseases, are unwilling to give up their "comfort foods," if a drug can be taken that promises to offset their detrimental effects.

The American diet, high in meat protein, fat and simple carbohydrates — notably refined sugar and white flour and other foods with a high glycemic index — is ideal for inducing diabetes. Fast-food fare typifies public consumption. Combining this faulty diet with a sedentary lifestyle lacking regular exercise has created a virtual epidemic. Sixteen million Americans have been diagnosed with diabetes, with more than 90 percent of them having type 2; another 5 million have it and don't know it. By the time many people receive a diagnosis, permanent damage to their health has already taken place. (*Newsweek*, September 4, 2000)

External Metabolism and the "Diseases of Civilization"

During his early years of practice in Bielefeld, Max had decided that the practice of healing could not consist of a collection of specialists with distinctly separate domains — just as the human organism is not simply the sum of an individual's body parts. Medical specialization tends to lead real healers away from the goal of restoring total health, because physicians focus on one particular disease symptom with the goal of eradicating its apparent single cause. This viewpoint is akin to examining a tree or a set of leaves and then deciding that one can now understand the composition and function of an entire forest, though ignoring its complex totality.

Like Dr. Schweitzer, Max Gerson showed concern for all living creatures and their good health — plants and animals, as well as human beings. He realized that all life was ultimately interconnected, and that changing some aspects of the environment, the living conditions, of one kind of creature might well affect the health of others, whether at that time or in a distant future. He regarded the body and mind, too, as a totality, a sum of many intricate parts that ideally should exist and work together in harmony. Thus his approach to treating each individual who came to him in a state of ill health involved restoring, if possible, the integrity and integration of all the body's functions, right down to the cells carrying out the metabolism that converts food into energy — therefore into life itself. A patient's strong faith in the body's innate healing powers, along with confidence in the healer, would also factor into the ultimate result.

And like Dr. Schweitzer, Dr. Gerson was deeply concerned about increasing environmental degradation. Both men took great interest in the adverse effects of modern foods, new agricultural practices and dietary habits, especially in their apparent effects on the African natives at Schweitzer's remote outpost in the world.

A basic principle evident to Dr. Gerson was that the human organism had evolved over many millions of years by drawing its basic sustenance from the plants that grew out of the soil. Without plants, there could be no animal or human life. All minerals, enzymes, vitamins, proteins, fats and carbohydrates that our bodies need for metabolism — that continuous, crucial energy- and growth-generating mechanism that functions on the cellular level — essentially derive from the soil, through the medium of plant growth. Even the carnivores, exclusive meat eaters, consume creatures that themselves are herbivores, who feed on plants. Thus, all the complex proteins found in animals are actually plant-based; their simpler forms, such as amino acids and peptides, are generated in plants when photosynthesis in leaves, using energy from sunlight and the carbon dioxide and nitrogen in air, combine with the minerals and water that the roots absorb from the soil. Plants also create vitamins, enzymes and an astounding array of special biological chemicals (now called *phyto-chemicals*) that are vital or helpful contributors to animal and human health.

Dr. Gerson examined this human dependency on soil and plants in several essays he wrote. "The Significance of the Content of the Soil to Human Disease" would later be included within his book, A *Cancer Therapy*.

> The familiar expression "mother earth" is justified. When we take from and rob the earth we disturb the natural equilibrium and harmony, producing sickness of the soil, sickness of the plants and fruits (the common nutrition), and finally sickness of both animals and human beings.

> As a physician who has spent much of his life investigating the nutritional aspects of disease, I have often had occasion to observe a definite connection between dietary deficiencies and diseases, and between dietary deficiencies and a sick or poor quality soil.

> The relationship between soil and plants on the one hand and animal and human nutrition on the other is to me a fascinating subject. This relationship is a natural cycle in which one may distinguish two great parts:

> I. The first part, which may be called "external metabolism," is comprised of the following:

> (a) Plants and their fruits.

> (b) Composition of the soil in which they grow — this being the real basis of all nutrition.

> (c) Transportation, storage and preparation of these foodstuffs.

> II. The second part, known as "internal metabolism," consists of all the bio-chemical transformations that take place when such foodstuffs enter the animal body and support the nutrition and growth of its cells and tissues.

> When foodstuffs are ingested, their metabolism is influenced directly by the biochemical changes of the individual body and indirectly by the condition of the soil from which they came. The type of metabolic change thus directly affects the nutrition and growth of the body tissues. There is an external and an internal metabolism upon which all life depends; both are closely and inextricably con-nected with each other; furthermore, the reserves of both are not inexhaustible. (pp. 175-176)

Dr. Gerson regarded the soil as the foundation and thus explanation for both health and sickness. Since our daily food may be termed an essential part of our external metabolism, the health of the soil that it derives from, directly or indirectly, is inseparably connected with our internal metabolism and human health. In "Are Soil, Food and Metabolic Disturbances Basically Responsible for Cancer Development?," his second article on the subject, he wrote:

[M]odern man treats the all important soil, which produces the food for our bodily existence, plunderingly at the present and without any forethought for the future. All too often man forgets to give back to this benevolent donor what she so readily produces for lavish harvests. What the defenseless soil is robbed of, it cannot give to the plants. Thus deficiencies, which are not easily detected and are difficult to correct, originate in the soil, and are passed from the soil to the plant and from plant to man and animal.

In my opinion, the well-being of man and the prevention of diseases is closely connected with the handling and maintenance of the age-old natural condition of the soil and its natural flora. Our body has, of course, reserves. When the reabsorption system in the intestinal tract functions properly, the liver can well combine, store and reactivate foodstuffs, so that body damage remains small and can, over a longer period of time, endure, without the symptoms of disease. In many cases, the clinical symptoms only become apparent when the reserves are used up.

But only few people have completely healthy and perfectly functioning body-systems at present. Therefore, we should turn our full attention to the soil with its biological conditions and its flora, since it should be considered as our "external metabolic apparatus." This is the basis or the furnishing agent for our internal metabolism which supports and governs all the functions of our body and rules over its well-being or inclination to disease to a great extent. . . . (c. 1955, The Gerson Foundation for Cancer Treatment, Inc.)

As was his habit, Max Gerson spent most of his so-called leisure time perusing research literature, making special note of such findings as these in A *Cancer Therapy*:

It seems that cattle fodder is supervised more carefully than human nutrition. There are interesting experiments made on rats, which show the following: When rats are feeding from organically grown soil, they have perfectly healthy organs through many generations. Other groups of rats, living on ordinary food in the United States and Britain, developed, within one generation, all the degenerative diseases and pathology known to human beings. (See *Prevention* Magazine, April 1957.)

Rats feeding on large quantities of organically grown substances have been found to have better fur, to be more peaceful among themselves and less aggressive towards other animals. Other experiments showed that rats susceptible to cancer showed a decline of incidence of cancer when given proper nutrition from the time of their birth. (p. 146)

Max Gerson, as a European transplanted to the New World, took notice of the still-ample lands that were barely settled, and especially not converted yet into urban and suburban sprawl. Yet in the vast agricultural acreage in different regions of the United States, he saw trouble for soil that had once been fertile when covered by meadows or forests or prairie grass:

> There exist abundant supplies of nearly all natural resources in the United States and especially of soil. Enough injury to the soil has taken place to indicate a pressing need for adjustments of agricultural people to the soil upon which they live. Since there are many soils these relationship are too complicated to be resolved by a few simple slogans or programs. (p. 148)

During the 1950s, Max Gerson would make frequent pronouncements about the connections between human health and soil biochemistry. Since he worked increasingly with cancer patients, he was especially convinced that foodstuffs lacking particular minerals, vitamins and other micronutrients predisposed people to conditions of deficiency that led ultimately to cancer. A weakened immune system and a damaged liver could not fend off microbes, toxins and abnormal cell development. He also recognized the essential function of trace minerals (not just the nitrogen-phosphorus-potassium, or N-P-K, the three-mineral formulas that typify commercial fertilizers), and understood the importance of the soil's living organisms, such as the nitrogen-fixing bacteria and earthworms, both of which were harmed, even destroyed, by harsh chemical fertilizers.

In these and other ways Max Gerson was adding a physician's voice to a growing chorus of Americans, most notably the popular novelist Louis Bromfield, who achieved additional renown as the popular publicist of natural-farming methods at his Malabar Farm in Ohio; and J.I. Rodale, the prime promoter of organic farming in commercial agriculture and home gardening. Their philosophic antecedent had been Sir Albert Howard, the British agricultural scientist who in the 1930s wholly rejected the new "agrichemical" technology, recommending a universal return to natural farming and introducing the concept of composting organic materials for recycling back into the soil. In the early 1940s, Rodale founded the successful Rodale Institute, whose activities involved experimental farming on acreage in western Pennsylvania. He also launched the company that specializes in publishing magazines and books devoted to nature-based or "organic" or "regenerative" living and health, a company that continues to be directed by his descendants. In the 1950s Dr.

Gerson would independently join the growing vanguard of people who were going to be called environmentalists, ecologists, nutritional therapists, health activists . . . and holistic health practitioners.

In the training years for his medical career, Max Gerson had taken a keen interest in pathology, the medical science that detects diseases and injuries by studying their manifestations in tissues of both living and deceased persons. He had often participated in autopsies of people who had died inexplicably or from assorted diseased conditions, and on whom pathological studies were then done. The hearts available for this sort of investigation particularly struck him. Rather than having the appearance of healthy heart muscle, these had the appearance of soft brown soap. Initially, he assumed these hearts were from very elderly people and was shocked to discover that the average age of the cadavers was in the mid 40s. How could the hearts of relatively young people deteriorate that badly at so early an age? He could not imagine any more common and all-pervasive cause than defective nutrition, especially in inhabitants of large cities.

For Dr. Max Gerson the growing prevalence of cancer and other degenerative diseases was scarcely mysterious or surprising. Since his years as a young physician in Germany, he had warned people about the health consequences caused by new agricultural and food technology and the concurrent indifference to the dangers connected it. Gerson had expressed concern over people's increasing reliance, especially in cities, on preserved foodstuffs and processed grains, from which most vitamins and minerals had been removed, resulting in widespread multiple nutrient deficiencies in most people. He observed this in the microcosm of his own medical practice, but also was aware of the problem from reading clinical research reports and epidemiological studies. His opinion was confirmed whenever his friend Albert Schweitzer wrote or told him directly, or sent him one of his newsletters from his clinic about the degenerative diseases that began appearing after many of the natives had abandoned their traditional fresh, indigenous foods.

Dr. Schweitzer's practice for years had dealt with diseases of malnutrition, infection, parasites and epidemics. But when his reputation and the lure of his clinic drew visitors and new settlers to Lambaréné, a vigorous trade in refined and processed foods arrived as well. In 1936 he had written Max about a disturbingly dramatic incident at his clinical outpost that illustrated the powerful effect that food processing could have on living organisms.

> An interesting story: one of our missionaries had two young leopards. One day, when he had nothing else to feed them, he gave them meat from a good can from which he also ate. The next day, both leopards were dead.

Salt, too — which in the past had been in short supply and not considered essential in cooking — was brought in, and its use became habitual. Dr. Schweitzer was now seeing diseases largely unknown in the past. In his 1954 *Letter from Lambaréné* , the newsletter that Schweitzer sent out to friends, supporters and contributors all over the world, he wrote:

> I have to point out a happening in the modern civilization of the Hospital something which happened on March 27th of this year. On this day we had to perform the first appendicitis operation on a native of this region. How it turned out that this so frequent sickness of white people did not occur cannot be convincingly explained. Probably its still exceptional occurrence is reducible to a change in the nutrition. Many natives, especially those who are living in large communities do not now live the same way as formerly — they lived almost entirely on fruits and vegetables, bananas, cassava, ignam, taro, sweet potatoes and other fruits. They now begin to live on condensed milk, canned butter, meat-and-fish-preserves and bread. . . .
>
> The date of the appearance of cancer, another disease of civilization, cannot be traced in our region with the same certainty as that of appendicitis. We cannot state decisively that formerly there was no cancer at all, because the microscopic examinations of all tested tumors, revealing their real nature, has only been in existence here for a few years. Based upon my own experience, going back to 1913, I can say, if cancer occurred at all it was very rare, but that it became more frequent since. However, it is not spread as much as among the white races of Europe and America.
>
> It is obvious to connect the fact of increase of cancer with the increased use of salt by the natives. In former years there was only available the little salt extracted from the ocean, which came up to the Hinterland. There was a very limited traffic only. The salt had to be transferred by the dealers of the tribes living at the coast to those tribes living next to them upstream. Then European salt was shipped in small sacks of a few pounds. Still, at the time of my arrival in Lambaréné salt was so precious that it prevailed as the most valuable and the most general type of remuneration. Whoever had to make a trip on the river or travel along the paths of the virgin woods did not take along money but salt (and also tobacco leaves imported from America), thus trading bananas and cassavas for his oarsmen or carriers. By and by the consumption of salt increased. Still today it is much less used among the colored than among the whites. The patients fed by us in our hospital receive a few grams a month and are satisfied with this small amount.
>
> So it is possible that the formerly very seldom and still infrequent occurrence of cancer in this country is connected with the very little consumption of salt and the still rare use of it. Curiously enough, we did not have any cancer cases in our hospital.

It should be mentioned that the infectious diseases among the whites gradually [appeared here]. It remains questionable if tuberculosis was spread formerly as much as now, even if it occurred at all times. According to my observation, it became more frequent after the First World War. (from typescript of translation hand-corrected by Max Gerson)

The connection made by Schweitzer between the rise of cancer incidence and the increase of salt usage was, of course, especially intriguing to Dr. Gerson, since he had long considered salt detrimental in the diet, especially with ailing persons. He, too, was also seeing a much greater number and variety of what Schweitzer called "diseases of civilization" in his patients in the New York City area.

Dr. Gerson, like Dr. Scweitzer, also recognized a "pre-cancerous" era when this disease was not rampant:

Our modern civilization has brought about such widespread changes in our nutrition that some cancer authors speak about a so-called pre-cancerous condition. I feel it must be expressed more generally as a pre-*morbid* condition. For our task it is important to know that we have no longer a *natural* nutrition; therefore, the therapy is more difficult. (p. 133)

Agriculture had been the basis of civilization, because its surpluses, as storable crops, enabled people to evolve from a tribal existence, in which most time and effort went into searching for food, to a system of production in which specialists could begin developing crafts, trades and learned professions. Through the millennia, in different parts of the world, civilizations were constructed, each enabling multiplying advances in technology, along with the arts and sciences, including medicine. By the mid 20th century astonishing accomplishments were made by humans, accelerating further developments which, among other things, tended to insulate and protect them from uncertainties and dangers in the natural world.

Dr. Gerson looked at the underside of such advances as they affected the food supply and public health. He usually traced a patient's deteriorating health back to disturbances in the immune system and malfunctions in the digestive tract, primarily the liver:

There, the damage is done by a permanent daily poisoning brought about by our modern civilization. This starts with the soil which is denaturalized by artificial fertilizers and depletion, thus gradually reducing the topsoil. In addition, the soil is poisoned by sprays with DDT and other poisons. As a consequence, our nutrition is damaged by a decrease in the important K [potassium]-group content of fruit and vegetables grown on such poisoned soil. Furthermore, the food substances are damaged as they are refined, bottled, bleached, powered, frozen, smoked, salted, canned, and colored with artificial coloring.

Carrots are sold in cellophane bags after having been treated for better preservation. Other foods contain damaging preservatives; finally, cattle and chickens are fed or injected with stilbestrol to accumulate more weight and be quickly "ready for market."

Denatured and demineralized soil produces food less capable of sustaining life and health. But the interference only starts there. The food industry receiving the poisoned and deficient fruit, vegetables and meat then subjects them to processing plants to be further damaged by cooking, canning, freezing, bottling, smoking and otherwise manipulating the raw material. To simulate a tasty food experience, flavor enhancers, most notably sodium compounds, especially salt, are added. Chemical emulsifiers of many kinds solidify or attempt to replicate the original textures of foodstuffs. Food coloring restores the food's appearance, which suffers badly during processing, and preservatives are added to prevent food spoilage during the long storage periods to which it may be subjected. These and other food additives have been approved by the Federal Drug Administration. The result is food virtually devoid of the vitamins, minerals and enzymes needed to sustain our health but which contains hundreds of substances that are poisonous in doses not much larger than we are getting.

After briefly reviewing the history of the technique of food canning and other forms of preservation, Dr. Gerson looked toward the future and asserted:

> The canned food industry has grown into an important factor in our modern civilization. Thus, the nutrition and feeding of families has been put on a mass production basis. The cans stay in the foreground and the mistakes in that respect, no matter how insignificant they may appear, become an ever-increasing calamity in our present day society.

Max Gerson was not known for making political pronouncements, whether about specifics or in generalities. But in the following statement, while offering his opinions about soil misuse, and beyond it the whole future of food production and human health, he showed a highly positive belief in the power of an active citizenry within a democracy. If educated and well informed, people could effect necessary changes by reversing the decisions and procedures of special interests, whether these were "experts" in science and technology or government bureaucrats.

> Soil science has a contribution to make toward the future, but certainly not by itself. Since science itself has become so specialized, it is difficult to see science as a whole and its relationship to politics, art, business, and agriculture. More and more, modern education seems to make people specialists — members of a group of clique — and leads them away from the masses, from real democracy. The kind of science that is super-specialized cannot lead people to

better relationships with each other and the land, nor can so-called "pure" science, which is too cold or too snobbish to face the real problems. Some see a danger that farmers as well as other people may turn their problems over to some special group, some special bureaucracy, rather than to think out the problems for themselves and make their decisions by the democratic method. (p 147)

Max Gerson was clearly not the only person in the United who fretted over the effects of deficient, toxic and contaminated soil and food on health. His preoccupation with how various environmental factors affected human health is demonstrated in the titles of a few of the books and other publications that he was reading, and obviously valuing, during the late 1940s and '50s: *Studies in Deficiency Diseases* by Robert McCarrison (1945); *What Price Civilization?* by Charles Eliot Perkins (1946); *The Living Soil* by E.B. Balfour (1948); *Our Plundered Planet* by Fairfield Osborn (1948); *Road to Survival* by William Vogt (1948); *Nutrition and Physical Degeneration* by Weston A. Price (1949); *Degeneration Regeneration* by Melvin E. Page (1951); *Organic Gardening* by J. I. Rodale (1955); *Our Daily Poison* by Leonard Wickenden (1955); *Hunger Signs in Crops: A Symposium*, American Society of Agronomy. Dr. Gerson cited all these titles in a chapter on "Directions for General Nutrition" in his book A *Cancer Therapy*.

Chemical Pollution

"When we interfere with the transfer of nutrients from the soil to our hungry bodies, we do so at our peril," Dr. Gerson warned. Likewise, when livestock and poultry are fed or injected with antibiotics and hormones, and if fish are raised in waters poisoned by heavy metals, pesticides or other chemicals, we can expect consequences, perhaps dire ones over time, to our own well-being if we consume animal products — not just meats and seafood, but also milk, milk products and eggs. The tendency of toxins to bind with fats increases the risk of eating and then storing chemicals that may cause cancer or other degenerative conditions.

Dr. Gerson had seen human interference with natural foods increase rapidly, from the time in his childhood when he had watched earthworms fleeing chemicals added to the soil. Artificial fertilizer adversely altered topsoil chemistry, resulting in loss of the plants' natural resistance to diseases and pests. The scientific response to these problems was the application of more and more fungicides and pesticides to the plants, killing both pests and beneficial organisms. In particular, during the years after World War II, the comparatively cheap and convenient-to-apply DDT was becoming the standard pesticide for all-purpose use around the planet, most widely in eradicating the mosquitoes that carried malaria. Dr. Gerson read reports on *in-vivo* laboratory experiments that implicated it in ultimate health consequences to humans, as well as to the biosphere of animals. In his book on cancer, he would cite such research:

In experiments of the Federal Food and Drug Administration with insecticides "five days after feeding showed the insecticides in the gizzard, the liver and the kidney, the tissues of the heart and brain and sciatic nerve fiber."

With larger doses, FDA scientists have also shown that it is possible to store many times the amount in the body-fat that would be acutely fatal intravenously in a single dose. Since DDT mobilizes from the body fat into the blood stream, the intravenous dose is the logical comparative one. Cumulative intoxication from extremely small amounts in food can thus be as dangerous as direct exposure to much larger amounts.

Studies had proven repeatedly that certain known poisons, including heavy metals, accumulate over time, especially in liver and fat tissue. A number of chemical compounds, or particular elements in widespread usage, such as lead, mercury and chlorine, were already identified as presenting problems that affected the reticuloendothelial (or immune) system and liver function; they also might be implicated in causing cancer and other degenerative disease. Additionally, chemicals that may seem relatively innocuous or are declared harmless by the food industry can build up to dangerous levels, or else combine with other chemicals to create potent internal toxins or carcinogenic substances. Moreover, it may take years for adverse effects to appear. By then who is to say what actually caused the health problem. Awareness would soon grow about the possible harm of ubiquitous substances such as asbestos, lead in gasoline and cleaning fluids, and the chemicals "outgassed" from household furnishings and construction materials. As if symptomatic of a major breakdown in public health due to overexposure to a flood of environmental chemicals, on the increase were extreme and chronic allergic or hyperintolerant reactions to various foods, rubber goods and microscopic allergens such as pollen, mites and dander.

When Dr. Gerson considered to the defects of people's diets and the problems posed by elements in the "external metabolism" of contemporary civilization — the pollution of water and air by industrial processes, solvents, household chemicals, paints, adhesives and a host of other chemicals — he was amazed at the reasonably healthy status of most people.

Environmental medicine was in its early stages, as physicians and biomedical researchers began to acknowledge the phenomenon of multiple chemical sensitivity — another unwelcome, degenerative byproduct of civilization that required a new diagnostic framework. Dr. Gerson realized from his own reactions to synthetic substances that many things with strong smells had a toxic effect, such as gasoline, disinfectants, solvents, carpet backing, paint, formaldehyde and a host of other volatile substances. His patients, as they recovered from illnesses by undergoing detoxification, found that they had become so sensitive to these items that they literally could not remain in the same room with someone with perfume, scented skin cream or hair spray, or with smokers, even when they weren't smoking. Then, as now, it was hard to determine whether people's particular reactions to ingested or inhaled substances or skin contact involved allergies or came from an acquired multiple chemical sensitivity, for often the symptoms and effects were the same. Some people's damaged immune systems have become so unduly sensitive to almost everything around them that they need to live in a sterile environment.

During this same period in the 1950s, a research biologist and author, Rachel Carson, had begun building a strong case against the indiscriminate use of many pesticides, herbicides and hormones. Her attack on the chemical industry, agribusiness and governmental blinders in her book *Silent Spring* would finally elicit a loud chorus of public concern about damages, many of them irreversible, to the delicate chain of life that had evolved. Her book, published in 1963, became a bible for the new environmentalist movement, which continues in full force to this day.

New Threats to Health in the Nuclear Age

Busy with his medical practice, Dr. Gerson had little if any time to contact personally other researchers who had become equally concerned about environmental perils, though he was aware of at least some of their work and deeds. Had he formed connections and friendships with other health advocates and agitators, he would have discovered a supportive camaraderie. Also, he would have witnessed the same sort of persecution and vilification of others that he himself had experienced from the medical establishment. Insults and banishment, even death threats, were visited upon those scientists and physician activists, as well as ordinary citizens, who were starting to speak out, in the various media, in books and on public platforms, about the damages to human, animal and plant life caused by toxic synthetic chemicals.

Yet another area of alarm and protest at mid century was the genetic damage and cancer induction now acknowledged to be caused by radiation coming from an immoderate use of X-rays in medicine — in diagnostic tests such as routine dental examinations and mammograms, and in treatment, such as in eradicating cancerous tumors or even subduing facial acne. Innovative diagnostic tracking and cancer treatment techniques were also using compounds containing radioactive isotopes of elements. The worst offense, however, had been the ignorant offering of fluoroscope machines in shoe stores, where children stood for long periods of time watching their toes wiggle inside shoes.

During the 1950s Dr. Gerson obviously was paying attention to this new problem of overexposure to radiation. He had cause for concern, because many patients came to him badly damaged by X-rays that had been used in futile cancer treatments. "Scientists Term Radiation a Peril to Future of Man" was the title of a chapter in A *Cancer Therapy*, in which he summarized a report that he had read in the *New*

York Times on "Biological Effects of Atomic Radiation," based on a presentation to the National Academy of Sciences in June of 1956. As he commented:

> The committee concluded in agreement with geneticists that radiation, no matter how small the dose, shortens life in some degree. . . . Exposure to radiation should be held down to 10 roentgens for the first 30 years of a person's life. A roentgen is a unit for measuring the harmful gamma ray from medical and dental x-ray equipment, nuclear weapons explosions and from natural causes like cosmic rays and natural radium....
>
> Radiation causes mutation or harmful changes in the genes or germ cells of the reproductive organs. Damage manifests itself in the shortening of the life span, reduces ability to produce children, and sometimes, but not often, produces deformed or freakish children.
>
> Even if the mutation is in one gene, there is some harmful effect that mutation will go on through every generation until the line that bears it becomes extinct. (pp. 85-86)

During the 1950s the most adamant protests came over the involuntary exposure of the public to radiation through the reckless, uncontrolled nuclear testing being carried out by the various world powers engaged in the Cold War between capitalism and communism. They were intent upon developing bigger and better weapons, and more of them than their opponents. People everywhere were being exposed to some degree of radioactive fallout, no matter how distant they were from the testing sites. As atomic bombs, then hydrogen bombs, were exploded in above-ground tests, radioactive particles entered the atmosphere, to be carried by wind and clouds to places both near and far. When these particles fell to earth, people breathed them in, and they also touched the skin. The soil received them, plants that grew on them and the animals that fed upon these plants were contaminated, eventually moving up the food chain through unnaturally ionized elements such as carbon-14 and strontium-90. Radioactive isotopes were present in the milk that children drank, coming from cows that had consumed irradiated fodder.

Max Gerson's concerned voice joined that of others who, like him, worked both inside and outside of the "establishment" of their professions, whose organizations and leaders attempted to enforce conformity, complacency and silence upon their memberships — and all too often used the financial support of profit-protecting corporations to influence the press and legislators in creating the illusion of consensus and political correctness.

The witch-hunt against outspoken scientists who protested against the government and corporate behavior was particularly evident in the attacks on Dr. Linus Pauling, who had received the 1953 Nobel Prize in Chemistry. By the mid 1950s, Pauling was devoting half his time to peace efforts, especially to educating the public as to the health dangers in the above-ground and atmospheric weapons tests, which would inevitably increase birth defects and incidences of cancer worldwide. He circulated an international petition that called for the cessation of nuclear testing. Presented to the United Nations in 1958, ultimately it was signed by some 13,000 scientists — including Max Gerson's friend Dr. Albert Schweitzer, whom Pauling had visited the year before in Lambaréné, especially to discuss the world's nuclear problems. Dr. Pauling was joined by other courageous and outspoken individuals and by activist organizations such as Committee for a Sane Nuclear Policy and Physicians for Social Responsibility.

Max Gerson would not live to see Pauling's efforts acknowledged by his being given the Nobel Peace Prize for 1962 — belatedly awarded in 1963 on the very day that the international Limited Nuclear Test Ban Treaty went into effect. Nor did he live to witness Professor Pauling's work as the champion of the alternative health movement through his advocacy of nutritional treatment of common diseases, from the common cold to cancer, in such publications as *Vitamin C and the Common Cold* and *Vitamin C & Cancer*. That same year, biologist Rachel Carson published her epochal *Silent Spring*, but alas, Carson's potent pen was permanently halted in the following year by her death from cancer. After a previous surgery, her physician had deliberately withheld from her the information that the tumor was malignant, believing — as so many doctors did then — that patients, especially females, would suffer extreme distress.

The New Nutrition

The many citations in the technical papers Max Gerson drafted in this period, whether or not they ever were published, indicate that the physician was attentive to work being done by nutritional biochemists and research dietitians. New scientific journals were originated to accommodate their findings, theories and recommendations. In the 1950s came a surge of public interest in the subject of applied nutrition, not just for the healing of disease but for its prevention, health maintenance and extending the life span. During this era, nutritionists began to influence the food-buying and cooking habits of at least a portion of the population. Nutrition studies were published not just in various Department of Agriculture and dietetics journals, but also were read, interpreted and explained to lay people. Notable among the healthy-diet popularizers were Adelle Davis, author of the books *Let's Cook It Right* and *Let's Eat Right to Keep Fit*, and Carlton Fredericks, with his regular radio program and publications. Their basic dietary principles were in accord with many of Max Gerson's assertions, though they did not prohibit salt and milk, for example. They based their recommendations on an impressive array of research findings in medicine and biochemistry and on statistical studies coming from the new field of nutritional epidemiology. During this period, small health-food stores in urban areas, which stocked organically grown foods, whole grain products and vitamin supplements, were established on a trial basis. A powerful nutritional-therapy influence upon the American public also came from the health magazine *Prevention*, published by the Rodale enterprise, along with its companion publication *Organic Gardening*.

By the mid 1950s, Max Gerson began to realize that his best hope for helping people with cancer and other diseases would *not* come by persuading physicians about the merits of his dietary therapy, but through contacting the public itself, directly or indirectly. Thus *Prevention* magazine became an important vehicle for him in conveying his curative messages to a number of American households. A number of his new cancer patients came to him because they or some friend or family member had read something by or about Max Gerson in *Prevention*.

Although frustrated and upset by being stonewalled by the medical establishment, Max Gerson tended to be philosophic in his understanding of the intransigence in science and medicine to accept new theories — and, in his case, demonstrable *results*, as he wrote *in* A *Cancer Therapy*:

> As soon as one of Nature's secrets is uncovered, apprehension and skepticism appear.
> The history of medicine is filled with tragic errors which allowed such a long time to elapse between the time of discovery of a basic principle and the actual medical application of the discovery for the good of mankind. (p. 59)

He hoped that people themselves — as inevitable food consumers — would come to their senses before it would be too late:

> I fear that it will not be possible, at least in the near future, to repair all the damage that modern agriculture and civilization have brought to our lives. I believe it is essential that people unite, in the old conservative manner, for the humanitarian purpose of producing nutrition for their families and future generations as natural and unrefined as possible.
> The coming years will make it more and more imperative that organically grown fruit and vegetables will be, and must be, used for protection against degenerative diseases, the prevention of cancer, and more so in the treatment of cancer. It will not be long before the entire population will have to decide whether we all die of cancer or whether we will have enough wisdom, courage and will power to change fundamentally all our living and nutritional conditions. (pp. 3-4)

In this concern and orientation, Gerson revealed himself to be a domestic traditionalist. He was far more in tune with the emerging "back to the land" lifestyle movement of the Hippies, with their throwback agricultural communes, wholegrain, home-baked breads and health-food products, than he would have been with the succeeding generation, with its notably fast-paced, success-oriented, fast-food consuming and glitzy urban lifestyle amidst the high-tech, biotech, "dot-com" workplaces. In the last two decades of the 20th century and the entry years into the "Y2K" era, there would be little time for shopping and preparing foods in the prescribed Gerson way in family homes where both parents worked full time or overtime, whether out of choice or economic necessity. In this context, Dr. Gerson's millennial vision seems remote, sadly:

> We will again need real housewives, not eager to save kitchen time, but homemakers who will devote their lives to the benefit of all, especially the task of developing and maintaining a healthy family. Babies would no longer be fed by a formula but would have the natural mother's milk; they would grow up without being afflicted with a fatal disease such as leukemia, and without being mentally retarded, both conditions which are increasing rapidly at present.
>
> For the future of coming generations, I think it is high time that we change our agriculture and food preservation methods. Otherwise, we will have to increase our institutions for mental patients yearly, and we will see the hospitals overcrowded with degenerative diseases even more rapidly and in greater numbers than the hospitals themselves can be enlarged. Seventy years ago, leukemia was unknown in the United States. Fifty years ago, lung cancer was so seldom observed in clinics and autopsies that every case was worthy of publication. But today — what a change for the worse. (p. 4)

Perhaps only when someone becomes seriously ill with cancer or some other intractable disease, which conventional medicine has thus far failed to cure, will a desperate person consider undergoing the Gerson diet as a last-ditch therapy. Used earlier as a basic preventative measure, it could have been carried out in a far less stringent form, and with more guaranteed positive outcome.

Viewed on a much wider scale, however, it is apparent that human societies, and the regimes that govern them, should recognize that to ensure their own survival they must pay close attention to their public's health — both physical and mental, from "womb to tomb." This means not only educating each person well about proper nutrition, from early childhood on, but also making it possible for everyone to be able to access the foods necessary for achieving good health. A truly healthful diet should not be a cure, affordable only to the affluent class; it should be a common birthright.

~19~
Whole Body Medicine
(1953–1954)

Totality or "Holism" in Science and Medicine

Max Gerson's determination now either to prevent cancer or to overcome its lethal presence in people already suffering from it revived his earlier interest, while still living in Germany, in *Ganzheit* — or *totality*. Possibly Max's talk with Albert Schweitzer during his 1949 stay in New York had inspired him to take a philosophical look at his dietary and detoxification therapy . Indeed, sometimes he explained the effectiveness of the therapy an almost nonmaterialistic and mystical way.

If we approach the cancer problem from a more practical viewpoint — the clinical side — based on the concept of totality, we learn two things: firstly, we have to live near nature, according to our natural development. Secondly, science cannot help us to solve the deep, underlying cause of cancer. . . .

Albert Schweitzer recognized the greatness of the "awe for life" [reverence for life] or the need to have the deepest respect for everything that is alive (*Die Ehrfurcht vorm Leben*). The living being, whether large or small, plant or animal, is in every respect perfectly created or developed, in all its functions and in all its parts, best in its totality.

Everybody respects and needs science, research, and laboratory work, but their conclusions should not be overestimated. Particularly, the direction of therapeutic action should always be based on the idea of the body as an entity, which has to be supported and restored in its silent perfection.

It is unnecessary to understand the whole life in its minute biological particles and effect — but it is necessary that, for the problem of therapy, the entire sick human organism be attacked in its totality, especially in degenerative diseases. It would be a great mistake to apply the therapy only as far as we understand the corresponding biological reactions or as far as they can be proven in animal experiments. In particular, in degenerative diseases and in cancer, we should not apply a symptomatic treatment or only one that we can fully understand; we need a treatment that will comprise the whole body as far as we know or can imagine it. These thoughts were well known by the physicians of Greece and Rome; the ancient physicians knew that there are no sicknesses but only sick human beings. ... The best pharmacologists realize how difficult it is to understand the actions of the pharmaca and often must use practical or clinical experience.

Modern technology has almost unlimited possibilities but it cannot transfer these accomplishments into the biology of the human being. (pp. 37-39)

Max Gerson was firmly grounded in medical science, but believed that the best route to effective treatment was to look at the individual body as a whole, an entity of intricate parts, which was situated in the human context of society as well as the biosphere, and also within the universe of matter and spirit. He traced this concept of totality back to both the legendary Greek physician Hippocrates and the 16th-century Swiss alchemist and physician Paracelsus. About Paracelsus, Dr. Gerson could sound almost impassioned, to the extent that he would devote an entire chapter in A *Cancer Therapy* to presenting his particular (and sometimes peculiar) physiological and dietary ideas:

Everywhere in his writings it can be perceived how he would like to dissect everything into the finest particle (atoms) and find an interpretation; it seems as if he would like a penetrating power to enable him to look into things microscopically. The layman only sees the surface; the physician must be able to visualize the inside and the hidden facts which combine to form the whole, regardless of whether it is a piece of wood or bone. Marvelous are his ideas about the chemical reactions and his passionate love for all chemical occurrences which he applied to the reactions of the body long before his time. Paracelsus seeks to develop everything from its origin. In that he always observes three things: the heaven, the earth and the microcosm; it is similar with healing. Man can only be comprehended through a macrocosm; not through himself alone. Only the knowledge about this harmony perfects the physician.

This short condensation does not take a critical stand in the historical sense towards the statements of Paracelsus as measured against the knowledge of this time. It merely seeks to show how stimulating his writings are and the wealth of ideas which shines through everywhere, how intense his urge to find causal connections or at least to intimate them in his passionate way and bring them in accordance with the eternal laws in nature outside of the body and the same laws ruling inside the microcosm. (p. 53)

Max Gerson's use of the word *totality* to characterize his own approach to treatment closely resembles what is widely known now as holistic medicine. And in using this particular term in a more general sense, whether for medicine or other professional pursuits, he was scarcely alone.

The Spiritual Dimension

Over the years Max Gerson made a number of loyal and strongly supportive friends who understood his absorption in his work. Some of these friends were also German-speaking exiles; others were Americans. Some were researchers, like medical biochemist Rudolf Keller, and medical technicians, such as the radiologist Dr. Heinrich, people with whom he worked on a steady basis — professionals who not only respected his work, but were awed by it, since no other physicians they dealt with were getting such extraordinary results. One of Max's best friends was Dr. Stanley P. Reimann of Philadelphia's Lankenau Hospital Research Institute, who sometimes referred patients to him.

Other friends began as his patients. Surely one of the most important friendships made during Max's American years was Henry Schaefer-Simmern, an art professor on the faculty of the University of California–Berkeley. Like Max, he was a German; he had escaped the Gestapo in Frankfurt and emigrated to the United States. In fact, Max had heard of him while still in Europe. Henry, who was a tall, heavy-set man, combined the vocations of art creator, educator and psychologist. He stressed the importance of cultivating visual imagination and expression in children to encourage the development of a creative spirit and humanitarian outlook, ensuring that they would grow into well-rounded adults. Besides being an inspirational innovator in art education, the professor was also an early advocate of using children's art work both to diagnose emotional disturbances and to work through traumas of many kinds.

The transcontinental friendship began in this way: While Schaefer-Simmern was visiting New York during the early 1940s, he suffered several heart attacks during the course of a week. He was 45 years old at the time. On his first visit with Dr. Gerson, he had blue lips and minimum circulation. Right away Max learned that this new patient of his was a ferocious, five-packs-a-day smoker and that his diet was scarcely salubrious. Dr. Gerson proceeded to educate him about his lifestyle principles. Obviously, the cardiovascular crisis indicated that his overall health was seriously deteriorating. If Schaefer-Simmern wished to recover permanently from his presenting condition, he would have to make radical changes in his diet and other habits, particularly requiring giving up smoking and indulging in fat-rich foods.

Dr. Gerson might have explained to Schaefer-Simmern the background for his treatment approach in this way:

It is important to realize that in our body all the innermost processes work together, depend on each other, and will be deranged with each other in diseases. That is the reason why all of them together have to be attacked for healing purposes at the base and in combination. My clinical experiences revealed that this is the surest way to the success of a therapy.

Schaefer-Simmern stopped smoking completely on the very day he met Dr. Gerson and agreed to follow the strict dietary regimen imposed. Dr. Gerson arranged for him to stay at the home of a doctor friend, where some other patients of his were lodged, partly to enable them to follow Gerson's therapeutic diet. After about four weeks, Henry's serious heart condition had improved enough for him to go home.

Though Henry never resumed smoking, his desire for his old friends the cigarettes never left him. From time to time he would pull out an unlit cigarette and hold it between his lips. His wife, whom he married some years after his heart-attack siege, gave up her own smoking habit to accommodate him. Apparently, he also obeyed Gerson's dietary instructions for the rest of his life; he lived for about three more decades, outliving his good friend Max by nearly twenty years.

"A close, lasting friendship developed with this professor," Mrs. Gerson said in her memoir of her husband. Probably from the start of their association, physician and patient recognized a similarity in their basic thinking about totality. The two men must have discussed, in their native German, many of the professor's ideas as well as Max's, and this convergence of ideas was doubtless the basis of their lasting friendship. At this time, Henry "S-S" was working on his book, *The Unfolding of Artistic Activity*, which would be published in 1950. Toward the beginning of his own book, *A Cancer Therapy*, published eight years later, Max mentioned Henry's book, quoting from it in the second chapter, entitled "The Concept of Totality—Decisive in Cancer and Other Degenerative Diseases."

In his book Henry Schaefer-Simmern applied the concept of totality to the fields of art and psychology, but Max Gerson regarded it within a much wider context:

> It is not only in biology where the idea of totality is to be regarded as an entity of the natural processes; it is also the rule in art, in philosophy, in music, in physics, where the most learned scholars found the concept of totality alive in their fields of research and work. I would like to mention first Henry Drumond's philosophical work *Natural Law in the Spiritual World* (1883). The basis of it is expressed in his words: "The continuity of the physical world to the spiritual." This means the coherence of the physical inorganic powers as they are transformed basically into the organic world of plants and animals. In man, there are electrical potentials outstanding in the life of the cells. They are eventually accumulated in the nervous system, which is ultimately the "spiritual organ" capable of creating progress and great accomplishments.

In physics, Albert Einstein's first great work was *Relativity of Space and Time*. At first the theory was considered fantastic. Later it was generally accepted. Einstein's advanced studies dealt with a transformation of light and the photo-electric effect. Finally, his "transformation theory" attempted to include gravity, magnetism, and electricity into one basic physical system, which he called the Unified Field View — *most difficult to prove.*

In art, as an example of this concept, is the work of Schaefer-Simmern, who took the application of art out of the narrow limitations of the old rational principles and demonstrated that art is a "creative power," inherent in our brain functions, developing according to the body's growth, mental, emotional and intellectual maturity. Schaefer-Simmern said that "The creative potentialities of men and in women, in business and the professions, are always present as an entity," united with all other powers of the body. Schaefer-Simmern used art to "unfold the inherent artistic ability in the education of children," since it may become the decisive factor in the groundwork of a culture that rests on the creative nature of man. (p. 13)

When Max Gerson cited Henry Drumond's words when considering totality in his book A *Cancer Therapy*, he was apparently recognizing the existence of "spiritual" aspects in the body itself, its connection with physical and mental health, creativity and healing. In scientific or medical terms, Max may have partly attributed this spiritual element to electrochemical pathways through brain cells and neurons, or to genetic or endocrine factors at work or at play. Nevertheless, his willingness to acknowledge this special ingredient in his concept of totality places him early and very strongly within the revivified philosophical camp of *holism* (or wholism, as it is sometimes spelled) in ecology and particularly in medicine, about to be taken up in the latter half of the mid-20th century, and in time finding a medical explanation in the provocative new research-based, multidisciplinary field of psychoneuroimmunology.

As certainly many CAM (complementary and alternative) physicians and other health practitioners now believe, much of true healing in individual patients appears to have a spiritual component. This may come from an absolute trust in the practitioner, from a strong religious faith in some "higher power" or from an extremely positive mindset about outcome, possibly invigorated by special healing-directed psychotherapy. Thus it is possible that Dr. Gerson's extraordinary personal success in effecting cures in seemingly hopeless cases may have partially derived from a unique aspect in his character that gave extra potency to his therapeutic methods.

When the Gersons began taking vacations in California, they sometimes were able to see Schaefer-Simmern and his wife, who also occasionally came to New York City for professional and social visits.

Max often wrote to his California friend to share both his triumphs and frustrations, as in this note sent in 1946:

Confidential: I now have greatly improved 5 brain tumors [cases] and one intramedullary spinal cord tumor which I myself considered almost impossible. [1/2/46]

Or this letter written in 1948:

Some of my articles were refused, but I am not depressed and I know how it goes. The results in the treatment of cancer are so far developed and there is such a great amount of improved patients that it would fill a book, which no one up to now could demonstrate. There are many more results around, but they [the patients] do not come back, partly to save money and partly because I have no one to follow up all these cases or to go to these patients and see how they are. [7/7/48]

In the following year, Max commented in a note:

When I read yesterday in the last issue of the New England Medical Journal that physicians think that bringing down the blood pressure by diet is something close to a miracle, I learned for the first time in my life what it will mean to these physicians when they find that diet can also help in cancer. [2/18/49]

And two years after that, Gerson reported to him:

May I tell you that the wonderful advice you gave me was given to me first by myself. I learned that only persistence will bring something to a successful end, and the persistence has to be very great with the medical profession in such an outstanding field as cancer and malignancies are.

I now have so many wonderful results which I can prove and demonstrate with x-rays, biopsies, etc., that no longer can anything destroy my confidence and [certainty] in my treatment. [7/31/51]

Then in another three years:

One thing I can tell you is that the results in the past months are much farther reaching and quicker, so good that I myself am very often astonished whether such a thing is really possible or whether it is only a dream. I do the utmost to be as objective as possible in my writings and explanations. We all know that objectivity is the most important part of any progress....

I now have several . . . cases where no physician on earth would touch the case and they come through. The new publications will be filled with these extraordinary results.

The trouble with the medical profession is that it does not make decisions according to the objective facts but, more or less, to save reputation and the income of the surgeon, x-ray man and hospitals. [4/27/54]

"S-S always thought the world of Gerson, believed him to be a great man and admired him without reservation," Charlotte Gerson has commented. "He tried to help my father as much as he could in setting up contacts with legislators and industry leaders who might take interest in promoting his therapeutic methods, especially in curing cancer."

For example, in 1953 the UC-Berkeley-based Henry Schaefer-Simmern wrote a letter to Henry Kaiser, whom he knew was much involved, in his nearby Oakland building, in creating a new model for improving public healthcare delivery in a nonprofit health maintenance organization (HMO), as well as in establishing a medical research-funding foundation. After introducing himself as a former patient of Dr. Gerson's who was in "closest contact with him and his work," S-S broached the subject of Gerson's important medical innovation:

> His results with the cure of cancer, I mean the cure and not only the treatment, is so beyond the grasp of the official medical profession that most physicians do not know what to do with it. According to statistics, there are eleven hundred cancer operations daily in New York City. You can well imagine what the attitude of those surgeons is who know of Dr. Gerson's treatment without surgery. In spite of the fact that Dr. Gerson's sanatorium in Nanuet, New York, is full of patients from all over the country and Europe, in spite of the fact that many physicians must recognize that their own patients who were given up by them, returned home being in normal conditions, the fight against Dr. Gerson goes on with all possible and impossible means. And yet, this man's inner believe [sic] and extraordinary faith in the meaning of his life as a helper for mankind is not affected by all these attacts [sic]. However, as his work must finally be extended to the degree that mankind may have the benefit from it, I turn to you.
>
> I know enough of you that you are a man who has made the assumed impossible possible, a man who has no fears and an unlimited courage. You have the means and the facilities, the hospitals and the physicians who are well able to bring Dr. Gerson's noble work into full action. I even believe that I am a tool in the hand of fate to direct your attention to that task which may be the greatest task you ever can fulfill. And so, I beg you whole-heartedly to do what is in your power to make this task possible as you did with so many other problems. If it would be possible for you to send one of your leading physicians to New York to study Dr. Gerson's treatment and observe the results with his patients you would get the necessary evidence for your further actions.
>
> I pray that fate may give you that deep insight in the unmeasurable tasks which you can realize as a helper of mankind. [7/20/53]

While S-S was trying to contact Henry Kaiser, Max Gerson on the other coast attempted to get the former Senator Claude Pepper, a friend of Kaiser's, to resume interest in his cancer therapy. He wrote him, reminding him of the 1946 Senate sub-committee hearing and asking for a letter of recommendation to Kaiser. Among various statements he made were these:

> As you know from [the] history of inventions and especially that of medicine how many difficulties and hindrances a new solution of an essential problem has to encounter, you will understand how many personal attacks and enemical [sic] oppositions I [have] had to go through. . . .
>
> The American Medical Association is still opposed to my treatment and renders it impossible for me to publish any article, a number of which have been returned.

No record has yet been found of any response from Henry Kaiser to this rather fulsome yet ingenuous plea from Professor Henry Schaefer-Simmern. Nor is there evidence of a reply from Claude Pepper to Gerson's plea. But how interesting it would have been if some of the Kaiser hospitals, with their many, many thousands of cancer cases over the years, summoned the unorthodox courage to at least *offer* patients the option of choosing the Gerson therapy, instead of undergoing the standard drastic treatments, to determine whether they might replicate Max Gerson's positive results, under carefully controlled and supervised conditions.

Fortunately, Henry Schaefer-Simmern kept Gerson's letters, and after his death his widow presented them to the Gerson family. Unfortunately, few of the art professor's own letters to Max Gerson have survived. Max did keep among his papers a sheet of paper on which Henry had copied several paragraphs that he knew would interest his freind that he had found them in a book by Kurt Goldstein, *Human Nature*, published by Harvard University Press in 1940. At the bottom he inscribed it with "Greetings. S-S."

> In the approach toward healing today we are no longer preoccupied with the innumerable single phenomena in disease; we know that these phenomena are not the essentials of disease. More and more we approach the conviction that the essential element of disease is the shock to the disturbance of the well-regulated functioning of the organism by disease. If restoration is out of the question, the only goal of the physician is to provide the patient with the possibility of existing in spite of his defect. To do this one has to consider each single symptom in terms of its functional significance for the total personality of the patient. (page 6)
>
> If the organism is a whole and each section of it functions normally within the whole, then in the analytic experiment, which isolates the sections as it studies them, the properties and functions of any part must be modified by their isolation from the whole of the organism. Thus they cannot reveal the function of these parts in normal life. (page 10)

During the 1950s Max Gerson was exploring both verbally and in his treatment of patients the domain of totality in medicine as it applied to cancer. Inevitably he questioned the whole basis and rationale of orthodox allopathic medicine and its focus on addressing the symptoms of disease, not the cause:

Medical science has broken the totality of natural laws in the human body to little pieces. It has studied and re-studied single processes and overestimated them. The symptoms of a disease became the main problem for research and clinical work. The medical theory of the old and middle ages to combine all parts in a body to a biological entity was pushed aside almost involuntarily, and finally became very far removed from our thinking. How such thinking of total-ity will help us to find the cause of cancer can best be seen in practical exam-ples—not animal experiments—in the nutritional field of peoples who do not get cancer, and, on the other hand, of those who get it in greater or increasing amounts....

Everybody would ask, "What should we do with the idea of totality in the practice of cancer treatment?" My thinking is that all organs and their cells depend mostly on nutrition. It is essential for their function, regeneration and division to maintain the life of the whole body at the same time. Therefore, we should start with the restoration of the intestinal tract and its anexa, especially the liver and the pancreas. It should not be forgotten that almost all diseases start with intoxification. Thus, the detoxification has to be effected as the first therapeutic application to revive the most essential functions of the body. This entails the elimination of toxins and poisons, the restoration and refilling of the essential organs with minerals, vitamins, hormones and oxidizing enzymes. All these together build the important basis for the stimulating of the healing power. This way we can bring the healing power to function in a short while by restoring the intestinal tract with the help of a special nutrition and some med-ication. (from unpublished article, "The Problem of Cancer Based Upon the Law of Totality," c. 1956)

Luckily for Max Gerson, in the early 1950s he was offered the opportunity to present to a large group of physicians his ideas about totality in medicine and how they were applied in his clinical practice.

Triumphant Return to Europe

Dr. Max Gerson was invited to lecture and demonstrate his nutritional cancer therapy before the International Congress for Totality-Treatment in Malignant Diseases, which would take place at Berchtesgaden, Germany, in October 1952. Max had not set foot in Germany since his nearly accidental escape from the new Nazi regime almost 20 years earlier. Though he was not especially eager to return to his homeland, he was curious about the changes that had taken place there. To him it must have seemed almost a lifetime, since the intervening years spanned the Holocaust, World War II, the early years of the Cold War between Eastern and Western Europe (symbolized by the contentious division within the city of Berlin), and West Germany's extraordinary postwar reconstruction. Understandably, Max was further bothered by the association between Berchtesgaden and Adolf Hitler, who had lived there before his takeover of the German government; and, after that, Hitler had kept a chalet there, called "Eagle's Nest," to which he retreated for R&R.

But Germany, after all, was the place from which Gerson had achieved his Europe-wide approbation and fame, his publication and success — things he had scarcely known since arriving in the United States of America. Also, he almost always accepted professional invitations. So he agreed to give a presentation at the *Ganzheitsmedizin* (Totality Medicine) conference after being specially urged to do so by Dr. Ralph Bircher, the author of a book he much admired about the long-living Hunza people of Kashmir, in the Himalayas. Ralph Bircher was a younger relative of Max Oskar Bircher-Benner, among the first physicians to promote a vegetarian diet in healing, and also the origi-nator of the healthful breakfast cereal called Muesli. In the 1920s he had founded the Bircher-Benner Clinic in Zurich, Switzerland; famous all over Europe for many decades, it is still in existence. In 1935 Trudy Gerson had studied clinic management for a time at this facility while her parents lived in Paris. And Dr. Bircher-Benner himself had even traveled to Dr. Gerson's Hôtel du Parc sanatorium in Paris to observe his therapy.

Max had been both touched and honored when Ralph Bircher told him that he would give up his own speaking slot if necessary so as to get him on the program. This assured Gerson that he would be treated with great respect and that his pre-sentation, bound to be provocative, would be well attended and seriously received. There was an additional personal inducement: his lecture, on the third and last day of the conference, was going to take place on his very birthday, October 18. What better way to celebrate the completion of his 71st year of life?

Max Gerson traveled across the Atlantic on an ocean liner instead of taking an airplane. His eldest daughter, Johanna Oberlander, accompanied him on this trip, having returned from living in Germany after her remarriage several years earlier. Gretchen Gerson, who normally accompanied her husband to most places, chose not to go, since she was subject to seasickness and also was taking care of several grandchildren. Furthermore, she was unable yet to forgive Germany for the Holocaust. Both Gersons had become American citizens in 1944 and no longer wished to think of themselves primarily as Germans. Charlotte Gerson, who as a girl had witnessed and experienced directly the anti-Semitism in her birth country and in Austria, well understands this abiding feeling of revulsion on the part of many Jews, including her mother:

I can speak for myself. I have been invited three times to speak in Germany, twice for the Waldthausen Verlag, which published a re-translated version of my father's book into German. I did go, but always left as quickly as possible and was glad to be gone — even after all these years! I can sometimes see, perhaps in some railway employee in uniform, a possible concentration camp guard and everything that implies. Once, driving down the Autobahn, we passed a sign for an exit leading to the town of Dachau. It made me sick.

Though Max had once been forced to flee Nazi Germany, his arrival by steamship at Hamburg now made front-page headline news, with newspapers prominently noting the return to Germany of the physician who had found the cure for *lupus vulgaris*.

Over 200 physicians from various European nations would attend the three-day conference. Dr. Gerson's presentation was scheduled for the afternoon of the third day. Despite Max's long absence from Europe, many of the physicians attending the conference remembered his sobriquet, "Diet Gerson." Never short of material to demonstrate the results of his dietary and detoxification regimen, Max had brought many X-rays, slides and charts. His presentation was received with wonderful enthusiasm. As he later happily reported to his friend Henry Schaefer-Simmern about the conference and meetings:

> At first the top scientists there were naturally very critically inclined, and they sent the best roentgenologist to thoroughly verify my original X-ray plates. However, the mood soon changed, and there was great enthusiasm for everything that I could tell them of my experience, particularly in Berchtesgaden. When I had to stop after two hours, I was asked to present the therapy in as much detail as possible later. I did it at 8 o'clock in the evening. The hall was overflowing. Many colleagues had to stand, and I finally had to stop answering the numerous questions and requests for scientific explanations at 12 o'clock. A great number of colleagues want to come here in order to observe and learn the therapy. (M.G. TO H.S-S, January 6, 1953, translated by Charlotte Gerson)

But at Berchtesgaden the doctors were not yet finished with Dr. Gerson. The next day, many of them showed up at his hotel, wishing to talk with him further. Dr. Josef Issels, a German physician who was particularly intent upon learning more, took copious notes and stayed to ask detailed questions as long as Dr. Gerson would answer them. There was good reason for Issels' intense persistence. He wanted to understand Gerson's ideas and results so that he might adopt them for use at the First National Clinic for the Internal Treatment of Cancer that he had founded a year earlier at Rottach-Egern on the Tegernsee, in Upper Bavaria in Germany. There he would elaborate on features in Gerson's methods, developing his own variation of the metabolic therapy he had so admired at Berchtesgaden. As in Dr. Gerson's practice,

95 percent of Dr. Issels' patients were "terminal" cases; and like Gerson, he showed unquestionably positive results. His clinic grew and prospered. But in time he, too, would encounter problems within his profession because of this very success in dietary treatment of cancer and other grave diseases.

Deeply touched by the honor and respect that he had been paid in Europe, particularly after being so long rejected, slandered and attacked in the United States, Max Gerson later told his friend Henry:

> After the tremendous success in Berchtesgaden my inhibitions or complexes or call them what you will, completely disappeared. Several colleagues told me that I did not have any idea how great my achievements were, and I did not need to be at all modest....

Dr. E. Wildhagen, a physician attending the Totality medical conference in Berchtesgaden, wrote in the Hamburger *Abendblatt* about Dr. Gerson's presentation of the main elements of his therapy and its positive outcomes with patients. Translated into English, the article was later published in an American magazine, *Nature's Path*. As Dr. Wildhagen recounted the event:

> The talk by Dr. Gerson, which was followed by a very animated discussion, was the highlight of the conference. Result: Dr. Gerson's Diet means new hope for cancer sufferers.
>
> Dr. Gerson, who will be 71 years old today, reported about a number of hopeless cases. These concerned poor unfortunates, whom the best physicians in the United States could not help any further. These sick people had been sent home to die. First of all, it required a particular kind of courage to take up their treatment. ...
>
> There was, for example, a woman who had undergone seven operations and who was many dozen times subjected to X-rays and radium rays. At the end she weighed but 87 lbs. and was deathly tired when she was told that she had cancer metastases in the lungs and at the left chest. This was in April of this year. Since then she has returned to life. Nothing to speak of has remained of the cancer nodules.
>
> There is John Heeter of Akron, Ohio, who already had the dreaded metastases, the implantations of cancer. The operating surgeon counted 50 nodules on the surface of the liver, the largest one the size of a fist. Today he is all right, he has gained weight and he feels well.
>
> Another patient had cancer of the esophagus. The esophagus had become so narrow that he could swallow water only if administered in a teaspoon. Today after eleven weeks he can eat vegetables and bread.
>
> Other cases, 20 in all out of 40, which Dr. Gerson had in mind, were reported

on, these cases having been supplied with all the clinical, X-ray and microscopic data supplied by American experts and hospitals. Nearly 200 sufferers have so far been treated with surprisingly quick and far-reaching results.

Dr. Wildhagen then attempted to explain some of Gerson's main theories regarding the genesis and growth of cancerous lesions as well as his dietary and detoxifying therapeutic methods:

> With many of the patients the success was so surprisingly rapid that the absorption of the cancer tumor had a dangerous effect, because the body was inundated by the poisons of the cancerous tissues. Therefore, important supplemental factors were necessary . . . to relieve the liver, which is overburdened in the removing of poisons from the body. The restoration of the liver function is the principal task of therapy. Of great importance is the preparation of the meals. Only natural foods — best if from naturally fertilized soil — are used. (Initial translation in typescript uncredited)

At the end of his article, the physician-reporter told how during intermission he had asked several well-known scientists about their opinion of Max Gerson. He quoted Professor Kollath, an early advocate of natural living: "There is undoubtedly something very good in this, with further development here and there. Everything should be done to get Dr. Gerson to stay here in Germany."

It had been difficult enough for Max Gerson to return to Germany, if just for a few days. He was unlikely to be persuaded to remain there — even though, had he done so, he doubtless would have been treated with far more respect for his work than he had received from his medical colleagues in the United States for a decade and a half now. There Dr. Gerson's work, scarcely admired within the medical profession, was known to comparatively few people.

But Max was not going to forget that most Germans' acceptance of and involvement in Nazism had destroyed his earlier chance for professional success in Europe, forcing him and his family into a difficult exile, in which they uprooted themselves from Berlin to move from Vienna to Paris to London, until finally settling permanently in New York. So he did not travel anywhere in Germany other than Berchtesgaden. Since he no longer had pleasant associations with Bielefeld, Kassel and Berlin, he did not wish to return to any of them for nostalgic purposes. As for his birthplace, Wongrowitz in Posen, it was now within Poland and behind the nearly impenetrable Iron Curtain. Besides, all his relatives had departed long ago; any Jewish acquaintances remaining there after World War I would have left later or else ended up in Nazi death camps.

From Berchtesgaden, Dr. Gerson continued on to Zurich, Switzerland, where he was invited to address the staff at the University Clinic. In private meetings with the staff, Professor Schintz, considered perhaps the foremost cancer specialist in Europe, inspected Gerson's X-rays and case histories. After thorough examination, the professor said, "Dr. Gerson, your colleagues in the United States must be very proud that you discovered the cure for cancer there. And this is a certainly a cure, let there be no doubt about it."

After 15 years of unwarranted abuse at the hands of the American medical establishment, this appreciation coming from Dr. Gerson's European colleagues was received like nourishment by a starving man. As Max wrote to Henry:

> I have always believed that it must be possible to help all the cancer patients who have been given up and sent home to die. Naturally there is no such belief in medicine, particularly with these "hopeless and terminal" cases. The theory is not much trouble for me. I have derived it from my results to the greatest of my ability, and always try to stand solidly on the facts. Many cancer theoreticians were very satisfied with [my presentation] in Berchtesgaden and in Zurich. Professor Dr. Werner Kollath, one of our best thinkers, now in Freiburg im Breisgau, inscribed his new nutrition book to me with the dedication: "Presented in the memory of his lecture in Berchtesgaden and with gratitude for his teachings: 'Incurable is curable.'" The Hippokrates publishing house immediately asked me for a cancer book. (from letter cited above)

It is probable that Dr. Gerson's participation in the conference in Berchtesgaden led to the invitation to contribute a chapter in F. Johannes Scala's book, *Handbuch der Diätetik mit Rezeptanhang*, published in Vienna in 1954. In his chapter, "Diet Therapy in Malignant Diseases (Cancer)," Dr. Gerson made a series of provocative statements:

> That one can change the cells of the body with chemical substances so tremendously that they show an uncontrolled ability to grow, and that this and other characteristics are inherited from generation to generation, seems to me one of the greatest wonders of nature. (p. 125)

> I do not believe … that it is possible to assign a single cause to all manifestations of malignant tumors because there are too many biological problems that are factors. To find the general foundation is a sufficient basis for thinking and therapy. (p. 128)

> Malignant degeneration of cancer cells cannot be reversed. The cells must be killed. However, with those that have degenerated in the clinical sense or have begun to degenerate: that [condition] is reversible, and can be reversed. (p. 130)

> In a body with normal metabolism no cancer develops or grows, or no cancer tissue can maintain therein its living conditions. (p. 138)

The liver only loses its resistance to cancer metastases after it has lost a substantial portion of its potassium. The human liver contains approximately 30 percent of all the body's potassium, while the muscles house 50 percent of this important mineral. (p. 134)

Liver Investigations

The organ in the human body most fascinating to Max Gerson was the liver; he regarded it as occupying the central position in achieving and maintaining totality in health. It contained the primary detoxifying mechanisms that enabled the body to nullify and expel toxins of many kinds. It stored glucose and several vitamins for future need. It aided in the complete digestion of foods and the recycling or elimination of waste products. Some of its functions were connected to the immune system in a partnership crucial to health, such as preparing the immune system's complex complement cascade that destroys invasive organisms and abnormal cells. Alone among the body's organs, it could regenerate itself if only a portion of it remained intact. But the liver had vulnerabilities. It was the body part most subject to damage from poisons in the environment and in foods. Certain infectious diseases, such as various forms of hepatitis, could weaken and even permanently injure it. Cells issuing from primary cancerous tumors often initially metastasized to the liver. Moreover, the liver was bound to be eventually affected, perhaps badly disabled, by a defective or micronutrient-deficient diet.

No wonder, then, that Max Gerson devoted so much attention to protecting, improving and restoring essential hepatic functions. Sometimes when he talked or wrote about the liver, he tended toward eloquence:

Most of our life is built upon the activation and maintenance of the living processes. These are based on the mineral metabolism and function of the liver — which acts like the chlorophyll in plants — accepting ions from the sun and transforming them as "life begets life." What Nature does in that wonderful, subtle form by transformations and combinations with these ions *we* cannot imitate biologically. (ACT, p. 96)

Dr. Gerson regarded the liver as the crucial organ for combating an incipient cancerous condition and the organ to restore in his cancer therapy, for if its functions could not be reactivated, the patient was eventually doomed. Metastases from other areas of the body often lodged first in the liver, especially tumors located in the gastrointestinal tract, since the portal vein, conducting the bloodstream issuing from the walls of the colon, went directly there; it brought not just a new influx of nutrients to be metabolized, but also a variety of ingested toxic substances to be dealt with. By the time a tumor is discovered elsewhere, the liver itself may already have been invaded by metastases, with its essential duties compromised. Yet because the organ is so hardworking and durable, it can carry on for some while before faltering:

> The liver weighs seven to ten pounds [sic] and has a functional capacity far in excess of ordinary needs. Before the functional reserves are used up, it is very difficult to detect a deterioration of liver function. The liver is a dynamic, active organ, and has manifold functions. Most of these are intimately associated and correlated with the activities of the other organs. It is impossible to test a liver by a single function, even by several, to find the degree of hepatic deterioration. That is the reason why the initial development of cancer remains hidden for such a long time; this interval may be called the "pre-cancerous or pre-symptomatic period." If a person gets nervous, feels weaker, has less energy and loses weight during that time, no physician can make a specific diagnosis as a cancer test does not exist and there is no early specific symptom complex. Physician and patient have to wait until a tumor is far enough developed in one or another area of the body to show local symptoms or signs which can no longer be overlooked clinically. (p. 36)

Max Gerson constantly read reports of laboratory and clinical epidemiological studies, keeping file folders full of clippings, handwritten notes, carbon copies of communications and retyped copies of interesting observations and conclusions, which he drew on for illustrations in his articles:

> The Bantu population in South Africa has twenty percent primary liver cancers. Their diet is of a very low standard, consisting chiefly of cheap carbohydrates, maize and mealy meals. Relatively seldom they have fermented cow's milk. Meat is eaten only at ceremonies. Two physicians, Drs. Gilbert and Gillman, placed rats on the diet of the Bantus with the result that in almost all animals the liver was affected and twenty percent cirrhosis developed later.
>
> When an extract of the Bantu liver was painted on the backs of mice, benign or malignant tumors developed. (from unpublished article, "The Problem of Cancer Based upon the Law of Totality," c. 1956)

Dr. Gerson had long believed that a healthy liver could overcome cancer, but he lacked the experimental proof to bolster his contention. For years, he had proceeded on this assumption and had fortified ailing patients' liver functions through diet and supplements, with good results. Still, he was very aware that it was an assumption. It was virtually impossible to find a healthy liver in a cancerous body: after all, the whole assumption that he was trying to prove precluded that possibility. If he was right, a healthy liver would have done away with the cancer, so there would be no disease present upon which to experiment.

Finally, he came up with an idea. If the bloodstream of a healthy body could be coupled with that of a body sick with cancerous tumors, a healthy liver would now be functioning within the linked system to handle the disease. Dr. Gerson arranged to have an animal laboratory perform this experiment with rats, but it was difficult to execute. When the rats' bloodstreams were finally linked, the animals would have to be completely immobilized to prevent the delicate vessels from being torn apart. In addition, the area where the vessels were extracted and connected had to be kept shaved for accessibility and sterility. The skilled technicians at the laboratory, however, managed to carry out the experiment as Gerson had specified.

Within weeks, the healthy rat's liver had significantly reduced the tumors in the cancerous rat. However, the experiment could not be continued, as the hair began to regrow at the connection site, irritating it and causing the rats to bite and scratch at the delicate vessels. The rats had to be destroyed, but not before they proved Dr. Gerson's contention that a healthy liver was able to reverse cancerous tumors. Furthermore, at autopsy they found no evidence of metastatic cancerous growths within the healthy rat.

Dr. Gerson continued his work with human patients — his theory now a fact. Word of the results of the experiment had filtered out of the laboratory to the patient population at his office clinic and sanatorium. The husband of one of the cancer patients approached Dr. Gerson with an unusual request: he wanted to connect his bloodstream with that of his wife so that his healthy liver could help her body recover. He had already found that their blood types were identical. Though his experiment with the rats had succeeded, Dr. Gerson declined the man's request. That the animals had been destroyed was secondary. The experimental procedure would require the two people to be completely immobilized for weeks — which the doctor declared a totally unacceptable state of affairs. Instead, the woman was placed on the usual Gerson cancer-therapy regimen, with good results.

The New Sanatorium at Nanuet

For several years Max Gerson had been well pleased with both the accommodations and the beautiful rural setting at West Point Farms, the Central Valley sanatorium that the Appisons had made available to his patients. Dr. Gerson was achieving astoundingly good results with many of his cancer patients. Then around 1952 something happened that soured his working relationship between the proprietors. Although he was most surely dismayed by this disturbing turn of events, he spent little or no time venting his feelings or trying to determine what or who had caused this problem. Other members of his family and his friends were apt to be more convinced of a possible conspiracy within the American medical establishment against him and his work.

When it became obvious that West Point Farms was no longer a hospitable place for patients who needed round-the-clock attentions from a competent and knowledgeable staff, Dr. Gerson once again began looking for a new facility. In a letter written in early 1953 to his friend Henry "S-S", Max told how he was preparing to open a new sanatorium sometime in the spring. This time he would own the facility, where he could welcome, not only his patients, but also the European physicians who had asked to see his regimen in practice. The Gersons found an ideal setting for the new sanatorium in a town called Nanuet, about five miles west of the Hudson River, at the Tappan Zee, between Nyack and Spring Valley. It was around 30 miles and 45 minutes from the Gersons' residence on Park Avenue. Though located in New York state, it was usually accessed from Manhattan via roads going through New Jersey. As Charlotte Gerson described the property purchased by her parents:

The property was on a quiet street, about a mile or so north from the main road between Nyack and Suffern. The facility itself was a rather sprawling structure which probably had originated as a farmhouse and then been added to over the years. Basically it consisted of three interconnected buildings. The biggest one, with the main entrance, had three stories and beautiful, large rooms; the other building was smaller, with two stories. The two structures were connected by a long catwalk, which also had smallish patient rooms on one side. All the bedrooms had baths, which of course was essential for the detoxification therapy. In the main house were a huge kitchen, a good-sized pantry converted into the juice room and a spacious common area where Gerson would hold his demonstrations. Since this was the staff headquarters, there were also some smaller office rooms used for such things as bookkeeping and dispensing stored medications. Trudy, who basically ran the sanatorium, lived in this staff area, too, with her son Peter.

A large rainbow-shaped driveway led up to the place. The buildings were surrounded by large lawns and beautiful tall oak and other trees, offering many shady places for patients to sit. My father loved the trees, of course. On warm Sundays Howard and I, often visiting there on Sundays, might be found up in one of the "blood beech trees," having climbed up to sit on one of the stronger middle branches to test our wits with the Sunday New York Times' crossword puzzle.

The Gersons came to Nanuet every weekend, going up on Friday afternoon and returning home on Sunday afternoon to their Park Avenue apartment/office. While my father made the rounds with his patients there and gave his customary talks and patient presentations, my mother often devoted herself to accounting tasks and checking over the supplies of foods and medications.

Usually two nurses were on staff to carry out Dr. Gerson's directions during his absence. Since young doctors who wished to work with him were regularly discouraged from doing so, he was almost always on his own, without any trained assistant physicians.

This time, Max Gerson had decided to keep the management of his sanatorium within the family, since he apparently could no longer rely on erstwhile benefactors like the Seeleys and the Appisons. Now Trudy Gerson Selten would preside at Oakland Manor Cancer Clinic, as the facility was officially called. Her mother's presence there on weekends often gave her a needed break from superintending the day-to-day operations. Local people were hired and specially trained to work with Gerson therapy patients. In fact, it often proved better to employ persons without any or much formal medical-service training. Licensed nurses, for instance, were inclined to resist or argue with aspects of the treatment, based on their own education and experience within the medical establishment.

A reporter for the Maywood, New Jersey newspaper, *Our Town*, wrote a long article about Joe Panebianco, a man who had miraculously recovered from terminal cancer after undergoing treatment from Dr. Max Gerson. Since Panebianco had initially stayed at Nanuet, the reporter decided to visit the sanatorium. As he described his time there:

> The writer of this article visited Gerson's home in Nanuet and was intensely impressed by what he observed. A normal number of patients was there, approximately a dozen. Each had a fascinating story to tell of hope, in most cases a remarkable recovery.
>
> There was a gentleman from California, given up to die with cancer of the bone, who was preparing to return home after a month's treatment, a changed person. There was a young West Virginia mother of three, who had rebelled against a 10th operation for tumors, and had come to Gerson. In less than a week she had found new hope, had experienced the disappearance of a large tumor. In speaking to this woman, we were left without a doubt was to the genuineness of what had taken place.
>
> The home was a strange place, tenanted by people on the brink of death (for, unfortunately, most of Dr. Gerson's patients are those of last resort, mostly terminal cases) and yet there was hope in their faces. It was a serious place, but there was a positive glimmer of restrained happiness.
>
> The saddest note of all was the fact that Dr. Gerson himself was [so] elderly a person that one wondered (even as you spoke to the dedicated physician) who would follow in his footsteps. His treatment has not been accepted by the general medical world and yet it has proven itself so many, many times that it must be recognized and perhaps, in the future, it will. (article quoted in S.J. Haught's "Censured for Curing Cancer," p. 35)

Dr. Gerson always tried to maintain contact with patients who lived outside of the New York area beyond the purview of his immediate care. He would ask them to get blood and other tests every several weeks, as he might then need to adjust the medications and dietary instructions in response to these results. If they were not too distant, patients would sometimes return to New York to be reexamined. All considered, it was not an optimal way to continue follow-up patient treatment and tracking, but it was the best that one physician with a widely dispersed patient population could handle. One such patient was Bill Schickel whose case is told in A *Cancer Therapy*: William (Bill) Schickel: Case No. 18 ("Mr. W. S., age — 32, married, three children").

In May of 1951 Bill Schickel felt a mass on the right side of his abdomen. Surgery, performed soon afterward, probably was initially expected to involve the removal of an inflamed appendix — a routine appendectomy. But the operation turned out to be far more complicated. After the incision, surgeons found and removed some enlarged retroperitoneal glands along with the fibrotic appendix. Diagnosed as suffering from large cell lymphosarcoma, over the following months the patient was given radiation treatments and spleen extract injections, and he modified his diet. But more and diffused tumors began appearing in his abdomen and groin areas. Now there was also a pain in his lower back, and he developed a bronchial cough. Clearly, the cancer had metastasized.

Bill Schickel's physicians gave him a prognosis of two to six months more months of life. Instead, he decided to consult with Dr. Max Gerson in New York City, even though he lived hundreds of miles away, in Cincinnati. Forty-seven years later, in 1999, he recalled that difficult period in his life:

> My wife had read some mention about Dr. Max Gerson and his work with cancer, probably in *Prevention* magazine. She and her family members were always interested in nutrition, so Dr. Gerson's form of treatment made a lot of sense to her. Besides, I had no alternatives by then. So we just put our three young children in the car and drove all the way from Ohio to New York City, where we could stay at a friend's apartment.
>
> By the time I saw Dr. Gerson in March of 1952 I was pretty far gone. ["Patient was normal, was calm outside but inwardly emotional and easily excitable," was Dr. Gerson's observation after he had carefully examined him.]
>
> My first impression of Dr. Gerson was of a stately, venerable man who was considerate and honest. He asked me a lot of questions and looked carefully at all the medical records I had brought with me.
>
> He didn't build my hopes up, like some doctors might. But he said maybe I had a 30 percent chance, and was very cautious about saying this. That of course appealed to me, because 30 is sure better than zero.
>
> He gave me two choices: go to his sanatorium in upstate New York and stay there for some weeks; or do the therapy myself. Money was tight then, so we went for the home treatment. Dr. Gerson gave me a little yellow book with

exact instructions about what to eat, what not to eat and how to do everything, which I was told to follow to the letter. He also ran a lot of laboratory tests while I was there.

Then I returned home with all those instructions about the diet and so forth. Every so often I was supposed to get various tests and X-rays done in a lab, and the results were to be sent to him in New York. At the same time I should send the yellow booklet along so that he could adjust the diet.

For a while I got worse. I had to stay in bed and couldn't work. Dr. Gerson had warned me that might happen before my body started to heal. And, sure enough, within a few weeks I started to feel better.

In September of 1953 I took the bus back to New York because Dr. Gerson said he wanted to examine me again. The X-rays taken then showed only some scar tissue in my lungs. He found only three small hard glands left in my abdomen, and assured me that they'd go away if I stayed on the diet for some while longer. It wasn't too difficult, because the whole family had started eating that way, too.

That was the time I didn't have enough funds to get back to Ohio. When he found out about this, he actually lent me the money for the bus fare! (from HS's interview, 1999)

Dr. Gerson's conclusions about "W.S." in A *Cancer Therapy: Results of 50 Cases* were these:

Since this treatment started, patient remained free of any recurrence or other discomfort after the restoration of his body in about 6 to 8 months. Since that time he felt better than ever before and was working full time and with good results. He himself and his family stayed on the diet most of the time as many other families do....

Last report, July 29, 1957: "I have been feeling really very well ever since I stopped sending in my treatment book and have been carrying on a full program of work."

Unfortunately, most members of the American medical profession were either unwilling to talk directly to a number of "terminal" Gerson patients who fully recovered, as Bill Shickel did, or else unable to read about them because of a long-standing prohibition of publication of 'case histories' in respected medical journals.

~20~

The Politics of Cancer
(1955–1957)

The National Cancer Institute

In 1952 Charlotte and Irwin Straus planned a short vacation trip for the week between two national holidays: Lincoln's and Washington's birthdays. (This was long before the two days were combined in "President's Day," a single holiday conveniently taking place on a flexible Monday so as to create a three-day weekend.) They would drive down the coast, from New York to Virginia, and visit the famous country residences of two U.S. presidents, George Washington and Thomas Jefferson. They looked forward to a relaxing time. They wouldn't have their two children, Peggy and Howard, then five and nine years old, squabbling in the back seat, since Grandmother Gretchen had volunteered to look after them.

Since their route toward Monticello would pass almost directly through Bethesda, Maryland, Irwin got the idea that they could take copies of some of his father-in-law's patient records to the National Cancer Institute (NCI), the federal government's primary center, established within the structure of the National Institutes of Health (NIH) during the 1940s for initiating, performing and tracking cancer research nationally and internationally. They would turn the folders over personally to a reasonably senior person after providing a verbal introduction to Dr. Max Gerson's work. Agreeing to this new tactic in trying to interest the people at the NCI in his work, Max carefully prepared the documents, along with a cover letter.

Lotte and Irwin arrived at the Institute close to 5 p.m. on Friday afternoon. They were almost surprised to find a senior official still in his office. Dr. Raymond F. Kaiser, Chief of the Cancer Control Bureau, graciously agreed to see these impromptu visitors, despite the lateness of the hour. After introducing themselves, Lotte told Kaiser about Dr. Gerson and his work with cancer, including his unparalleled results. Then she handed him the five case histories that her father had selected to submit to the NCI.

Kaiser flipped open the first case file. It was that of Gertrude Hartmann, Gretchen's sister. Their mother had developed breast cancer in the late 1920s, ultimately with fatal results. Then in 1945, Gertrude, at exactly the same age, had similar symptoms. The lab report indicated that the positive biopsy results on cells in tissue removed from her breast were not absolutely certain. But wishing to take no chances, Gertrude had undergone the Gerson treatment for cancer, and now, seven years later, was alive and well. (She lived for many more years, dying at age 86.)

With visible relief, Dr. Kaiser said, "This one probably wasn't even cancer," as Charlotte recalls. Kaiser became distinctly uncomfortable as he examined the second file. It contained thoroughly documented biopsy results, not from a laboratory under Gerson's control, but from Memorial Hospital. The case records showed clearly that the cancer had been cured by the Gerson therapy. The other three files showed similar results: diagnoses and biopsies from different leading cancer specialists and treatment centers in the country, including their written prognoses of weeks or months until death; and yet the patient was now evidently totally recovered and had been alive for five years or more — the medical profession's own definition of certainty of a *cure*.

Kaiser was silent for a long time as he pored over the files, Charlotte recalls. Finally, he looked up at his visitors. "Well," he said, "sometimes these European refugees come to America and simply want to make a splash. So they go ahead and cure cancer." Lotte and Irwin were absolutely stunned by this extraordinary statement from an official of the national institute dedicated to finding the cure for cancer. Dr. Kaiser had just acknowledged that Dr. Gerson had cured cancer, while at the same time he treated this achievement flippantly.

Finally Irwin spoke. "Dr. Kaiser, we should make it clear to you that Dr. Gerson is not asking for any money from NCI. He has a deep distrust of government funding because he thinks that it slows progress. He always expects to pay for his own research, although several nonprofit organizations have occasionally helped to support his studies. He is only asking that the NCI give this extraordinary data careful examination. We think that, considering what we have placed in your hands, further study into the therapy by researchers at your Institute is certainly warranted. You did say yourself that apparently he actually *cured* cancer."

Kaiser seemed reluctant to speak but finally he said, "Of course, five cases aren't enough to make any kind of decision. We will need at least 25 more cases to really evaluate the treatment." As Charlotte explains, Kaiser assumed that it was impossible for this lone physician, with no outside funding, to have that many cured cancer patients.

Although they were not received as heroes for bringing evidence of a cure for cancer to the NCI, Charlotte and Irwin believed they had placed the data in the right hands. All Dr. Gerson had to do now was to provide the 25 additional cases, so that his therapy would finally be properly examined. This, after all, was what Max had hoped for when the Senate Subcommittee hearings took place in 1946, six years earlier.

With renewed optimism, Dr. Gerson carefully selected 25 more cases to submit to NCI scrutiny. He prepared the histories meticulously, selecting only those for which he had positive proofs of malignant disease, whose prognoses were for brief terminal periods, and who were alive more than five years afterward, showing no sign of cancer. He included the most complete documentation possible, including case outlines, medical charts, biopsies, before-and-after X-rays, photographs and test results — done by reliable and respected medical centers and laboratories. Then he sent them all off to the National Cancer Institute, a few weeks after Lotte and Irwin's visit.

Patiently, Dr. Gerson waited for some response. Three months elapsed, then six. Nine months later, there still was no word from the NCI. Finally he wrote a letter to the NCI inquiring about the results of their investigation of these cases. Several more months passed before a reply arrived: "Twenty-five cases is really not enough for the NCI to make a positive and definitive statement on the efficacy of a therapy. In order to do that, we will need a hundred more cases." Sorely disappointed once again, Gerson declined. Now, whenever the National Cancer Institute received an inquiry about Dr. Gerson's therapy, they responded, "Dr. Gerson was asked to submit cases for investigation, but refused to do so." The American Medical Association and the American Cancer Society responded similarly. NCI did not return the case records or ever acknowledge that they had read them. Years later, when Gar Hildenbrand at the Gerson Institute tried to use the Freedom of Information Act to extract these records from the NCI, they said that files were routinely destroyed after five or six years. In a somewhat similar situation and using the same act, a few years ago Pedro Aponte Vazquez, author of *Cronica de un Encubrimiento*, tried to retrieve from the Army records of C.P. Rhoads' atomic, biological and chemical experiments on human subjects. He was told that: (a) the records were not available because they routinely destroy old records, and (b) it would be too difficult anyway to find any such information in the huge warehouses full of old records.

Another disappointment for Max Gerson came in 1953, when the Commerce Committee of the House of Representatives conducted hearings on the subject of special funding of innovative cancer therapies. He had been approached initially about his willingness to testify, and he responded affirmatively, hoping to give a presentation similar to the one he had done in front of the Senate subcommittee in 1946, but in the end he was not invited to attend the hearings.

By the mid 1950s Dr. Gerson was absolutely convinced that some sort of conspiracy had been formed against him years before. Although he might appear paranoid in his suspicions, there were ample reasons for this feeling. A publisher of a respected medical journal once called Dr. Gerson to say that he wished he could publish an article he had submitted because it was tremendously interesting, but that he had been warned by other subscribing physicians that if he ever published an article by Dr. Gerson, his journal would be boycotted by these physicians. When he had offered to hold lectures for other physicians, he had been shunned. When radio broadcasters like Reaymond Swing praised his work, they were chastised or fired. When he himself was interviewed on the radio, he was severely censured. At times he even suspected that some of his recovering patients had been subjected to some drug or procedure by other healthcare personnel in order to reflect poorly on his therapy.

Possibly if Dr. Gerson had been able to devote himself to publishing in lesser American medical journals, such as those connected with the different regional medical societies, he might have gotten more of his papers published. He could also have submitted papers to new professional journals devoted to various aspects of biomedical research and to nutritional biochemistry, which might have responded differently than the editors of mainstream physician journals.

Nevertheless, Dr. Gerson did resume publishing papers in European medical journals that were peer-reviewed — the criterion for scientific acceptability. It was still easier for him to write in German than in English. Papers accepted with alacrity in Europe could eventually be translated, distributed and possibly even republished in the United States. His European reputation may have prompted *Prevention* magazine to publish "The Gerson Treatment for Cancer" in the August 1955 issue. If not recognized by scholarly journals, Dr. Gerson was praised by this holistic health magazine:

> One out of four! That is this year's prediction for cancer incidence by the American Cancer Society. One out of every four Americans will get cancer. The last report was "one out of every five." Will it be "one out of every three" five years from now? And in the next decade "one out of every two"?
>
> Max Gerson, M.D. of New York City, believes that cancer can be prevented and cured. His life is a living testimony to that belief, for Dr. Gerson cures cancer by diet. This is a dangerous, heretical thing to say in present-day America, but from the evidence that we have studied there seems to be no doubt that Dr. Gerson cures cancer. Advanced cases. So-called "terminal" cases. What about early cases — patients who have malignant growths but have not had surgery, X-ray or radium treatments? We are told that these cancers disappear under Dr. Gerson's treatment just about as easily and as speedily as a bad case of sniffles might.

The author of this article defended the Gerson therapy against the charge that the preparation of foods and juices was too complex and labor intensive:

True, it is a difficult diet to follow, from the practical point of view. The vegetables and fruits must be raw, as fresh as possible and is it too much trouble for a cancer patient to follow the diet at home?

Some patients have found that it is. But think a moment. We are talking of a diet that cures cancer. Could anything be too much trouble for that? We are living in a land and a time where housewives spend uncounted hours of time rolling and cutting out cookies, baking pies, decorating cakes with colored icing, making fancy sandwiches, cutting curls into radishes, stuffing celery and so forth. *Is it possible that following a diet to cure cancer could be too much trouble?*

The author did not hesitate to declare his or her belief in the efficacy of the Gerson diet after talking with the doctor and interviewing some of his patients at the Nanuet sanatorium:

Meeting Dr. Gerson helps you to understand how the long patient years of research, disappointment and courage in the face of disappointment temper a man and make him strong. Dr. Gerson's presence is electric. He speaks rapidly, warmly, brilliantly. His many European years as an honored member of the medical profession there qualify him to speak in words so technical that no layman could understand them. Instead, he waves his arm around the room and says, "Here are my patients. Ask them. Get their stories. Talk to them."

We did. And we came away convinced that Dr. Gerson is curing cancer in a way little short of miraculous. We were reassured as well that those of us who want to prevent cancer are on the right track. It is interesting to note that other degenerative diseases succumb to the diet treatment, just as cancer does....

Talking to people like this makes you feel humble, awed and thankful. Talking to Dr. Gerson and his staff about his treatment is a revelation. For the treatment is living proof of our belief that the most important single factor in good health is the right food grown in the right soil. And disease occurs in bodies that have not had this kind of food. Not in a matter of days or weeks, but after years of nutritional abuse.

This article ended with an urgent plea for readers to demand answers from various organizations and people to these provocative questions:

Whether or not someone near you has cancer, the finest thing a *Prevention* reader can do to help along this good cause is to write to the American Medical Association, to the American Cancer Society, to your local congressman, to the magazines you read, to your newspaper telling them all about the Gerson treatment and asking *why*, WHY is this treatment not taught in medical schools and *why* is it not investigated by the American Cancer Society and the American Medical Association?

Several other articles in *Prevention* helped to publicize Max Gerson's promising cancer treatment widely; and in April 1957, Dr. Gerson wrote an informative article at the magazine's request, "Can Cancer Be Prevented?"

Probably the best nationwide publicity that Dr. Gerson ever received came when he published the article "Can Cancer Be Prevented?" in *Prevention*, the best-known popular publication promoting a healthful lifestyle. His message was in accord with what J. I. Rodale, the magazine's publisher and editor-in-chief, was already telling the American public: that chemicals used in agriculture were very harmful to humans, that organic farming and gardening were healthy practices, and that, for the sake of their children's health and the future of the nation, Americans needed to change the way they ate and lived. As Dr. Gerson write in his article: "Modern civilization first damages the soil by artificial fertilizers, sprayings, etc., correspondingly our nutrition is denaturalized and partly poisoned (see Wickenden, *Our Daily Poison* and other authors), while our bodies are adapted, through millions of generations, to the natural food.

He then articulated for the public the 'theory' of cancer he had been developing over the past decade:

Where there is no modern civilization, there is no cancer....

The question of whether cancer can be prevented has to be generally answered as "no." To really wipe out cancer, it would be necessary to change our agriculture by avoiding artificial fertilizers and all types of sprays. In addition, it would be necessary to change the ways of preservation and distribution of foods and to avoid depriving them of their natural, vital values. That means: not to can, bottle, refine, or subject food to other damaging methods. I think that only some individuals will be able to accomplish the difficult task of avoiding or reducing to a minimum all methods which modern civilization has brought upon us. On the other hand, great revolutionary transformations would be necessary, pressed by the strongest demand of a great part of the population to accomplish this vital task for the well-being of our future offspring.

As long as all the historical observations and those of our present time remain "paper warnings" only, we cannot speak about prevention of cancer. Such paper warnings, even given in the strongest and most convincing way, did not save old Persia, the ancient Egyptian people, the culture of Greece, and the people of the Roman Empire (Roma eterna). All these and many more had to go down after "their modern civilization" ruined the simple habits of life and nutrition, but increased degenerative diseases.

In the United States, our upward rise went quicker than in all other ancient countries, and degenerative diseases with cancer and mental sicknesses have increased much faster too. In the last years degenerative diseases appear in our babies and children, especially in the form of leukemias. It is an illusion that the clinical attempt to detect early symptoms means prevention of cancer. Prevention is possible *only* if we know the cause of cancer. In my opinion it is based upon the degeneration of the liver and I repeat: the beginning degenerative changes in the liver do not show any symptoms for a long period. For that reason, the removal of one or several cancer symptoms (growths) by operation, or X-rays or radium does not remove the underlying cause, therefore the tumors regrow sooner or later. . . .

The treatment (a combined totality regime) has to make good what modern civilization and other methods and occurrences have ruined before, in the liver and whole digestive tract. (from *Prevention* magazine, April 1957)

Dr. Gerson summarized his regimen for diet and supplements, and afterwards provided four unpublished cases that "show the effectiveness of this method."

We have no idea how many people read this article and changed their diet accordingly, but by now, Dr. Gerson had gained a reputation, albeit a somewhat subterranean one, as a physician with a an amazing ability to cure people afflicted with seemingly hopeless cancerous conditions. Increasingly, these patients came to him from other states as popular magazines like *Prevention* articles spread the word.

During this period, Max Gerson turned his attention to writing a comprehensive book on his therapy.

Max worked hard on this manuscript, spending almost all his waking hours apart from his medical practice on writing. His customary procedure was to write some notes, then dictate the text to his secretary, Mrs. White, who would then transcribe it, chapter by chapter, into typescript form. She also helped him assemble 50 of his best cases for a case history section. Mrs. White had been with Dr. Gerson for about five years, since he left the Madison Foundation.

Considering his relatively uncompromising approach to life and to diet, Max Gerson had an uncharacteristic weakness. In the late afternoon, he suffered from low energy — a combination of low blood sugar and lethargy, further compounded by his advanced age. To combat this daily droopiness while continuing his demanding work, he began taking a cup of coffee in the afternoon, which supplied both caffeine as a quick stimulus and added sugar for glucose. If this single cup of coffee each day that Dr. Gerson depended on could be called an "addiction," it was a very minor one indeed. Mrs. White routinely prepared and brought him his coffee.

In 1955 Gerson was just short of completing the book manuscript when he fell mysteriously ill. Though he was 74 years old, until then he had been in robust health, never taking so much as a day off due to illness. Now he felt extremely weary and weak and suffered from recurrent diarrhea. He canceled his patient appointments and stayed around the apartment. He could not determine what this mysterious, debilitating problem was, but of course used his own painstaking methods to regain his ability to function. He had always drunk freshly pressed juices; now he drank even more. Yet, surprisingly, he did not take any coffee enemas, though his body, particularly his liver, would have benefited from being detoxified. (According to his daughter Charlotte, to her knowledge Dr. Gerson never gave himself a coffee enema during his entire life — a clear case of "Do as I say, not as I do" — or, in this case, "as I *don't do*.")

A few weeks later, when Max finally returned to his office to put the finishing touches on his book, he discovered that his notes and the entire typescript of the book he was working on had been removed from his desk — apparently stolen. The book containing the distillation of his life's work was gone, as were the case histories he compiled. Mrs. White disclaimed knowledge of the whereabouts of any of the materials. For Max, this felt like a repetition, but with far worse consequences for him, of his previous experiences with the Madison Foundation when his patient files were taken from him. He dismissed Mrs. White immediately, holding her responsible for the theft of his materials.

Since no backup carbon copies of the book manuscript had been made for safe storage elsewhere. Max faced the prospect of having to start his entire book from the beginning. He worked on it during the next two years, amid numerous other calls upon his time and energy.

Max Gerson, his family members and friends concluded that Mrs. White apparently had been influenced by Dr. George Miley in an effort to derail Gerson. In 1955 — the same year as his illness and the manuscript theft — Dr. Gerson had hired a public relations specialist, Cyril Maire, hoping that Maire's expertise would help to overcome the AMA's refusal to allow him to publish his work. Max shared files, X-rays and results with him, but Maire not only failed to produce any positive results, but actively participated in undermining Gerson's work. An intriguing section of a letter written by Max in July 1955 to his friend Henry Schaefer-Simmern indicates his perception of this conspiracy:

> You will be interested to know that we had to dismiss Mr. Cyril Maire. He did not accomplish anything. I spent so much time with him, gave him the best pictures and reports, put all together to be give to Mr. Moran [perhaps connected with the AMA], but he did not do it and I could not get [them] back from him. Finally, we heard that he worked together with Dr. Miley and Mrs. Seeley who are, as you know, my archenemies and most probably paid by the AMA. They also succeeded in bringing my former secretary, who was here five years, on their side, so that she worked in my office as their spy, notifying them about all cancer patients, here in New York and abroad. That was another bad experience with human beings. Maire told everyone that he worked for

humanitarian purposes, but got $500.00 a month personally from me. In reality, he worked only for other companies actively.

He made, also, as we know from several friends, including Mr. Mowinkel, derogatory statements about my person, mostly not about my cancer work. . . .

The most difficult and inhuman part of the attacks directed against me is that the physicians fall in with this policy and take my best and furthest-recovered patients away, bring them into the hospitals and let them die there. In this way, I continually lose about 25-30% of my best cases. This happens particularly here, in the New York and New Jersey area, as far as they can be controlled through their "family physicians." They know every case I treat or continue to treat in Nanuet, of course, since I need the patients' prior surgery and biopsy reports.

Max Gerson and his family often considered other behind-the-scenes figures might be responsible for preventing his work from gaining any recognition within the medical community. As Max wrote in a 1954 letter to his friend Albert Schweitzer:

My main opponent is C. P. Rhoads, director of Sloan Kettering hospital here. He controls the AMA and Academy of Medicine since he also controls millions of dollars annually from cancer collections, etc.

Those who would like to befriend me are saying quite openly that they are not allowed and cannot do so. They are sorry that they cannot help me or else they would lose their position and hospital privileges and laboratories. I have long given up hope of any kind of recognition. Nevertheless, I continue on my straightforward path. (10/1/54; translated from the German by Charlotte Gerson)

The questionable political motives and ethical behavior of the established cancer research and treatment facilities in the 1950s has been exposed by Ralph W. Moss in his book *The Cancer Industry*. Dr. Max Gerson was a decidedly anti-establishment and even threatening figure in this "industry."

Gerson's New Foundation

Around the time of the stolen book manuscript, some of Max Gerson's former patients and ardent supporters decided to start a new organization, the Foundation for Cancer Treatment. The foundation intended to raise funds for Dr. Gerson's continuing medical research and for enabling low-income patients to receive a full course of therapy at the Nanuet sanatorium or to supplement their incomes so as to pay for juicing supplies and supplements during home-based treatment. Another main function was educational: to acquaint both health professionals and the public with Dr. Gerson's work. Initially, the official address was Dr. Gerson's apartment on

Park Avenue. Foremost among those who agreed to serve as directors of the foundation was Dr. Albert Schweitzer, who could only furnish nominal assistance by lending credibility through his excellent name.

A concerted effort now seemed to be made by other people to connect Dr. Gerson and his work with the lay public. For instance, engagements were set up for him to talk directly to business persons, as in a luncheon program for over 200 attendees given in December 1955 at the Hotel Martinique in Manhattan. If Max Gerson could not persuade the medical profession to pay attention to the results of his therapy, he could at least give lectures about his success in treating cancer to intelligent and concerned persons in other professions.

When Johanna Oberlander, the Gersons' oldest daughter, began serving as the administrator of this new foundation, it started operating out of her home in Kew Gardens. She fielded telephone inquiries and answered letters about Dr. Gerson's work, and referred people to his office, to make appointments to see him. She wrote newsletter-style articles about Dr. Gerson's work and about other therapies, such as that of Dr. Issels in Germany, which utilized many techniques of the Gerson therapy. She arranged to duplicate or print some Gerson papers that hadn't been accepted by reputable American medical journals, and arranged for some German ones to be translated, for distribution to interested people. Also, for patients' convenience, she handled sales of the Gerson-recommended K & K juicer at $150, close to the wholesale price, earning only a small profit for the foundation. During this same period her sister Trudy was running the Gerson sanatorium at Nanuet.

In 1956 Dr. Gerson corresponded with a philanthropist in Chicago interested in knowing more about his cancer therapy. Dr. Gerson responded with a comprehensive description of his "theory" of cancer before making a an implicit plea for funding the Nanuet sanatorium:

> According to my experiences I developed the following theory: cancer is one of the degenerative diseases, the visible or hidden malignant formations are symptoms only, regardless of their origin. I do not treat the pathology of the symptoms but their underlying cause, which I found to have several pathological changes in the whole metabolism, especially, the liver. This conception brings us back to the older doctrine of the law of totality in the body — effective in both health and sickness.
>
> The practice of the treatment is too complex to be described here in a letter. Part of it you may find in former articles and in the article "Cancer, a Problem of Metabolism."
>
> Of the cancer cases that come to my clinic 95% are so called terminal cases, sent home to die after operations and other conservative treatments in the best renowned cancer hospitals had been futile. The majority of these given-up cases

have improvements fast and lasting results, if the intestinal apparatus and the essential organs especially the liver are not too far destroyed directly by too many metastases, or indirectly damaged by toxins, poisons and also long series of X-rays, cobalt, etc. Results are poor in leukemia, specially after many blood transfusions. I see the best results in the most malignant cases, when the whole body can be quickly detoxified with the help of the liver and that organ reactivated.

In the last ten years I have been investigated 5 times as a member of the A.M.A. by the best experts of the A.M.A. The result was that they could not do anything against my favorable successes but they still are withholding my publications and demonstrations. This is the reason why I like to invite you to visit my cancer clinic without any physician who is connected with the A.M.A. and dependent on their rules and accepted therapeutic methods.

At present I have in the cancer clinic in Nanuet, N.Y.: 23 beds, one assistant physician, M.D., two nurses, one specially arranged diet kitchen and one well equipped room for the preparation of juices. What is needed: hospital facilities for about 50 to 60 beds, a modern laboratory, an X-ray installation for examination only, not for treatment, and organic gardening facilities for the summertime and hothouse for wintertime. I don't know what these projects might cost but let us estimate $650-750,000. There are large enough grounds in Nanuet planted with wonderful trees. . . .

I thank you so much for your well known benevolent interest in that humanitarian problem and my cancer work in particular.

Among the patients who stayed at the Nanuet sanatorium was a young man named Eddie Braun. Forty-three years later he recounted to me some of his experiences with Dr. Gerson and his therapy. Ed Braun is Case #11, "E.B.," in A Cancer Therapy.

In 1956 I was in big trouble with cancer. I was a young guy, 30 years old — married, with a couple of small children. The cancer probably came from when I was in the Army over 10 years earlier, during the Second World War. I had been stationed at Los Alamos, New Mexico, where the scientists were making those first atomic bombs. We were sent in to check everything at the site soon after that first test bomb was detonated. In those days they didn't know much at all about the dangers of being exposed to radioactive fallout.

Anyway, the disease process started with a cancerous tumor on a testicle. The surgeons removed that, but then tumors developed in other places. One was on my penis; a couple of inches long, it was wrapped around it. No wonder cancer means "crab." It got so I could barely urinate. So they did some more surgery, but it didn't help much. Then they tried deep X-ray treatment. I was just fried — cooked, like you wouldn't believe.

The doctors then wanted to do still more surgery. In the hospital they gave me sedatives and prepped me for the operation. But they also took some X-rays, and these showed that the cancer had metastasized to both lungs. So the operation got cancelled. The prognosis? — Hopeless. I was sent home to die. But they said they'd give me morphine to make it easier on me. They also told me to take care of personal things, like a will, insurance and so on, right away . . . because I'd probably go within six weeks. So it was pretty tight.

Well, my wife's sister had read about Dr. Gerson and his cancer therapy in *Prevention* magazine. Though I was reluctant to do it, my wife and other people were pushing me to give it a try. After all, I had nothing to lose. So I left Wisconsin for New York in March or April of '56. First I called up Dr. Gerson, talked with him and set up appointment to see him at his office on Park Avenue. When I got there, Dr. Gerson looked me over and took my medical history. Then he said he thought he could help me. Nobody had said that before. I had a tempered belief that he could, too. I was grasping at straws.

My doctors back home of course had been unhappy about my going away like that. They warned me, "Hold on to your wallet!" I was very concerned about whether we could afford the treatment. I can't remember offhand how much that first office visit cost. It was very reasonable, maybe five dollars. Overall, too, the price per week for staying at Nanuet was very fair. So I decided to do it.

That day I had to get from the city to Nanuet on my own. It was my first time in New York, so I felt a bit overwhelmed by the circuitous route involved. I took a cab to the Port Authority, then caught a bus, and so on. I got to the sanatorium about suppertime, and immediately started on the therapy. I stayed there for a month.

At Nanuet, I was quite impressed by how many people were really being helped — though of course there were those who couldn't be helped. Then there was the man who had to sneak around to smoke his forbidden cigarettes.

When Dr. Gerson came up to Nanuet on the weekends, after a meal the patients would gather in the sitting room, right next to the dining room. He would talk to us for an hour or more. It was really interesting — and encouraging, because he would give weekly presentations of patients who were recovering or already recovered, and had come back for a checkup or a visit. To demonstrate the results of his regime, he'd point out the changes from their original conditions.

He'd do little things that showed he was a kindly man, like doing doctoring even with the people who worked there, the nurses and attendants — taking care of their aches and pains. Yet there was something else about him, too. I won't use the word arrogant to describe him, but he had a demeanor that was single-minded. He was going to help people with cancer, and no one was going to tell him that the way he did it wasn't the right thing, the best thing, for everyone to do.

After a few weeks, one day when I was urinating some blood came out with the urine. The tumor was no longer hard and began dissolving. It disappeared almost totally within days, so I could urinate normally. After a month I returned to New York, taking a bus with several other patients. We went to get X-rays taken by some man that Dr. Gerson used all the time because his X-rays were better than anyone else's; he said he was "an artist." Well, my chest X-rays looked great. In one lung that had had 12 metastases, they were reduced down to four; the other one was totally cleared. I could tell that I could breathe much better already, so I was pretty happy.

I went home and stayed on the therapy for about two years. By then the X-rays showed that the tumors in my lungs had turned into scar tissue. It took a couple of years more before nothing showed up anymore.

I've been totally healthy ever since coming back here from New York. I'm now 76 years old. And I lived to raise our three children.

The Wienberger Bill

Max Gerson rarely traveled farther away from New York City than his sanatoriums nearby, but now and then he went to some other cities for specific purposes. For instance, in Pasadena, California, in 1953 he gave a lecture on "Cancer Development and Treatment" at a meeting of the American Academy of Applied Nutrition, and even presented some of his recovered patients in addition to showing X-ray and other documentary evidence of cures. At one lecture he characterized his therapy, well accepted in Europe, as the standard treatment for strengthening the immune system of weak patients — "from the simplest of postoperative hospital patients to Adolf Hitler." Max Gerson took a certain grotesque pride in knowing that the Nazi leader and some of his chief advisors had followed the Gerson diet. He also traveled to Pittsburgh for the controversial fluoridation hearings there. Not surprisingly, he was adamantly opposed to water fluoridation for public health reasons, whether or not the citizens themselves had voted for it. He was concerned, too, about the health effects of using chlorine to disinfect public water supplies. The two chemicals, he believed, would damage people's health in various ways over time.

Dr. Gerson attended a major trial in California concerning the popular but notorious "Hoxsey Family Formula" based on an old remedy long used by Harry Hoxsey's farming family in self-administered cancer treatments. A number of people, including some politicians and even a few physicians, claimed that they had seen cancers healed by the combination this formula, a combination of herbs such as red clover and prickly ash bark with the pharmacological substance potassium iodide in an internal tonic, or in an external paste, with bloodroot, antimony trisulfide and zinc chloride. At the least, the Hoxsey formula was harmless compared to the drastic measures that conventional medicine usually employed in treating cancer.

The Hoxsey formula was one of the cancer treatments discussed at the volatile hearings conducted in San Francisco in early May of 1958 by members of the California legislature in an effort to revise and revive the "anti-cancer-quack" Weinberger Bill. Some high-powered witnesses from the medical establishment attended, including Dr. Cornelius Rhoads from the Memorial Sloan-Kettering Institute and Dr. Raymond Kaiser from the National Cancer Institute, as well as representatives of the American Medical Association and the Food and Drug Administration. At the three-day hearing officials debated with supporters the highly controversial issues regarding the efficacy of various different "alternative" methods currently claimed as treatments for cancer. Detractors, which included most of the medical establishment, wanted them legally banned from the public marketplace, including advertising. They also intended to disbar licensed physicians from utilizing them with cancer patients.

A prime hearing target was Harry M. Hoxsey's well-known herbal nostrum, though Hoxsey did not attend the hearings to defend his treatment. Another closely examined cancer cure was the secret chemical formula called Krebiozen, invented and manufactured by the Durovic brothers of Yugolavia. This formula was validated in person at the hearing by a reputable Chicago physician, Professor Andrew C. Ivy, whose advocacy was destroying his high standing in the medical community. Dr. Gerson was well aware of certain parallels between these cases and his own situation, yet there was a notable difference in his dietary and detoxification treatment regimen: he sold no profit-making substances or devices, and indeed provided access to information so that cancer patients might undertake it on their own.

Although the Weinberger Bill had initially met defeat, it was later passed in 1959 in an amended form, largely due to public attention to the San Francisco hearings, where the orthodox medical men — not unexpectedly — won the day. As Maurice Natenberg, who attended the San Francisco hearings, wrote soon afterwards in his admonitory book *The Cancer Blackout*:

> The original Weinberger bill had been defeated, but its proponents had refused to let it die. This bill is highly important to every citizen, not only in California but in the entire United States, for it may augur a revolutionary attempt to dictate the trends of events in the treatment of cancer and eventually of all other diseases. Not only the life and health of everyone may be involved, but the professional destinies of thousands of practitioners and investigators are also in the balance. When certain approaches to the treatment of a disease are authorized and all others become illegal, every mode of treatment and every avenue of investigation will be narrowly restricted. (p. 1)

Other states soon followed suit, banning all cancer treatments that did not meet the approval of the American Medical Association and its subordinate regional organizations. The sale across state lines of some of these treatments, even certain information about ways to treat cancer, also became illegal, to be enforced by the U.S. Post Office and the FDA. The use of unapproved cancer treatments by licensed physicians and other health practitioners also became subject to raids by the FDA, which included the permanent confiscation of equipment, supplies and records. This circumstance persists to this day, and definitely affects the ability to offer a treatment center using the Gerson Therapy.

Max Gerson at Rest

Max and Gretchen tried to take at least two vacations every year: one during winter in a warmer climate to give them relief from New York's frigid season, another in the summer to escape for a time the oppressively hot and muggy weather. In wintertime they usually spent two or three weeks in Miami, Florida. Their summertime vacation took place from late August into September so that allergy-prone Gretchen could avoid the city's worst hay-fever period. They often stayed with friends in New Hampshire, where ragweed pollen was absent. During the later 1950s, the Gersons began spending their late-summer vacations at Dr. Bernard Jensen's Happy Valley Health Ranch in Escondido, California, northeast of San Diego, located in a beautiful valley surrounded by the rolling, golden, oak-covered hills that characterize central and southern California's landscape. To Mrs. Gerson's relief, ragweed was absent. "It was considered a sanctuary, a place to come to, to learn how to live a more natural life," was how Dr. Jensen described his health spa.

Bernard Jensen, a licensed chiropractor, not a medical doctor, was becoming well known for his work in iridology, a healthcare practice that used a study of the eye's iris to determine a patient's health status and make diagnoses. Dr. Jensen had come to New York earlier in the 1950s to visit the Nanuet clinic to learn more about Dr. Gerson's methods. Impressed by what he saw, he adopted some elements of the Gerson therapy for use at his health ranch, notably eating organic vegetarian food and administering colonic cleanses. He was interested in helping people with minor illnesses and did not claim or attempt to treat cancer.

For various reasons Max Gerson truly enjoyed his time at Jensen's ranch. He could get the special salt-free, organic vegetarian cuisine he required for his health. The ranch was a lovely place to relax and to socialize with like-minded people committed to healthful living like Dr. Jensen. Max especially enjoyed looking at the hundreds of artistic photographs of flowers that were hung around the large ranch house — all taken by Jensen, who was a talented photographer. Over a half century later, Bernard Jensen — by then in his early 90s, the author of numerous books and the recipient of many international honors — recalled the Gersons' visits:

> Dr. Max Gerson and his wife came to the ranch two times that I know of, and probably a third as a short visit. They had a very amiable relationship and seemed to have gotten along very well while staying here. He had come to the health ranch because he needed a rest and wanted to get away from his work for a while. He was also interested in having some good nutritious food. In fact, one of his first statements when he picked strawberries out of our garden was that he didn't get any allergies from them, which he usually did. He was quite adamant about getting foods with no sprays.
>
> Dr. Gerson was very enthusiastic about the ranch and how it was operated. It had been founded to teach others how to live and then go home and do the right thing, especially in the art of nutrition. It operated year round. People could come without seeing a doctor; however, many doctors referred patients to the ranch. I was the doctor on staff and oversaw everything, from growing the foods to supervision of treatments. In fact, I grew as much as 3,000 pounds of carrots a month just for vegetable juices for my patients.
>
> Dr. Gerson was eager to build up his own health while he was here. We did not go into his health problems. He looked as if he needed some rest. He complained a bit about being tired. But he didn't want my advice particularly. He was pretty well set on what he should do for himself. We tried in every way possible to get the specific foods he wanted prepared for himself.
>
> He was in harmony with our surroundings and we spent some hours talking about our philosophies and the methods we used to treat our patients. He was an assertive person with very definite and individual ideas. But he also could listen to other people's opinions and experiences. Our association naturally grew into a friendship because I was so much in harmony with his theory and practice of healing.

Although at Escondido Dr. Gerson was on vacation from his medical work, he sometimes was visited socially by ever-grateful former patients of his. Occasionally he also gave rather informal talks to residents at the Jensen Ranch.. When he lectured on "The Cure of Advanced Cancer by Diet Therapy: A Summary of 30 Years of Clinical Experimentation," his talk was tape-recorded. A transcription of this talk shows how Max could readily explain the origin of his special cancer therapy to lay people, without using abstruse medical jargon. In his narrative he first told of his initial successes and failures in treating a few cancer patients while he was still in Europe, notably his first three cases in Bielefeld, all of them successful, followed mostly by discouraging results. Then he took up the story upon his arrival in America:

. . . I had no idea what cancer was. If somebody asked me about the theory, just what it was I was doing, I had to answer, "I don't really know myself."

Some time later I came to this country. I couldn't get the cancer problem and the cure of the first three cases out of my mind. I kept thinking, "It must be possible, it would be a crime not to do it." But it wasn't so easy. When I came here, I had no clinic. I didn't even have a license to practice medicine. When I had taken the exams and could take patients, I had to treat them at home and that was hard work. The patients didn't like to obey the diet, to do it at home. They were accustomed to save kitchen time and not to work hard to make all the juices necessary for the treatment as it had been worked out. . . .

All the material was there, nothing was lost. But it didn't work. Then I found out through a physicist that in the liquefier, in the center, there is positive electricity and in the fluid there is negative electricity. This electricity kills the oxidizing enzymes. And that is also true for the centrifugal juicer and the other apparatus. . . .

The patients must drink a lot of those juices. They have to have the Hippocrates soup. I can't go into all the details. The evening would not be long enough for that. But very important for the detoxification are enemas. I felt that the detoxification as suggested in the book of Hippocrates was a most important part.

Finally, I had a clinic. The patients saw that also the more advanced cases and even some terminal cases, very far advanced cases, could be saved. They brought me more and more of these terminal cases. I was forced into that. On the one side, the knife of the AMA was at my throat, and on my back I had only terminal cases. If I had not saved them, my clinic would have been a death house. Some of the cases were brought on stretchers. They couldn't walk. They could no longer eat. It was very, very difficult. So, I really had to work out a treatment that could help these far advanced cases. Again, I was forced into it.

On the need of where to put the emphasis: reading all the literature, I saw that all the scientists treat the symptoms. These, I thought, are only symptoms. There must be something basic behind them. It has to be impossible that there are symptoms in the brain, others in the lungs, in the bones, in the abdomen and in the liver. There must be something basic, or else this is impossible.

Already, through my work with tuberculosis, I learned that in tuberculosis and in all other degenerative diseases, one must not treat the symptoms. The body — the whole body — has to be treated. But that is easily said. How will you do it? Little by little I came to the conclusion that the most important part of our body is the digestive tract. For all our intake to be properly digested, and for the other organs of the digestive tract to function right and help in the digestion to the end product — and at the same time eliminate all the waste products — all the toxins and poisons must be eliminated so that nothing will accumulate in our system. I thought that this was the most important thing in the tuberculosis treatment. It must be the same in all the other degenerative diseases, too. And still, up to the present, I am convinced that cancer does not need a "specific" treatment.

Cancer is a so-called degenerative disease, and all the degenerative diseases have to be treated so that the whole body at first is detoxified. In my tuberculosis work . . . I saw that the liver plays the important role. It eliminates the toxins from the body, prepares them so they can enter into the bile ducts, and can thus be eliminated with the bile; that is not an easy job. In addition, the liver helps to prepare the stomach juice with the help of the visceral nervous system. The liver helps to prepare the pancreas, trypsin, pepsin, lipase, the digestive enzymes — all that is regular with the help of the visceral nervous system. The liver has many, many more very important functions. One of them is the reactivation of the oxidizing enzymes. . . . It is very important to note that oxidizing enzymes are at a low level of function in cancer patients.

Now let us anticipate the theory. During these years the idea occurred to me that there are two components in cancer which are of particular importance. One is the whole body, the general component. The other is a local one, the symptom. The treatment has to be applied to the general component. When we are able to bring this into balance, the local one disappears. What is the general component and what does the treatment have to do to bring it into balance. I should like to devote this evening mostly to that question.

Dr. Gerson went on to explain the elements of the therapy: the juices and the saltless, fatless and vegetarian diet; the use of coffee enemas in detoxification; the addition of certain supplements — notably potassium, thyroid, iodine drops in Lugol's solution, certain digestive enzymes and raw calves' liver juice. He even presented two recovering patients of his, a young boy who earlier had suffered severe leukemia and a man who had had metastatic prostate cancer. Then he answered questions from his audience, including this well-informed one: "What metabolic tests do you do before and after to further prove recovery systematically as well as clinically?"

I examine in all these cases the urine, the complete blood count, basal metabolism or protein-bound iodine, and potassium in serum and tissue. To see how the liver functions, I found it best to examine the end product of the protein metabolism, urea nitrogen and uric acid. When these are normal and stay normal, then I assume that the patient is all right. But potassium in serum does not give a characteristic picture and makes it difficult to judge. The patient can be cured yet the serum potassium still shows low because the tissues take it away.

The final question put to Dr. Gerson that evening was, "How can we prevent cancer?" His response was cautionary, simplistic in its solution — and, as might be expected, adamant:

Cancer must be prevented by preventing damage to the liver. The basic measure of prevention is not to eat the damaged, dead, poisoned food which we bring into our bodies. Every day, day by day, we poison our bodies. The older people still have a better liver and resistance from the food they had when they were young. The younger people get worse and the babies, now the second generation on canned baby foods, are still worse. They get leukemias. First of all, eat as much as you can of raw food, keep the potassium level up and take some iodine.

Still, in spite of the highly positive relationships that Dr. Gerson formed with ordinary people — such as his patients and their families, and other persons he met who wished to learn how best to maintain or regain good health — the doors of organized medicine in the United States had been slammed shut against his entry, and remained so. That is why Max Gerson would sometimes compose political action-soliciting letters such as this one, written in 1956 to a patient's daughter:

I am glad that your dad came home in such an excellent mental and physical condition. I am pleased that they continue the treatment to cure him entirely. . . .

I think that it would be advisable that you write of your own accord to your Senators and Congressmen to tell them that it is a crime to suppress such an effective cancer treatment and that the AMA do not permit Dr. Gerson to publish his papers or let more people be informed about his treatment. Write the story in your own words, and tell them they must do something against this crime. [letter to Mrs. Becker, May 28, 1956]

Max Gerson's continuing fight with the medical establishment, which clearly wanted to hide his successes and squelch his voice, was not about to end. In fact, a year after he wrote that letter, it would get even worse.In his letters to Henry Schaefer-Simmern Max Gerson continued to convey his great appreciation for his friend's frequent efforts in his behalf in trying to promote his cancer therapy. He also reports on his interactions with medical associates — including times when they sat in judgment of his practice, as when the Medical Society of the County of New York repeatedly subjected him to professional inquisitions. He had learned over the years how best to conduct these grueling sessions. However, the grim reality of his publication situation was confirmed by physician informants:

I thank you whole-heartedly for your wonderful letter and even more for all our deep devotion and great activity for my work.

If you think that I am scolding at physicians you are mistaken. I was very polite and friendly when the investigators were here. After the fourth investigation the N.Y. Medical Society even thanked me for my readiness and correct handling of all cases, and friendliness to the other colleagues.

Also at the fifth investigation I refrained from saying anything against their thinking and feeling, showed only my results and answered their questions. If they were of another opinion, I did not contradict in order to avoid any sharp discussions. You are right, the opposition can only be broken down with results.

In the last two weeks two physicians told me that the more results I show the greater will be the opposition to let me demonstrate or publish.

Still, Dr. Gerson, who inherently was optimistic, was getting such positive results in many patients that he had good reason occasionally to share with Henry of his high hopes for the future. Best of all was when another physician expressed the desire to work with him in furthering his cancer therapy — which never, alas, got realized or lasted for long:

I discussed the matter recently with Dr. L.W. Tomarkin of Spring Valley, who was until a few years ago the president of the International Cancer Committee. I know him from Germany where we once had dinner together at Sauerbruch's home. He now admires my work after I showed him a few patients in Nanuet and will come immediately into the Foundation and devote all his working power and time to bring my cancer treatment through, something which has been a great desire all his life. He knows all the big leading cancer workers and will give us all the advice in which way we can best break through resistance and let the public know my results.

There are many more good features here in the making which are too early to report but it will be very favorable for us in the future.

We should not forget that the difficulty of applying this treatment and keeping it up, is to many physicians and patients a great hindrance to start and continue it. [2/3/55]

~21~
The Perils of Publicity
(1957–1958)

The "Long John" Radio Show

Because so many of his patients now came to him because they had heard about him, directly or indirectly, from publications like *Prevention* magazine, Max Gerson began to realize that the best way to spread the information about his cancer therapy was not to keep trying to convince physicians of its efficacy through demonstrations and publications in respected medical journals, but to write and talk directly to the public. These people might then begin insisting that their own doctors learn about Gerson's methods so that they could supervise their application; if they refused to do so, their patients might well go to someone else for treatment, even travel a great distance to see Dr. Gerson himself.

Dr. Max Gerson was invited to serve as a panelist on the "Long John" Nebel talk show on January 15, 1957. The WOR radio program customarily went from 11 p.m. to midnight. The invitation had come about because an active member of Gerson's Foundation for Cancer Treatment, Joe Neumark —himself a recovered cancer patient (case #25 in A *Cancer Therapy*) —knew that Nebel, a highly popular New York radio talk-show host, regularly interviewed physicians on his late-night program. In a roundtable format, they discussed health matters that concerned the public.

That night the host and his guests were scheduled to talk about the overuse of elective surgery. Joining Dr. Gerson on the panel were Jim Donnelly, a perennial Long John guest, and Joe Neumark. Mrs. Gerson accompanied her husband to the studio but sat on the sidelines, not participating in the talk. Fortunately for those who are interested, this panel discussion was audiotaped, and two tape cassettes are available from the Gerson Institute.

Introducing Dr. Gerson, Long John ran briefly through his medical credentials. He then asked a few questions on the subject that the discussion was intended to explore: excessive use of surgery. Dr. Gerson's responses were based on his observations and experiences in the area of his greatest recent expertise — namely, cancer. It soon became clear that Dr. Gerson thought many surgeries for cancer, with the exception of those that could immediately resolve life-threatening situations (such as intestinal blocks or abscesses), were not only unnecessary, but did not have the desired effect of eradicating the cancer. He quoted several medical authorities, surgeons with years of experience in the surgical treatment of tumors, who had come to the conclusion that they had achieved little during their long careers to solve the problem of cancer. Dr. Gerson also cited a physician in a recent article in JAMA who had stated that statistics showed an increase in the incidence of cancer, while the problem of hopeless cases may remain for many years to come, because science is pessimistic about finding a cancer cure soon, despite costly research work in experimental chemotherapy. However, Dr. Gerson said that he didn't agree either with this pessimism or with the direction that medical research and treatment had taken in the past 200 years, all over the world, with millions of dollars already spent on the attempt to treat cancer where it appears in the body.

Dr. Gerson then launched his first intense monologue of the evening, occasionally interrupted by a leading question or provocative comment from his host. As medical practitioners and researchers generally do, Dr. Gerson employed the language of combat when describing his particular "war on cancer," staying in the attack mode while waxing eloquent on several of his favorite subjects, totality and the human liver. A number of the things Gerson said or quoted anticipated passages in the ambitious book he was currently completing, A *Cancer Therapy*.

> We should not attack the symptom by itself, locally. Cancer is a so-called degenerative disease. In all degenerative diseases, not only in cancer, like in chronic arthritis, hardening of arteries, even in cardiopathy, muscular dystrophy, diabetes, tuberculosis to a certain degree — in all these degenerative diseases we have to attack the whole body.

> And I would say there is a law of totality in the whole body, not only in mathematics, physics, art and philosophy, but also that is effective in human beings, in biology. We have therefore to attack the whole body. A few prominent physicians have had that idea. But they didn't know exactly how to attack the whole body to get at the symptoms. In my endeavor to do this in the past 30 years in tuberculosis and other degenerative diseases I found finally that we can attack that problem, also cancer finally, by attacking the whole metabolism.

> And something more: the whole metabolism is to the highest degree concentrated on our liver. To explain that problem it would be first necessary to say something consistent with the life problem: cancer is consistent with the life problem. What is it, what does it mean for the human being? Look, in plants life is maintained through the chlorophyll and the rays of the sun and the split

atoms; it is the only substance in the living world which is able to take up the split atom and transform it into living substances for the plant.

Now where do we have in our body such an organ that can maintain life? We have it in our liver. The liver is the organ in our body that can activate and reactivate our oxidizing enzymes. And that means maintain our life. That is the most important part of the function of our liver. The liver is to a certain degree a filter of the whole metabolism. It is also a storage place. The liver activates the metabolism. Everything is activated, ionized, to some degree. We cannot use potassium, our most important mineral in the body, if it is not activated, ionized: not K-39 but K-41. That is the active mineral in our body — ionized potassium. In cancer, K-41 is terribly reduced. . . .

We know that now. But what could we do to bring this about? We have to help our liver. The best authorities in our country say that the most damaged organ in the cancer body, in the tumor-bearing body, is the liver. It is damaged and cannot reactivate the oxidizing enzymes normally. When this happens, when the intracellular oxidizing mechanism in the body is damaged, then cancer can grow. That is known since 1930 with the wonderful work of Otto Barber.

What can we do now? Give therapy to reestablish the function of the liver. The therapy has to reestablish the function of the liver. I found especially in the last 10 years that if we are able to restore the function of the liver, we can cure cancer, even in far advanced cases. But if that is not possible any more . . . then sorry, the patient is licked. And we can't help it.

Clearly fascinated, Long John now began asking Dr. Gerson closely about his claim that he had gotten "favorable results" with terminal cancer patients through his dietary and detoxifying methods. The round-table discussion quickly became an interview between Long John Nebel and Max Gerson, with Mr. Donnelly bowing out of the conversation. At first, Nebel sounded like the model of a hard-hitting, skeptical broadcast journalist, asking sharp questions, then sounding incredulous. Yet Dr. Gerson had documentation for all of his statements. Some even pertained to panel member Joe Neumark.

LJN (Long John Nebel): Dr. Gerson, if you really have a solution for cancer — and I am not saying you do, I am not a medical man — but if you do, why isn't the AMA publishing your work?

MG (Max Gerson): I don't know why.

LJN: Well, if they think that you are — and I don't want to use too strong a word here — a fake, why don't they throw you out?

MG: Now, look here. I have been investigated five times by the Medical Society of the County of New York. But I bring them patients the investigators themselves sent home to die. Here, I say, this person you sent home to die, cured! Another, you sent home to die, also cured! They can do nothing. I have the proof.

LJN: Well, what were the results of the investigation?

MG: I don't know. They will not release them to me or to anyone else.

LJN: I don't understand. Why don't you publish your findings?

MG: I have tried many times to publish in this country, but nobody will publish any of my articles. I sent the same articles to scientific journals in Europe, and they are accepted and published with great thanks! When I was invited to lecture at the University of Zurich in 1952, I brought with me X-rays and records, biopsies performed in the great medical centers of the United States, Mayo, Sloan-Kettering, proving the patients had cancer. The most eminent and acknowledged cancer specialist there said, 'Dr. Gerson, your colleagues in the United States must be very proud that you have found a cure for cancer. And nobody can claim that it is not a cure.' But here I cannot get a single paper published.

LJN: Do they acknowledge your treatment in Europe, then, Dr. Gerson? I mean, is it a standard treatment there?

MG: Some doctors do. Most do not. But at least it is accepted as a valid treatment.

While Long John probed Dr. Gerson's opinions, the discussion covered many subjects connected with cancer and its treatment. For instance, the radio host mentioned a *Life* magazine article about the controversy over Hoxsey's supposed cancer cure. Dr. Gerson remarked that he had read his book and saw that "most of his cases are not scientifically presented enough," whereas he himself showed clinical reports, biopsies, X-rays done in the best hospitals. He was even able to cure some people who had been operated on five, seven or 12 times. And when Nebel asked whether some of these operations might have brought about the actual cures, Dr. Gerson countered with specific examples of patients who had been brought to him in a variety of dreadful conditions, after being given up by other physicians; yet, amazingly, they recovered after undergoing his therapy.

Dr. Gerson also introduced his long-standing opinion that the use of salt and processed foods was increasing the occurrence of cancer and other degenerative diseases, citing some of Dr. Schweitzer's observations about Africa, then the example of the long-lived Hunzas in the Himalayas, "who don't permit food grown in any other country to be brought in." No poisons, sprays or fertilizers either. Modern medicine, through vaccinations, antibiotics and other means, had diminished infectious diseases, infant mortality and the death rates after operations, increasing overall life expectancy, "but other diseases only increase, such as mental diseases," Dr. Gerson asserted. Many modern psychiatrists have decided that degenerative brain disorders are caused by "changes in our whole metabolism, so they are now tackling the problem from that point." Again, Dr. Gerson remarked how cancer was also increasing. Seventy years ago leukemia was unknown; now even many babies have it.

The Long John Nebel show was normally a call-in talk program, but for this discussion, Long John had decided that there would be no on-air calls. Nonetheless, calls started pouring in. Though callers were not put directly on the air, written questions were passed into the studio by the staff. Dr. Gerson did his best to answer people's questions in a thoughtful and modest way, making no claims that he could not support with either cases or documentation. One caller pointed out that there were cancer cases in Europe 200 years earlier, before there were canned foods, bleached flour, synthetic products. Dr. Gerson concurred, saying that cancer had indeed existed for thousands of years, with descriptions of it in Ancient Egypt, but cancer has never occurred anywhere to the present degree. He said that it might be initiated by exposure to some toxin, infection, injury or radiation, or be influenced by a genetic factor. Cancer could even be produced within 10 days or two weeks by painting some coal-tar substance on the skin of laboratory animals. "We know that 100 to 200 years ago there were many poisons that came on human beings, and there were liver diseases a long time ago. When they had a special type of poisoning, then cancer developed."

When the men began discussing the growing suspicion that tobacco, or smoking, could cause cancer, Dr. Gerson expressed the belief that tobacco smoking alone, especially of cigarettes, wouldn't produce cancer, but it was another form of poisoning. "Patients accumulate many other poisons too. And heavy smokers have more cancer than nonsmokers. . . . I am of the opinion that cancer is produced, developed, by an accumulation of many different types of poison. Tobacco is only one. Two hundred years ago there were mercury and other toxins, meat and fish poisoning, infectious diseases."

When Nebel asked whether today's food processing might be eliminating most potential poisoning, he provoked a strong response from Dr. Gerson:

> When we refine the food and make canned food, *live* substances are taken out of nutrition. Our body needs living substances. Minerals, enzymes must be alive in our body and kept alive. We should not have as our nutrition these processed foods. Our food must be natural foods, grown in a natural way, and alive. Not all food must be alive, but a great part. When I was a young physician in Germany, cancer was a rare disease. I saw it in people 50 and more years old. But here are cancer cases at 24, 28, 31, 41 years old. Older people with cancer . . . we even have more.

Nebel remarked that Dr. Gerson, at 75 years of age, looked extremely healthy, but added that there were people who lived to be 110 years old and smoked five cigars or drank a bottle of whiskey a day. Dr. Gerson commented that because he was not born with a hardy constitution and had a poor health history as a young man, he was initially prompted to make his therapeutic discoveries just to maintain his own well-being:

> Some people have such a strong body, such good liver and intestinal tract function, that even with smoking and drinking you can't ruin them too much. No, I didn't have them. When I was a young student and got jaundice, I was given up; my mother saved me with plenty of enemas detoxifying the body and a strict diet. And later, I had plenty of migraine headaches and skin diseases. The migraines were inherited from my mother's side, for four generations. I have through the disease inherited a weak liver; I was forced to work with good nutrition. I learned most of all on own body.

When Nebel probed Dr. Gerson's relationship with the AMA, Dr. Gerson recounted the incident when the *Journal of the American Medical Association* had printed a section of the January 8, 1947 issue discussing the Gerson therapy among cancer "frauds and fables" — a discussion that was deleted in the final printed issue when Dr. Gerson that was Gerson sent a telegram to the AMA through a lawyer, threatening a lawsuit, and those pages were omitted from the final printed issue:

LJN: If they thought you were a fraud, why are you allowed to practice medicine?.

MG: They could not prove it, even though they didn't accept my treatment.

LJN: If they don't take away your license to practice medicine, then in my humble opinion you're not a fraud.

Dr. Gerson also recounted his presentation of patients to the Senate subcommittee in 1946 that was investigating possibilities in cancer research and treatment for the purpose of securing future government funding:

MG: I showed them cases that proved that my treatment did it. Raymond Swing is a well-known commentator. He came there. He wanted to see what I could do. Many physicians told him, "That Gerson will break our head and bones, would finish our research work. We are lost. We would have to go into an entirely different career." He gave on the radio a wonderful speech about my treatment. What was the consequence? The radio station told him they would not let him talk again. They warned that all would be against him, not be permitted to speak at all on radio. I tell you only what I know. A well-known cancer man under request of AMA wrote to Raymond Swing; he gave me the letter. And he did not give in.

LJN: Does anyone have a job for a promising young radio host named Long John Nebel? Because after tonight, I may be out looking for a job.

But Nebel sounded less glib and more agitated as Dr. Gerson laid the blame for degenerative diseases on the industries that processed and refined foods or produced tobacco, alcohol, drugs, artificial fertilizers and other chemicals. Dr. Gerson backed up his trenchant statements with documentation from scientific articles. Nebel realized that Gerson was pointing an accusing finger at the industrial sponsors who paid the bills at WOR "Your own statements," Nebel remarked, "not too many programs would permit you to make them. I'm not preventing you from making them, not putting my finger up to your mouth to shush you and ask you to be quiet. Do you really feel that drug manufacturers are so badly hit in the pocket that they can't stand it?"

As this topic of discussion came to a close, Nebel asked how Dr. Gerson planned to promulgate his message. Dr. Gerson pointed to his book A *Cancer Therapy*, then almost completed:

LJN: What are you doing now? You are sold on this; believe in this. What are you going to try to do to try to get it accepted by the American medical profession? You don't look like the kind of man who's going to give up on this.

MG: No. How could I, when I have seen such wonderful results? Impossible. First, I write the cancer book, and in it I will bring in as many cases as possible sent home to die. Every physician here in the country can read. I will have it translated into many languages. All over it can be read. The treatment will be described in the book in the best way I can, even in all details, so that nobody can say that I keep something away. Of course I work with large experience; and every physician would have to acquire such experience and to see how we can purify the whole body. We give the patient plenty of enemas: we use coffee enemas. We use also in some cases, especially in cases when it is difficult to detoxify the whole body and especially the liver —

LJN (interrupts to caution MG): Please do not state over the air what your treatment is. Many people who are listening may try the treatment. I think you will agree with me that they should have some competent physician with them.

MG: Oh yes, they need the help of a physician.

LJN: Don't describe it in too much detail.

MG: The treatment will be so described that nobody can say I keep something away, from the medical profession and even from the people. This is my deepest desire and all of my endeavor will go in that way, so that all physicians all over the world will know it and (this is the) purpose on which the foundation is founded. To give that treatment to all physicians who want it and to all people who can urge their physicians to apply it.

LJN: Associated with a hospital?

MG: I have my own, because here in the hospital they didn't do it. It is too difficult to put it in a large hospital. Hospitals would have to be reformed to bring in such a treatment where the patients get fresh vegetable juices (and this will tell something more about the treatment) from morning to night. It is not an easy job, that treatment. Especially to give fresh calves' liver juice. Calves' liver has to be bought from a slaughterhouse; it must be fresh. No other livers will do it; we tried but had no results. And it has to be prepared in a special way.

The midnight hour that usually marked the end of the Long John Nebel show came and went, with no letup in the call volume. Long John decided just to stay on the air. When it became two o'clock in the morning, he finally decided to end the program. Nebel concluded the long session with a disclaimer statement, repeating that the opinions expressed on the program did not necessarily reflect those of "Yours Truly" or of the radio station. And — "Do not go out on your own to accept or reject theories brought out by Dr. Gerson. Talk to your own physician. Get more information about the subject from Dr. Gerson, c/o Long John, WOR. Requests will be turned over to Dr. Gerson and the foundation." Earlier in the show, Nebel had offered similar words of caution, mixed with respect for Dr. Gerson:

> Max Gerson has nothing to sell: no special powders, a magic flower, nothing grown in a basement to sell at a price. This doctor who is 75 years of age wants to give information to others in his profession, but up to the present time they are reluctant to accept. There's more to it than that they don't believe in it. I'm not a medical expert myself. People listening can make their own decision. But I will say this: You should remember the name—Dr. Max Gerson. I hope that no member of your family is suffering from cancer. If . . . talk to your own physician. Send a letter to Dr. Max Gerson, c/o Long John, WOR, New York 18.

When he ushered Dr. Gerson out of the studio, Nebel asked if he would return the next night to answer some of the questions that he had been able to handle during this interview. Dr. Gerson happily accepted. But the next afternoon, as he was gathering materials for the evening's radio program, he received a telephone call from WOR canceling this invitation. Apparently, the station's largest sponsors — food processors, tobacco companies, beer producers, manufacturers of over-the-counter remedies and chemical-manufacturing companies — had called WOR to censure Dr. Gerson. Censorship action by big advertising interests on the news media has been repeated, of course, many times over the years in innumerable situations. Commercially sponsored media, then as now, are almost wholly dependent on the revenues of their biggest advertisers, who use this power to quash stories that they perceive as inimical to their promotional and profit-earning interests.

Another Trial Summons

In the autumn of 1957, almost a year after he appeared on the Long John Nebel talk-radio program, Dr. Max Gerson received a summons by the Medical Society of the County of New York. Inevitably, it reminded him of the severely worded summons sent to him long ago by the Westphalian Medical Association when he was practicing in Bielefeld:

> You are hereby directed to appear before the Trial Committee of the Comitia Minora of The Medical Society of the County of New York on the 4th day of November, 1957, at four o'clock in the afternoon, at the office of The Medical Society of the County of New York, Room 52, in the Academy of Medicine Building, No. 2 East 103rd Street, Borough of Manhattan, City, County and State of New York, and at the time and place appointed above, to make answer to the annexed charges, either in writing or verbally. Your failure to obey this summons without a satisfactory excuse shall constitute case for discipline.

Attached was a document specifying the Medical Society's particular charges against Dr. Gerson:

> The undersigned, FRANK H. PETERS, M.D., Secretary of the Censors of The Medical Society of the County of New York, having been directed so to do by said Censors acting upon information received and obtained by them from sources other than written charges, which in the opinion of a majority of said Censors, justifies the preferment of these charges, hereby prefers written charges against Max Gerson, M.D., pursuant to Article 4 of Chapter VIII of the bylaws of The Medical Society of the County of New York and alledges [sic], upon information and belief, as follows:
>
> FIRST: Max Gerson, M. D., is, and at all times hereinafter mentioned was, a duly licensed physician and a member of The Medical Society of the County of New York.
>
> SECOND: On the morning of Tuesday, January 15, 1957, or the morning of Wednesday, January 16, 1957, at or about one thirty o'clock of said morning, a radio program was broadcast over radio station WOR, New York, sometimes known as the "Long John" program. Such program is a continuing program in which the individual known as "Long John" acts as master of ceremonies and from time to time interviews guests on this program.
>
> THIRD: Dr. Max Gerson appeared as a guest on said Long John program broadcast over station WOR as aforesaid Tuesday, January 15, 1957 or Wednesday, January 16, 1957.
>
> FOURTH: In the course of such broadcast statements were made that Dr.

Gerson was graduated from medical school in Freiburg, Germany, that he was licensed to practice medicine in the State of New York and that he was a member of The Medical Society of the County of New York.

FIFTH: Dr. Gerson explained on said broadcast his theory of the causes of cancer and a development of a cure by Dr. Gerson for cancer.

SIXTH: Dr. Gerson, in the course of said broadcast, enumerated cases which have been given up as hopeless victims of cancer by the rest of the profession which he had cured by his treatment.

SEVENTH: Dr. Gerson, in the course of said broadcast, stated that he had cured Dr. Albert Schweitzer's wife and daughter.

EIGHTH: Said broadcast over station WOR was made primarily to the laity. It was not made under any accredited medical auspices or with the advice or consent of this Society or of the The Medical Society of the State of New York.

NINTH: Said broadcast was arranged with radio station WOR and/or the individual known as John Long [sic] by the Foundation for Cancer Treatment which Foundation is built around Dr. Gerson's treatment for cancer. The avowed purpose of the Foundation for Cancer Treatment is [sic] arranging said broadcast was to obtain contributions to the Foundation which in turn would defray in whole or in part the cost of treatment of cancer patients by Dr. Gerson.

TENTH: As a further result of said broadcast, Dr. Gerson received several inquiries from prospective patients.

WHEREFORE, it is respectfully submitted that Max Gerson, M.D. has violated and set at naught the provisions of Sections 4 and 5 of the Principles of Professional Conduct of The Medical Society of the State of New York and of Section 5 of Appendix One of the By-laws of The Medical Society of the County of New York, each binding upon the members of The Medical Society of the County of New York and upon Max Gerson, M.D., as such member, and therefore said Max Gerson, M.D., should suffer discipline, as provided by the Constitution and By-laws of The Medical Society of the County of New York.

At the direction of the Censors,
Frank H. Peters
Secretary of the Censors

Although these statements themselves were certainly true, the actions they referred to violated nothing. Dr. Gerson had not arranged for the radio program, nor had he solicited business on the program that might be construed as advertising — at that time against the profession's rules of proper conduct. Certainly the resulting inquiries to the radio station regarding how to get in touch with Dr. Gerson were neither solicited nor invited by him. He was simply attempting to share his knowledge with the world, since the medical profession during his entire American medical career had blocked all other avenues.

Dr Gerson's act speaking up in public had now given cause enough for the Medical Society of the County of New York to "discipline" him by suspending his membership. Quite sensibly yet irately, Dr. Gerson returned the letter to the Society along with a notice of his resignation of membership. He received the following response, sent on February 27, 1958:

> Under date of February 17, 1958, I sent to you by registered mail, return receipt requested, formal notification of the action taken by the Comitia Minora on February 10, 1958, suspending you from the rights and privileges of membership in the Society for a period of two years. You saw fit to refuse to accept my letter, which was then returned to me with notice of your rejection from the Post Office Department. A copy of my letter is enclosed.
>
> Receipt is acknowledged of letter signed by you on February 19, 1958, in which you purport to resign from membership in this Society.
>
> Please be advised that your resignation cannot be accepted by this Society nor can it become effective without acceptance under the provisions of Articles 10 and 11 of Chapter [sic] of the By-Laws. These two Articles provide in substance that a member in good standing but not a member not in good standing may resign from the Society; that any member who is under charges shall not be considered a member in good standing of this Society; and that when written charges shall have been preferred against a member, he is deemed to remain under charges until final decision on such charges and on any appeals therefrom shall have been made.
>
> As you will note from the enclosed copy of letter sent to you on February 17, 1958, the time granted to you to appeal from the decision of the Comita [sic] Minora will expire on March 3rd next. Upon your failure to take such an appeal, you will then have the status of a member of this Society suspended from the rights and privileges of his membership. In such event, you would not be considered a member in good standing.

Dr. Gerson was not even allowed to *resign* his membership in this society. The logic defies reason.

The Case of Gail Allen Brogue

Despite these harassments from the Medical Society of the County of New York, Dr. Gerson continued to give special care to his patients. In 1999 I spoke at length with Gail Allen Bogue about her experiences as a young patient of Dr. Max Gerson in 1957. She welcomed the opportunity to recall that difficult period:

What better cause is there to talk about in the entire world? The Gerson therapy is an answer to what everybody fears will happen to their body — not just cancer, but other degenerative diseases. It's so obvious and so simple, but we've really been indoctrinated in the American medical way of thinking. Societies with no doctors available to them rely on things like grandparents' wisdom, common sense and herbs. But here in this country the treatments we're given "follow the money."

I'm frustrated almost every time I try to explain to people that they should try the Gerson treatment on themselves or someone they know who's really sick with something. I've found that the ones who are the most "schooled" are actually the most close-minded. But it makes sense to simple people who live close to nature, and to farmers or anyone who works with animals. They understand because on a day-to-day basis they see the connection between food or diet and health.

I was around seven years old when I first met Dr. Gerson. That must have been in late 1957. But he wasn't the first doctor I had seen. This is how it came about: I had been fooling around with my sister and somehow my left leg got hit. The pain in my ankle was excruciating. My mother took me to the hospital, and after they did some tests the doctors told her I had bone cancer — giant-cell sarcoma of the left tibia. The head of surgery said they'd just take it out. So I went into surgery the next day. When I woke up, the whole top of my leg and the hip were all packed in. They had removed an enormous amount of my left hip. It hurt a lot and I was really upset. "Couldn't you have just told me what you were going to do to me?" I asked the surgeon. "You didn't need to know," he said. He hadn't bothered to tell Mother, either.

After a few days I went home. Six weeks went by, and I came back for the follow-up X-rays. We learned that some of cancer had started to return. The only thing the doctor told Mother to do was to see that I stayed very still. Which wasn't too hard to do because it hurt just to lie there, let alone move around any. We waited another six weeks before the next visit. The doctor now looked out at Mom and said to her: "She needs another operation right away." She asked, "What are you going to do?" "We're going to amputate the leg at the hip." "But if she didn't do well after the first operation, how's she supposed to do after the second one?" "Well, probably not well at all. But it will be an easier death than if you just let it go." And I was right there when he said it!

Mother knew something about empowerment —that believing in something helps you get better and that people should have choices about what happens with their own bodies. So she turned to me and asked, "What do *you* think we should do?" And I said, "If I'm going to die, I want to die in one piece." Then she said firmly to the doctor, "We'll just go home and pray about this. She's not going to die." And the doctor told her, "If you don't go ahead with this, you are a murderer." This, after he had already said I was going to die!

I'll tell you how we first found out about Dr. Gerson. We lived in a town in New Jersey, on an out-of-the-way street. One day a salesman came by, selling a product called Green Life, made from wheatgrass sprouts grown on organic soil; they were ground up into a powder that you mixed with water. When he found out from Mother about my condition, he handed her a jar and said, "Give it to her. It will help." Then he told mother about a Dr. Max Gerson in New York whom he'd heard about, who was curing people with cancer. That very day Mom called and made an appointment.

We learned that Dr. Gerson was a very exacting person, the first time we went in. If he told you 9 o'clock, you'd better be there at 9 o'clock. My mom hadn't gotten me into his office until 10:30 or so. When we strolled in, Dr. Gerson literally took my mother by the ear, shook his finger at her and said, "When I tell you something, you must do it absolutely." Dr. Gerson had wanted a picture of the tumor before it shrank, and the man who was to take the X-rays had come there at 9.

He told Mother he was pretty sure he could help me. But when Mother wanted him to explain his methods to her, he said, "I don't have time to explain everything to everybody. You must do as I say — no questions asked, ever again." His confident, authoritarian manner impressed Mother to the core. Also, of course, his saying he probably could save my life. She trusted him. So she never questioned again whatever he said or did. I'm sure she was one of the most diligent caregivers that Dr. Gerson ever met in his work with patients.

Dr. Gerson wanted me to stay at the sanatorium in Nanuet for a few weeks. My parents were very poor. My dad said, No way. But my mom said, No way we're not going to do this. She really believed that Dr. Gerson was going to save my life. So they mortgaged their house, and Mom wrote to all their relatives and to all the friends she'd ever had, saying, "We're in this for the long haul. Whatever you can send now, whatever you can send on a monthly basis, please do it. Our child's life is at stake."

The first day I was at Nanuet Dr. Gerson came around carrying a glass with a thick, brownish looking liquid in it. He looked at me and said, "You will drink this. Do it quickly, and *now*. Put the lemon in your mouth first and it won't taste so bad. So that is how you will do it. Every day." Then he turned and walked away. It was the raw liver juice that was so important in his therapy.

Sometimes I've heard people say that Dr. Gerson could almost heal with his eyes. There may be something to this. I've taken courses in iridology, and it's interesting for me to remember those eyes of his. They were deep blue and unclouded, even though he was in his late 70s by then. You could see the clear part on top of the irises' color. As a child, I trusted those eyes of his. His gaze was unwavering — usually calm and kindly, yet somehow penetrating.

Another thing I remember about Nanuet was when they brought a woman in on a stretcher. They were giving her juices and enemas every hour, and Dr. Gerson was always going in to check on her. "What is going on?" I asked someone. "They're trying to keep her from dying; she's so close to it." And she actually did survive and get better.

After two weeks I left Nanuet and went home. I wasn't in pain anymore, and soon I could even run around. I had no more trouble taking the liver juice, but the castor oil floating on top of black coffee gave me trouble. And I also fussed about the needles with the injections. Everything else, I just did it. Because I knew that was how I would be able to live.

It's very hard to do the Gerson therapy without good help from other people. I am still amazed that my mom could have done it. Dr. Gerson had warned her that she would be physically unable to do it. After all, she had three other children besides me. "It takes one person to do the therapy itself, and it takes another person to do the shopping, all the kitchen work and other assistance," he said. And yet my mother managed to do it all, I don't know how. I remember that whenever she stood still, like when she was washing the dishes, she'd fall asleep. I once asked her, "How can you do all this?" She told me, "Well, you go to bed at night and you pray, and the next morning you just start out again and just keep praying. Then night time comes and you're closer to where you want to be. You just don't stop."

Initially I visited Dr. Gerson for check-ups every month, then every six weeks, then about every two months. After I had been going to see Dr. Gerson for about a year, I was doing fabulously well. There was no sign at all of the cancer; it had just disappeared. We were eager to share this outcome with that first doctor, thinking he would be delighted. We went in and showed him the latest X-rays and he examined my leg briefly. Then he said to us: "This result is just a fluke, a one-in-a-million thing. If she really is better, it is only because of the X-ray therapy we gave her." But the only radiation I had actually had all this time was three sets of X-rays: ones with him at pre-op, then with Dr. Gerson at six months, and finally at 12 months!

I guess that's what most doctors say when people who have been helped by the Gerson therapy come back later, maybe after two years, and are quite well. "Sure," they said, "we gave you all that chemo first, before all that weird diet stuff." Or they gave radiation or surgery. And you say, "No, no — it's because of what I did . . . something else!" And then they say, "Get out of my office. I don't want to hear any more." Because what you've just done is demonstrate how wrong everything is that they've learned at such expense and effort, and that now sustains them in their medical practice. In effect, you're showing them that it's *they* who are the real murderers.

Still, if doctors have goodwill, they'll listen to you and open their minds a bit. I'm now 50 years old, so it's well over 40 years since I got treated by Dr. Gerson. And I'm noticing that more doctors than ever before seem to be using alternative ways of treating cancer and other diseases. Or at least they're willing to hear and think about them. People can read much more about these therapies, too, in so many places. Which wasn't at all possible back then when I was so sick.

But here's the near-tragic part of my story about being a patient of Dr. Gerson's when I was a child. After staying in the program for about a year and a half, I was doing so well that he said I'd be finished by the end of two years. But then Dr. Gerson passed away before the two years were over, and there was no doctor who would pick up his practice and patients. We lost our supply of the nutritional supplements and supplies we needed: the potassium, niacin, iodine, raw liver extract, needles and so on. My mother continued doing what we had been doing with the juices and the rest of the diet, but without all those other things. So there was a gradual deterioration. I began getting sick again. My leg began to swell and hurt, and we were very worried about a recurrence of the bone cancer.

The new problem may have come partly from a psychological blow. Because Dr. Gerson had provided the answer to curing me. And we know much more now about how important your belief system is in supplying that wonderful quality called hope. So after he died, for a while we lost a lot of our hope.

Mother didn't want to take me to a regular physician again and go through the standard sort of treatment that hadn't helped me earlier. But finally we found another doctor, Dr. Vallan, who was able and willing to help us by supplying those things for the therapy. We also had Dr. Gerson's book as a guide, of course. And so I got better again. I stayed on the Gerson program for a total of seven years. The cancer never came back. And when I grew up, I got married and had two children. I also kept both my legs. The very fact that I was alive at all was because of Dr. Gerson.

~22~

Censured for Curing Cancer
(1957–1958)

The National Enquirer's Exposé

I n February 1958 Max Gerson was anticipating the publication, at long last, of his book, A Cancer Therapy . This same month, S.J. Haught, a reporter with the National Enquirer, read a lengthy letter that had come into the newspaper's office from a woman who claimed to have been cured of cancer by a Dr. Max Gerson. The letter, "To Whom It May Concern," had a dual purpose: its author hoped that the Enquirer would publish the story of Dr. Gerson and his unorthodox cancer treatment; and, on a more practical note, she desperately sought financial assistance, since she and her husband lacked funds to continue the Gerson dietary therapy for the required additional year. She said she had already applied for support from the various charitable and government agencies that helped cancer patients unable to pay the costs of their therapy, but her plea for assistance was rejected by the organizations because they did not approve of Dr. Gerson's approach.

Though Haught was accustomed to all manner of odd and even crazy letters, this woman's letter struck him with its sincerity and pathos. Its author, he decided, had been bilked of all she had by a cancer quack, who then turned her out on the streets to die. Haught found that the letter kept disturbing him. The woman was still alive — long after the time she was supposed to die. He finally went to his editor for permission to explore the case further in preparation for the article he intended to write, "The Unveiling of a Quack."

An experienced and thorough reporter, Haught first wrote to the American Medical Association requesting their opinion of Dr. Gerson's cancer treatment. He was certain that they would be only too happy to help him unmask this fraud in their role as protector of the American public from medical miscreants. The letter he received in return was more puzzling to him than the letter that had sparked his investigation. After some brief biographical information on Dr. Gerson, the AMA's letter continued:

We have been informed that he has been suspended from membership by his local medical society for a period of two years, beginning March 4, 1958. The specific charge was his use of a radio interview to discuss his work in the treatment of cancer.

We have had record of Dr. Gerson and his diet treatment for various diseases for a considerable period of time. We commented on Dr. Gerson, and his reluctance to reveal the details of his treatment, in an editorial in The Journal for Nov. 16, 1946. We are sorry we do not have tear sheets or reprints available. Therein it was pointed out that although Dr. Gerson had been requested to do so, he had failed or refused to acquaint the medical profession with the details of his treatment.

The letter was signed by Oliver Field, Director of the AMA's Bureau of Investigation.

The reporter's eye quickly caught the apparent discrepancy. If a physician had been "unwilling" to reveal the details of his treatment to the medical profession, why would he go on a talk show for several hours to talk about this same treatment? Wouldn't that public exposure put him in jeopardy, especially if he had something to hide?

When going through Gerson's files, Haught read a response to an inquiry that the AMA had written on July 28, 1949, which seemed to be the bedrock for the organization's claim to inquirers, such as Haught, that Gerson withheld information.

We have no knowledge of any report published in medical literature describing the medication or the course of treatment sponsored by Gerson, nor do we know of any other investigators who use his methods. Gerson has been invited by this Association to give information on these items, but so far he has never done so.

For a man bent on keeping his curative therapy a "secret," Dr. Gerson had published a surprising number of articles and books. Haught had seen the books and articles himself. He also saw other evidence of Dr. Gerson's willingness, even eagerness, to share his knowledge and experience with other physicians, and to demonstrate his work so that it might be fairly judged by them.

For instance, four years earlier, on May 3, 1954, Dr. Gerson had written to Dr. Samuel Klein, Special Committee chairman of the Medical Society of the County of New York. The letter showed Gerson's polite response to yet another investigation. It also expressed his desire to present some of his patients to the investigating committee and then publish a report about these cases in the society's journal.

In answer to your letter of April 15, I am enclosing a photostatic copy of the letter of May 28, 1953, which will speak for itself.

As to the complaints mentioned, of which I would like to have a copy, I wish to say that the records in my office can be looked into by the Committee.

As I have always stated to the medical profession and any investigating body, I am eager to interest them in the results of my cancer treatment; therefore, I highly appreciate your desire to see the real proof, the records and the X-rays of these results.

The questions posed in your aforementioned letter are answered in one of my most recent publications, a reprint of which is enclosed. Also enclosed is my treatment book. The treatment I am using is described therein, and a more detailed description will be found in a subsequent article now in the process of printing.

I would like to have some assurance that after my presentation before your special subcommittee I will be given an opportunity to make a demonstration of these cases before the entire medical society and that these cases will be published in the New York State Medical Journal. I am obviously not seeking to suppress it to the attention of the medical profession.

I feel that I am justified by the facts in making these reasonable suggestions, as the success of my cases has never been disproven by renowned cancer experts, here and elsewhere. Even after the most searching examinations I have not been successful in having them published in the American medical journals so that they could be brought to the attention and before the scientific critic of the entire profession.

Following is a brief review of my demonstrations:

In July, 1946, by invitation, I demonstrated some cases in Washington, D.C., before the United States Senate subcommittee holding hearings on the Pepper-Neely bill.

In February, 1947, at the request of the Medical Society of the County of New York, I presented fourteen cases before Doctors Hanford and Twembly, and about thirty other invited physicians.

Again on invitation I published some articles and demonstrated twenty cases out of forty cases prepared at the Cancer Congress in Berchtesgaden, Germany, October, 1952. Thereafter I was invited to demonstrate a number of cases in the University Clinic in Zurich, Switzerland.

In 1953, I complied with a request of the censors to show films and records to Dr. Edward Tolstoi, one of the censors of the County Medical Society. The only tangible result of this cooperation was the letter from Dr. W. Laurence Whittemore, Chairman of the Board of Censors, expressing Dr. Tolstoi's appreciation of (my) courtesy and frankness in discussing with him (my) methods of treatment. See enclosed photostat. If desired I will gladly submit a review of the published articles of my cancer work.

In view of the foregoing I feel it not unreasonable to expect that you and your associates on the special subcommittee after examining and evaluating my cases, should be inclined in the interest of truth and medical progress to recommend that I be granted the opportunity of a demonstration before the whole society and publication in the official journals.

In closing, I wish to express my profound gratitude for your reassurance of the complete objectivity of the society and its subcommittee.

Certainly when confronting adversarial attitudes toward his work, Dr. Gerson's manner was courteous, calm and confident. He had also learned that finally in the United States the correct politics among peers could play an enormously expedient role in simply being able to practice medicine —especially when one was a maverick.

S.J. Haught next asked the American Cancer Society about Dr. Gerson. A preprinted sheet provided some historical and biographical notes, ending with the statement: "The American Cancer Society can find no acceptable evidence that the treatment proposed by Dr. Max Gerson produces any objective benefit in the treatment of cancer." The ACS letter had referred to an article in the January 8, 1949 issue of *Journal of the American Medical Association*. Haught looked up the infamous JAMA article, "Frauds and Fables." Haught could see why, because of its strange and unorthodox methods, the Gerson therapy would be looked on with disfavor by the medical establishment. But why then, he asked, wouldn't the medical authorities take some remedial action if the treatment didn't work and was downright charlatanism?

The reporter then wrote to the Medical Society of the County of New York, asking if they approved or disapproved of Gerson's cancer treatment. The reply was less than satisfactory:

It is not within the province of the Medical Society of the County of New York to pass on the efficacy or adequacy of any doctor's treatment of his own patients.

Doctor Gerson is a member of this Society but is presently under suspension from the rights and privileges of membership as a result of personal publicity.

Haught found this answer strange. On the one hand, the Society would not utterly condemn Gerson, who was a member. On the other, they made sure that Haught knew he was under a cloud.

Haught next phoned the woman who had written the letter asking for help during her recovery from cancer. She related the story of her ordeal. She told him about how she was sent home to die, after the doctors and hospital had done what they could. They gave her the prognosis of death within two to six months, at most. No specialist or surgeon was willing to touch her further. "With this kind of tumor," they said, "you go quickly." She had then heard about Dr. Max Gerson. After five days on his dietary therapy, her large tumor had shrunk to the size of a golf ball, and within two months it was gone. Now, over six months later, she was virtually recovered, back to doing her housework and taking care of her daughter on weekends. But the food still required in maintaining Gerson's strict diet was costing her almost as much as her husband could earn — $50 a week.

She had applied to the Red Cross, the American Cancer Society, the Welfare Department and every charitable organization she could think of —all in vain. As soon as they heard that she was seeing Dr. Gerson, the door was firmly closed in her face. Even her own minister had turned her down. "I guess society wants me to die of cancer," she told Haught. "They would rather I died than to be cured the 'wrong' way!"

Questions were building in Haught's mind as he contacted Dr. Gerson's office to set up an interview. His first two attempts to see the doctor were unsuccessful, as Max's secretary told him that the doctor was "busy with patients." Sure, Haught reasoned, this weasel would be terrified of the power of the press. Or else he would try to smooth-talk him into believing some ridiculous story. He described his thoughts prior to his first meeting with Gerson in his book *Censured for Curing Cancer: The American Experience of Dr. Max Gerson:*

> A quack, I felt, would do one of two things. He would refuse to see me, or he would do just the opposite —roll out the royal rug of welcome and charm me with stories of the wonderful things he had been doing with cancer, hoping that I would return to my office and write a glowing account of his accomplishments.
>
> Mentally, I had Dr. Gerson pictured as a dark, ferret-faced man —the kind of cancer quack you see on television —who had a "good thing" going for him and was terrified that the press wanted a word with him about one of his patients. Naturally, he wouldn't want me prying into his affairs.

Then a surprise: Dr. Gerson's secretary called Haught back with an appointment time. Haught now faced the man "whom the power of the press would squash like a bug." He could see at once that his mental image of him had been wrong:

> He was an old man! But he was tall and spare, with blue eyes and white hair, and spoke with a German accent. He was neither eager nor reluctant to answer my questions. As a matter of fact, I asked very few questions. It was he who did most of the talking. Very early in our discussion I got the impression that Dr. Gerson had been all through this before. Not once, but many times. But kindly and patiently he endured my comments, many of which, I'm afraid, were not well founded. Dr. Gerson was willing to go along with me —up to a point. Then he exploded. "Can't you understand that this type of cancer has

never been cured?" he yelled. "That never in the history of medicine has such a patient been cured! That she is well now and working. Here, here are the X-rays. I will explain them to you!"

Later the 77-year old doctor smiled. "They do not like for me to cure cancer," he said. "They say it is not possible. I say it is possible, and I do it!"

Haught now asked why Gerson had not revealed the details of his treatment to the American Medical Association. In response, Gerson showed him many of the rejection letters he had received from medical journals for papers he had submitted to them. If the AMA and other medical groups had wanted to learn more, they would have published his papers. Furthermore, they could now read his recently published book, A *Cancer Therapy*, a copy of which Gerson showed Haught.

The reporter began wondering to himself:

Why the need for a new method unless —unless he believed in it? And Dr. Max Gerson looked to me like a man who believed what he was saying. He was shy, a little awkward because the English words did not come easily to him, but a man of obvious dedication and integrity. I doubt if a quack would have shouted at me like that! He would have been too anxious to make a good impression on a reporter.

The story that I had already written in my mind about Dr. Gerson was coming apart.

"Five times," Dr. Gerson told him, "they sent a committee here to investigate my methods, the Medical Society of the County of New York. I let them see patients, X-rays, records, everything."

"And what were the results of those investigations?"

"I do not know," Max replied. "They have never revealed them."

Haught was very disturbed by this statement. If these competent authorities really did thorough investigations of this physician when looking for evidence that he was engaged in unethical or illegal practices, and then found them, surely they would have informed Dr. Gerson himself about their findings, as well as the AMA. If they had any reason to believe that he was a quack, why would they permit him to continue committing his fraudulent treatments? Was it not their duty to protect the public by rescinding his license to practice and removing him from the ranks of the medical profession?

Or could it be possible that these examiners had actually witnessed, while going over Dr. Gerson's records and gathering visual and anecdotal evidence of recovery from patients themselves, how effective the Gerson therapy actually was? Yet, having failed to prove that Gerson was a quack —quite the contrary! —they certainly didn't want to trumpet the opposite evidence of true healing by giving it an airing in a written statement that Dr. Gerson might use to his advantage. Hence, though there had been five investigations of Max Gerson over the years, no report had ever been given to Dr. Gerson himself.

But, Haught reasoned, if they had actually found that Gerson's therapy had any value at all against this terrible and thus far incurable disease, cancer, would it not be equally incumbent upon them to publish the information far and wide? The secrecy that surrounded this matter grated on the newspaperman's nerves, especially when the doctor told him that he had recently been suspended from the Medical Society, ostensibly for having appeared on the Long John Nebel radio show on WOR. He found it curious, he said, that many other physicians had also been featured on Long John's program, but none had been suspended or disciplined in any way.

Haught now knew he had to see the results of the five investigations of Gerson that performed by physician-members of the Medical Society of the County of New York. The reports, he was sure, would answer many of the as yet unanswered questions, including the biggest one: Why weren't their investigators' findings revealed?

As he chased down various byways on the Gerson story, S.J. Haught, using the *National Enquirer* letterhead, wrote to the Medical Society of the County of New York:

> We have not yet published a story concerning Dr. Max Gerson because every organization we have contacted says it does not pass on the efficacy of a doctor's treatment. They further explain that there are channels through which a doctor can go to present any new treatment, and that Dr. Gerson has not done this.
>
> From the Foundation for Cancer Treatment I learn that Dr. Gerson has repeatedly tried to go through these proper channels, and each time has been rebuffed. His articles have been rejected, and apparently he has no other way to turn. I understand that a committee of doctors from your society has investigated Dr. Gerson on a number of occasions —seen X-rays, examined patients, etc. —and that none of these findings has ever been made public.
>
> We have no feelings one way or the other concerning Dr. Gerson's treatment except that of public responsibility. Is there any way we can be advised of the nature of your findings?

The reply from the Medical Society of the County of New York was reasonable. They informed Haught that due to the privileged nature of the information and to protect the physician, he would have to get written permission from Dr. Gerson to have the results of the investigations released to him. He soon secured the doctor's okay in writing. Haught was very excited. Soon he would get those reports, and then could wrap up the story. He was mistaken. The reply from the Society was brief:

> This office has received a letter from Doctor Max Gerson, M.D., authorizing us to release to you the results of our investigations.
>
> The results are that Doctor Max Gerson was suspended from the rights and privileges of membership, as a result of personal publicity.

Haught had initially been told that the suspension was the result of personal publicity because of Gerson's appearance on the Long John Nebel radio show, but now the Society was telling him that the investigations spanning a period of over 12 years were the reason for the suspension. He tried a different tack:

> I assume that you have changed your mind and do not intend to release the information to me as you promised. I did not need an authorization from Dr. Gerson to learn from you that he has been suspended; you told me that the first time I wrote to you about him. Then, however, you told me he had been suspended because of unfavorable publicity. Now you tell me it was a result of your findings. If you will not send me the results of your investigation, can you not send them to Dr. Gerson himself?

Their answer to Haught's note was less than cordial:

> We received from Doctor Gerson a letter giving you the authorization to receive from us the results of the several investigations referred to in your letter. You will note that we are authorized through this letter by Doctor Gerson to give you the results of the several investigations. This we have done.

As Haught acknowledged later:

> Their reply was to embark me on the strangest, most frustrating story of my life ... the story of a man who by absolute record had cured people of cancer, including children, and his incredibly courageous and lonely fight against the forces of organized medicine.

S.J. Haught was seriously doubting his initial assessment of Dr. Gerson as an unscrupulous quack, but even more disturbing to him now was the way this doctor was being treated by the medical profession. Evidently the stonewalling was due to the reluctance of the established authorities to provide information. But was this because they were protecting a member from damage by the press ... or because ....? The mystery remained.

While reading the JAMA editorial on "Gerson's Cancer Treatment" from November 1946, Haught came across a reference to Dr. Gerson's testimony before the Senate hearings earlier that same year. He was impressed that Dr. Gerson had been so honored — evidently the first time in history that any physician had been invited to present patients at a formal Senate hearing. He was puzzled, however, at the total lack of any reference in the contemporary press to this testimony. The sub-committee's report, 227 pages long, had never received public airing, either. Haught resolved to obtain a copy of the published report, informing Dr. Gerson that he would be contacting the appropriate agencies in Washington.

"They will not send it to you," Gerson stated with firm conviction.

"Of course they will," Haught protested. "I'm a newspaper reporter."

But his estimation of the power of the press was brought into sharp perspective when he attempted to retrieve the report. Medical-industry lobbyists had apparently managed to suppress even an official report of the United States Senate. Both the Superintendent of Documents and a senator's office informed him that no more copies remained. Eventually, with Mrs. Gerson's help, Haught was able to locate a copy. When he realized the importance of Gerson's testimony during the hearings, he was shocked at the length of time — a dozen years — that had elapsed with absolutely no action taken by the cancer-research establishment, particularly the National Cancer Institute, to explore the effectiveness of the Gerson therapy.

During the process of researching this story, S.J. Haught became a great admirer of Dr. Gerson. The two men were quite friendly. Haught was convinced that Dr. Gerson was a genuine healer and that he was not hiding his therapy from the medical profession's scrutiny. He had examined copies of the dozens of articles by Gerson, both published and unpublished, written over the course of 30 years, plus three books and a chapter in a fourth. He had seen a list of lectures that Dr. Gerson had given at major universities in Europe. There were hundreds of case records. Scores of letters expressing the deep gratitude of patients and their families — evidence of how many lives this physician had saved.

When Haught first proposed an article or series of articles about a fraudulent cancer cure based on a weird diet, his editor at the *National Enquirer* approved that story, but as he investigated Dr. Gerson's work, the story became a crusading piece. Haught championed Dr. Gerson and questioned the medical establishment. Haught was not surprised when his editor withdrew the article from that weekly tabloid which, then as now, is infamous for sensationalist, yellow journalism. Undeterred, S.J. Haught later published the story as a book, though not without difficulty.

~23~
A Healer's Passage
(1958–1959)

Academic Honors

During 1957, Max Gerson received a letter from the University of Vienna offering him the Chair in the Department of Nutritional Medicine. Although he felt honored by this prestigious offer so appropriate to his background, accomplishments and interests, he declined it for several reasons. At the advanced age of 75, with his energy and health declining, Max did not wish to uproot himself and his wife in a return move to Europe, abandoning his current patients and the medical practice he had begun in New York City almost 20 years earlier. His three daughters and his six grandchildren would doubtless remain in the United States, and he and Gretchen wished to be close to them all. In addition, Max felt that the Austrians had not yet confronted, much less renounced, their nation's history of Nazi sympathy. He did not relish a return to a country with a history of anti-Semitism.

The atmosphere in the United States, however, was not much more hospitable, though for vastly different reasons. In June 1957 Gerson wrote a letter of condolence to Albert Schweitzer, on hearing the news of the death of his patient and Dr. Schweitzer's wife, Hélène. He then vented some of his grievances against the all-powerful medical establishment in America, at the same time acknowledging a growing number of advocates who believed in the value of his therapy, whether or not they dared to advocate it publicly or professionally:

> My dear Dr. Schweitzer,
>
> We were very saddened when we heard this week that your dear wife is no longer with us. We all admired her simple, wise, unassuming manner. She devoted herself to your work with all her energy. She bore each burden and her long illness without complaint!
>
> She deserved her eternal rest and will be always in our loving thoughts.
>
> As I wrote you in my last letter, I would like to thank you again for your

supportive words. It will probably interest you that there is a great and increasing opposition here to an effective cancer treatment. Physicians in America, particularly the leading policy makers, are predominantly "dollar-minded" (money- driven). The so-called AMA, American Medical Association, will not allow facts to be decisive.

The public is very angry about this, but can't do much since the general press is entirely dependent on the AMA.

The decent physicians have to toe the line in order to maintain their hospital affiliation. A number of physicians have come to me as patients. The first thing they say is, "Please don't use my name because if it were known that I came to you, I would be thrown out of my position at the hospital."

A number of open-minded celebrities have gotten together to publicize the suppressed truth. Miss Gloria Swanson, a popular and well-known movie actress, is one of these celebrities.

She is in Europe at the moment, and wants to visit you sometime in the next few weeks. She asked us for an introduction to you. She wants to have a look at your great humanitarian achievements.

My cancer book is well under way, and will hopefully be done in late autumn.

All of our best wishes for your continuing good health and well-being.

Your devoted friend,

Gerson

A Cancer Therapy

In his mid 70s, Max Gerson set out to recreate his definitive book on cancer, undaunted by the mysterious disappearance of the first draft two years earlier in 1955. Though Max knew it would be difficult to rewrite the book, given his age and his still rather weakened condition, he was determined to do so, dedicated to this mission of providing healing information to others. A Cancer Therapy: Results of Fifty Cases would be his ultimate "show and tell" in publication form as he first explained his theory of cancer then provided 50 case studies. Thus the title and the two part structure of the book. "All the explanations in this book about the healing of cancer as well as other presentations would be not much more than words, if we were not able to demonstrate the corresponding clinical facts of real healings. But after these facts are achieved, these conceptions are explanations for our clinical observations." (p. 133)

Part I (A Cancer Therapy) is a collection of a large number of his opinions and conjectures, based on his scientific observations, clinical experiences and reading. Extant handwritten and typescript drafts indicate that some of the 33 chapters in Part

I (about 250 pages) had probably originated as articles he had drafted for submission to medical or scientific journals. Other chapters seem to have been written when he was seized by some inspiration or line of thought he was pursuing at the time, with frequent footnoted references to scientific and medical papers and monographs. Part I thus reads somewhat like a miscellany, though the first draft of the book may have been more logically structured. The 33 chapter titles, given in sequence here, show the wide variety of subjects he undertook to discuss, technical, theoretical and practical:

1. The "Secret" of My Treatment; 2. The Concept of Totality — Decisive in Cancer and Other Degenerative Diseases; 3. Directions for General Nutrition; 4. Development of the Combined Dietary Regime in Cancer (Survey); 5. The Theory; 6. A Few Similar Cancer Theories; 7. Paracelsus' Dietary Regime; 8. Different Authors' Cancer Therapies by Diet (Survey); 9. Early Cancer Symptoms; 10. Cancer and Liver; 11. Survey of Treatment of Liver Pathology by Several Authors; 12. Development of Liver Medication in Chronic Degenerative Diseases; 13. Scientists Term Radiation a Peril to Future of Man; 14. Mineral Metabolism in Degenerative Diseases; 15. Distribution of Enzymes in Organs; 16. Mineral Accumulations in the Thyroid; 17. The Healing of Cancer; 18. Role of Allergy in the Healing Process of Cancer; 19. Introduction to the Diet; 20. Introduction to Nutrition and Diet; 21. The Saltless Diet; 22. Salt in Cancer Diet; 23. Insecticides; 24. The Significance of the Content of the Soil to Human Diseases; 25. Cancer Diet and Its Preparation; 26. The Practice of the Therapy; 27. Reactions — Flare Ups; 28. Short Practical Explanation of the Medication; 29. Rehabilitation of the Cancer Patient; 30. Most Frequent Mistakes of Patients in the Application of the Treatment, and Check List for Cancer Patients on the Gerson Therapy; 31. Medication —Some Failures; 32. Tables / Total Treatment of a Typical Case / Hourly Schedule of Typical Treatment; 33. Combined Dietary Regime / Special Notes to Physician

Part II (about 140 pages) presents the "Results of Fifty Cases," which were identified briefly in the table of contents by sequential case numbers followed by each patient's most serious presenting circumstances of cancer and other disorders, if relevant. For example, Case # 4 is labeled "Spongioblastoma, left part thalamus," and Case #23, "Myosarcoma, followed by osteomyelitis, subtrochanteric pathologic fracture of left subtrochanteric area." Within the text itself the patient's identity was disguised by initials, but age at start of treatment and possibly life circumstance are noted: for example, "Case No. 3 — Miss M.K., age 17"; "Case No. 11 — Mr. E.B., age 31, married, three children."

In his very short Chapter I, "The 'Secret' of My Treatment," Dr. Gerson admits in the first sentence, "Of course, there is none! The heading is used because I am asked frequently, often reproachfully, by physicians about it." In the second paragraph, he introduces the underlying theme of the book and indeed his whole practice of medicine:

> The harmony in the metabolism of all internal organs and systems must be maintained; it reflects the eternal mystery of life, expressed in our health and continuance. . . .The onset of metabolic disturbance constitutes the beginning of disease. (p. 5)

Chapter 2 is an elaboration of his concept of totality, his integrated view of the body's organs, systems and functions, as it applies to cancer and other degenerative diseases. Although the term "holistic" as alternative or complementary medical concept was not yet in use among physicians, Dr. Gerson finds similar terms for his purposes. (All italicized words here are Dr. Gerson's.)

> [T]he biological fact [is] that not one factor alone or a combination of single factors is decisive, but what is decisive is how they influence the *whole body, mind and soul in their entirety.*
>
> To the great complexity of the biological functions of the body belongs also its *capacity of adaptation.* A healthy body can adapt itself to different types of nutrition. It reabsorbs the necessary minerals, vitamins and enzymes as we know from experiments to determine the time for the clinical appearance of one or another vitamin deficiency. A sick body has lost this capacity. The deficiencies cannot be restored as long as the essential organs are poisoned. That is true in cancer also, as demonstrated by clinical observations.
>
> Cancer, the great killer, will be prevented and can be cured if we learn to understand the eternal laws of totality in nature and in our body. Both are combined and have to be united in an effective treatment for cancer; in that way we can learn to cure cancer in a higher proportion, even of advanced cases. The limitations of the totality of functions of the whole body, however, also come into action here. The totality of functions is lost if *one or another* vital organ is too far destroyed. (p. 18)

In Chapter V, "The Theory," Dr. Gerson further defines this notion:

> My theory is not presented to give a general scientific explanation of the cancer problem, nor to compare it with the many existing theories and explanations. It is supposed to be a guide which helps physicians to apply the treatment properly. The theory was derived from clinical observations during which was recorded what was most characteristic of the disease and what seemed to be most decisive in the course of the treatment. In short, it is this: What is essential is not the growth itself or the visible symptoms; it is the damage of the whole metabolism, including the loss of defense, immunity and healing power.

It cannot be explained with nor recognized by one or another cause alone.

In my opinion, cancer is not a problem of deficiencies in hormones, vitamins and enzymes. It is not a problem of allergies or infections with a virus or any other known or unknown microorganism. It is not a poisoning through some special intermedial metabolic substance or any other substance coming from an outside, so-called carcinogenic substance. All these can be partial causative agents in man, contributing elements, called secondary infections, etc. Cancer is not a single cellular problem; it is an accumulation of numerous damaging factors combined in deteriorating the whole metabolism, after the liver has been progressively impaired in its functions. Therefore, one has to separate two basic components in cancer: a general one and a local one. The general component is mostly a very slow, progressing, imperceptible symptom caused by poisoning of the liver and simultaneously an impairment of the whole intestinal tract, later producing appearances of vitally important consequences all over the body. The process in the pre-stage of cancer has not been proven clinically. . . . In the poisoning of the liver, clinical symptoms are not noticeable for a long period of time, even for many years. . . .

The local component is caused, in my opinion, by abnormal cells, immature cells, formerly damaged cells, transitional cells when they fall back or are forced to fall back into a type of embryonic life, because they are no longer supported sufficiently by the activated (ionized) minerals of the potassium group and a sufficient amount of reactivated oxidizing enzymes simultaneously united with the normal regulations of hormones, vitamins and the impulse of a normal functioning visceral nervous system. Finally the functions of subcutaneous, reticular lymph cell tissue and reticulo-endothelial system [the immune system] are diminished in function and defense power. (pp. 35-37)

A lifetime of study underpinned this theory of cancer. Max Gerson's reasoning was derived from his knowledge of human physiology, nutritional biochemistry and electrochemistry, but his wisdom was fully empirical and his methods stochastic – he tried various kinds of treatment, then tried to figure out why they were beneficial or detrimental. And so he developed the Gerson diet and detoxifications regimens. During the ensuing decades considerably more has been learned about human physiology, biophysics and biochemistry, immunology, genetics, molecular biology and other aspects of medical science that confirm or disprove a number of Dr. Gerson's postulations. Regardless of whether his theories proved right or wrong, many of his patients benefited greatly from this form of treatment. Even when Dr. Gerson's patients died because the damage to certain vital organs, particularly the liver, eventually proved irreversible, they usually lived longer and suffered less than when undergoing the standard treatments offered by the medical establishment.

Rewriting A *Cancer Therapy: Results of 50 Cases* took nearly a year. In order to secure the time needed to complete this work, Max took a leave of absence in 1957 from tending his patients, both at his New York office and at the Nanuet sanatorium, and spent some weeks at the home of a doctor friend in Florida. Periodically, Max wrote to his good friend Henry "S-S" (Shaefer-Simmern) about his progress on the book, as well as his hopes for its effect on his reputation.

> The ocular reports for the brain tumor cases, as far as they are decisive and necessary, will be written by Professor Ray Franklin, professor of ophthalmology at Columbia University. The X-ray reports are all written by Professor Ziegler, who is one of the foremost authorities in this field.
>
> The most important and ultimate proof for all cases is the fact that almost all of them were operated once or even several times. We will publish all their surgery reports and clinical findings. No serious physician will dare to bring up any valid objection against these. I shall keep the clinical section as precise and short as possible in order not to tire physicians or lay persons with it.
>
> When lay persons or physicians call the Academy of Medicine here, they are always told that I am not an authority and that my reports cannot be trusted. This will finally have to stop. In spite of this, my small clinic is overloaded so that I can only accept some of the applicants.

Not surprisingly, given that medical doctors sat on the board of directors or editorial boards of major book publishers, Max Gerson had difficulty finding a publisher, as he explained to "S-S":

> Three of the best publishers have rejected my book again, because first of all cancer books are not good business; nobody wants to read about hopes, promises and results of bioassays any more, the great majority of people are fed up with that. They want to see facts and form their own judgments from them.
>
> I omitted all judgments and enumerations of cancer theories, and try as far as possible to present the scientific foundation for my philosophy. Also, as far as I can, to present scientific proof for my ideas. That is not a simple project because, even when one reaches the basics of the cancer problem, everything is still more or less contradictory or unknown or misunderstood.

Max had hoped that Albert Schweitzer would write an introduction to the book, but to his great disappointment his old friend declined:

> I am not a medical authority but only a modest Horse and Buggy doctor in the African backwoods. No scientific work was published during all the years of my practice here.
>
> Only an authority in the cancer field should be able to express a judgment

about your significant work. You know how I always was and still am interested in your clinical achievements and what significance I attribute to them, but only as a scholar, not as an authority.

Your book does not need any introduction. The facts will speak for themselves. The time is over when people believe in introductions. The reader does not want any recommendation but wants to judge by the unbiased facts.

Eventually, Max Gerson did find a publisher. Whittier Books, in New York, agreed at least to issue his book, but only after being assured by the author that he would cover all its production costs. A *Cancer Therapy: Results of Fifty Cases* was published in the spring of 1958. It was clothbound and had 402 pages. The second part of the book, containing the case histories, was amply illustrated with "before and after" X-rays and revelatory photographs of patients' original and healed cancerous growths on skin, organs, bones.

No promotional events were scheduled for the book by its publisher, for the publisher acted here only as a printer. Now his daughters Trudi and Johanna, through the Gerson Foundation for Cancer Treatment, assumed an active role in publicizing and marketing the book. They worked on the sales and distribution of their father's book, to such good effect that the first edition of 3,000 copies was nearly sold out even before it appeared. Most of the initial buyers were former patients and their acquaintances.

Review copies were sent out to various medical journals, but not surprisingly, it received sparse notices. One appeared in the *New York State Journal of Medicine*, written by E. Mendelson.

It is Gerson's theory that there is no cancer in a normal metabolism, that a disturbed metabolism frequently results from the modern processing of food products, and that it is possible by the use of the rather extreme and restricted diet which he has developed to improve the body metabolism, and, in this way, help the body combat the abnormal cancer metabolism. The development of this theory, I must admit, has confused this reviewer.

Some of the end results reported in these 50 cases are definitely startling, particularly the relatively long-term alleviation mentioned in several cases of melanosarcoma and carcinoma of the cervix.

This book may be read because of its unusual approach to the therapy of inoperable malignancy. The author has promised to document at least 400 more cases treated by his diet. Certainly it would seem that this is necessary to convince a skeptical medical profession.

Newly energized, Dr. Gerson had plans to write a second book featuring more of his best cases —a full hundred of them —as he stated in A *Cancer Therapy*. However, he would not live to do so.

Flax Oil

While Max Gerson was preoccupied with writing his book, less time and energy was given to running the sanatorium in Nanuet. In the spring of 1958, when *A Cancer Therapy* was about to be published, Trudy, who had been managing the facility for five years, proposed closing it down, and her father agreed. Because his book was now available, explaining his theory of cancer, describing the Gerson diet and detoxifying procedures, and providing the scientific or medical reasons for these treatments, it became feasible to turn over more responsibility to patients themselves and their caregivers. And since *A Cancer Therapy* was partly a textbook, it relieved Dr. Gerson somewhat of that ever-pressing desire to pass his wisdom on to a younger generation of physicians.

Nevertheless, Dr. Gerson's inquiring mind did not rest. An inveterate researcher, he remained on the lookout for other promising micronutrients and food constituents to introduce into his basic dietary therapy so as to test their efficacy. His choices were usually determined by some prior research-based evidence of their possible value.

Dr. Gerson had long searched for a substance he could give his patients to supply the essential fatty acids (EFAs) that were not available in the constituents of fruits, vegetables and greens in his diet therapy. He experimented with various kinds of oil, including safflower, sunflower, olive, almond and other nut oils, corn oil and even raw, unsalted butter. Each oil was cautiously administered to patients, invariably those who had had easily visible tumors, such as breast, lymph nodes, melanoma —yet only in cases where the tumors had already disappeared or dried up. Each time the addition of oils or butter caused tumor recurrences. Dr. Gerson reluctantly concluded that *all* fats and oils needed to be excluded from the cancer patient's diet for at least 18 months He had put that cautionary note into his book in emphatic, bold print.

Shortly after *A Cancer Therapy* was completed and printed, Max came across the work of Johanna Budwig, Ph.D., a German nutritional researcher who was recommending the use of flaxseed oil in therapeutic diets. For more than a half-century Dr. Budwig had researched the healing benefits of particular fats, especially flaxseed oil, and the dangers in consuming saturated fats. She is said to have revolutionized medical thinking about the relationship between fat metabolism and cancer. Dr. Budwig was nominated at least seven times for the Nobel Prize. Among her books are *Flax Oil as a True Aid Against Arthritis Heart Infarction, Cancer and Other Diseases* and *The Oil Protein Diet Cookbook*.

Dr. Gerson was intrigued by this research, especially flaxseed oil was probably the only edible oil and fat that he had not tried in all his clinical experiments in adding EFAs in his patients' diets. He immediately tried flaxseed oil cautiously on a few patients. When it did not cause new tumor growth, he tried it on patients who still had tumors, and the tumors did not increase. In fact, Dr. Gerson observed that they actually shrank faster than those in patients not given the oil. As he wrote his friend Henry Schaefer-Simmern in November of 1958: "The results with the cancer patients given flaxseed oil have developed further, to my great satisfaction, as they are faster and much more far-reaching."

Max felt like kicking himself for not having thought of flaxseed oil before; after all, flax oil had been a main product of his father's oil press in Wongrowitz. He had watched the oil being squeezed out from the tiny brown seeds saved after the fibrous stalks in the highly useful flax plant had been removed for conversion into linen thread for fabrics. The seeds were sold either for pressing into linseed oil for industrial and commercial uses at mills like Bernard Gerson's; or they were sold to housewives for food use. Most home kitchens had a small oil press for flaxseed oil production, and it was often used to prepare a fresh, delicate oil for use on salads or vegetables. The oil did not lend itself well to storage as a kitchen-grade oil, since it quickly became oxidized or rancid. Nor was it good when heated in cooking.

When Dr. Gerson looked further into the biochemical processes that were taking place as a result of ingesting flaxseed oil, he found that this oil helped to transport vitamin A (in the form of beta carotene) to the tissues. It was an aid in dissolving and eliminating vascular plaque, thus improving circulation and oxygenation. It also supplied the essential fatty acids so important in cell metabolism. (It is now known that the oils constituting flaxseed oil are "cis-fatty acids", as opposed to "trans-fatty acids," and are the same "omega" factors that have gotten so much attention in fish oils. Linoleic, linolenic and oleic acids constitute about 70% of the flax oil. Flaxseeds and flax oil, including capsules for use as supplements, are now widely available, especially in health stores.)

Homecoming

In mid September 1958 Max returned from a late-summer vacation at Dr. Jensen's health ranch in California. On this trip Max had accepted the invitation of some friends to visit an interesting natural cave not far from Escondido, but this excursion proved to be injurious to his health. When he returned to New York he did not look rejuvenated, as Charlotte Gerson recalls:

> My first indication that something was terribly wrong was seeing my father arrive at the New York airport. He should have looked rested and well after his vacation, as he usually did when coming home. Instead, he looked terrible. His face was thin, his skin sallow, his eyes sunken, with black circles.
>
> But he never complained, never said anything about not feeling well. On the contrary, he continued his regular office hours, seeing patients. It was not until about three months later, in December, that he had a mental lapse; he didn't

know where he was, wasn't coherent. Since the episode passed without apparent further problems, it was discounted, and he continued to work. However, he was tired, more than usually weary before the end of the day. And he was beginning to have breathing problems.

Dr. Gerson was self-treating his condition, but was getting no better. Just after Christmas he was admitted to Mt. Sinai Hospital for two weeks. His care was not all that beneficial, as Gretchen explained in a letter to Henry Schaefer-Simmern:

> The physician there has a reputation for being very capable, but he refuses to treat [a patient] at home. And you know what to expect from the hospital: for one, Max was given meat daily and fish. Juices, soup and enemas I brought him twice daily, as agreed. But it is, of course, difficult for a physician to allow himself to be treated by a therapy which he would not have allowed for his own patients. So, this doctor was terminated and Max returned home. He was well rested but still spends much time I bed. He had worked himself to total exhaustion and didn't listen to any warnings. So he self-treated for about 2-3 weeks without medical help. It didn't work. There was no diagnosis up to now from any of the 6 doctors.... At this time, he has a little appetite but he is, of course, very weak and feeling down. He is constantly lying down in his hospital bed and has a night nurse for 12 hours. Our children are touching and spend as much time here as their other duties permit.

The rest in the hospital helped him to recover his strength somewhat, though. From his bed at home, Max dictated in German his own letter to his good friend Henry "S-S":

> Yesterday I returned home from the hospital. My women — whom I now call my Amazons — had a violent fight with me to get me to the hospital on the recommendation of the consulting physician. However I finally had to obey the Amazons.
>
> After a cold, double bronchopneumonia set in, which was soon eliminated. It went faster at home than in the hospital, where it took 10 days to return to therapy that I had begun at home. Now, however I am again very much better.
>
> Next week, I'll see the most urgent cases and then I plan to spend a few weeks in Florida. (1/6/59; translated by Charlotte Gerson)

While recuperating, Max received an invitation to promote his work in the Soviet Union, which posed an attendant dilemma, given the difficult Cold War political scene throughout the 1950s, as he explained to "S-S":

> About 2 weeks ago, a Russian physician who is employed here with the United Nations, and his wife who works in Russia in a cancer institute, were

here for the second time. The wife speaks fluent German, French, English and Russian, is intelligent and active. She was highly pregnant and the baby was probably born in the meantime. At the end of our conversation they asked me to write an article for a Russian medical journal, in German or in English. They will place it in the journal with my name.

My wife is strictly opposed, and my daughters have different opinions. I am still considering it. Here the atmosphere against me is very negative; yet, on the other hand, I must consider that I have been given the opportunity to an immigrant to work and build a lucrative practice. S, it is possible that my passing on to the Russians the answer to the cancer problem to give to mankind could be interpreted as a trick or stab in the back against the local [medical] circles. They could also brand me a "communist" and cause me still more problems that have not had a great effect on me so far.

The history of medicine shows that it has always been like that and I do not believe that people have improved or have become more humanitarian. If the Russians take the material from the book by themselves and publicize it, nothing can be said against it; it can't be avoided. The Russians already know that further progress has been made and has been added to the German edition.

May I ask you to consider the problem carefully and give me your opinion.

Max also received less promising information about the spread of knowledge of this cancer therapy in a letter from a Fresno, California-based physician:

Dear Dr. Gerson:

I am taking the liberty to send you a copy of a recently published pamphlet entitled "Unproven Cancer Treatment Methods," put out by the Cancer Commission of the California Medical Association.

Since your name appears on page eight, I believe you will be interested in seeing the pamphlet.

It is a shame that organized medicine cannot see the good in many new methods, and pursue them for their merit with an open and unbiased mind.

With best regards,
Clement A. Tavares, M.D. (1/29/59)

Not surprisingly, the booklet's brief description of the Gerson treatment method quoted the Conclusions of the Bureau of Investigation, American Medical Association: "It is of the opinion of the Bureau that the Gerson method of treating cancer is of no curative value." What surely cheered the seriously ailing Max Gerson, however, was this evidence of physician, unknown to him, who practiced in a medium-sized city clear across America, was concerned enough about this issue to contact Dr. Gerson directly.

Plans to travel to Florida and any decision concerning publishing an article or excerpt from his book in a Soviet medical journal were, sadly, deferred because of further ill health. Max couldn't understand why he continued to be ill — this went far beyond any manifestations of the normal "aging" process. He tried to discover the source, suspecting that something in his environment was causing an abnormal sensitivity reaction. He asked that a 24-hour urine test be taken, to see if he and any conferring physicians could determine the cause of his health problem. When the test results were finally given to him, they showed that he was suffering from arsenic poisoning.

At first, this was completely baffling since he had never experienced any significant exposure to arsenic in his food or environment. Then Max began to suspect that someone may have poisoned him. Whatever the source of the arsenic, there was nothing anyone could do anything about it now. Arsenic, an almost tasteless and low-cost cumulative poison, had damaged the cells in his liver, lungs and other tissues so slowly and imperceptibly, except for his increasing weariness, that he hadn't noticed the effect. Curiously, arsenic was an element that the alchemist Paracelsus, whom Gerson much admired, had particularly favored, using it in minuscule amounts in combination with other basic substances —some, like arsenic, well known to be toxic in larger doses.

As his lungs deteriorated, Max began to have more difficulty breathing. When he became agitated, his doctor gave him Valium — which calmed him, though it caused gastrointestinal problems. Compounding the effects of arsenic poisoning was an infection Max had contracted while touring the cave in Calfornia on his last vacation, as Charlotte Gerson explains while recalling that difficult period in the Gerson family's life:

> After my father came home from the hospital in January of 1959, he even returned to seeing patients for a limited number of hours. (After all, his office was just next door to the apartment, so he didn't have to travel anywhere.) But he was getting weaker, wearier, needed more rest. Pretty soon, he had little appetite and frequent episodes of diarrheas, which weakened him more. Toward the end of the month, he had to spend almost all of his time in bed, so was unable to see patients.
>
> By this time, every day before going to our own office, I would stop by the apartment at 815 Park Avenue to see him. One terrible day, when he was trying to show me that his breathing was quite all right, he expanded his barrel chest —but he was not breathing! No air went in, it was just a muscle exercise. I was shocked.
>
> Too weak to walk, he was taken in a wheelchair to a radiologist's office in his building to have a chest X-ray made. When he saw this X-ray picture, he expressed his own death sentence: "With those lungs, I cannot live. The second book will not be finished."

More tests were made and a new, little-known virus was found. It had been described in the medical literature only a short time before: an organism that lived in bat droppings and could be contracted by breathing the dust in moist caves. So he had brought the infection back with him from his Escondido vacation. No wonder we thought he looked so worn out and ill!

My father saw in the X-rays the terrible damage caused by the virus. The disease had literally eaten holes in his lungs. He directed me to get a specific book from his office, for he wanted to look up antiviral agents that might help him. He tried, but found nothing, so gave up. Another shock, and now fright.

Max Gerson soon after died, attended to the end by his loving family, as Charlotte continues:

The next few weeks were just a whirl of pain for us all as his weakness increased and his condition worsened. Finally, during the first week of March, his body, specifically his lungs, gave out. He was placed into an oxygen tent. I remember seeing him, semi-conscious, pearls of sweat on his brow, struggling to breathe. He was no longer talking. And then, on March 8th, he stopped struggling, stopped breathing.

I was there in the apartment when the men came to take his body away. A huge black void opened. My mother was there, crying. She was not in good condition herself; her heart was acting up. I remembered that his last words to me had been, "Take care of Mother." I reassured him, "Yes, we are all here." (But as it turned out, before my mother died, both of my sisters — her two older daughters —preceded her.)

Then came the arrangements, the announcements, the funeral. The sons-in-law took over some of these sad duties. My father's body was resting at a funeral home in the East 60s. I was struck with one detail. The room next to the one where my father's body was lying, in his closed coffin, was overflowing with visitors who were paying their respects to some high official in the New York City Police Department. But few mourners came to my father's room —apart from all the family, of course. They were mostly patients who had heard of his death. Here was this genius who had shown the way to healing "incurable" diseases for all humanity, but he was virtually unknown in his own community.

The death certificate stated that the cause of Dr. Gerson's death was chronic pneumonia. No autopsy was performed. But a final professional insult came from the physician who had done Dr. Gerson's chest X-rays. While the plates clearly showed holes in his lungs caused by the viral invasion, this doctor claimed, without the benefit of evidence from either a biopsy or an autopsy, that the X-rays he had taken proved that Max Gerson died of lung cancer.

In Memoriam

A nondenominational funeral service for Max Gerson was conducted two days after his death, on March 10, at the Universal Chapel in New York City — not at a synagogue, since he was a secular Jew. The eulogy was spoken by a minister, the Rev. Dr. Erwin Seale, who had been a friend of Max (and was thanked by him for his help with the cancer book):

> Dr. Gerson was unostentatious. He was not given to effusiveness or display. He was humbly dedicated and deeply devoted to the healing art. He gave himself unstintingly to his practice and to the alleviation of pain and misery. He was a conscientious Jew, but he was a universal soul. He never concerned himself with creeds and classifications. People in trouble were his great care. So many grateful patients will praise him forever for their health. They will hear of his death with tremendous shock and sadness. Others who do not yet know how much they are indebted to him for the extension of human knowledge, will one day praise him with all their hearts. As with all original discoverers, he was ahead of his time and time must pass for his great work to be fully appreciated. I myself not only admired him; I loved him. . . .
>
> Life must go on and his work must go on even as his spirit goes on. We all must nerve ourselves to complete the dear unfinished tasks of his and therein he may comfort us.

As Charlotte recalls some details of the funeral, though her grief understandably has left the memories sketchy:

> I can hardly remember the details of the funeral, except that a Reverend Seale (who was not Jewish) spoke some consoling words before the trip to the Kew Gardens Cemetery. There, the soil was still frozen hard, so it had been difficult to dig the grave into which his body was lowered.
>
> I could only think that he was surely deserving of his rest after his many years of exhausting work. But, of course, he hadn't wanted to rest at all: he wanted to finish his second book, about another hundred recovered people, returned to life from terminal cancer. He had not actually started writing it, but had already made a list of the cases in his collection of patients that he wanted to publish.

Dr. Max Gerson was mourned by hundreds of his cured patients and many others who were aware of his unacknowledged contributions to medical science. Significantly, some of the condolence letters sent to Mrs. Gerson came from physicians —showing that not all doctors, by any means, had joined "organized medicine" in America to oppose the Gerson therapy. For instance, Dr. Maurice H. Kowan, a physician and surgeon who practiced in Los Angeles, wrote:

One of my patients…told me a few days ago of the sudden passing of Max. I was broken hearted and really did not know what to do. I felt that I would like to write you a note, expressing my deepest sympathy as well as my great appreciation for having known such a wonderful man.

He spent his entire life trying to help others and finally, in my opinion, found a solution to this dreadful disease called cancer. As all courageous explorers he received the hatred of those who pose as leaders of the medical profession, but in reality are interested only in the economics of their profession and apparently do everything in their power to destroy anyone who would prove their position wrong.

Mrs. Gerson received this note from former Senator Claude Pepper of Florida:

Your announcement of the passing of Dr. Gerson grieves me very much. I shall always remember his appearance before my committee holding hearings upon my bill to appropriate One Hundred Million Dollars to remain available until spent for research into the cause and cure of cancer.

Dr. Gerson dedicated his life to the mastery of this scourge of cancer and all should honor his great work.

And then there were telegrams from patients who had grown close to Mrs. Gerson's husband, such as this one:

DEEPEST SYMPATHY IN YOUR GREAT LOSS I HAVE LOST NOT ONLY THE BEST DOCTOR I EVER HAD BUT ALSO A GOOD FRIEND
    SINCERELY =
    ESTHER KRAMER =

Of all the condolence letters, notes and telegrams received by Mrs. Gerson, probably none was touching as a message posted from a medical clinic in the interior of French Equatorial Africa, written in German:

March 10, 1959

Dear Mrs. Gerson,

A little while ago your husband wrote me that he would like to see me again and that I should let him know when I would be in Europe. Gladly I made a note of this, for I, too, had the desire to sit down again wit him quietly…. And now he has passed away!

I was moved that you sent me a cable as if I belonged to the family. How I take part in the loss you suffer you know; and that I mourn a friend in the departed, whom I counted among my closest, you also know. I owe him such gratitude for all that he did for my wife. Without him, she would have died when our child was small. How gratefully she always thought of him!

But in the hour when I received the news of his death, I also thought about what he has meant to the world. I see in him one of the most eminent medical geniuses in the history of medicine. He possessed something elemental. Out of deepest thought about the nature of disease and the process of healing, he came to walk along new paths with great success. Unfortunately, he could not engage in scientific research or teach; and he was greatly impeded by adverse political conditions. In ordinary times he would have been able to expound his ideas for many years as professor at one of the important German universities; would have taught pupils who could carry on his research and teachings; would have found recognition and encouragement.... All this was denied him.

His was the hard lot of searching and working as an uprooted immigrant to be challenged and to stand as a fighter. We who knew and understood him admired him for working his way out of discouragement again and again, and for undertaking to conquer the obstacles.

Many of his basic ideas have been adopted without having his name connected with them. Yet he has achieved more than seemed possible under these adverse circumstances. He leaves a legacy which commands attention and which will assure him his due place. Those he cured will now attest to the truth of his ideas. I hope that he also gained some pupils in the New World who will do this for him.

We who knew and valued him mourn him already today as a medical genius who walked among us and as a man who was destined to be a fighter who proved himself in this adverse fate.

With loving thoughts, your devoted

Albert Schweitzer

On May 12, 1959 — two months *after* his death — the New York Academy of Sciences invited Dr. Gerson to become a member of this prestigious organization. When they received no reply, the following letter arrived, addressed to Dr. Max Gerson:

On May 12, 1959, our Executive Director, Eunice Thomas Miner, extended to you an invitation to membership in the Academy. We have had no reply from you and are interested in learning what your decision has been.

May we hear from you regarding this matter? If you have decided to become a member, we shall be glad to present your name to the Council at its next meeting.

Dr. Max Gerson had at last been accepted into the American medical establishment.

~24~
Dr. Gerson's Legacy
(1959–)

Family Matters

When Max Gerson's deteriorating health made it obvious that he would never return to practice, his secretary returned all files to his patients. Then only a few months after his death, his widow gave up the large apartment on Park Avenue, since she had no need for the attached office and other extra rooms. Her three daughters helped her pack the furnishings and books collected over a long, rich lifetime and helped her move into a smaller apartment on the corner of Third Avenue and 72nd Street.

That summer, Mrs. Gerson decided to revisit Europe, as she had not been back since the family's flight from the Nazis, though Max had been back once, to speak at the 1952 holistic conference at Berchtesgaden. Besides meeting with some scattered relatives and friends, Gretchen wanted to visit Dr. Schweitzer, who was in Europe at the time. She solved the problem of being very shy and somewhat anxiety-prone by inviting me, her grandson, then 16 years old, to accompany her. The trip included time in Hamburg, Hanover, Gretchen's home town of Verl, Gütersloh, Freiburg im Breisgau, Paris, Gunsbach (Schweitzer's European home in Alsace-Lorraine), Donaueschingen and Lugano, Switzerland. My proficiency in German and French improved significantly during this time, as Gretchen depended on me to deal with the various interactions necessary for such a trip.

I remember visiting the Thyssen villa in Lugano with her, a very beautiful and well-stocked art museum. She noted to me that, though the villa and art were quite beautiful, the Thyssens had been a big and early supporter of the Nazis (Thyssen Steel). I know that she was very aware of the Nazi presence that hovered like a ghost. After all, it was only 14 years after the end of the war and the Holocaust.

We visited grandmother's home town Verl, in Westphalia, where old friends and some distant relatives still lived; all her close relatives had been exterminated or else managed to escape. The aftermaths of the war and of the Holocaust were still very much present. Grandmother pointed out the Hope house, her parents' house where she grew up. Down the street there is a Holocaust museum commemorating the Jewish families of Verl . . . and a small stone marker in the memory of the Hopes has been erected behind the store. When I visited these relatives again in 1967 they told me that, although they were Catholic and only one-eighth Jewish, their barn had been fired and painted with swastikas and the legend "Jew Wester-Ebbinghaus" — their surname. The oldest son, Pütti, had spent 10 years in a Russian POW camp, had just returned four years before our first visit in 1959.

We paid a visit to Mrs. Steinhaus, the woman in Gütersloh whose rheumatoid arthritis Max Gerson had cured in the late 1920s and spent a pleasant day at Freiburg im Breisgau with Herrmann Luft of Hyperion Verlag, the publisher of the German edition of A *Cancer Therapy*. From there, we went to see Dr. Schweitzer in Gunsbach. As might be expected, that experience left a deep impression on me. Dr. Schweitzer invited us for lunch and to spend the day with him. He provided a very simple farmer's lunch of potatoes, sauerkraut and ham. At the table, besides Dr. Schweitzer, his secretary, and us were two Swiss farmers, one of whom had been named Albert Schweitzer after the great man, and now wanted to meet his namesake, as well as a harpsichordist named Wanda Landowska, who is credited with repopularizing the harpsichord in the 20th century.

Schweitzer had engaged a car to drive him after lunch to the next town, where he had a meeting and where we were staying. As we were standing there waiting for the car, Dr. Schweitzer engaged me in conversation, brief and simple due to my deficient German and his lack of English. But he clearly wanted to know if I planned to go into medicine, like my grandfather. I'm afraid he was a bit disappointed by my answer. As we drove out of Gunsbach, a tiny little village, and across the fields, about a mile out of town a dirt road crossed the two-lane country road we were on and disappeared into the fields on either side. A signpost had been erected at the intersection, large enough for the legend "Rue Albert Schweitzer." Dr. Schweitzer plucked my sleeve to get my attention. "Look," he beamed, "they named a street after me." The man's humility and goodness were powerful, even for a callow 16-year-old.

Max Gerson had never really been much of a companion for his wife. They never went together to movies, rarely to the Metropolitan Opera or the New York Philharmonic, and almost never socialized with other couples. Gretchen had developed a fair degree of independence, with a network of a few friends whom she would visit weekly. After her husband's death she rarely felt lonely.

One thing became plain. She had not enjoyed the severe dietary restrictions that her husband's health sensitivities and belief system had demanded of her cuisine. After her husband's death, she felt she had no reason to continue to deprive herself of certain culinary pleasures. Born and raised as she had been in Westphalia, these included a liking for beer and for ham and other delicacies, but before very long, she began having her own health problems. The first of these was arthritic joints, which on her hands interfered with her daily piano practice. I had always enjoyed my grandmother's piano music, but now, before she could comfortably play, my grandmother needed a half hour of massage to loosen up her finger and wrist joints — a task that I was happy to perform.

Their daughter Johanna continued working at the Foundation for Cancer Treatment, where she had been largely responsible for selling out the first printing of A *Cancer Therapy* — 3,000 copies altogether — before her father's death. A second printing was ordered, with the production costs again wholly paid for by Max Gerson, not the publisher. Johanna also became involved in trying to find replacement physicians for her father's patients. She managed to find a doctor to monitor the conditions and prescribe medications for those in the New York City area. As Charlotte Gerson recalls, "In 1960 Dr. Lance Vallan, a doctor who lived on East 79th Street, in my sister's neighborhood, took over some of our father's patients and got their files. His work with them was considerably supported by Johanna, who helped patients by giving explicit directions for doing the Gerson therapy, obtaining the special medications for them, purchasing the right juicer, etc." Dr. Vallan himself, though, was scarcely a model for the Gerson lifestyle. He was an extremely heavy smoker. He had a huge ashtray on his desk, easily 8 inches square, usually brim full of cigarette butts. Only about two or three years later Vallan suffered a gall bladder attack and had surgery; following the surgery, when he was already up, he had a fatal hemorrhage.

In the mid 1960s Mrs. Gerson had to endure the illnesses and deaths of her two oldest daughters, when they were only in their late 40s — first Trudy, then Johanna. Neither had adhered to their father's dietary principles when they became adults, in part because their husbands refused to consume such Spartan fare. Despite her father's warnings about the health consequences, Trudy had smoked cigarettes for some time before giving up the habit. Only a few months after she remarried in 1964, Trudy experienced a relatively common side effect of the high-dose birth control pills she was taking. She suffered a blood clot, which caused a stroke, followed by her death.

Johanna had never been in robust good health, even as a child. In the 1960s, not long after Trudy's death, she was diagnosed with colon cancer. She went to Austria, where a doctor treated her using the Gerson therapy. Having failed to get better, she died in 1967 near Vienna — the first city of the Gerson family's exile after fleeing from Berlin in 1933.

Fortunately, the Gersons' youngest daughter remained in excellent health. Charlotte has carried on her father's work in her own inimitable way. Lotte had followed the guidelines of her father's therapy to the extent that she could, given a husband who insisted upon meat at every meal. (In 1966 she and Irwin Straus were divorced.) If she strayed far from the regimen, she would get migraine headaches, an undesirable and avoidable consequence.

Charlotte often tended to her mother's needs — a responsibility previously shared with her sisters. As Gretchen grew older, the frigid East Coast wintertime became harder for her to endure, with its icy sidewalks particularly difficult for her to navigate safely. Her lifelong hay fever worsened; moreover, the polluted air in New York City made it difficult for her to breathe. Her dietary changes had resulted in a heart attack, then in a stroke. In 1969, following the stroke, Charlotte persuaded her mother to move to a retirement home in Monterey, on the central California coast, where the moderate year-round weather and the cleaner air would be far more agreeable. An extra inducement was that I lived nearby, so could often visit with her and take her on outings.

On May 10, 1971, Mrs. Gerson died in her sleep, a week before her 79th birthday. It was a sudden death caused by a stroke. For her age, she had been in relatively good health. Only the day before she had celebrated Mother's Day in a happy reunion with several of her grandchildren.

The Gerson Institute

Max Gerson's therapy did not perish after his death in 1959. His continuing legacy as a healer is in good part attributable to the many years of dedicated work done by his third daughter, Charlotte, as she explains.

> The survival of the Gerson therapy was up to me. The first thing I decided was that A Cancer Therapy would have to remain in print. Since the Long Island vitamin-distribution company which had reprinted the book earlier was unwilling to republish (they had been threatened by the FDA), I arranged to have 3,000 copies printed and stored. But having the books was of little use; I had to find a way to distribute them.
>
> In the meantime, several groups had emerged that pushed freedom of choice in medicine, especially publicizing various nontoxic cancer treatments. One of these was the IACVF (International Association of Cancer Victims and Friends), in San Diego. They developed several chapters, of which the Los Angeles one and the New York one split off. The L.A. one is now known as The Cancer Control Society, headed by Lorraine Rosenthal, and is active and quite effective. The New York chapter is headed by Ruth Sackman (now in her 80s); they call themselves ACT, or Alternative Cancer Treatments.

There were numerous chapters of those groups, and I made myself available to lecture at meetings: for instance, in Long Island, Manhattan, Detroit, Chicago, Florida, San Diego, Los Angeles. And of course I sold books there when I lectured. Patients started to clamor for a place to get the Gerson Therapy.

Eventually, a few doctors became interested in setting up clinics. The first one was in Los Angeles, but the doctor bowed out within a few weeks, no doubt under extreme pressure from his professional peers, so I had to close. Next I had a clinic in South Bend, Indiana, but there the doctor was harassed and quit in six months. (She later died under extremely suspicious circumstances, probably a murder victim.)

Finally, a doctor named Tom Siaw planned to start a hospital in Tijuana that would use the Gerson therapy. He had deduced from his wide reading that nutrition was one of the major keys in the healing of degenerative diseases. He contacted Charlotte Gerson and Norman Fritz.

In 1977, 18 years after her father's death, Charlotte Gerson Straus decided to launch a nonprofit organization that would enable her to publicize the Gerson Therapy. She had been urged to do so by Norman Fritz, who already had valuable experience with International Association of Cancer Victims and Friends (IACVF). The Gerson Institute was founded in 1977 and received its nonprofit status in the following year. Charlotte acted as president from its founding to 1998. Norman Fritz served as co-founder and vice-president. Fritz was also president of the San Diego IACVF — now called International Association of Cancer Victors and Friends. Vice president of the Gerson Institute for nearly 20 years, he is now president of the Cancer Control Society in Los Angeles.

The nonprofit organization's principal missions were to educate people about the Gerson therapy, to train practitioners in providing it and to provide supportive assistance to individuals and groups who desired to practice the Gerson diet and lifestyle principles. The Gerson Institute started its existence and continued in Bonita, California, halfway between San Diego and the Mexican border, but has since moved its offices to San Diego. The Institute set up a Gerson clinic across the U.S. border in Mexico. There it was possible to treat people for cancer in unorthodox ways that were regarded as illegal and indeed criminal by the American medical establishment, beyond the reach of persecution not only by national, state and local medical societies, but also confiscatory raids and arrests by the police, the FDA, the FBI and even the U.S. Postmaster General.

The original Gerson clinic was located in an old motel called La Gloria between Tijuana and Playas de Tijuana. Many of the physicians and facility owners with whom the Gerson Institute and staff had to work over the years were ethically questionable, to say the least. But Charlotte Gerson and the Institute did the best they could, keeping it as clean as possible, building a reputation for quality, integrity and demonstrable results that other, less ethical operators try to trade on to this day. One day, a disgruntled employee set the offices on fire, destroying many of the medical records of years of treatment. The facility then moved to a motel closer to the beach called Del Sol.

When Charlotte was still supervising the Gerson clinic at the Del Sol Hospital in Tijuana, she was surprised by the arrival there one day of Dr. Joseph Issels. At the age of 82, he had high blood pressure, extremely high cholesterol and a severely arthritic hip. He had given up his practice in Germany, and wanted to recover from these debilitating conditions. Gratifyingly, he responded quickly and left the clinic much improved.

The Trial of Dr. Joseph Issels

In the two decades following Max Gerson's death, physicians made occasional attempts to utilize his dietary and detoxifying approach to treating diseases, especially cancer. These usually involved modifications of the diet and other aspects of treatment (such as the coffee enema). The earliest, most ambitious and best known of these experiments with the Gerson therapy was done by Dr. Joseph Issels.

One of the attendees at the 1952 Totality conference in Germany that Dr. Gerson attended, Dr. Issels had been so impressed with Gerson's presentation of his methods and results that he wanted to try them at the First National Clinic for the Internal Treatment of Cancer, which he had founded in the previous year at Rottach-Egern in Upper Bavaria, Germany. Dr. Issels gradually elaborated on facets of Dr. Gerson's approach, developing his own variation of the metabolic therapy he had so admired at Berchtesgaden. As in Dr. Gerson's practice, 95 percent of his patients were "terminal" cases, and, again like Dr. Gerson, he showed unquestionably positive results overall. His clinic grew and prospered.

Then on September 15, 1960, Dr. Issels was arrested for fraud and manslaughter. The charge of fraud was based on the allegation that he had promised cures to dying patients so as to get them to check into his clinic for the "outrageous" cost of DM1,700 (U.S. $425) per month, which included treatment, room and board. He was also charged with manslaughter because the district attorney was able to produce three cases of patients who had died but might have lived longer, he said, if orthodox treatments had been used before or instead of the Issels therapy.

Professor Dr. Schulten, one of the most respected medical experts in Europe, claimed that only a world medical congress could render final judgment about the results and utility of Issels' methods. Consequently, the judge barred any evidence concerning the effectiveness of the methods that Issels used, thereby denying it a public airing. Other startling evidence emerged, however. A dentist formerly on Issels' staff at the clinic admitted that he had been paid DM10,000 (U.S. $2,500) by an unnamed interest group to collect material that could prove damaging to Issels. These documents were eventually used to initiate the lawsuit.

The trial took place in Munich in the summer of 1961 and lasted almost seven weeks. Every newspaper, tabloid and magazine in Europe and many other countries, except for the United States, reported on this criminal court proceeding. The issue on trial was a most explosive one in medicine: Can a doctor explore new ways of treating terminal cancer patients other than those prescribed by orthodox medicine?. The German press daily carried detailed descriptions of the action, offered editorials and elicited letters to the editor from the public. The letters, which arrived from people in all walks of life and in all socioeconomic levels, expressed almost unanimous objection to the trumped-up charges against Issels. Many condemned the fact that a court of law could assume jurisdiction over an area of science that had not yet yielded its ultimate secrets.

The results of the trial were inconclusive. Charges of fraud were dropped, but Issels was sentenced to one year in prison for manslaughter, a sentence that was immediately suspended. Issels appealed the sentence at once, because at least one of the witnesses for the prosecution had committed perjury. Though Issels was imprisoned until his appeal was heard, the conviction was eventually overturned due to the perjured testimony of one of the prosecution's key witnesses.

The Gerson Therapy Trademark

Shortly after Dr. Issels' visit, the Gerson hospital moved into a new six-story facility, now named CHIPSA (Centro Hospitalario Internationale del Pacifico, S.A.). Cooperation with the Gerson Institute became strained as Charlotte tried to keep the treatment as close as possible to Gerson's, whereas the physician-owners kept trying to introduce their own ideas and modifications, often at the patients' expense, both monetarily and recovery-wise. The rift eventually led to a split, with the Gerson Institute no longer sending patients to CHIPSA. Instead, an arrangement was made with the Meridien Hospital in Tijuana to set up a special Gerson ward.

The separation from the Gerson Institute and Charlotte Gerson's supervision obviously created a crisis for the CHIPSA people, who had little credibility of their own. They hired Gar Hildenbrand, who had recently left the Gerson Institute under a cloud to help them market their services. Hildenbrand's coup was to convince Dr. Issels, now 87, to come to Mexico, lend his name and reputation to CHIPSA, and begin providing what they claimed was the "Gerson-Issels" therapy. Issels died less than two years later.

The split between the Gerson Institute and CHIPSA caused the Institute to decide to apply for a trademark on the term "The Gerson Therapy," but CHIPSA trademarked the name in Mexico, where the first applicant usually gets the trademark. The legal battle over the trademark continues, both in Mexico and the United States.

The Gerson Healing Newsletter, circulated by the Gerson Institute to interested persons, was started by Gar Hildenbrand when he was the Institute's executive director. After Hildenbrand's departure, I assumed editorship of the newsletter, and *The Gerson Healing Newsletter* evolved into its current bimonthly 12-page format. Its main features are articles relevant to Gerson Therapy, from the dangers of soy or root canals or Ritalin® to common mistakes or questions about the therapy. Gerson patients' recovery stories are also recounted, of course. Announcements of lectures and conventions of interest are posted. People automatically receive the newsletter for a year after their stay at the Gerson clinic. Naturally, other subscribers interested in or involved with the Gerson Therapy are welcomed through the Gerson Institute's website.

In 1993, when the Internet was mainly a curiosity for computer-savvy hobbyists, I saw the opportunity to distribute Gerson Therapy information electronically without the constant threat of censorship from the advertising-addicted commercial media. In my capacity as a member of the Institute's board of directors, I recommended an Internet site. The site soon became a primary means of reaching patients from around the world and a primary resource for patients undergoing treatment. Today, the site contains patient histories, photographs, newsletter articles, history, resource listings and historical information, as well as information about the regime and the authorized provider hospital.

The Gerson Healing Center, Sedona

In late 1996, the Gerson Institute's board of directors decided that, due to changes in the social, legal and medical climate in the United States, it was time to open another Gerson Therapy clinic in this country. The clinic could not be in located California since laws instituted there make the provision of such a therapy a felony, and the state vigorously prosecutes offenders. The California Medical Association has a body that judges the medical competency of physicians, with the power to cancel medical licenses if necessary. This power is often used to intimidate alternative and complementary physicians, but seldom to discipline truly incompetent physicians.

Arizona's laws seemed the most hospitable at the time, the main attraction being that MDs, naturopaths (NDs) and chiropractors (DCs) each had their own state boards, so that the MDs could not block the establishment and operation of a Gerson clinic. No treatment or medication that was illegal in the U.S. would be used.

A supporter promised financial backing up to $150,000, and the Gerson physicians at the Meridien Hospital in Mexico agreed to consult weekly at Sedona. I went off to Arizona with a check to start the venture. Half of an underutilized nursing home was procured, with the advantage that it already had the necessary licensure, under which the new clinic could easily operate.

The story of the Gerson Healing Center is an amazing one. The staff came miraculously out of the woodwork, ecstatic that they could finally do what their hearts had always told them to do. Some even commuted up to two hours from Phoenix and Flagstaff. The Gerson Institute sent patients to us. A physician and nursing staff were trained. The patients did very well.

Although the financial backing was always late and less than promised, the operation also went well until the "dirty tricks" department of the opposition kicked in. The medical doctor we had hired, who was operating under his naturopath's license, started to turn on us. Television interviews and stories were never aired. Health insurance companies refused to cover our treatments, placing inordinate strain on the already financially drained cancer patients. In the end, the owner of the nursing facility diverted most of our financing, such that we could no longer sustain the facility. Sadly, the Gerson Healing Center went bankrupt just 15 months after its opening.

Hospital Oasis de Esperanza

At this time, only the Hospital Oasis de Esperanza, owned and managed by the well-known medical family of Dr. Ernesto Contreras provides the highly effective, scientifically proven treatment Dr. Gerson intended for cancer patients.

This Gerson clinic exists for the purposes of providing the comprehensive Gerson therapy and concurrently instructing patients and their accompanying caregivers in how to continue the therapy regimen at home. Over the past quarter of a century, Charlotte Gerson and her staff at the Gerson Institute have labored to maintain the quality and integrity of the name Gerson at each of the clinics that she has helped to initiate. She has taken personal pride in the operation of the kitchens, the training of the physicians and nurses, and the patients' instruction, since they will have to continue the therapy when they return home. Her efforts have established the Gerson name as one with the highest levels of integrity and effectiveness among alternative therapy centers.

Unfortunately, other practitioners with less idealism have represented themselves as providing the Gerson therapy while providing either a badly diluted or unwisely altered treatment regimen, often at the expense of the health and well-being of patients who trusted the name Gerson without checking into the bona fides of the clinic they were entering.

Besides this clinic, the Gerson therapy has been administered with outstanding results in sanatoriums and hospitals in Manhattan, Nanuet and Spring Valley, New York; Los Angeles, California; and South Bend, Indiana. In recent years, the Gerson Institute has offered a practitioner course that has trained health care professionals from all over the world in the methods of administering the Gerson therapy to patients with all manner of degenerative diseases. At the Gerson clinics supervised by Charlotte Gerson, dozens of degenerative diseases besides cancer have been successfully treated over the years, including all four of the top killers in the United States — heart attack, cancer, stroke and diabetes — and even conditions that have defied diagnosis and have no names. Drug addiction yields easily, quickly and painlessly to this therapy. Long-festering wounds heal quickly and cleanly, chronic pain disappears in hours, painful conditions like rheumatoid arthritis and fibromyalgia can be reversed and the patient relieved using Dr. Gerson's methods.

The Gerson Books

For some years after Dr. Gerson's death in 1959, people who undertook the Gerson therapy on their own had to rely on acquiring the essential information from his book, A *Cancer Therapy*, which he had written for more the guidance of physicians than for use by patients. Fortunately, the book is accessible even for the medically unsophisticated and subsequent appendices have made it even more so.

The first changes made to A *Cancer Therapy* were the additions of Appendices I and II in about 1975. Appendix I is an essay by Charlotte Gerson, "Restoring the Healing Mechanism in Other Chronic Diseases," which attempts to overcome the limitations caused by the title, "A Cancer Therapy," and recognize the Gerson therapy as effective for other disease conditions. Her essay also speaks of dietary modifications for different diseases, offering instructions for putting together a less intensive diet for non-malignant diseases and a maintenance diet after the end of the intense therapy period. Appendix II is a transcript of a lecture given by Dr. Gerson in Escondido in 1956, "The Cure of Advanced Cancer by Diet Therapy: A Summary of 30 Years of Clinical Experimentation." (Freeman Cope published this item in *Physiological Chemistry and Physics*, just before his death.) Appendix III, added in 1989, contained an explanation of the omission of liver juice in the current therapy, titled "Contemporary Concerns in Raw Liver Juice Therapy." Further changes explained changes in the diet necessitated by the omission of the liver juice, such as the addition of Coenzyme Q-10. Flaxseed oil was added to supply EFAs, or essential fatty acids. Over the years the cover has been redesigned and updated several times. X-rays were digitally enhanced in the mid 1990s.

Over 350,000 copies of Gerson's book have been printed, in five languages, including German, Japanese, Rumanian and Korean translations. Over 90 percent of the books are in English. All publications of the English-language editions have been done by either Charlotte Gerson or by the Gerson Institute. The initial German-language edition, available for years but not wholly reflective of the original English version written by Max Gerson, was published by Hyperion Verlag in Freiburg im Breisgau, Germany. A few years ago, a new and complete German translation was issued by Waldthausen Verlag in Ritterhude bei Bremen, Germany. The Japanese edition was printed by Takuma Shoten, Tokyo. A sixth edition of the English version is scheduled for future publication.

The first book about Dr. Gerson, an expanded version of S.J. Haught's profile of the man and his therapy for a feature article in the *National Enquirer*, has endured a somewhat checkered publishing history. The *National Enquirer* declined to print Haught's positive appraisal of Dr. Gerson's character and his therapy, which was decidedly critical of the medical establishment's mistreatment of Dr. Gerson. After Dr Gerson died, S.J. Haught decided to develop his article into a book, but despite his diligent efforts, no mainstream house wanted to publish it. He finally succeeded in getting it issued by the London Press, in 1962, under the provocative title, *Has Dr. Gerson a True Cancer Cure?*

Apparently this publisher was a paperback house that specialized in pornography and fetishes. When Norman Fritz started to correspond with them about the copyright, he started getting mail advertising these books, with S.J. Haught's book at the bottom of the list! The publisher later changed his own name, several times. The copyright reverted to Haught because he was never paid royalties, and he sold the copyright to the Gerson Institute in 1983. The directors of the Institute didn't think that the original title was very snappy, but any change needed to stay within British law. In England, where many Gerson patients and prospects live, one can't even imply that there is a cancer cure without running afoul of the law. As long as the title was phrased as a question or imperative, rather than a statement, the title was "legal." Hence the new title of Haught's book became *Cancer—Think Curable! The Gerson Therapy*. When former Gerson Institute director Gar Hildenbrand reissued the book in 1991, having added some comments as well as pictures to it, it was retitled, *Censured for Curing Cancer: The American Experience of Dr. Max Gerson*.

This book is still in print, available from the Gerson Institute. The original publisher once claimed that the number of copies sold was in excess of 200,000, in 12 or 14 printings, but there was never any substantiation for these numbers. S. J. Haught, by the way, is a pseudonym. Having seen for himself what happened to people who openly gave their names in support of Dr. Gerson and his therapy, the reporter decided not to identify himself when publishing the book, initially or in subsequent editions. He still fears being known as the author of the Gerson book. The power of the opposition is awesome.

A very different book was written by Beata Bishop about the Gerson therapy. The Hungarian-born author took up residence in England after World War II, eventually becoming a psychotherapist and BBC documentary scriptwriter. A *Time to Heal*, published in Great Britain in 1985, summarized her experience in overcoming metastatic melanoma — one of the most intractable of cancer conditions — by undergoing treatment using the Gerson therapy, after surgery proved futile in halting the disease. She read A *Cancer Therapy*, conferred with Charlotte Gerson's daughter in London, Margaret Straus Dego, and lined up two physicians open to alternative cancer treatment modes who were willing to monitor her condition. Then Bishop traveled to Tijuana, Mexico, for a two-month stay at the Gerson clinic there, and afterwards returned to London and faithfully continued the difficult dietary regimen, despite numerous obstacles, for the requisite year and a half.

Beata Bishop, now a woman in her early 70s, is alive and well, without a recurrence of cancer and still sticking to the modified Gerson diet. The caption "Triumph over cancer . . . The therapy of the future" accompanies the author's photo on the book's dust cover. As she maintains,

> My basic tenets are unchanged. I know that dietary therapy works. I believe that there will be no real breakthrough in the treatment of the killer diseases of civilisation until food is recognised as the most basic vital key to health, the womb-to-tomb factor that determines are well-being, energy level, resistance to disease, state of mind, behaviour, rate of ageing and lifespan. In the light of what is already known about the impact of nutrition, it seems crazy to try and tackle chronic degenerative diseases without analysing minutely patients' eating habits — and knowing how to correct them. Yet that is happening today. The doctors' only excuse is ignorance. Nutrition is barely touched upon in medical training.
>
> I suspect that medicine's corporate indifference to diet springs from the probably unformulated macho view that diet equals food equals kitchen equals woman's work, and that makes it inferior by definition and unworthy of scientific interests. In other words, food is yet another feminine value that has been degraded and banished from its proper place by our overweeningly masculine order. Now it must be restored. Doctors will have to learn how to use diet as a tool of prevention and healing, if only to keep up with their better-educated patients and with the growing number of non-medical practitioners who already use dietary therapy successfully.
>
> Once they have broken through the barrier of their own indifference, doctors may realise that nutrition is too important to be left to the profit-centred processing industry, and that the heavily advertised junk foods that flood the market actually create an overfed but undernourished population. Perhaps they will begin to question the use of countless chemical additives whose cumulative effects are unknown, and denounce the dreadful meals served in so many hospitals, schools

and old people's homes. Some doctors might even consider the revolutionary possibility of treating addiction and rehabilitating the old through correct feeding, two topical areas that need urgent exploration. Enlightened doctors would have a great deal to do. They might even stop living on junk foods themselves and improve their health.

From where I sit today, all that seems a dizzily ambitious scenario. Yet even if it came true tomorrow, our health problems would only be eased, not solved, for we would still be up against a poisoned ecosystem which is in turn poisoning us. (pp. 260-261)

Several other patients healed of degenerative diseases have written books about their recovery experience, including a Japanese medical professor who cured his own colon cancer that had spread to the liver and an American medical professor who cured her own breast cancer, both using Gerson's book as their guide.

Max Gerson's life and career have also been portrayed in a documentary novel by Giuliano Dego, an Italian-born poet and professor of literature at the University of London, who is married to Charlotte Gerson's daughter, Margaret (Peggy). In *Doctor Max* he combines the telling of Dr. Gerson's own life story and the Gerson Institute with a complex, largely European-set suspense plot concerning nefarious attempts over many decades to suppress knowledge of the Gerson therapy, which includes persecuting and killing people who actively promote it. The cover of *Doctor Max* announces it as "The story of pioneering physician Max Gerson's acclaimed cancer therapy and his heroic struggle to change the way we look at health and healing." The stories pertaining to Max Gerson's own career as a physician are based on facts and documents; the introduced characters are fictional and the plot connecting them with Dr. Gerson are fabricated. First published in 1997 in the United States, an Italian version of the biographical novel later appeared in Italy, where Dego won the coveted Premio Nazionale Latina per il Tascabile, or the Latina National Paperback Book Award in 1999.

Charlotte Gerson and the well-known health writer Dr. Morton Walker have co-authored a book, published by Kensington Press, that extends the clinical experience of Dr. Gerson, adding to it the results of 25 additional years of treatment. *The Gerson Therapy: Healing Cancer and Other Degenerative Diseases* is written for those who wish to undertake the Gerson therapy, featuring discussions of disease treatments described besides those for cancer, with the therapy adapted specially for them; practical information for doing the therapy; recipes for Gerson therapy and maintenance diet. There are many inspiring recovered-patient stories. The book has no X-rays or formal medical case histories, as in A *Cancer Therapy* — which Dr. Gerson wrote more as a textbook for other physicians than as a guide for patients.

Other authors have favorably presented the work of Dr. Max Gerson, notably

Ralph W. Moss in *The Cancer Industry* (a new, updated edition of "the classic exposé of the cancer industry," published in 1996, of *The Cancer Syndrome*, which originally appeared in 1980); Maurice Natenberg in *The Cancer Blackout* (published in 1959 and later reprinted); and a chapter by Katherine Smith on "Dr. Max Gerson's Nutritional Therapy for Cancer and Other Diseases" in *Suppressed Inventions & Other Discoveries*, a volume edited by Jonathan Eisen, which includes chapters on several other controversial cancer therapies (Avery Publishing Group, New York, 1999).

The Gerson therapy is the oldest, best documented, scientifically based and proven of the holistic therapies. Virtually every book or publication that catalogs diet and health, particularly with respect to cancer, touches on the Gerson therapy or its principles — although acknowledgment of that fact often is not given by authors or editors, who may not even be acquainted with Dr. Gerson's work. Most diet-based cancer therapies are based directly or indirectly on the Gerson diet, most notably is the Kelley treatment, advocated and offered by Dr. Nicholas Gonzales.

Dr. Gerson's Reputation

In the 1980s Dr. Patricia Spain Ward, one of the most eminent medical historians in the United States, was commissioned by the U.S. Congressional Office of Technology Assessment (OTA) to evaluate alternative methods of cancer management. After reviewing all relevant literature pertaining to Dr. Gerson's work, she wrote a report on the "History of the Gerson Therapy," citing the proven value of this treatment regimen and describing the unjust attacks by the medical establishment on Max Gerson . However, the OTA administrative staff suppressed the circulation of the report to OTA advisors, an action which was vigorously protested by Gerson therapy advocates before the cause was taken up by Senator Charles Grassley of the Technology Assessment Board, who helped to force the belated publication of the report in 1988.

Dr. Ward's report on the "History of the Gerson Therapy" provides a telling coda to the story of Max Gerson's life and career as it parallels the development of complementary and alternative medical treatments for serious disease conditions like cancer. As Dr. Ward begins her report:

> It is one of the least edifying facts of recent American medical history that the profession's leadership so long rejected as quackish the idea that nutrition affects health (JAMA 1946, 1949, 1977; Shimkin, 1976). Ignoring both the empirical dietary wisdom that pervaded western medicine from the pre-Christian Hippocratic era until the late nineteenth century and a persuasive body of modern research in nutritional biochemistry, the politically minded spokesmen of organized medicine in the U.S. remained long committed to surgery

and radiation as the sole acceptable treatments for cancer. This commitment persisted, even after sound epidemiological data showed that early detection and removal of malignant tumors did not "cure" most kinds of cancer (Crile, 1956; updated by Cairns, 1985).

The historical record shows that progress lagged especially in cancer immunotherapy–including nutrition and hyperthermia–because power over professional affiliation and publication (and hence over practice and research) rested with men who were neither scholars nor practitioners nor researchers themselves, and who were often unequipped to grasp the rapidly evolving complexities of the sciences underlying mid-20th-century medicine.

Nowhere is this maladaption of professional structure to medicine's changing scientific context more tragically illustrated than in the American experience of Max B. Gerson (1881-1959), founder of the best-known nutritional treatment for cancer of the pre-macrobiotic era. A scholar's scholar and a superlative observer of clinical phenomena, Gerson was a product of the German medical education which Americans in the late 19th and early 20th centuries considered so superior to our own that all who could afford it went to Germany to perfect their training (Bonner, 1963). As a medical graduate of the University of Freiburg in 1909, Gerson imbibed all of the latest in scientific medicine, with the emphasis on specificity which bacteriology had brought into western medical thought in the preceding decades. Gerson subsequently worked with leading German specialists in internal medicine, in physiological chemistry, and in neurology (U.S. Congress, 1946, 98). . . .

Trained in the theories of specific disease causation and treatment that began to dominate western medicine–for the first time in history–as bacteriological discoveries multiplied in the late 19th century, Gerson was at first uneasy about using a single therapy in such seemingly disparate conditions. But he was committed to the primacy of clinical evidence, which he liked to express in Kussmaul's dictum: "The result at the sick-bed is decisive" (quoted in Gerson, 1958, 212). In later years, after research began to provide explanations for Gerson's clinical observations, he quoted Churchill on the mistaken course of action he had thus avoided: "Men occasionally stumble over the truth, but most pick themselves up and hurry off as if nothing had happened" (Gerson, 1958, 212). Gerson persisted.

After detailing Gerson's professional qualifications, summarizing his work in treating tuberculosis through dietary measures and describing his gradual involvement with cancer patients, Dr. Ward expounds upon the scientific underpinnings of the rationale for the Gerson therapy:

Gerson constantly sought explanations for his observations in the scientific literature, where he read widely in several languages (Gerson, 1958). In 1954, in Cancer, a Problem of Metabolism, he credited J. Maisin (1923) and B. Fischer-Wasels (1929) with advancing physiological explanations of general predisposition toward tumor formation and abandoning the theory of cancer causation by local irritation. For the next few decades (according to Gerson's account of the evolution of cancer concepts) there was a tendency to interpret cancer in terms of constitution and diathesis, as was done with diabetes, gout and tuberculosis. It was Caspari (Nutrition and Cancer, 1938) who turned to metabolic explanation of the kind Gerson ultimately favored (Gerson, 1954, 1). He devoted an entire chapter of his book to a review of efforts, largely by German researchers, to alter metabolism by diet (Gerson, 1958, 89-104). He found special appeal in Otto Warburg, The Metabolism of Tumors, (London, 1930), in G. von Bergmann's Funktionelle Pathologie (Berlin, 1932), and in Frederick Hoffman's massive compilation, Cancer and Diet (Baltimore, 1937).

Gradually, out of his bedside experience and his reading, he formed a unitary theory of degenerative disease (including cancer) which rested on one of the oldest and most pervasive concepts in the history of medicine: the vis medicatrix naturae or healing power of nature (Neuburger, 1926 and 1944; Warner, 1978). Endlessly seeking out the latest researches and theories in physiology, biochemistry, and–increasingly–immunology, Gerson rapidly integrated these massive bodies of new detail into the larger framework of what he called "the physician within", that is, the natural powers of resistance, which we today call the immune system.

Gerson believed that cancer changes the body's normal sodium/potassium balance, already disturbed by modern diet. Thus his therapy used foods low in sodium (no salt added), high in potassium, and rich in vitamins A and C and oxidizing enzymes. He excluded fats and dairy products for the first four to six weeks, considering them dangerously burdensome to the digestion in the extremely sick patients who usually came to him only after having exhausted conventional measures. Above all it was essential for patients to eliminate excess sodium, which Gerson believed responsible for altering cellular electrochemistry in favor of cancerous growth.

Dr. Ward notes that various investigations had confirmed some of Dr. Gerson's tenets since his death in 1959:

> There is now a great deal of research suggesting possible mechanisms for the efficacy of Gerson's high potassium/low sodium diet. As he suspected and we now know, hypokalemia often accompanies cancer of the colon, and alterations in electrical and mineral states occur often in cancer patients (Newell,

1981, 87). Cone has furnished experimental proof of a correlation between the level of electrical potential across somatic cell membranes and the intensity of mitotic activity (Cone, 1971), a finding supported by Zs.-Nagy and his colleagues in studies so human thyroid cancer (Zs.-Nagy, 1983). Ling's association/induction hypothesis is based on laboratory studies which show that damaged cells partially return to their normal configuration in high potassium/low sodium environments (Ling, 1943), perhaps explaining the remarkable tissue repair which Gerson sometimes saw in his formerly debilitated patients (Cope, 1978). Lai has suggested that intracellular sodium and potassium levels may furnish the mechanism for regulating cellular differentiation and transformation (Lai, 1985).

To supply active oxidation enzymes and potassium-rich minerals, Gerson's patients drank hourly glasses of freshly prepared vegetable and fruit juices. As early as 1933-34, while living in Vienna, Gerson had begun giving injections of liver extract, as another means of stimulating the patient's liver (Gerson, 1958, 31-32). In later years he had patients drink two to three glasses daily of the juice of calves' liver pressed with carrots. In addition to beta-carotene/vitamin A, this would supply iron and copper, both of which affect peripheral T cell functions and other peripheral lymphocyte subpopulations (Keusch, 1983, 345- 347).

Although the AMA Council on Pharmacy and Chemistry labeled as a "false notion" the idea that diet can affect cancer, recent researchers have found that "nutritional status plays a critical role in immunological defense mechanisms at a number of important levels" (Keusch, 1983, 345) and that nutritional factors "can have profound influences on . . . the development and manifestations of cancers" as well as other diseases (Good, 1982, 85). In "The Cancerostatic Effect of Vegetarian Diets" (1983), Siguel describes as the ideal way to strengthen bodily defenses against neoplastic cells a diet similar to Gerson's: high in carbohydrates and vegetables, low in protein.

Like von Bergmann, Gerson believed that "every defense and healing power of the body depends on the capacity of the body to produce a so-called 'allergic inflammation' — a truth long recognized by surgeons, but somehow forgotten by medicine during the heyday of microbiology. To Gerson this capacity to produce inflammation was "the decisive part of the body's 'weapon of healing power'" (Gerson, 1958, 127-28).

Dr. Ward gave credibility, too, to the efficacy of the unpleasant, seemingly regressive "flare-ups" or healing reactions that Dr. Gerson believed were crucial in destroying cancerous tissue. She explained why the recovering body, from Gerson's perspective, must be assisted by rapid detoxification and supported by the constant infusion of nutrients. From her point of view, even the much-derided coffee enema made sense:

Noting that fluid from a normal inflammation metabolism kills cancer cells, but that blood serum does not, von Bergmann concluded that a cancer metabolism occurs when the body can no longer produce this healing inflammatory reaction (Gerson, 1958, 120- 121). Gerson agreed, but in contrast to von Bergmann and most of his contemporaries, Gerson believed it was often possible for the physician to help restore the vital power of inflammation, even in anergic patients with advanced cancer. If cancer was a degenerative disease caused by the cumulative effect of inadequate nutrition with foods grown in soils depleted by artificial fertilizers and poisoned by toxic insecticides and herbicides, doctors must respond by replenishing the entire human organism. For a condition that represented an ultimate failure of equilibrium in a poisoned metabolism, removal of tumors by surgery or radiation was merely superficial, symptomatic treatment. "Medicine," Gerson said, "must be able to adapt its therapeutic methods to the damages of the processes of our modern civilization" (Gerson, 1958, 199).

Gerson set about doing this by altering the basic diet he had used earlier in other conditions. Through meticulous observation of his patients in New York (where he passed state boards in 1939), he perfected a regimen of detoxication and diet requiring a high degree of compliance by the patient, heroic devotion by the patient's family, and close attention and frequent adjustment by the physician. His therapy aimed to detoxify the body and restore its healing apparatus, especially the liver, the visceral nervous system, and the reticulo-mesenchymal system.

Gerson first encountered the idea of detoxication in cancer in the version of Hippocratic regimen which he read with his first cancer patient in Bielefeld in 1928 (Gerson, 1958, 404). After losing several cancer patients to hepatic coma rather than to direct effects of the disease (Gerson, 1958, 191), he realized that "The digestive tract is very much poisoned in cancer". The liver and pancreas failed to function: "nothing is active" (Gerson, 1958, 407). To stimulate the liver, he began to use coffee enemas, which O.A. Meyer of Goettingen had found effective in opening the bile ducts in animals and which American surgeons in that period were using in acute adrenal insufficiency and in shock from post-operative hemorrhage and bleeding peptic ulcer (Beeson, 1980, 90, 96; Rothstein, 1987, 124). As he watched the progress of his patients, he found that he could accelerate detoxication by giving coffee enemas more frequently, with the addition of castor oil, by mouth and by rectum (Gerson, 1958, 81).

Although Gerson used caffeine enemas primarily to facilitate excretion of toxic wastes, especially from necrosing tumors, we now realize that these enemas also promoted the absorption of vitamin A, a process requiring the action of bile acids (Simone, 1943, 64). Thus the enemas that brought ridicule from

Gerson's enemies actually enabled his patients to use the enormous amounts of vitamin A which his diet provided (recently estimated at about 100,000 IU daily: see Seifter, 1988). Vitamin A, in turn, plays a vital role in immune function, perhaps by causing the helper cells to induce the production of interleukin-2, or by causing killer cell precursors to activate cytotoxic mechanisms, or by causing suppressor T cells to eliminate down regulation (Keusch, 1983, 330-331).

Gerson also found that caffeine enemas greatly reduce pain, a particular boon in his regimen, which avoids the use of opiates and other painkilling drugs that might overtax the liver at a time when its limited capacity is needed for immune functions and for eliminating the toxic products of tumor breakdown.

Dr. Ward explains why Dr. Gerson added some 'new' vitamins and minerals to the Gerson diet:

One of these was niacin, which he believed would help restore proper intracellular potential, raise depleted liver stores of glycogen and potassium, and aid in protein metabolism (Gerson, 1958, 32, 99-100, 209). [It also opens capillaries and therefore promotes circulation.] Another was iodine, which Gerson initially used only in cases of low metabolic rates. When he found that "The best range of healing power" was a BMR of + 6 to + 8 (monitored by organic iodine in blood serum), and that iodine seemed to counteract the neoplastic effect of hormones, he incorporated iodine into the basic regimen, at first in the form of thyroid extract, later as inorganic Lugol's solution (iodine plus potassium iodide) (Gerson, 1958, 32, 409; U.S. Congress, 1946, 114). Several researchers have showed that thyroid raises natural resistance to infection by augmenting the power of reticuloendothelial cells and by increasing antibody formation – thus supporting Gerson's hunch that iodine was a decisive factor in the normal differentiation of cells (Lurie, 1960; Thorbecke, 1962).

Dr. Ward's report also challenges the 1949 JAMA article that had attacked the Gerson dietary therapy as highly questionable.

Although the AMA Council on Pharmacy and Chemistry labeled as a "false notion" the idea that diet can affect cancer, recent researchers have found that "nutritional status plays a critical role in immunological defense mechanisms at a number of important levels" (Keusch, 1983, 345) and that nutritional factors "can have profound influences on . . . the development and manifestations of cancers" as well as other diseases (Good, 1982, 85). In "The Cancerostatic Effect of Vegetarian Diets" (1983), Siguel describes as the ideal way to strengthen bodily defenses against neoplastic cells a diet similar to Gerson's: high in carbohydrates and vegetables, low in protein.

Then, one by one, Dr. Ward touches upon salient incidents in the long succession of Dr. Gerson's problems with the medical establishment, which appeared to begin after his first publication, in 1945:

> Despite the fact that he had no inpatient facility until 1946 . . . Gerson managed, through his thriving Park Avenue practice and an affiliation at Gotham Hospital, to amass enough data to publish a preliminary report in 1945. He presented his rather remarkable case histories modestly, concluding that he did not yet have enough evidence to say whether diet could either influence the origin of cancer or alter the course of an established tumor. He claimed only that the diet, which he described in considerable detail, could favorably affect the patient's general condition, staving off the consequences of malignancy and making further treatment possible (Gerson, 1945).
>
> Gerson may have struck an Establishment nerve with his statement that many physicians use surgery and/or radiation "without systematic treatment of the patient as a whole" (Gerson, 1945, 419). But it seems more likely that it was his growing success in practice, or perhaps even his opposition to tobacco, that first drew the wrath of organized medicine. (Philip Morris was then JAMA's major source of advertising revenue: see Rorty, 1939, 182-194).
>
> In any case the AMA did not openly attack Gerson until November 1946, a few months after he testified in support of a Senate bill to appropriate $100 million to bring together the world's outstanding cancer experts in order to coordinate a search for the prevention and cure of cancer. At hearings before Senator Claude Pepper's sub-committee in July 1946, Gerson demonstrated recovered patients who had come to him after conventional methods could no longer help. Dr. George Miley, medical director of the 85-bed Gotham Hospital, where Gerson had treated patients since January, 1946, gave strong supporting medical testimony (U.S. Congress, 1946).
>
> In a surly editorial response, JAMA said it was "fortunate" that this Senate appearance received little newspaper publicity; the AMA was clearly outraged that Gerson's appearance had become the subject of a favorable radio commentary, broadcast nationwide by ABC's Raymond Gram Swing (U.S. Congress, 1946, 31-35; JAMA, 1946). The JAMA editorial focused on Gerson, even though it was not Gerson but a lay witness, immune to AMA retaliation, who had called Gerson's successes "miracles" and urged the Senators to secure their future cancer commission against control by any existing medical organization (U.S. Congress, 1946, 96,97).
>
> It was not Gerson, but Dr. Miley, who told the Senators that a long-term survey by a well-known and respected physician showed that those who received no cancer treatment lived longer than those who received surgery,

radiation or X-ray (U.S. Congress, 1946, 117). Perhaps because Miley was a Northwestern medical graduate, an established physician licensed in four states, and a fellow of the AMA and state and county societies of Pennsylvania and New York, Morris Fishbein did not attack him personally. Instead, he limited himself to intimations of fiscal impropriety in the Robinson Foundation, which owned Miley's Gotham Hospital, and to the scandalous revelation that the director of the section on health education of this Foundation (which was promoting "an unestablished, somewhat questionable method of treating cancer") was not an M.D. at all, but a Yale University professor of economics!

Compared to Miley's testimony, Gerson's was innocent, concentrating on the histories of the patients he brought with him and on the likely mechanisms whereby his diet caused tumor regression and healing. Only under pressure from Senator Pepper did Gerson state that about 30% of those he treated showed a favorable response (U.S. Congress, 1946, 115). Nonetheless, JAMA devoted two pages to undermining Gerson's integrity (JAMA, 1946). Showing no restraint where Gerson was concerned, Fishbein, contrary to fact, alleged that successes with the Gerson-Sauerbruch-Hermannsdorfer diet "were apparently not susceptible of duplication by most other observers." He also falsely claimed that Gerson had several times refused to supply the AMA with details of the diet. (Fishbein said he could provide them in this editorial only because "there has come to hand through a prospective patient" of Gerson a diet schedule for his treatment.) Fishbein emphasized, without comment, Gerson's caution about the use of other medications, especially anesthetics, because they produced dangerously strong reactions in the heightened allergic state of his most responsive patients.

Fishbein attempted to tie together this strange patchwork of slurs against Gerson and against research supported by lay-dominated industrial corporations with his accustomed mastery of innuendo: "The entire performance, including the financial backing, the promotion and the scientific reports, has a peculiar effluvium which, to say the least, is distasteful and, at its worst, creates doubt and suspicion" (JAMA, 1946, 646).

Through no fault of his own, Gerson was again portrayed favorably in the news in 1947, when John Gunther, in Death Be Not Proud, credited Gerson with extending the life of Gunther's son during the boy's ultimately unsuccessful struggle with brain cancer. Beginning that same year the New York County Medical Society staged five "investigations" of Gerson and eventually suspended him for "advertising" his "secret" methods.

At this point Gerson's life took on a nightmare quality. The Pepper-Neely bill met defeat and, with it, the hope for coordinated cancer research free of prior restraints against investigations of anything other than "established" methods. In

1949 the AMA Council on Pharmacy and Chemistry, in a report entitled "Cancer and the Need for Facts", rehashed material from the earlier editorial, adding that the Gerson diet was "lacking in essential protein and fat" and that Gerson's concern about the dangers of anesthesia was "wholly unfounded and apparently designed to appeal to the cancer victim already fearful of a surgical operation which might offer the only effective means for eradication of the disease." Without benefit of either a literature search or new clinical or laboratory research, the Council labeled as a "false notion" the idea that "diet has any specific influence on the origin or progress of cancer." They concluded that "There is no scientific evidence whatsoever to indicate that modifications in the dietary intake of food or other nutritional essentials are of any specific value in the control of cancer" (Council on Pharmacy and Chemistry, 1949, 96). Gerson lost his hospital affiliation and found that young doctors who wanted to assist him and learn from him could not do so, for fear of incurring Society discipline. He was denied malpractice insurance, because his therapy was not "accepted practice" (Moss, 1980, 178; Natenberg, 1959, 136).

In the early fifties Gerson submitted five case histories to the NCI, requesting an official investigation. He was told that they would need 25 cases, which he promptly supplied, with full documentation. More than a year later the NCI demanded 125 case histories, saying that the 25 they had previously requested were insufficient to justify investigation.

According to a 1981 publication of the Gerson Institute, headed by his daughter, Charlotte Gerson, a manuscript for a book he was writing about his therapy disappeared from his files in 1956 (Healing, 1981, 19) At the age of 75, isolated from medical colleagues and unable to find assistants, Gerson undertook the work of rewriting the entire manuscript in order to show "that there is an effective treatment of cancer, even in advanced cases" (Gerson, 1958, 3). It was published in 1958, as A Cancer Therapy: Results of Fifty Cases. Gerson died of pneumonia the following year, before finishing a second volume. His ideas have gained wide distribution through subsequent editions of his book (1975, 1977, and 1986); through a 1962 publication called Has Dr. Max Gerson a True Cancer Cure? [since renamed Censured for Curing Cancer: The American Experience of Dr. Max Gerson], which had reportedly sold more than 250,000 copies by 1980 (Moss, 1980, 178); and through the publications and physician-training programs of the Gerson Institute in Bonita, California, and the Hospital de Baja California.

In 1980 a reformed JAMA carried a commentary called "The 'Grand Conspiracy' Against the Cancer Cure" by William Regelson of the Department of Medicine of the Medical College of Virginia. Surveying a series of "inappropriate judgments [that] have resulted in injury to good observations," Regelson said, "We may shortly have to ask if Gerson's low-sodium diet, with its bizarre coffee enemas and thyroid supplementation, was an approach that altered the mitotic regulating effect of intracellular sodium for occasional clinical validity in those patients with the stamina to survive it" (Regelson, 1980, 338).

Disregarding such suggestions and resting its case instead on the claim that the NCI had "found no convincing evidence of effectiveness" during a review of ten Gerson cases some forty years earlier, the American Cancer Society in 1987 stated that "The Gerson method of cancer treatment is not considered a proven means of cancer treatment, and on the basis of available information, the Institute does not believe that further evaluation of this therapy is called for at this time" (American Cancer Society, February 5, 1987).

Dr. Ward closes her report by mentioning a then-ongoing cancer-treatment program initiated in 1984 in Austria that was testing, with closely matched patients as controls, "a modified form of Gerson's therapy." In Max Gerson's view, the nutrients omitted from this 'modified' regimen (such as niacin, iodine and liver juice) and the lack of detoxification programs (as with coffee enemas) would have disqualified the study, yet after four years, outcomes appeared quite favorable in a number of the Gerson patients. For some patients, this meant extending their life span, reducing pain and improving overall quality of life. As Dr. Ward observes, "It is an irony of both history and geography that the first comparative study of Max Gerson's therapy should take place at the hands of surgeons, in that part of the world which Gerson fled as a Jewish refugee half a century ago and that the results, while not so outstanding as those he seemed able to produce, are most encouraging in patients with severe damage to the liver, the organ he considered central to recovery." Although Dr. Ward lamented the lack of interest on the part of the American medical establishment in a truly objective, scientific investigation of Max Gerson's cancer treatment methods in a clinical setting, she saw hope in this Austrian study:

> Testing is underway, however, outside of the U.S. Since 1984 a modified form of Gerson's therapy has been in use at the Second Department of Surgery of the [Landesk]rankenhaus in Graz, Austria. Omitting liver juice and niacin, using thyroid only in hypothyroid patients, and limiting caffeine enemas to two per day, Peter Lechner and his colleagues, all of them surgeons, have been testing the Gerson method as an adjunct, often with chemotherapy or radiation, in 60 postoperative cancer patients, male and female, ranging in age from 23 to 74, and representing many different forms of cancer. By pairing each patient who was willing to use the Gerson method (GP) with one of similar age and condition who chose not to try it (NGP) and observing the comparative progress of the disease in the two groups over a four-year period, Lechner and his colleagues have approximated a controlled study of admittedly imperfect structure (Lechner,

1987). Their findings show that the Gerson therapy made a notable difference in several forms of cancer.

In 1990, Drs. Lechner and Kronberger published a follow-up report, "Experience with the Use of Dietary Therapy in Surgical Oncology," in *Aktuelle Ernaehrungsmedizin* (*Topical Nutritional Medicine*), where they concluded:

> It can be seen that the patients treated with the adjuvant nutritional therapy are in a better general condition, with less risk of complications, and they also tolerate radiation and chemotherapy better than patients who do not follow the diet. To what extent nutritional therapy yields benefits with regard to the basic disease process and to life expectation will have to be established over a long period of time by studying a larger number of patients.

This long-term Austrian study being conducted by surgeons involved the use of radiation and chemotherapy following surgery—all modes of treatment that Max Gerson opposed, except for the use of surgery under certain essential conditions. The patients in this study who had enrolled in the special-diet program apparently remained in better condition, despite the damage being done to them by the standard slash/burn/poison tactics.

Properly conducting a clinical trial of the Gerson therapy on cancer patients would be very costly indeed as well as time-consuming. Trials would have to take place in a highly supervised residential clinical setting for a period of at least a year and a half in order to determine its effectiveness in bringing about significant remissions that possibly might lead to cures (five-year survivals without cancer recurrence). It would not be possible to employ double-blind clinical trials, since anyone undergoing or administering the Gerson therapy would be aware of it. Nevertheless, in some clinical situations an effort has been made to use matched controls: that is, patients with comparable conditions who chose not to follow the Gerson restrictions and instead undergo the suggested standard treatment for particular types of cancer. Similarly, comparisons have occasionally been made between Gerson cancer patients and comparable patients undertaking other forms of treatment or not receiving any treatment at all, in terms of pain levels, progression or regression of tumors, overall mood and outcome (including survival time).

Despite the difficulty of conducting statistical studies of Gerson patient outcomes, some studies have been done. Probably the most notable one was done by Gar Hildenbrand on melanoma, which indicated that the Gerson therapy was considerably more effective on metastatic melanoma than the conventional treatments. In advanced disease stages that are preponderantly fatal when no treatment or standard treatment (surgery, chemotherapy, radiation) is given, the Gerson patients did markedly better. The Hildenbrand melanoma study, published in the peer-reviewed journal *Alternative Therapies in Health and Medicine* (September 1995,) used five-year survival rates as a measure of efficacy. In early stage I and II melanoma, the Gerson therapy was as effective as more conventional therapies, but in the later, more difficult stages the Gerson therapy results began to outstrip allopathic methods. In stage III melanoma, 82 percent of the patients were alive after five years, as opposed to 41 percent for conventional medicine, and in stage IV — melanoma that was widely spread or metastasized to internal organs—39 percent of Gerson patients were alive after five years, compared with only 6 percent of those who had been treated by the most successful standard methods. Interestingly, no patients with melanoma above the neck had survived five or more years.

Like Dr. Ward's report, these results can no longer be ignored by the medical community. As S.J. Haught speculated:

> The history of medicine is a story of almost incredible stupidity, and a story of almost incredible genius and perseverance. Nearly every single advance, nearly every single discovery, has met with such furious opposition by the medical fraternity that one wonders how medicine has advanced at all. Years, decades, sometimes centuries were allowed to elapse between discovery and approval, and millions of lives were lost because of it. Medical pioneers have been imprisoned, executed, hounded, and driven insane for their genius. Their names are now the names of heroes, and every schoolboy knows them.
>
> Does Dr. Gerson's name belong on the list?
>
> Tomorrow, will the world say of him, "He was a fool who offered hope where there was no hope, and life when there was no life to give?"
>
> Or will they say, "He could look at the evidence planted in the universe and from it derive a new concept, and a greater thing than this no mind can accomplish."

The Future of the Gerson Therapy

Since Max Gerson's death in 1959, degenerative diseases have certainly not decreased. The majority of us will experience some degenerative disease in our lifetime, and someone close to us will surely die prematurely from cancer, diabetes, cardiovascular disease, or some other preventable disease. Our children are increasingly prone to cancer, diabetes, drug addiction and obesity—and at ever-earlier ages. Antibiotics, the wonder drugs of the post World War II era, have been so overused in medicine and in food animal husbandry that most organisms against which we were once protected can no longer be controlled by these once-powerful substances. We have become an "addictive" society. Most people are 'addicted' to one or more drugs, ranging from prescription and over-the-counter drugs to stimulants and 'recreational' drugs — coffee, alcohol, tobacco, marijuana, cocaine and heroin. Obesity has assumed epidemic proportions, to the point that half the population in the United States is overweight and one in five people grossly so. Chronic pain and non-healing wound clinics are thriving. Previously unknown diseases are surfacing: HIV/AIDS, hantavirus, Legionnaires' disease, Lyme disease, chronic fatigue syndrome and hepatitis C, among others. Public health nightmares like Ebola and Marburg viruses are poised to spread throughout the world. Even tuberculosis, once nearly eradicated in the United States, is spreading rapidly again in strains that are resistant to most antibiotics. Tuberculosis was one of the first diseases that Dr. Gerson was able to cure — there is no way for tubercle bacilli to develop a resistance to a strong human immune system.

As Dr. Gerson recognized, at the root of these disorders is a single but complex factor: the nature of our food supply. Blame goes not so much to the monstrous volume of calories taken in daily (largely from fats and sugar), but to the paucity of nutritional value and the presence of toxins in what people consume. Man-made, often carcinogenic chemicals, undesirable hormones and antibiotics are introduced at all points along the food production line, from soil and water through the feed lot and processing plants to supermarket shelf. In the developing world, people's extreme vulnerability to infectious diseases is definitely linked to gross malnutrition and the changeover from wholesome, well-balanced native food to the high tech diet of the so-called developed world.

As a society we are extremely concerned about educating our children: making sure that they can capably read, write, do arithmetic and operate computers. However, our obligation to teach them the very rudiments of nutrition, so as to ensure their future well-being, is woefully neglected. We fail not just in providing them with healthy food (including prenatally), but also in serving as role models in the purchase, preparation and consumption of food. As a culture we have also become commercially programmed to believe that eating Big Macs and drinking soda pop are desirable human habits.

However, a substantial minority of us have become so dissatisfied with the perennially empty pronouncements of the established medical authorities that we have shown ourselves increasingly willing to entrust our health care to complementary and alternative medical (CAM) practitioners, despite the direst warnings of many physicians. The growing popularity of unorthodox or alternative medicine was highlighted in a 1999 study in the *Journal of the American Medical Association* showing that 42.1 percent of Americans go beyond the traditional medical establishment for treatment, a 50 percent increase since 1990. In 1999, Americans spent $27 billion on alternative medicine consultations, treatments and medications. While these expenditures were largely out-of-pocket because such treatments are not covered by health insurance policies, some insurance companies and HMOs (health maintenance organizations) have begun to recognize the competitive advantage of offering certain select CAM benefits, such as chiropractic, to their subscriber-members. Experiments by medical insurance carriers in this area have shown a 10-fold short-term and up to a 20-fold long-term return on investment when nutritional methods are used as health management tools rather than relying solely on drugs and surgery.

Special research programs focusing on unorthodox treatment methods are now being set up in medical and health science centers. The majority of American medical schools have instituted courses in alternative medical practices – botanical or herbal medicine, homeopathy, traditional Chinese medicine, acupuncture and acupressure, mind/body medicine, hydrotherapy, detoxification and nutritional therapy. And research is pointing toward the effectiveness of the methods Dr. Gerson pioneered years ago — and for which he was so viciously attacked. Report after report announces that substances found in fresh fruits and vegetables act to prevent cancer. The same authorities now recognize that environmental toxins irritate, if not cause, cancer conditions.

While the Dr. Gerson's therapy may not be a panacea, this medical program has been shown over the past 60 years to cure (yes, *cure*) serious degenerative diseases, relieve chronic pain and promote healing. The amount of suffering that could be immediately alleviated by the widespread administration of this treatment is immense, even without considering the *preventive* benefits of the Gerson diet and detoxification regime. One of the most controversial aspects of the Gerson therapy, the coffee enema may yet prove to be one of the most effective contributions ever made to the therapy of degenerative diseases. There is no other means known of detoxifying the liver so powerfully or so quickly. There is little danger of overdose or toxic reaction. The cost is pennies per dose. The pain relief aspects alone should make it a standard treatment for cancer and migraine.

By treating the degenerative diseases that threaten us, Dr. Gerson showed his understanding of the origins of disease and health. Cancer and most of the other degenerative diseases have at their roots the deficiency and toxicity of our contemporary food supply. This results in a progressive degeneration of the body's ability to fight off abnormal cells or other conditions, and leads eventually to cancer or one of the other dread diseases. More than one in three people in the United States will at some time suffer from cancer. This percentage is rising, not falling, despite technological advancements in medical treatments.

Treating a degenerative disease at the site of the symptom with surgery, radiation or chemotherapy, as is the current medical practice, is no more useful than mopping the floor during a rainstorm without fixing the gaping hole in the roof. Until medicine changes its basic direction, there can be no overall restoration of the body's ability to respond to disease and heal itself. If we were to judge only by their methods of approaching illness, allopathic physicians would appear to believe that disease is caused by an excess of body parts and a deficiency of drugs.

Dr. Gerson conducted his medical practice and his research according to Kussmaul's dictum, "The result at the sickbed is decisive." Dr. Gerson arrived at his conclusions by observing what worked for his patients, not what worked for corporate sponsors. Although he was rigorous in his search for a scientific explanation for the effectiveness of his therapy, he never jeopardized the well-being of any patient in a double-blind or otherwise controlled study for fear that a patient might suffer unduly or die prematurely without undergoing the Gerson therapy. The ongoing suppression of information about the Gerson therapy by the government and medical authorities betrays a deep insecurity that people would choose this low cost, low tech, and low profit method of treatment if they had the data. In fact, that is what is now happening. The availability of information about the Gerson therapy on the Internet has helped to defeat efforts to censor Dr. Gerson's discoveries and censure the man, as has the growing corps of cured patients who have become vocal advocates for the therapy. Longevity and good health lend these former patients credibility unmatched by the statements of the medical and pharmaceutical industries.

Dr. Gerson has left us gift beyond measure — a therapy that works to cure and prevent degenerative diseases, that improves overall health and performance, that works as an anti-aging regime, that improves mental acuity, that stops heart attacks and strokes, and that boosts the function of the immune system — all the while reducing our medical bills. Dr. Gerson has left us the knowledge and the methods needed for each one of us to take charge of our own health. Beyond the mechanics of the therapy itself, Dr. Gerson has left us a profound holistic understanding of the connection between our external metabolism, the Earth, and our internal metabolism, the Body. If a large proportion of the population were to adopt his dietary methods, our agricultural industry could feed the planet while producing more topsoil than it consumed, providing our children and their children with a fertile land and sustainable agriculture for the foreseeable future. In the age of high technological achievement, our health is, ironically, a matter of returning to nature and using common sense. At least in the matter of degenerative disease, technology is the *problem*, not the solution, as Max Gerson first discovered as a child when he watched earthworms flee from artificially to organically fertilized soil in his grandmother's potato patch.

As Dr. Albert Schweitzer wrote in a eulogy for his good friend, "Dr. Max Gerson is one of the most eminent geniuses in the history of medicine. He has achieved more than seemed possible under adverse conditions. Many of his basic ideas have been adopted without having his name connected with them. He leaves a legacy which commands attention and which will assure him his due place. Those whom he has cured will attest to the truth of his ideas."

Gretchen and Max Gerson, 1958

Bibliography of The Gerson Therapy

Alexander, H. "Treatment of Pulmonary Tuberculosis with Salt-Free Diet." *Münch. med. Wochnschr.* 77:971, Jun. 6, 1930.

Ahringsmann, H. "Historische Bemerkung zu der neuen Diätbehandlung der Tuberkulose nach Gerson-Sauerbruch-Herrmannsdorfer." *Münch. med. Wochnschr.* 76:1565, Sep. 1929.

Apitz, G. "Treatment of Tuberculosis of Lungs and of Other Organs with Salt-Free Diet." *Deutsche med. Wchnschr.* 55:1918, Nov. 15, 1929.

Axmann. "Dietary Treatment in Tuberculosis of the Skin." *Münch. med. Wochnschr.* 77:707, Apr. 25, 1930.

Bacmeister, A. "Interne Behandlung der Lungentuberkulose." *Med Welt.* 4(14):474-476, Apr. 5, 1930.

Bacmeister A.; Rehfeldt, P. "Phosphorlebertran und die Gerson-Herrmannsdorfersche Diät zur Heilung der Tuberkulose." *Deutsche med. Wchnschr.* 56(12):480-481, Mar. 21, 1930.

Baer, G.; Herrmannsdorfer, A; Kausch, H. "Salt Free Diet in Tuberculosis." *Münch. med. Wochnschr.,* Jan. 4, 1929.

Banyai, A.L. "The Dietary Treatment of Tuberculosis." *Am. Rev. Tuberc.* 23:546-575, May 1931.

Barát, I. "Gerson's diet in treatment of pulmonary tuberculosis." *Orvosi hetil.* 74:877-879, Aug. 3, 1930.

Barát, I. "Über den Wert der Gersondiät in der Behandlung der Lungentuberkulose." *Beitr. z. Klin. d. Tuberk.* 76:588-591, 1931.

Beck, O. "Herrmannsdorfer Dietary Treatment of Tuberculosis: Theoretical Basis." *Monatsschr. f. Kndrheilk.* 48:276, Oct. 1930.

Bentivoglio G.C. "Le variazone del riflesso oculocardiaco nei banbini in seguito al trattamento dietetico di Gerson." *Pediatria.* 41:1457-1483, Dec. 1933.

Bertaccini, G. "A proposito della dieta aclorurata Gerson-Herrmannsdorfer-Sauerbruch nella tuberculosi: richerche sulla influenza del cloruro di sodio nella infezione tubercolare sperimentale del coniglio." *Gior. ital. di dermat. e sif.* 73:1775-1778, Dec. 1932.

Bertaccini, G. "A proposito della dieta Gerson-Herrmannsdorfer-Sauerbruch nella tuberculosis recherche sulla influenza del cloruro di sodio nella infezione tubercolare sperimentale del coniglio; infezione cutanea." *Gior. ital. di dermat. e sif.* 74:1469-1486, Dec. 1933.

Blumenthal, F. "Treatment of Tuberculosis of Skin with Special Consideration of Dietary Therapy." *Med. Klin., Berlin* 26:1432, Sep. 26, 1930.

Bommer, S. "Dietetic Treatment of Tuberculosis of Skin." *Münch. med. Wochnschr.* 76:707, Apr. 26, 1929

Bommer, S.; Bernhardt, L. "Dietary Treatment of Lupus Vulgaris." *Deutsche med. Wchnschr.* 55:1298, Aug. 2, 1929.

Bommer, S. "Neue Erfahrungen auf dem Gebiete der Hauttuberkulose mit besonderer Berücksichtigung der Gersondiät." *Strahlentherapie* 35:139-148, 1930.

Bommer, S. "Dietary treatment of skin tuberculosis. *Am. Rev. Tuberc.* 27:209-215, Feb. 1933.

Bommer, S. "Beitrag zur Diätbehandlung von Lupus vulgaris. *Med. Klin.* 28:209-215, Feb. 1933.

Bommer, S. "Capillaroscopic study of skin following administration of Gerson-Herrmannsdorfer-Sauerbruch diet in treatment of injuries to skin." *Dermat. Wchnschr.* 97:1367-1372, Sep. 23, 1933.

Bommer, S. "Zur Frage der Wirkung von Sauerbruch-Herrmannsdorfer-Gerson-Diät." *Deutsche med. Wchnschr.* 60:735-739, May 18, 1934.

Bommer,,S. "Salzarme Kost im Gefässystem (G.H.S.-Diät)." *Klin. Wchnschr.* 13:148-158, Oct. 27, 1934.

Brezovsky. "Sauerbruch-Gerson diet in treatment of tuberculosis of skin." *Budapesti orvosi ujsag.* 28:769-773, Jul. 17, 1930.

Bruusgaard, E; Hval, E. "Gerson-Sauerbruch-Herrmannsdorfer diet treatment in skin tuberculosis and its results." *Norsk mag. f. laegevidensk.* 92:1157-1175, Nov. 1931.

Bruusgaard, E. "Über die Herrmannsdorfersche Diätbehandlung von Hauttuberkulose." Acta dermat.-venereol. 13:628-642, Nov. 1932.

Bussalai. "La dieta di Gerson-Herrmannsdorfer nel Lupus. (Nota preventi). Con presentazioni di ammalati, di'preparti microscope e di fotografie." *Gior. ital. di dermat. e sif.* (supp. fasc. 1) 1:10-13, 1931.

Canal Feijoó, E.J. "Régimen ácido Como tratamiento de la tuberculosis pulmonar." *Rev. med. latino-am.* 16:981-992, Apr. 1931.

Canal Feijoó, E.J. "Régimen ácido Como tratamiento de la tuberculosis pulmonar." *Rev. españ. de med. y gir.* 16:124-128, Mar. 1933.

Cattell, H.W. "Diet in Treatment of Tuberculosis." *Internat. Clin.* Vol.1, 41st Series, 1931.

Clairmont, P.; Dimtza, A. "Dietary Treatment in Tuberculosis." *Klin. Wchnschr.* 9:5, Jan. 4, 1930.

Conrad, A.H. "Lupus Vulgaris." *Archiv. Dermat. Syph.* 24:688, 1931.

Cope, F.W. "A medical application of the Ling Association-Induction Hypothesis: the high potassium, low sodium diet of the Gerson cancer therapy." *Physiol. Chem. Phys.* 10(5):465-468, 1978.

Crosti, A; Scolari, E. "La dieta di Gerson-Herrmannsdorfer-Suerbruch nella tuberculosi cutanea. Osservazioni cliniche e recherche biologiche." *Gior. ital. di dermat. e sif.* 72:897-945, Aug. 1931.

Crosti, A. "La dieta Sauerbruch-Herrmannsdorfer-Gerson nella tuberculosi cutanea; reperti clinice, biochimici, istopatologici (con dimostrazioni di fotografie)." *Gior. ital. di dermat. e sif.* (supp. fasc. 1). 1:13-16, 1931.

Csapó, J.; Péterfy, M.; Palfy, E. "Urinalysis in tubercular children kept on Sauerbruch-Herrmannsdorfer-Gerson diet." *Orvosi hetill.* 75:1090, Nov. 7, 1931.

Csapó, J.; Péterfy, M.; Palfy, E. "Harnuntersuchungen bei der Diät nach Sauerbruch-Herrmannsdorfer-Gerson." *Arch. f. Kinderh.* 96:231-235, 1932.

Curschmann, W. "Beobachtungen bei Gersonscher Diät." *Beitr. a. Klin. d. Tuberk.* 80:120-131, 1932.

Curschmann, W. "Ein klärendes Wort zur Ablehnenden Kritik der Ernährungsbehandlung der Tuberkulose. Erwiderungen auf die Aufsätze von Sauerbruch und Herrmannsdorfer." *Münch. med. Wochnschr.* 77:2196, Dec. 19, 1930.

Curschmann, W. "Ergebnisse salzloser Diätbehandlung nach Sauerbruch und Herrmannsdorfer bei Lungentuberkulose und Knochentuberkulose." *Beitr. z. Klin. Tuberk.* 77:540-590, 1931.

Curschmann, W. "Beobachtungen, bei Gersonscher Diät." *Beitr. z. Klin. Tuberk.* 80:120-131, 1932.

Danholt, N. "Culture of Tubercle Bacilli from Lupus Lesions of Patients under the Gerson-Herrmannsdorfer-Sauerbruch Diet." *Acta dermat.-venereol.* 13:617, Nov. 1932.

(Directives). "Richtlinien für die Heilkostbehandlung der Tuberkulose nach Gerson-Sauerbruch-Hermannsdorfer." *Med. Welt.* 3:1229, Aug. 24, 1929.

de Raadt, O.L E. "Factor responsible for curative value." *Wien. Klin. Wchnschr.* 43:752-753, Jun. 12, 1930.

de Raadt, O.L.E. "Reply to Korvin's article." *Wien. Klin. Wchnschr.* 45:146-147, Jan. 29, 1932.

Doerffel, J. "Clinical, Experimental and Chemical Studies on the Influence of Diet on Inflammatory Changes in Healthy and Diseased Skin." *Arch. Dermat. Syph.* 162:621, Jan. 24, 1931.

Doerffel, J., Goeckerman, W.H. "Effect of a Diet Low in Salt in Cases of Tuberculosis of the Skin." *Proc, Mayo Clinic* 7(6):73-78, Feb. 10, 1932.

Doerffel, J. "Effect of a Diet Low in Salt in Cases of Tuberculosis of the Skin." *Arch. Dermat. Syph.* 26:762-764, 1932.

Doerffel, J.; Passarge, W. "Lokale Ektebinbehandlung der Hauttuberkulose bei gleichzeitiger Kochsalzarmer Diät (Gerson-Herrmannsdorfer-Sauerbruch)." *Dermat. Wchnschr.* 99:1173-1179, Sep. 8, 1934.

Drosdek-Praktische. "Erfahrungen mit der Gerson-Sauerbruch-Diät." *Beitr. z. Klin. d. Tuberk.* 78:697-723, 1931.

Eckhardt, H. "Die Stellung der Krüppelfürsorge zur Gerson-Herrmannsdorfer-Sauerbruch-Diät bei der Knochengelenktuberkulose." *Ztschr. f. Krüppelfürsorge.* 28:79, May-Jun. 1935.

Egues, J. "Regimen dietetico en los tuberculoses pulmonares." *Rev. Asoc. red. Argent.* 46:1574-1581, Dec. 1932.

Elder, H.C. "The Influence of the Gerson Regime on Pulmonary Tuberculosis." *Trans. Med.-Chir. Soc. Edinburgh,* Nov. 1932.

Eller, J.J.; Rein, C.R. "The Value of an Equilibrated Salt Diet in the Treatment of Various Dermatoses: A Modification of the Herrmannsdorfer-Sauerbruch-Gerson Diets." *N.Y. State J. M.* 32(22):1296-1300, Nov. 15, 1932.

Emerson, C. "Treatment of Tuberculosis by Altering Metabolism Through Dietary Management. (Gerson-Sauerbruch Method.)" *Nebr. St. Med. J.* 14(3):104-107, Mar. 1929.

Falta, W. "Ist die Gerson-Diät bei Tuberkulose zu empfehlen?" *Wien. Klin. Wchnschr.* 43:148-149, Jan. 30, 1930.

Falta, W. "Ist die Gerson-Diät bei Tuberkulose zu empfählen?" *Aerztl. Prax.* 99-101, Apr. 1, 1930.

Fishbein, M., ed. "The Gerson-Herrmannsdorfer Dietetic Treatment of Tuberculosis." *J. Amer. Med. Assoc.* 93(11):861-862, Sep. 14, 1929.

Fishbein, M., ed. "Dietetic Treatment of Tuberculosis." *J. Amer. Med. Assoc.* 93(16):1237, Oct. 19, 1929.

Fishbein, M., ed. "Gerson's Cancer Treatment." *J. Amer. Med. Assoc.* 122(11):645, Nov. 16, 1946.

Fishbein, M., ed. "Frauds and Fables." *J. Amer. Med. Assoc.* 139:93-98, Jan. 8, 1949.

Formenti, A.M. "Studi sulla lipasi ematica nella dieta di Gerson-Herrmannsdorfer-Sauerbruch." *Riv. di. clin. pediat.* 36:319-350, Apr. 1938.

Foster, H.D. "Lifestyle changes and the 'spontaneous' regression of cancer: An initial computer analysis." *Intl. J. of Biosocial Rsch.* 10(1):17-33, 1988

Francois, P. "Le regime de Gerson-Sauerbruch-Herrmannsdorfer dans le traitement de la tuberculose lupeuse." *Bruxelles-med.* 11:1034-1038, Jun. 28, 1931.

Frontali, G. "La dieta di Gerson nel trattamento della tuberculosis infantile." *Lotta contro. la tuberc.* 5:818-830, Aug. 1934.

Funk, C.F. "Zur Therapie der Hauttuberkulose unter besonderer Berücksichtigung des Lupus vulgaris." *Dermat. Ztschr.* 68:87-96, Nov. 1933.

Funk, C.F. "Einflüsse der Sauerbruch-Herrmannsdorfer-Gerson-Diät auf den Effektoren-Bereich der vegetativen Neuroregulation." *Med. Klin.* 27:1139-1141, Jul. 31, 1931.

Gade, H.G. "Preliminary communication on treatment with Gerson's diet." *Med. rev., Bergen.* 46:385-399, Aug. 1929.

Gerson, M. Dissertation article: "Influence of artificial hyperemia and blood transfusions in the treatment of fractures of the hip joint", 1907.

Gerson, M. "Eine Bromoformvergiftung." (A Bromocol Poisoning) *Aerztliche Sachverständigen-Zeitung.* (Aus der innern Abteilung des Stadt. Krankenhauses im Friedrichshain zu Berlin). S. 7, 1910.

Gerson, M. "Zur Aetiologie der myasthenischen Bulbarparalyse." (Concerning the Etiology of Myasthenic Bulbar Paralysis) *Berl. Klin. Wchnschr.* 53:1364, 1916.

Gerson, M. "Reflex hyperthesia" *Zeitschrift für die Gesamte Neurologie und Psychiatrie.* 1918.

Gerson, M. "Über Lähmungen bei Diphtheriebazillenträgern." (Paralyses found in in Diphtheria Carriers) *Berl. Klin. Wchnschr.* 56(12):274-277, Mar. 24, 1919.

Gerson, M. "Zur Aetiologie der multiplen Sklerose." (Concerning the Etiology of Multiple Sclerosis) *Deutsche. Ztschr. f. Nervenh.*, Leipz. LXXIV, 251-259, 1922.

Gerson, M. "Über die konstitutionelle Grundlage von nervösen Krankheitserscheinungen und deren therapeutische Beeinflussung." (Constitutional Basis for Nervous Symptoms) *Fortschr. d. Med.*, Berl. 42:9-11, 1924.

Gerson, M. "Experiments attempting to influence severe forms of tuberculosis through dietetic treatment" *Munch. Med. Wchnschr.*, No. 2 and 3. 1926.

Gerson, M. "Die Entstehung und Begründung der Diätbehandlung der Tuberkulose." (Origin and Basis of the Dietetic Treatment of Tuberculosis) *Med. Welt.* 3:1313-1317, 1929.

Gerson, M. "Korrespondenzen. Rachitis und Tuberkulosebehandlung." (Treatment of Rickets and Tuberculosis) *Deutsche. med. Wchnschr.* 55(38):1603, Sep. 20, 1929.

Gerson, M *Meine Diät* (My Diet) Ullstein, Berlin, 1930.

Gerson, M. "Several factors in the dietary treatment of pulmonary tuberculosis." *Zeitschr. f. die Ärztl. Fortb.*, No. 11, 1930.

Gerson, M. "Phosphorlebertran und die Gerson-Herrmannsdorfersche Diät zur Heilung der Tuberkulose." (Phosphorelated Cod Liver Oil and the Gerson-Herrmannsdorfer Diet in the Treatment of Tuberculosis) *Deutsche. med. Wchnschr.* 56:478-480, Mar. 21, 1930.

Gerson, M. "Comment on Wichmann's article of December 17." *Klin. Wchnschr.* 9:693-694, Apr. 12, 1930.

Gerson, M. "Einige Ergebnisse der Gerson-Diät bei Tuberkulose." (Several Experiments with the Gerson Diet in Tuberculosis) *Med. Welt.* 4:815-820, Jun. 7, 1930.

Gerson, M. "Grundsätzliche Anleitungen zur "Gerson-Diät." (Basic approaches to the Gerson Diet) *Münch. med. Wochnschr.* 77:967-971, Jun. 6, 1930.

Gerson, M. "Salt association with migraine (an early factor in dietary treatment)" *Verhandlungen der deutschen Gesellschaften für innere Medizin*, 23:129, 1930.

Gerson, M. "Basic approaches to the Gerson diet." *Münchener Med. Wchnschr.*, 23:967, 1930.

Gerson, M. "Erwiderung auf die Arbeit; Die Gründe der Ablehnung der salzlosen Diät durch die Tuberkuloseheilanstalten von Prof. O. Ziegler." (Reply to 'Basis underlying discontinuance of salt-free Diet by Tuberculosis Sanatoria' by Professor O. Ziegler) *Deutsche med. Wchnschr.* 57:334-335, Feb. 20, 1931.

Gerson, M. "Einiges Über die Kochsalzarme Diät." (On the Low-Salt Diet) *Hippokrates.* 3:627-634, Mar. 1931.

Gerson, M. "Nicotine as a deterrent factor in the dietary treatment of lupus." *Verh. der deutschen Ges. f. innere. Med.*, 1931

Gerson, M. "Current dietetic problems in the treatment of lung tuberculosis." *J. State Med.*, Vol. XXXIX, No. 8, London, 1931.

Gerson, M. "Resume of varying sensory factors in the treatment of lupus." *Verhandl. d. deutsche Gesellsch. f. inn. Med.*, 1931.

Gerson, M. "Current dietary problems in the treatment of tuberculosis." *J. of State Med.*, XXXIX:8, London, 1931.

Gerson, M. "Erwiderung auf die Arbeit C. v. Noordens 'Kritische Betrachtungen Über Gerson-Diät in Besondere bei Tuberkulose.'" (Reply to C. v. Noordens 'Critical view on the Gerson Diet, in particular with Tuberculosis') *Med. Klin. Wchnschr.* 45:1116-1117, Sep. 9, 1932.

Gerson, M. "Blutsenkung bei Diätbehandlung der Lungentuberkulose." (Sedimentation in the Dietetic Treatment of Lung Tuberculosis) *Zeitschr. f. Tuberk.* 63(5):327-337, 1932.

Gerson, M. "Einige Resultate der Diättherapie bei Kavernen nach vorausgegangener chirurgischen Behandlung." (Some Results of Diet Therapy on Tubercular Lung Cavitations (Kavernen) after Prior Surgical Treatment) *Verhandl. d. deutsche Gesellsch. f. inn. Med. Kong.* 44:222-224, 1932.

Gerson, M. "Diätbehandlung bei Migräne und Lungentuberkulose." (Dietary Treatment of Migraine and Pulmonary Tuberculosis) *Wiener Klin. Wchnschr.* 45:744-748, Jun. 10, 1932.

Gerson, M. "The Gerson diet in chronic pulmonary spastic diseases and hypertension." *Wiener Klin. Wchnschr.*, No. 13, 1932.

Gerson, M. "Observations on the Gerson diet." *Wiener Klin. Wchnschr.*, Heft 9, No. 37, 1932.

Gerson, M. "The Gerson diet in practice." *Tech. Pharm. Ärtztzeit.*, No. 20, Vienna, 1932.

Gerson, M. "Gerson diet in pulmonary tuberculosis and migraine." *Mitteilungen des Volksgesundheitsamtes*, Heft 9, Vienna, 1932.

Gerson, M. *Diättherapie der Lungentuberkulose*, [Dietetic therapy of Lung Tuberculosis] Edition Franz Deuticke, Vienna and Leipzig, 1934.

Gerson, M. "Psychische Reaktionen während der Gerson-Diät bei Lungentuberkulose." (Psychic reactions during the Gerson Diet in pulmonary tuberculosis) *Psychotherapeut. Praxis.* 1:206-213, Dec. 1934.

Gerson, M. "Unspezifische Desensibilsierung durch Diät bei allergischen Hautkrankheiten." (Nonspecific Desensitization through Diet in Allergic Skin Diseases) *Dermat. Wchnschr.* 100:441, Apr. 20, 1935.

Gerson, M. "Unspezifische Desensibilsierung durch Diät bei allergischen Hautkrankheiten." (Nonspecific Desensitization through Diet in Allergic Skin Diseases) *Dermat. Wchnschr.* 100:478, Apr. 27, 1935.

Gerson, M. "Bemerkungen zum Aufsatz von Neumann 'Ernährung der Tuberkulösen.'" (Remarks on von Neumann's essay 'Nutrition of the Tuberculosis Patient') *Wien. Klin. Wchnschr.* 48:272-273, Mar. 1, 1935.

Gerson, M. "Rückbildung von Entzündungen bei Gerson-Diät unter besonderer Berücksichtigung der Tuberkulösen Entzündung." (Recession of inflammation in Gerson Diet with special reference to tubercular inflammations) *Wien. Klin. Wchnschr.* 48:847-853, Jun. 21, 1935.

Gerson, M. "Anmerkung zur obigen Ausführung von W. Newmann." (Remarks on the above comments by W. Newmann.) *Wien. Klin. Wchnschr.* 48:1069, Aug. 23, 1935.

Gerson, M.; von Weisl, W. "Lebermedikamentur bei der Diättherapie chronischer Krankheiten." (Administration of liver extracts in the dietary treatment of chronic diseases) *Wien. med.. Wchnschr.* 85:1095-1098, Sep. 28, 1935.

Gerson, M.; von Weisl, W. "Flüssigkeitsreiche Kalidiät als Therapie bei cardiorenaler Insuffizienz." (Potassium diet rich in fluids as treatment in cardiorenal insufficiency) *Münch. med. Wochnschr.* 82:571-574, Apr. 11, 1935.

Gerson, M. "Feeding of the tubercular." *Wien. Klin. Wchnschr.*, No. 9, 1935.

Gerson, M. "The Gerson diet in home practice." *D. Öster. Artzt.*, Folge 2, Jahrg. 2, 1935.

Gerson, M. "Feeding the German Army." *New York State J. Med.* 41(13):1471-1476, Jul. 1, 1941.

Gerson, M. "Some aspects of the problem of fatigue." *Med. Record.* 156(6):341, 1943.

Gerson, M. "Dietary considerations in malignant neoplastic disease; preliminary report." *Rev. Gastroenterol.* 12:419-425, Nov.-Dec. 1945.

Gerson, M. "Case histories of ten cancer patients: clinical observations, theoretical considerations and summary." *National Archives, Center for Legislative Archives*, Rec. Grp. 46, Rec. US Senate, Papers Relating to Specific Bills and Resolutions, S.1875, 79th Cong., 2nd Session. Box 110, 8E2 24/14/4, Jul. 1946.

Gerson, M. "The Jew and Diet." *The Jewish Forum*, New York City, Apr. 1948.

Gerson, M. "The significance of the content of soil to human disease." 1948.

Gerson, M. "Effects of combined dietary regime on patients with malignant tumors." *Exper. Med. & Surg.* 7:299-317, Nov. 1949.

Gerson, M. "Theorie der diätetisch-medikamentösen Krebs-Behandlung." (Theory of Diet and Medication in Cancer Treatment) *Der Wendepunkt*, Zürich, Switzerland, XXVI(12):379-386, Nov. 1949.

Gerson, M. "Cancer development and treatment." Lecture at the Academy of Applied Nutrition, Pasadena, California, 1952.

Gerson, M. "Kein Krebs bei normalem Stoffwechsel; Ergebnisse einer speziellen Therapie." (No Cancer in Normal Metabolism; Results of a Special Therapy) *Med. Klin.* 49(5):175-179, Jan. 29, 1954.

Gerson, M. "Krebskrankheit, ein Problem das Stoffwechsels." (Cancer, a Problem of Metabolism) *Med. Klin.* 49(26):1028-1032, Jun. 25, 1954.

Gerson, M. "Zur medikamentösen Behandlung Krebskranker nach Gerson." (Medications used in the treatment of cancer patients according to Gerson.) *Med. Klin.* 49(49):1977-1978, 1954.

Gerson, M. "Dietary therapy in malignant diseases." *Scala, Handbuch der Dietetik*, Franz Deuticke, Vienna, 1954.

Gerson, M. "Sind Boden, Nahrung und Stoffwechselschädigungen grundlegend fuer Krebsentwicklung?" (Are Soil, Food and Metabolic Disturbances the Basis for Cancer Development?) *Ernährungs-Rundschau*, II(6):128-130, Dec. 1955.

Gerson, M. "Can cancer be prevented." *Prevention Magazine*, 1957.

Gerson, M. "A New Therapeutical Approach to Cancer." *Herald of Health*, Apr. 1957.

Gerson, M. "Cancer – Reflected Symptom of Abnormal Metabolism." *Let's Live Magazine*, Los Angeles, CA, 1957.

Gerson, M. "A Cancer Therapy: Results of 50 Cases", *Whittier Books*, New York City, NY, 1958.

Gerson, M. "The cure of advanced cancer by diet therapy: a summary of 30 years of clinical experimentation." *Physiol. Chem. Phys.* 10 (5):449-464, 1978.

Gettkant, B. "Lungentuberkulose und Gerson-Diät." *Deutsche. med. Wchnschr.* 55:1789-1790, Oct. 25, 1929.

Gettkant, B. "Die Heilkostbehandlung der Tuberkulose nach Gerson." *Med. Welt.* 3:1349-1351, Sep. 21, 1929.

Gettkant, B. "Die Gerson-Diät im Lichte der Fachkritik." *Med. Welt.* 4:804-807, Jun. 7, 1930.

Gezelle Meerburg, G.F. "Gerson Herrmannsdorfer diet." *Geneesk. gids.* 8:381-392, Apr. 25, 1930.

Gibbens, J. "Gerson-Herrmannsdorfer diet; summary of recent experiences." *Brit. J. Tuberc.* 25:132-135, Jul. 1931.

Gloor, W. "Dietetic Treatment of Tuberculosis." *Schweiz. med. Wchnschr.*, May 17, 1930.

Golin, A; Domenighini, R. "La dieta di Gerson-Herrmannsdorfer-Sauerbruch nel trattamento della tuberculosi infantile." *Riv. di clin. pediat.* 33(3):257-300, Mar. 1935.

Grunewald, W. "Untersuchungen Über den Wasser und Chlorbestand der Organe des tuberkulosekranken Menschen." *Beitr. z. Klin. d. Tuberk.* 82:189-206, 1933.

Guy, J.; Elder, H.C.; Watson, C.; Fulton, J.S. "Influence of Gerson regime on pulmonary tuberculosis." *Tr. med. Chir. Soc. Edinburgh.* 1-20, 1932-1933.

Hagedorn, K. "Vitamine und Tuberkulose. Eine kritische Besprechung der experimentellen und klinischen Ergebnisse, einschliesslich der Diäten nach Gerson und Herrmannsdorfer." *Zentralbl. f. d. ges. Tuberk.-Forsch.* 34:665, May 2, 1931.

Hagedorn, K. "Vitamine und Tuberkulose." *Zentralbl. f. d. ges. Tuberk.-Forsch.* 34:809, Jun. 27, 1931.

Haldin-Davis, H. "The Dietetic Treatment of Lupus Vulgaris." *Brit. J. Med.* 2:539, Sep. 27, 1930.

Hashimoto, M. "Über die Diätetische Behandlung der Knochentuberkulose nach Gerson, Sauerbruch und Herrmannsdorfer." *J. Orient. Med.* 13:54, Nov. 1930.

Harms; Grunewald. "Treatment of Pulmonary Tuberculosis with Salt-Free Diet." *Deutsche med. Wchnschr.* 56:2-61, Feb. 14, 1930.

Henius, K. "Die wirksamen Faktoren der Gerson-Herrmannsdorfer-Diät und ein Rat zur versuchsweisen Anwendung." *Ztschr. f. Tuberk.* 55:319, 1930.

Herrmannsdorfer A. "La influencia de una alimentación especial sobre la cicatrización de las heridas y sobre las afecciones tuberculosas graves." *Rev. méd. german.-iber.-am.* 2:677-684, Nov. 1929.

Herrmannsdorfer. A. "Über Wund- und Tuberkulose Diät." *Jahresk. f. arztl. Fortbild.* (Hft. 8). 20:35-43, Aug. 1929.

Herrmannsdorfer, A. "Über Wund Diätetik." *Ztschr. f. ärtzl. Fortbild.* 26:580-587, Sep. 15, 1929.

Herrmannsdorfer, A. "Dietary Treatment in Tuberculous Diseases." *Med. Klin.* 25:1235, Aug. 9, 1929.

Herrmannsdorfer, A. "Dietetic Treatment Before and After Operation in Pulmonary Tuberculosis." *Ztschr. f. Tuberk.* 55: 1, Oct. 1929.

Herrmannsdorfer A. "Differences Between Gerson and Herrmannsdorfer Diets." *Ztschr. f. Tuberk.* 56:257, Apr. 1930.

Herrmannsdorfer, A. "Effect of Sodium Chloride-Free Diet on Tuberculous Process." *Ztschr. f. Tuberk.* 59:97, Dec. 1930.

Herrmannsdorfer, A. "Zehnjährige Erfahrungen mit der Ernährungsbehandlung Lungentuberkulöser. Zugleich ein Kritischer Beitrag zum gegenwärtigen Stande der Gerson-Diät." *Ztschr. f. ärtzl. Fortbild.* 32:673-678, Dec. 1, 1935.

Herrmannsdorfer, A. "Rückschau auf die mit der Sauerbruch-Herrmannsdorfer-Gerson-Diät erzielten Ergebnisse der Tuberkulosebehandlung." *Ztschr. f. Tuberk.* 100:316-322, 1952.

Hildenbrand, G.L.; Hildenbrand, L.C.; Bradford, K.; Cavin, S. "Five-year survival rates of melanoma patients treated by diet therapy after the manner of Gerson: a retrospective review." *Alt. Ther. In Health and Med.* 1:4:29-37, Sep. 1995.

Hindhede, M. "Gerson's tuberculosis diet." *Ugesk. f. laeger.* 91:1018-1022, Nov. 14, 1929.

Hoffschulte, F. "Ergebnisse der Gerson-Diät bei Tuberculose." *Med. Welt.* 4:928, Jun. 28, 1930.

Holm, E. "Versuche mit Gerson-Diät." *Acta Ophth.* 10:232-236, 1932.

Hval, E. "Microscopic study of capillaries of patients on Gerson-Herrmannsdorfer-Sauerbruch diet." *Acta dermat. venereol.* 13:593-600, Nov. 1932.

Jaffé, K. "Hämatologische Untersuchungen bei Hauttuberkulose während der Behandlung mit Gerson-Herrmannsdorfer-Sauerbruch-Diät." *Münch. med. Wochnschr.* 78:703-705, Apr. 24, 1931.

Keinung, E.; Hopf, G. "Die Bedeutung des Mineralsalzeinflusses für die pathogenische Beurteilung der Hauttuberkulose." *Dermat. Wchnschr.* 99:1397-1406, Oct. 27, 1934.

Keinung, E.; Hopf, G. "Wirkt kochsalzzusatzfreie Diät Tuberkulose-spezifisch?" *Ztschr. f. Tuberk.* 62:352-356.

Klare, K. "Warum muss die Sauerbruch, Hermannsdorfer Gerson-Diät bei Lungentuberkulose im allegemeinen versagen?" *Deutsche med. Wchnschr.* 57:928-930, May 29, 1931.

Koehler, B. "Dietary Treatment of Tuberculosis." *Münch. med. Wochnschr.* 77:1832, Oct. 24, 1930.

Korvin, E. "Zur Wirkungsweise der S.H.G.-Diät, Kritik der Ausführungen de Raadts." *Wien. Klin. Wchnschr.* 45:144-146, Jan. 29,1932.

Kremer, W. "Erfahrungen mit der Gerson-Herrmannsdorfer-Diät." *Med. Welt.* 4:354-356, Mar. 15, 1930.

Kremer, W.; Cobet, G.; Frischbier, G. "Erfahrungen mit der Sauerbruch-Herrmannsdorfer-Gerson-Diät bei Lungentuberkulose." *Ztschr. f. Tuberk.* 66:185-203, 1930.

Kretz, J. "Über die Diätetische Behandlung der Lungentuberkulose nach Sauerbruch, Herrmannsdorfer und Gerson." *Wien. Klin. Wchnschr.* 42:993-995, Jul. 25, 1929.

Kulcke, E. "Die Gerson-Herrmannsdorfer-Sauerbruchsche Diät und ihre Beziehungen zur Lahmannschen Diät." *Med. Klin.* 26:196-200, Feb. 7, 1930.

Lambotte. "Le régime de Gerson dans le traitement de la tuberculose." *Liége méd.* 23:1-12, Jan. 5, 1930.

Lana Martinez, F. "La dieta de Gerson Sauerbruch en el tratamiento do las tuberculosis cutáneas." *Clín. y Lab.* 20:550-552, Jul. 1932.

Lassen, O. "Gerson, Herrmannsdorfer diet in pulmonary tuberculosis." *Ugesk. f. laeger.* 92:445-451, May 8, 1931.

Lechner, P. "Dietary regime to be used in oncological postoperative care." *Proc. Oesterreicher Gesellsch. f. Chir,* Jun. 21-23, 1984.

van Leersum, E.C. "Phosphorlebertran und die Gerson-Herrmannsdorfer-Sauerbruchsche Diät zur Behandlung der Tuberkulose." *Nederl. tijdschr. v. geneesk.* 74:2854-2864, Jun. 7, 1930.

van Leersum, E.C. "Phosphorlebertran und die Gerson, Herrmannsdorfer, Sauerbruch Diät zur Behandlung der Tuberkulose." *Münch. med. Wochnschr.* 77:975-976, Jun. 6, 1933.

Leitner, J. "Blutdruck, Blutstatus und Blutsenkung bei der Diätbehandlung der Tuberkulose nach Gerson-Sauerbruch-Herrmannsdorfer." *Beitr. a Klin. d. Tuberk.* 78:331-336, 1931.

Levin, O.L. "The Treatment of Psoriasis by Means of a Salt-Free Diet." *Med. Journ. and Record* 134(4):179, Aug. 19, 1931.

Liesenfeld, F. "Klinische Versuche und Beobachtungen mit der Diätbehandlung der Lungentuberkulose nach Sauerbruch-Herrmannsdorfer-Gerson Während 1_ Jahren." *Beitr. z. Klin. d. Tuberk.* 72:252-259, 1929.

Lorenz, G.F. "Der Kochsalzgehalt der Gersondiät. Entgegnung aus dem Diätsanatorium von Dr. Gerson, Kassel-Wilhelmshöhe." *Med. Welt.* 4(38):1362-1363, Sep. 2, 1930.

Lubich, V. "La dietoterapia della tuberculosis (Rivista sintetico-critica sulle diete Gerson-Herrmannsdorfer-Sauerbruch)." *Lotto. contro. la tuberc.* 3:245-261, Mar. 1932.

Ludy, J.B. "Cutaneous Tuberculosis." *Med. Clin. North Amer.* 18(l):311-327, Jul. 1934.

Maag. "Über die Diätbehandlung chirurgischer Tuberkulose nach Sauerbruch-Herrmannsdorfer-Gerson." *Deutsche. Ztschr. f. Chir.* 236:603-610, 1932.

Maendl, H.; Tscheme, K. "Beobachtungen bei der Diät nach Gerson-Sauerbruch-Herrmannsdorfer an 40 Fällen von Tuberkulose." *Tuberkulose.* 10: 132-134, Jun. 10, 1930.

Mariette, E. "The Dietetic Treatment of Tuberculosis." *Annals of Int. Med.* Vol 5:793-802, 1932.

Mårtensson, A. "Gerson-Sauerbruch-Herrmannsdorfer diet in treatment of tuberculosis." *Ugesk. f. laeger.* 91:1063-1066, Nov. 28, 1929.

Mathiesen, H. "Gerson's tuberculosis diet." *Ugesk. f. laeger.* 91:1066, Nov. 28, 1929.

Matz, P.B. "Gerson-Sauerbruch Dietetic Regimen." *U.S. Vet. Bur. M. Bull.* 6:27-32, Jan. 1930.

Mayer, E.; Kugelmass, I.N. "Basic (Vitamin) Feeding in Tuberculosis." J. Amer. Med. Assoc. 93(24):1856-1862, Dec. 14, 1929.

Mayer, E. "Salt-Restricted Dietary With Particular Application to Tuberculosis Therapy." J. Amer. Med. Assoc. 97(26):1935-1939, Dec. 26, 1931.

McCarty, M. "Aldosterone and the Gerson diet – a speculation." Med. Hypotheses. 7:591-597, 1981.

Mecklenburg, M. "Sauerbruch-Herrmannsdorfer Diet in Chronic Pulmonary Tuberculosis." Ztschr. f. Tuberk., Leipzig 57147, Jun. 1930.

Mienicki, M. "An Attempt to Increase the Curative Effect of a Salt-Free Diet on Lupus Vulgaris." Przegl. dermat. 29:346, Sep. 1934.

Metz, G.A. "Über die therapeutische Wirkung von Lebertran, Sauerbruch-Herrmannsdorfer-Gerson-Diät und Heliotherapie bei Tuberkulose." Deutsche med. Wchnschr. 61:916-917, Jun. 1935.

Meyer, F. "Zur Gerson-Therapie (Medizinische Aussprache)." Med. Welt. 4(2)168, Jan. 11, 1930.

Meyer, M.; Irrmann, E. "Considérations sur le traitement diététique de la tuberculose d'après Sauerbruch-Herrmannsdorfer-Gerson." Strasbourg méd. 92:169-171, Mar. 15, 1932.

Meyer, M.; Irrmann, E. "Le Régime de Sauerbruch-Herrmannsdorfer-Gerson. Ses Bases Théoriques. Ses Résultats Dans la Tuberculose Externe." Gaz. d. hôp. 105(51):957-961, Jun. 25, 1932.

Meyer, M.; Irrmann, E. "Le Régime de Sauerbruch-Herrmannsdorfer-Gerson. Ses Bases Théoriques. Ses Résultats Dans la Tuberculose Externe." Gaz. d. hôp. 105(52):997, Jul. 2, 1932.

Michelson, H.E. "Lupus Vulgaris." Arch. Dermat. Syph. 24:1122, 1931.

Moeller, A. "The Dangers of Salt Withdrawal in Pulmonary Tuberculosis." Deutsche med. Wchnschr, Aug. 15, 1930.

Monzon, J. "Le régime de Gerson; un essai allemand de traitement diététique de la tuberculose pulmonaire." Presse Méd. 37:1251-1254, Sep. 25, 1929.

Müller, P. "Über die Behandlung der Lungentuberkulose mit salzfreier Kost und Mineralogen." Deutsches Arch. f klin. Med. 158:34-41, 1927.

Münchbach, W. "Gerson-Herrmannsdorfer-Sauerbruch-Diät." Beitr. z. Klin. d. Tuberk. 77:395-411, 1931.

Neumann. "Bemerkungen zu der Arbeit von Max Gerson." Wien. Klin. Wchnschr. 48:1069, Aug. 23, 1935.

Noorden, C. von. "Kritische Betrachtungen Über Gerson-Diät, ins Besondere bei Tuberkulose." Med. Klin. 28:743-748, May 27, 1932.

Noorden, C. von. "Reply to Gerson." Med. Klin. 28:1062-1063, Jul. 29, 1932.

Noorden, C. von. "Bemerkungen zur Gerson-Diät." Wien. Klin. Wchnschr. 45:708-709, Jun. 3, 1932.

Oulmann, L. "Lupus Vulgaris." Arch. Dermat. Syph. 34:317, 1931.

Ota, M. "Erfahrungen mit der Diätbehandlung nach Gerson-Sauerbruch-Herrmannsdorfer bei Hauttuberkulose." Jap. J. Dermat. & Urol. 39:82-85, May 20, 1936.

Pachioli, R.; Gianni, G. "Contributo ala cura della tuberculosi polmonare del bambino mediante il trattamento dietetico di Gerson, Herrmannsdorfer, Sauerbruch." Riv. d. pat. e clin. d. tuberc. 5:446-469, Jun. 30, 1931.

Pachioli, R.: Gianni, G. "Richerche sull meccanismo d'azione del regime di Gerson-Herrmannsdorfer-Sauerbruch nel trattamento della affezioni tubercolari." Riv. di clin. pediat. 30:664-680, May 1932.

Parreidt, R. "Behandlung der Paradentose durch Diät (nach Gerson)." Oesterreischishe Zeitschr. f. Stomatol. 27:969-972, Oct. 1929.

Pawlowski, E. "Erfahrung mit der Gerson-Herrmannsdorfer-Diät in der Behandlung der Knochen- und Gelenktuberkulose." Deutsche med. Wchnschr. 56:1870-1871, Oct. 31, 1930.

Pennetti, G. "La dieta de Gerson-Herrmannsdorfer-Sauerbruch nella affezioni tubercolari." *Riforma med.* 46:372-376, Mar. 10, 1930.

Pfeffer, G.; Stern, E. "Über die Wirkung der Sauerbruch-Gersonschen Diät bei Lungentuberkulose." *Beitr. z. Klin. d. Tuberk.* 67:742-747, 1927.

Pöhlmann, C. "Influence of Gerson's Dietary Treatment Continued for Four Months in Severe Pulmonary and Laryngeal Tuberculosis." *Münch. med. Wochnschr.* 77:707-708, Apr. 25, 1930.

Popper, M. "Dermatoskopische Befunde bei Lichtreaktionen der Haut unter dem Einfluss Sauerbruch-Herrmannsdorfer-Gersonschen (S.H.G.) Diät." *Strahlenther.* 45:235-246, 1932.

de Raadt, O.L.E. "Gerson diet; factor responsible for curative value." *Wien. Klin. Wchnschr.* 43:752-753, Jun. 12, 1930.

Rieckenberg, H. "Gerson-Diät bei Lungentuberkulose." *Deutsche med. Wchnschr.* 56:746-747, May 2, 1930.

Ritschel, H.U. "Die Diät nach Gerson in der Behandlung der chronischen Lungentuberkulose." *Beitr. z. Klin. d. Tuberk.* 68:394-398, 1928.

Rosen, K. "Herrmannsdorfer-Gerson diet in pulmonary tuberculosis." *Svenska lak. tidning.* 28:305-316, Feb. 27, 1931.

Sachs, W. "Die salzarme Kost nach Gerson-Sauerbruch-Herrmannsdorfer in der Behandlung der Lungentuberkulose." *Beitr. z. Klin. d. Tuberk.* 73:816-824, 1930.

Santori, G. "L'alimentazione di Gerson, Sauerbruch e Herrmannsdorfer nelia cura del lupus vulgare." *Bull. e atti* D.R. *Accad. med. di Roma.* 56:25-29, Jan. 1930.

Sauerbruch, F; Herrmannsdorfer, A. "Ergebnisse und Wert einer Diätetischen Behandlung der Tuberkulose." *Münch. med. Wochnschr.* 75:35-38, Jan. 6, 1928.

Sauerbruch, F. "Stellungnahme zu Gerson und Gettkant." *Med. Welt.* 3:1351, Sep. 21, 1929.

Sauerbruch, F. "Erklärung zur Ernährungsbehandlung der Tuberkulose." *Zentralbl. f. Chir.* 56:2306-2307, Sep. 14, 1929.

Sauerbruch, F. "Erklärung zur Ernährungsbehandlung der Tuberkulose." *Beitr. z. Klin. Chir.* 147:501-502, 1929.

Sauerbruch, F. "Erklärung zur Ernährungsbehandlung der Tuberkulose." *Deutsche Ztschr. f. Chir.* 219:381-382, 1929.

Sauerbruch, F. "Erklärung zur Ernährungsbehandlung der Tuberkulose." *Med. Klin.* 25:1272, Aug. 9, 1929.

Sauerbruch, F. "Erklärung zur Ernährungsbehandlung der Tuberkulose." *Deutsche. med. Wchnschr.* 55:1391-1392, Aug. 16, 1929.

Sauerbruch, F. "Erklärung zur Ernährungsbehandlung der Tuberkulose." *Münch. med. Wochnschr.* 76:1363, Aug. 16, 1929.

Sauerbruch, F. "Erklärung zur Ernährungsbehandlung der Tuberkulose." *Zentralbl. f. inn. Med.* 50:802, Aug. 31, 1929.

Sauerbruch, F. "Erklärung zur Ernährungsbehandlung der Tuberkulose." *Chirurg.* 1:933, Sep. 1, 1929.

Sauerbruch, F. "Erklärung zur Ernährungsbehandlung der Tuberkulose." *Med. Welt.* 3:1351, Sep. 21, 1929.

Sauerbruch, F. "Ein Klärendes Wort zur ablehnenden Kritik der Ernährungsbehandlung der Tuberkulose." *Münch. med. Wochnschr.* 77:1829-1832, 1930.

Schade, H; Beck, A.; Reimers, C. "Physiochemical Study of Action of Acid Food in Wound Healing: Effect of Gerson Diet on Wound Healing." *Zentralbl. f. Chir.* Leipzig 57:1077, 1930.

Schedtler, O. "Wirkt kochsalzzusatzfreie Diät Tuberkulose-spezifisch? Bemerkungen zu der Arbeit von Keining und Hopf." *Ztschr. f. Tuberk.* 63:337-338, 1932.

Scheurlen, F.; Orlowitsch-Wolk, A. "Vitamin therapy of Pulmonary Tuberculosis." *Münch. med. Wochnschr.* 77:976, Jun. 6, 1930.

Schiller, W. "Zur Frage der Kochsalzarmen Kost nach Sauerbruch-Herrmannsdorfer-Gerson bei Tuberkulose. *Tuberkulose.* 9:70-74, Apr. 1929.

Schlammadinger, J. "Gerson-Herrmannsdorfer-Sauerbruch diet in treatment of tuberculosis and chronic diseases of the skin." *Orvosi hetil.* 74:954-957, Sep. 20, 1930.

Schlammadinger, J.; Szép, E. "Erfahrungen mit der Gerson-Sauerbruch-Herrmannsdorferschen Diät bei einigen tuberkulösen und anderen entzündlichen Dermatosen." *Med. Klin.* 27:508-510, Apr. 2, 1931.

Schlesinger, W. "Die Gerson-Herrmannsdorfer-Sauerbruchsche Tuberkulose Diät." *Wien. med. Wchnschr.* 80:587-589, Apr. 26, 1930.

Schmiedeberg, H. "Herrmannsdorfer Diet in Tuberculosis in Children." *Monatsschr. f. Kndrheilk.* 48:230, Oct. 1930.

Schmitz, H. "Über die Gersonche Diät bei Lungentuberkulose." *Ztschr. f. Tuberk,* 47:461, 1927.

Schrick, F.G. van. "Haut und Knochentuberkulose unter dem Einfluss der Sauerbruch-Herrmannsdorfer-Gerson-Diät. *Ztschr. f. Orthop. Chir.* 61:388-394, 1934.

Schroeder, M.G. "Modern Dietetic Problems in Treatment of the Tuberculous." *Journal of State Med., London* 39:435, Aug.1931.

Schwalm, E. "Erfahrungen mit der Gerson-Diät bei Lungentuberkulose." *Klin. Wchnschr.* 8:1941-1943, Oct. 15, 1929.

Scolari, E. "Osservazioni cliniche e richerche sperimentali sulla dieta di Sauerbruch-Herrmannsdorfer-Gerson nella affezion cutanea." *Gior. ital. di dermat. e sif.* 76:665-701, Jun. 1935.

Sellei, J. "Gerson diet in treatment of skin diseases." *Gyogyaszat.* 70:453-454, Jun. 8, 1930.

Sliosberg, A. "Le traitement de la tuberculose par la méthode de Gerson." *Rev. do. phtisiol. méd. soc.* 10:564-574, Nov.-Dec. 1929.

Sossi, O. "Sulla cura dietetica di Sauerbruch-Herrmannsdorfer nella tuberculosi pulmonare." *Riv. di clin. med.* 30:1124-1149, Oct. 31, 1929.

Sprigge, S.; Morland, E. eds. "Dietary Principles in Tuberculosis." *The Lancet.* 217(2):617, Sep. 21, 1929.

Sprigge, S.; Morland, E. eds. "Dietary Treatment of Tuberculosis." *The Lancet.* 217(2):404, Aug. 24, 1929.

Sprigge, S.; Morland, E. eds. "The Gerson Diet for Tuberculosis." *The Lancet.* 218(l):1415, Jun. 28, 1930.

Sprigge, S.; Morland, E. eds. "Dietetic Therapeutics of Tuberculosis of the Skin." *The Lancet.* 219(2):311, 1930:

Sprigge, S.; Morland, E. eds. "Dietetic Treatment of Tuberculosis of the Skin." *The Lancet.* 220(l):610, Mar. 14, 1931.

Sprigge, S.; Morland, E. eds. "The Gerson Diet for Dermatoses." *The Lancet.* 220(l):1201, May 30, 1931.

Sprigge, S.; Morland, E. eds: 1931. "The Gerson Diet." *The Lancet.* 220(l):1366-1367, Jun. 20, 1931.

Sprigge, S.; Morland, E. eds. "The Gerson Diet." *The Lancet.* 222(l):629, Mar. 19, 1932.

Sprigge, S.; Morland, E. eds. "The Diet of Gerson." *The Lancet.* 222(l):708, Mar. 26, 1932.

Starcke, H. "Erfahrung mit der salzlosen Diät nach Gerson und Herrmannsdorfer bei Kindern und Jungendlichen." *Beitr. z. Klin. d. Tuberk.* 74:61-88, 1930.

Stein, H. "Erfahrung mit Diätkuren bei der Lungentuberkulose." *Ztschr. f. Tuberk.* 58:426-431, 1930.

Strauss, H. "Dietary Treatment in Pulmonary Tuberculosis." *Med. Klin.* 25:1383, Sep. 6, 1929.

Strauss, H. "Diät als Heilfaktor." *Med. Welt.* 4 (6):171-175, Feb. 8, 1930.

Stub-Christensen. "Dietetics and Tuberculosis, with Especial Regard to Calcium Metabolism and to Significance of Vitamins." *Hospitalsitdende, Copenhagen* 74:157, Feb. 5, 1931.

Stumpf, R. "Case of lupus vulgaris treated by roentgen therapy and Gerson diet." *Irish J. Med. Sci.* 254-257, Jun. 1930.

Stumpke, G.; Mohrmann, B.H.U. "Dietary therapy of Lupus and Other Skin Diseases." *Med. Klin.* 27:235, Feb. 13, 1931.

Sylla, A.; Schone, G. "Zur Ernährungsbehandlung der Lungentuberkulose nach Sauerbruch-Herrmannsdorfer-Gerson (S.H.G.)." *Beitr. z. Klin. d. Tuberk.* 78:678-696, 1931.

Symposium. "Die Bedeutung der von Sauerbruch, Herrmannsdorfer und Gerson angegebenen Diät bei der Behandlung der Tuberkulose." *Veröffentl. a.d. Geb. d. Med.-Verwalt.* 32:541-632, 1930.

Szold, E. "Treatment of Tuberculosis of the urinary tract with the Sauerbruch-Herrmannsdorfer-Gerson diet." *Orvosi hetil.* 75:1130-1132, Nov. 21, 1931.

Tesdal, M. "Die Diät von Gerson-Herrmannsdorfer-Sauerbruch und deren Einwirkung auf den Stoffwechsel." *Ztschr. f. klin. Med.* 121:184-193, 1932.

Tesdal, M. "Effect of Gerson-Herrmannsdorfer-Sauerbruch diet on metabolism in tuberculosis." *Norsk. mag. f. laegevidensk.* 93:1073-1082, Oct. 1932.

Timpano, P. "La dietoterapia e la radiumterapia del lupus vulgaris." *Rinasc. med.* 10:184-185, Apr. 15, 1933.

Traub, E.F. "A Case for Diagnosis (Tuberculosis)." *Arch. Dermat. Syph.* 30:592-593, 1934.

Unverricht. "The Influence of an Unsalted Diet upon the Gastric Secretion, and the Clinical Use of Such Diet." *Deutsche med. Wchnschr.*, Aug. 4, 1933.

Urbach, E. "Skin Diseases and Nutrition, including the Dermatoses of Children" (trans. F.R. Schmidt; Vienna: Wilhelm Maudrich, 1932.)

Urbach, E. "Skin Diseases, Nutrition, and Metabolism" (Grune and Stratton, New York, 1946).

Varela, B.; Recarte, P.; Esculies, J. "Sauerbasengleich und ionisiertes Kalzium im Blute der Tuberkulösen und ihre Veränderungen bei Mineral Diättherapie nach Sauerbruch-Herrmannsdorfer-Gerson." *Ztschr. f. Tuberk.* 57:380- 390, 1930.

Valagussa, F. "La cura dietetica della tuberculosi medianti il metodo Gerson-Herrmannsdorfer-Sauerbruch." *Bull. e. atti d. r. Acad. med. di Roma.* 56:15-24, Jan. 1930.

Van Kampen, F. "De Gerson-Therapie." *Nederlands Tijdschrift voor Integrale Geneeskunde* 8:53-57, 1985.

Van Kampen, F. "De Theorie van de Gersonbehandeling." *Nederlands Tijdschrift voor Integrale Geneeskunde* 10:199-204, 1985.

Vaucher, E.; Grunwald, E. "Le Traitement diététique de la Tuberculose Pulmonaire, Revue critique sur les travaux de G-S-H." *Paris méd.* 1:25-30, Jan. 4, 1930.

Volk, R. "Therapie des Lupus vulgaris und die Gerson-Diät." *Wien. Klin. Wchnschr.* 43:1461-1466, Nov. 27, 1930.

Volk, R. "Zur Diättherapie von Hautkrankheiten." *Dermat. Wchnschr.* 91:1869-1873, Dec. 20, 1931.

Volk, R. "La dieta sin sal según Sauerbruch-Herrmannsdorfer-Gerson en la tuberculosis extrapulmonar." *Rev. mex. de. tuberc.* 2:5-23, Jan.-Feb. 1940.

Watson, C. "Gerson Diet for Tuberculosis." *The Lancet.* 218(2):161, Jul. 19, 1930.

Watson, C. "Gerson Treatment of Tuberculosis." *Brit. Med. J.* 2:284-285, Aug. 23, 1930.

Watson, C. "Diet and nutrition with special reference to the Sauerbruch-Herrmannsdorfer-Gerson diet." *Med. Press.* 130:207-209, Sep. 10, 1930.

Watson, C. "The 'Vital' Factor in Diet: A theory of the Nature of Vitamins." *Edinburgh Med. J.* 3 8:91-104, Jan.-Dec. 1931.

Watson, C. "The 'Vital' Factor in Diet." *Nature*. 128:154, Jul. 25, 1931.

Watson, C. "The Gerson Regime in Pulmonary Tuberculosis: With a Note on the Radiological Findings by Dr. J.S. Fulton." *Trans. Med.-Chir. Soc. Edinburgh* pp. 6-20, Nov. 1932.

Wichmann, P. "Über die Beeinflussung der Hauttuberkulose durch die Diät nach Gerson." *Beitr. z. Klin. d. Tuberk.* 66:464, 1928.

Wichmann, P. "Ergebnisse der Diätbehandlung der Hauttuberkulose." *Klin. Wchnschr.* 8:2366-2368, Dec. 17, 1929.

Wichmann, P. "Reply to Gerson." *Klin. Wchnschr.* 9:694, Apr. 12: 1930.

Wichmann, P. "Verschlimmerung von Haut- und Schleimhauttuberkulose durch Gerson-Diät." *Beitr. a. Klin. d. Tuberk.* 73:825-828, 1930.

Wichmann, P. "Ergebnisse der Gerson-Sauerbruch-Herrmannsdorfer-Diät-Behandlung bei Haut- und Schleimhauttuberkulose" *Beitr. a. Klin. d. Tuberk.* 75:100-103, 1930.

Wise, O. "Erfahrungen mit der 'Diätbehandlung nach Gerson-Herrmannsdorfer-Sauerbruch' bei verschiedenen Tuberkulose Formen des Kindesalters." *Ztschr. f. Kinderh.* 51:119-126, May 1931.

Weisl, N. von. "Einiges Über die praktische Durchführung der Gerson-Diät." *Fortschr. d. Med.* 53:185-188, Mar. 11, 1935.

White, C.J. "Lupus Vulgaris (Treated by Gerson Diet). Lupus Erythematosus?" *Archiv. Dermat. Syph.* 24:323-324, 1931.

White, C.J. "Tuberculosis of the Skin." *Illinois Med. J.*, 6:1215-1218, Jul.-Dec. 1931.

Wohlfarth. "Erfahrungen mit HGS-Diät bei Lungentuberkulose." *Ztschr. f. ärtzl. Fortbild.* 29:559-563, Sep. 15, 1932.

Wolff-Eisner, A. "Die Gerson Sauerbruch Tuberkulose Diät im Urteil der Fachkritik." *Beitr. z. Klin. d. Tuberk.* 73:829-834, 1930.

Zelinka, J. "Gerson-Herrmannsdorfer-Sauerbruch diet in therapy of osseous tuberculosis." *Casop. lék. cesk.* 71:357, Mar. 18, 1932.

Zelinka, J. "Gerson-Herrmannsdorfer-Sauerbruch diet in therapy of osseous tuberculosis." *Casop. lék. cesk.* 71:391, Mar. 25, 1932.

Ziegler, O. "Die Gründe der Ablehnung der salzlosen Diät durch die Tuberkuloseheilanstalten." *Deutsche med. Wchnschr.* 57:11-13, Jan. 2, 1931.

QUARRY
HEALTH
B O O K S